D1521420

A Measure of Success

A Measure of Success

The Influence of Curriculum-Based Measurement on Education

Christine A. Espin, Kristen L. McMaster,
Susan Rose, and Miya Miura Wayman, Editors

University of Minnesota Press
Minneapolis
London

Published by the University of Minnesota Press
111 Third Avenue South, Suite 290
Minneapolis, MN 55401-2520
http://www.upress.umn.edu

Library of Congress Cataloging-in-Publication Data
    A measure of success : the influence of curriculum-based measurement on education /
Christine Espin ... [et al.].
    Includes bibliographical references and index.
    ISBN 978-0-8166-7970-6 (hc : alk. paper)
    1. Curriculum-based assessment. 2. Deno, Stanley L. I. Espin, Christine.
    LB3060.32.C74M43 2012
    371.26'4—dc23   2012008202

Printed in the United States of America on acid-free paper

Contents

Abbreviations

AAIMS	Algebra Assessment and Instruction: Meeting Standards
AYP	Adequate Yearly Progress
AA-AAS	alternate assessment based on alternate academic achievement standards
AA-MAS	alternate assessment based on modified achievement standards
ANCOVA	analysis of covariance
ANOVA	analysis of variance
BASA	*Basic Academic Skills Assessment*
BIC	Bayesian Information Criterion
BAFT	Behavior Analysis Follow Through
CTT	Classical Test Theory
CFI	comparative fit index
CLPM	correct letters per minute
CIWS	correct minus incorrect word sequences
CWPM	correct words per minute
CWS	correct word sequence
CEC	Council for Exceptional Children
CBA	Curriculum-Based Assessment
CBE	curriculum-based evaluation
CBM	Curriculum-Based Measurement
CBM-R	Curriculum-Based Measurement of Reading
DN-CAS	Das-Naglieri Cognitive Assessment System
DBPM	Data-Based Program Modification
DCD	developmental cognitive disability
DDS	DIBELS Data System
DIBELS	Dynamic Indicators of Basic Early Literacy Skills
EGRA	Early Grade Reading Assessment
EMR	Educable Mentally Retarded
EAHCA	Education for All Handicapped Children Act
ESL	English as a Second Language
ELLCOI	English Language Learner Classroom Observation Instrument
ELLS	English Language Learners

EBP	Evidence-Based Practice
FAPE	free appropriate public education
GOM	General Outcome Measurement
G THEORY	Generalizability Theory
GMORF	Growth Modeling Oral Reading Fluency Passages
IPT	IDEA Proficiency Test
IEP	Individual Education Plan
IEP	Individualized Education Program
IDEA	Individuals with Disabilities Education Improvement Act
IRLD	Institute for Research on Learning Disabilities
IES	Institute on Educational Sciences
IRT	Item Response Theory
KLDA	Korea Learning Disabilities Association
LD	learning disabilities
LD	Learning Disabled
LRE	least restrictive environment
MPS	Minneapolis Public Schools
MBST	Minnesota Basic Standards Test
MCA	Minnesota Comprehensive Assessments
MBSP	Monitoring Basic Skills Progress
MP³	Monitoring Progress of Pennsylvania Pupils
NCTM	National Council of Teachers of Mathematics
NCLB	No Child Left Behind Act
NWF	Nonsense Word Fluency
OSELA	Observation Survey of Early Literacy Achievement
OCR	Office of Civil Rights
OSEP	Office of Special Education Programs
ORF	oral reading fluency
PPVT-III	Peabody Picture Vocabulary Test—III
PSSA	Pennsylvania System of School Assessment
PSF	Phoneme Segmentation Fluency
PASS	Planning, Attention, Simultaneous, and Successive
PLAAFP	present levels of academic achievement and functional performance
PSM	Problem-Solving Model
RAN	rapid automatized naming
RAFT	reading words aloud from text in a fixed time
RIPM	Research Institute on Progress Monitoring

RTI	Research Triangle Institute
RTI	Response to Intervention
RMSEA	root mean square error of approximation
SPPS	Saint Paul Public Schools
SERT	Special Education Resource Teacher
SLD	Specific Learning Disabilities
SCRED	St. Croix River Education District
SAT	Stanford Achievement Test
SPSS	Statistical Package for the Social Sciences
SIT	student intervention team
SNAP	Students Needing Alternative Programming
SARF	Subskill Analysis of Reading Fluency
TONI	Test of Nonverbal Intelligence
TAKS	Texas Assessment of Knowledge
UNESCO	United Nations Educational, Scientific and Cultural Organization
USAID	United States Agency for International Development
WISC IV	*Wechsler Intelligence Scale for Children—Fourth Edition*
WPIC	Western Psychiatric Institute and Clinic
WJ-LW	Woodcock-Johnson Letter-Word Identification subtest
YPP	Yearly ProgressPro

Introduction

*Christine A. Espin, Kristen L. McMaster,
and Susan Rose*

Our goal in organizing this book was to put together a compilation of chapters that would reflect the impact that Curriculum-Based Measurement (CBM) has had on educational policy and practice over the past thirty years. We asked the authors of each chapter to reflect on the following question: "How has CBM research and development influenced policy and practice in _____?" The blanks were to be filled in with the topics addressed by the authors.

Although our primary purpose was to highlight the influence of CBM on educational policy and practice, it was clear from the outset that it was impossible to reflect on the contributions of CBM without reflecting on the contributions of the person behind CBM—Professor Stanley Deno. In collaboration with Phyllis Mirkin, one of his first graduate students, Stanley Deno conceptualized and developed the use of CBM progress monitoring and placed it within a problem-solving approach, in which the child's performance and progress would drive instruction rather than the child's diagnosis. Throughout the chapters, the influence of both Deno and his ideas come to light. Many of the authors refer to Deno with great admiration and affection. This book, then, is a tribute to not only the work that has been done on CBM over the past thirty years but also Stanley Deno, the person who began that work.

The chapters of the book address a variety of topics in a variety of ways. However, despite the variability in chapter content and approach, a common theme clearly emerges throughout the chapters: CBM, in all its simplicity, has influenced educational policy and practice in far-reaching ways—from the classroom to school to district to state levels; from elementary- to high-school levels; across core academic areas; in both national and international settings; in the fields of special and general education; and in the areas of teacher education, psychology, and school psychology. Recent educational reforms, such as Response to Intervention, reflect this broad influence as evidenced by their emphases on progress monitoring and data-based decision making. Next, we provide a brief overview of the parts and chapters included in this volume.

In chapter 1, Jenkins and Fuchs provide the foundation for this collection of writings through a discussion of the formation and evolution of CBM from its inception to present-day practices. Jenkins and Fuchs highlight the distinctiveness of CBM as a process that not only has significantly influenced a multitude of educational venues but also has increased the educational progress of individual students.

Part I features the contribution of CBM to educational policy. In chapter 2, Fuchs and Bradley describe Deno and Mirkin's Special Education Resource Teacher model. This model focused on moving students with disabilities up the continuum of service options toward regular classroom placements. The model focused on effective academic instruction and ongoing evaluation of that instruction. In chapter 3, Yell and Busch describe the critical role that CBM can play in constructing substantive Individualized Educational Programs to meet the letter and intent of the Individuals with Disabilities Education Act. As the authors illustrate, CBM provides a research-based tool that can be used to set measurable annual goals, monitor progress, and evaluate the effects of a student's special education program. Finally, in Chapter 4, Hosp and Hosp describe how CBM can bridge the gap between assessment and instruction by demystifying assessment data and facilitating collaboration among educational professionals.

Part II highlights the use of CBM at the school and district levels. Specifically these chapters highlight critical and beneficial relationships between universities and school districts as they worked together to solve problems and establish principles. In chapter 5, Marston traces the evolution of current educational practices in problem solving and Response to Intervention to Deno's leadership and to early collaborations with the special education program in the Minneapolis Public Schools. Marston describes the process used to develop CBM standards for screening students in general education settings and for comparing data for students in Title I, special education, and general education programs. In chapter 6, Germann describes the "Big Ideas" of a comprehensive problem-solving model that requires adherence to the principles of data-based decision making. Germann traces the challenges and successes in the development and implementation of district-wide use of CBM and problem-solving practices. Scaffolding on Marston's and Germann's chapters, in chapter 7, Gibbons and Casey highlight the use of CBM data throughout school-based organizational structures to support teachers and administrators in instructional decision making and the determination of effective intervention practices.

Part III encompasses chapters 8, 9, and 10, which focus on applications of CBM at the early elementary- and elementary-school levels. In chapter 8, Dion, Dubé, Roux, Landry, and Bergeron review studies that have extended the use of CBM to monitor first graders' progress in reading. In chapter 9, specific applications and examples of CBM uses in early intervention and prevention of reading difficulties are described by Good, Kaminski, Fien, Powell-Smith, and Cummings. Good and colleagues illustrate how principles of General Outcome Measurement and data-based decision making have guided the development and use of Dynamic Indicators of Basic Early Literacy Skills. In chapter 10, Lembke, McMaster, and Stecker trace the evolution of technological applications of CBM and describe how these applications can improve the efficiency and utility of CBM for data-based decision making, particularly at the elementary-school level.

Part IV focuses on the applications of CBM at the secondary-school level. In chapter 11, Foegen highlights Deno's influence on her work in developing progress monitoring measures for secondary mathematics. In chapter 12, Espin and Campbell describe Deno's influence on their development of progress monitoring measures for secondary reading, writing, and content-area learning and reflect on the potential contributions of CBM to secondary-school programming.

The next set of chapters, chapters 13 and 14, make up part V and focus on school-based applications within general educational settings and address the alignment of CBM to educational outcomes in general education settings. Chapter 13 by Kloo, Machesky, and Zigmond is a powerful description of one school's "challenge to change" and the implementation of progress monitoring to effect system-wide change. The authors describe the three-year process involved in implementing change and present the data that led to a change in the local headlines from "schools in distress" to "school success." In chapter 14, Speece provides a reflective perspective on the robust characteristics of CBM, as well as the vulnerability of the process, particularly as it applies to the "interplay of assessment and instruction."

Part VI, chapters 15 through 17, introduces recent applications of CBM to two unique populations: students who are English Learners (ELs) and students with cognitive disabilities. In chapter 15, Robinson, Robinson, and Blatchley describe the process developed in the St. Paul Public Schools to differentiate ELs with and without disabilities using CBM as the normative reference point. In chapter 16, Graves describes research in which CBM was used with first-grade ELs and their teachers. Graves highlights Deno's contributions to this work and establishes a platform for continued research with ELs. Finally, in chapter 17, Wallace and Tichá extend the definition of progress-monitoring practices through a discussion of the challenges and research paradigms used with students who have significant cognitive disabilities.

In part VII, the final chapters of the school-based applications, the links between CBM and state assessments are discussed. In chapter 18, Roberts, Wanzek, and Vaughn demonstrate the use of latent variable growth modeling to tie CBM scores to statewide standards and high-stakes testing. The results of a series of studies posit a new application for CBM as a predictor of success on performance outcome assessments. In chapter 19, Tindal highlights critical features of CBM that allow it to be used in conjunction with large-scale testing and describes how CBM data can be used to make systematic decisions about student participation in large-scale testing programs. In chapter 20, Shriner and Thurlow describe contributions of CBM to assessments within Individualized Education Programs, to state regular and alternative assessments, to decisions about accommodations and modifications on state assessments, and to use of growth modeling as part of an accountability system.

Part VIII addresses preservice and professional development of teachers as problem solvers and effective practitioners. In chapter 21, Sindelar, McLeskey, and Brownell describe how Deno's work has fundamentally altered teacher education and classroom practices, emphasizing the importance of preparing preservice teachers to be problem solvers and collaborators whose work is supported by efficient and reliable data. In chapter 22, Wagner and Scierka underscore the bottom-up approach to implementation of effective instructional practices by preparing teachers as data-based program implementation specialists and present a case example of one teacher's implementation of the CBM problem-solving process.

Part IX focuses on the contributions of CBM to the fields of school psychology and psychology. In chapter 23, Shapiro and Lentz trace how Deno and Mirkin's "Data-Based Program Modification" model shaped their careers as school psychologists and, in doing so, illustrate how CBM has shaped the field of school psychology in general. In chapter 24, Christ expands on Deno's influence on school psychology, using key excerpts from Deno's writing on problem solving to illustrate a vision of problem solving that addresses the "cultural imperatives" of schools. In chapter 25, van den

Broek and White describe challenges associated with measuring reading comprehension and show how CBM provides a valuable index of this cognitively complex construct.

Part X is devoted to CBM's international contributions. A number of researchers have exported the CBM paradigm to their own countries or to countries with which they are working to develop and improve systems for education and learning. Chapters 26 and 27 showcase CBM's reach to South Korea: Kim provides a review of CBM research, and Shin highlights the influences of Deno's work on research in the past, present, and future of South Korea. In chapter 28, Linan-Thompson describes efforts to introduce CBM into developing countries as part of an initiative driven by the United Nations Educational, Scientific, and Cultural Organization, using Nicaragua as a case example. Last, in chapter 29, Kendeou and Papadopoulos describe their work to better understand the underlying constructs measured by the CBM maze task in Greek.

The book concludes with a reflection by Mark Shinn. Shinn celebrates this volume—and Stanley Deno's work—by way of a "set of *Ps*." We encourage you, the reader, to discover each of these *Ps* yourself as you read the chapters in this book.

We would like to thank each and every contributor to this book. The authors have risen to the task of illustrating how CBM has influenced educational policy and practice and, in doing so, have showcased Stanley Deno's far-reaching impact, not only by describing how he has influenced education but also by revealing how he has deeply inspired the work of researchers who are dedicated to improving student learning. We end with a recent reflection from Professor Deno about his view of leadership:

> I've always thought that the deepest and most enduring approach to providing leadership is through teaching and mentoring. If successful, teaching and mentoring result in the development of individuals who understand who they are, what they believe, what they know, and what they can do in whatever roles they eventually occupy. I believe that people who possess these characteristics will create their own vision of what they hope they and their organizations will accomplish. One of my colleagues was once asked what he thought was the most effective approach to dissemination of educational innovations. On reflection, he replied that he thought education— teaching—possessed the greatest chance of bringing about lasting

social change. I have embraced that perspective in my own work and, while I have had some scholarly success, I have always believed that my first obligation has been to my students and to those colleagues whose lives I might influence by example. Many of my students now occupy significant roles in both higher education and the public schools. I take great satisfaction in their accomplishments and the leadership they are providing. I cherish the idea that the model I provided, and what the students learned while with me, has contributed to their successes. I also hope and expect that what they have learned from me they will pass on in similar fashion to their own students and colleagues. This is my view of leadership. (S. L. Deno, personal communication, 2009)

This book, we believe, is a testament to not only the ideas of Stanley Deno but also his leadership. His direct or indirect teaching and mentorship of the chapter authors (as well as many other educational leaders) will surely have an enduring impact on education and learning.

1

Curriculum-Based Measurement

The Paradigm, History, and Legacy

Joseph R. Jenkins and Lynn S. Fuchs

Dr. Stanley L. Deno did what few people do in their lives. He had a revolutionary idea: Simple indicators of academic competence could be used to capture the overall academic strength of an individual student at a given point of time, and such data could be used to track the trajectory of development. His emphasis was solidly on the idea of simplicity: Measurement had to be easy and time efficient to conduct so that educators might collect the data without much training and without the assessment competing for available instructional time. The vision was that educators would use these data as the dependent variable to assess the effects of their practice: that teachers would evaluate the effects of their instruction on individual students, thereby formatively building stronger academic programs student by student, and that schools and districts would distinguish generally effective from ineffective practices, thereby providing the basis for data-based education reform.

In this chapter, we remind readers about the distinctiveness of Curriculum-Based Measurement (CBM), trace the evolution of the idea for CBM, and provide an overview of CBM research as conceptualized and operationalized by Deno and as eventually practiced by so many researchers in the fields of special education, school psychology, and general education. We conclude by considering Deno's legacy, the magnitude of his contribution, and its continuing potential for enhancing the practice of education.

CBM's Distinctiveness

The obvious and conventional approach to classroom assessment is mastery measurement. With mastery measurement, teachers specify a hierarchy of instructional objectives constituting the annual curriculum and, for each objective in the sequence, devise a criterion-referenced test to assess mastery. When in the teacher's judgment a student achieves the mastery criterion for an objective, the teacher shifts instruction as well as assessment to the next skill in the hierarchy. In this way, learning is conceptualized as a series of short-term accomplishments, which are believed to accumulate into broad competence.

Stanley Deno's initial research on CBM highlighted several technical difficulties with mastery measurement (Fuchs and Deno, 1991). For example, to assess mastery of a specific skill, each mastery measurement criterion-referenced test addresses a single skill. Such testing is potentially misleading, however, because many low achievers can perform adequately when a skill is presented in isolation. That is, some students read consonant-vowel-consonant words accurately only when all words on the page conform to the pattern; similarly, some students can solve addition with regrouping problems if they know that all problems on the page fit that problem type. By contrast, when asked to read words with different phonetic patterns or to complete math problems of different types (as occurs on high-stakes tests and in the real world), these same students no longer perform the "mastered" skill competently. The potential lack of generalization to authentic tasks raises serious questions about mastery measurement's central assumption that demonstrating mastery on a series of short-term objectives, each assessed in isolation, accumulates into broad-based competence. Because improvement within a mastery measurement system often fails to reflect broad-based competence, the relation between number of objectives mastered during the year and end-of-year performance on more global assessments is compromised, lulling educators into a false sense that their students are making progress. Another important problem with mastery measurement is that the nature of the test changes each time the teacher begins to work on a new skill. This introduces complexity to the measurement system, which requires the teacher to administer multiple tests to assess students' retention of previously mastered skills.

To address these and other important problems associated with mastery measurement (see Fuchs and Deno, 1991 for a discussion), Deno (1985) offered CBM. Each weekly CBM is an alternate form, representing the performance desired at the end of the year. In this way, CBM circumvents mastery measurement's technical difficulties by requiring students to simultaneously integrate the various skills required for competent year-end performance on every weekly test. As students learn the components of the annual curriculum, their CBM score gradually increases. Because each weekly test is of comparable difficulty and conceptualization, the rate of weekly increase through a student's CBM scores (i.e., slope) can be used to quantify rate of learning. The slope of a line of best fit can also be used to gauge a student's responsiveness to the instructional program, allowing teachers to detect inadequate responsiveness and take action. Moreover, because the measurement system remains constant in difficulty and conceptualization as the student masters successive objectives, it addresses Deno's requirement for simplicity.

A key challenge in the development of CBM, of course, is to identify measurement tasks that simultaneously integrate the various skills required for competent year-end performance and that preserve the simplicity of the assessment. Two approaches have been used. One involves identifying a task that correlates robustly (and better than potentially competing tasks) with the various component skills constituting the academic domain. For example, Deno, Mirkin, and Chiang (1982) first identified reading words aloud from text in a fixed time (RAFT) as a key CBM task by showing that its correlations with valued criterion measures were high and exceeded correlations for other potential CBM tasks. Conceptually, it makes sense that RAFT is a robust indicator of overall reading competence because reading passages quickly and accurately is a complex performance that entails a reader's perceptual skill for automatically translating letters into coherent sound representations, unitizing those sound components into recognizable wholes and automatically accessing lexical representations, processing meaningful connections within and between sentences, relating text meaning to prior information, and making inferences to supply missing information (Fuchs, Fuchs, Hosp, and Jenkins, 2001). For this reason, RAFT produces a broad dispersion of scores across individuals of the same age, resulting in strong correlations with measures of reading comprehension, decoding, word identification, and vocabulary (e.g., Deno et al.; Marston, 1989; Hosp and Fuchs, 2005; Wayman, Wallace, Wiley, Tichá, and Espin, 2007).

The second approach to designing a CBM task involves systematic sampling of the skills constituting the annual curriculum to ensure that each weekly CBM represents the curriculum equivalently. Fuchs, Fuchs, Hamlett, and Stecker's (1990) math CBM illustrates this method. Each weekly test incorporates the same problem types in the same proportion: addition, subtraction, multiplication, and division of whole numbers and fractions on computation tests and number concepts, numeration, word problems, geometry, money, and measurement on concepts/application tests. As with RAFT, students have a brief, fixed time to complete as many problems as they can. The total test score, which is the indicator of overall math competence in the annual curriculum, is graphed; the rate of improvement over successive scores is used to depict slope (i.e., rate of learning). As with RAFT, this second approach to identifying a CBM task produces strong correlations with valued criterion measures and offers the added benefit of informing instruction by providing descriptions of individual skill mastery because each skill in the annual curriculum is systematically assessed on every weekly test (e.g., Fuchs, Fuchs, Hamlett, and Allinder, 1991; Fuchs, Fuchs, Hamlett, Phillips, Karns, and Dutka, 1997).

The Evolution of a Construct

Where do ideas come from? We can't ever be certain why and how an idea emerges, but it's sometimes possible to trace events and experiences that function as tentative landmarks in its development. In retrospect, several such landmarks, accompanied by countless conversations and periods of pondering, seem likely to have contributed in important ways to Deno's formulation of CBM. These include his graduate school training in classical measurement theory; his early studies of instructional objectives; the emergence of Precision Teaching; working with university practicum students in applying Precision Teaching in the Seward School Project; his emerging conceptions of common and distal measures of progress; the enactment of the Education for All Handicapped Children Act (Public Law 94-142) with its requirement for annual goals as a part of the Individualized Education Program (IEP); and the award by the federal government to the University of Minnesota establishing an Institute for Research on Learning Disabilities that provided research support for the development of formative measures of progress. We describe these landmark events in more detail.

The first landmark and perhaps most influential seed for the idea of CBM occurred during Deno's graduate studies at the University of Minnesota. There he enrolled in an educational measurement class taught by Jack Merwin and William Mehrens in which he came to grips with the classical measurement concepts of standardization, reliability, and validity. Years later, Deno would summon these measurement principles, recognizing that they were as important in the measurement of academic progress as they were for developing norm-referenced achievement and ability tests.

One of Deno's first lines of research addressed the relationship between learning outcomes and instructional objectives in the design of curricula, emphasizing the clarity and choice of instructional objectives (Deno and Jenkins, 1969; Jenkins and Deno, 1968; Neisworth, Deno, and Jenkins, 1969). In a way, the idea that expressing achievement goals in clear measurable outcomes could effectively guide teaching presaged Deno's work on the development of CBM.

In 1970, Ogden Lindsley presented his work on Precision Teaching to a group of University of Delaware faculty that included Deno. Prior to the development of Precision Teaching, most behavior analytic applications to schooling had focused on shaping motor and developmental skills (e.g., dressing), reducing troublesome social and classroom behaviors (e.g., non-compliance), and modifying proxies for academic learning (e.g., attending, completing assignments). Precision Teaching was a major advance in behavioral education, and Deno was intrigued by Precision Teaching's precepts, which he later adapted for CBM:

1. Pinpointing an academic skill
2. Collecting time-based repeated measurements of performance
3. Setting an aim for performance level and rate of growth
4. Representing performance visually on a graph
5. Examining performance level and rate of growth
6. Evaluating and adjusting instruction

The idea of measurement-guided instruction resonated with Deno's belief that student learning (should) shape teaching as much as teaching shapes student learning, and a technology that precisely measures change in performance would strengthen the reciprocity between teaching and learning.

Precision Teaching enjoyed something of a cult status among special education practitioners until Tom Lovitt introduced it to the scholarly community. In a series of articles, Lovitt convincingly showed how measuring performance daily could inform teaching and lead to better instruction for students with learning disabilities (Lovitt, Schaaf, and Sayre, 1970; Lovitt, 1975a, 1975b). He focused on direct teaching and measurement of academic skills—text reading, spelling, reciting math facts, and computing math problems. Lovitt's exciting work caught the attention of higher education faculty who soon began incorporating this data-based approach to instruction into teacher preparation and professional development programs.

Upon returning to the University of Minnesota, Deno worked with Jerry Gross, Minneapolis's director of special education, to develop a field-based training site at Seward School. There he introduced preservice special education teachers to Precision Teaching methods. Using a "general rounds" model, he met with groups of practicum students to review and discuss their children's performance charts. Although Deno found case-based problem solving to be beneficial in preparing teachers, he often left these sessions troubled by concerns about Precision Teaching's nonjudgmental acceptance of the skills worthy of teaching and measuring and the particular way Precision Teaching linked teaching and measurement.

Slogans like "if it's worth teaching, it's worth measuring" expressed the essential tenet of Precision Teaching—that linking teaching and measurement makes teaching more effective. Another hidden and less salutary implication was that the demands of a mastery measurement approach could easily get out of hand when teachers constructed complex lessons. For example, a reading lesson that included instruction and practice in phonemic awareness, letter-sound correspondences, word practice, text reading, vocabulary, and comprehension would require six measurements per student every day.

In addition, decisions about *what to measure* were dictated by decisions about *what to teach*. Thus the capacity of measurement to guide instruction for achieving long-term goals (i.e., overall proficiency) depended entirely on the wise choice of specific teaching/measurement pinpoints. In reading, for example, teaching/measurement pinpoints might include matching letters to pictures, circling a target letter every time it occurred in a random string of letters, writing a letter, naming a specific set of letters or letter sounds, blending specific letter combinations, "making words" from a specific set of letters, reading a specific set of words, answering a set of comprehension questions, and countless others. Unless teachers attended carefully to the validity of their teaching/measurement targets, they might consistently succeed in reaching their immediate teaching aim but might miss their overall goal of helping students become proficient readers. Ironically, because Precision Teaching was agnostic about what to teach, it put at risk the consequential validity of its measures for advancing reading proficiency writ large.

Another related concern was the diversity in *size and complexity of skills* pinpointed for instruction and measurement ranging from small and simple to large and complex (e.g., naming the sounds for two randomly ordered letters versus naming sounds for all randomly ordered letters and letter combinations; reading a set of five words versus reading the first grade Dolch words).

When teachers pinpointed highly circumscribed skills for mastery (e.g., naming the letters M and A), performance aims could be achieved relatively quickly and the next teaching target pinpointed. As a result, chances were slim that instruction on any pinpoint would last long enough for teachers to compare alternative treatments (interventions), thus limiting the potential of Precision Teaching to inform teachers and build practical knowledge about effective instruction. In essence, all of Deno's concerns about Precision Teaching centered on issues of feasibility, informational value, and validity of progress measurement, concerns that continued to percolate as he pondered ways to retain the powerful aspects of Precision Teaching.

The next significant event influencing Deno's work was the 1975 enactment of the Education for All Handicapped Children Act, a law that mandated every student with a disability receive an Individual Education Program (IEP). The law's requirement of specifying short-term objectives connected to annual goals would prove an important milestone on the road to CBM. Supported by a federal grant, Deno, working with Phyllis Mirkin (1977), designed a model to guide special education teachers in planning and delivering educational programs that were consistent with the newly mandated IEP. Three important assumptions undergirded their model of Data-Based Program Modification (Deno and Mirkin, 1977):

1. Educators cannot with any certainty prescribe specific and effective instruction for individuals. Prescribing a form of instruction for an individual should be treated only as a hypothesis that must be empirically tested to ascertain its effects.
2. Time-series analyses are uniquely appropriate for testing instructional hypotheses.
3. Progress monitoring should focus on those academic performances that represent "vital signs" of educational development (p. 14).

Data-Based Program Modification encouraged teachers to use an inductive individualized process to build more effective instructional programs for students. The Data-Based Program Modification process involved setting annual performance goals for vital academic skills, measuring performance daily, employing time-series analysis to evaluate the relative effectiveness of instructional variations on vital outcomes, and prompting instructional changes where needed, leading to stronger individualized programs. In suggesting measures that might potentially qualify as vital signs of educational development, Deno and Mirkin borrowed heavily from conventional Precision Teaching measures, especially those employed by Lovitt (1975a, 1975b) (e.g., for reading, words read correctly from text; for spelling, correct letter sequences written; for math, written answers to computation problems).

In the early 1970s, the University of Minnesota applied to the U.S. Office of Education and was awarded one of four national Institutes for Research on Learning Disabilities, quite possibly an existential landmark on the road to CBM, without which it may never have occurred. The Institute for Research on Learning Disabilities not only funded Deno's research program on performance measurement but also supported a number of remarkably talented and committed special education and school psychology doctoral students, several of whom continue the work on formative evaluation today.

The first critical turn from standard Precision Teaching was the move to establish feasibility and validity standards for measuring progress on vital outcomes. Not all measures represent vital signs of educational development, meaning that measurement options could be sharply circumscribed. This is the point at which CBM began to establish its distinctiveness. Drawing on his background as a teacher and his training in classical measurement, Deno proposed a set of feasibility criteria for progress measures (i.e., they had to be simple, time efficient, and inexpensive enough that teachers could employ them routinely), along with essential psychometric properties (i.e., standardization, reliability, and validity). His idea was to pare down Precision Teaching's infinite academic pinpoints to a finite set of *common measures* with which teachers could formatively evaluate students' instructional programs.

But would it even be possible to identify vital measures of academic progress? Could they be constructed so that teachers could employ them routinely? What would these measures be measures of? With the resources provided by the Institute for Research on Learning Disabilities, Deno, Mirkin, and a cadre of graduate students examined selected reading and written expression behaviors (e.g., oral reading in context) employed by precision teachers, along with their own alternatives (e.g., timed measures of isolated word and contextual reading, vocabulary, and cloze tasks), examining their reliability, growth characteristics, and concurrent validity using standardized achievement measures as the criterion. These studies determined that fixed time samples of oral reading in context and isolated word reading could be created that met all criteria for vital measures of both reading and written expression. The measures could be administered repeatedly throughout the year to monitor progress.

The next critical turn from standard Precision Teaching came with the idea that the content of measurements (i.e., test items) could be separated from the contents of daily lessons. Several studies asked how remote measures could be created from proximal instructed content. Essentially this was a question of how test samples should be drawn—should daily measurement samples be drawn from the words/text that teachers instructed in that very lesson (consistent with Precision Teaching conventions) or from more distal words/text domains of various sizes? For example, should daily progress measures be drawn from samples of words/text that students would encounter during the current two to three week period, from a larger set of words/text that students would encounter during their current grade level, or from an even larger set of words/text that students would encounter sometime during the primary grades? Findings showed that samples from the annual curriculum yielded the strongest information for instructional decision making.

At this point the basic idea of CBM had landed. Growth could be tracked using a finite set of standard measures, collected repeatedly. A set of standard measurement tasks had been identified for progress monitoring. In reading, measures consisted of random samples from grade-level content. Like Precision Teaching, the measures were collected daily, but unlike Precision Teaching they were not dependent on the content of daily lessons. Rather than allowing instruction to dictate measurement, measurement became the arbiter of instruction.

Much remained to be accomplished—extending the research to writing and math, specifying procedural features of CBM (e.g., length of timings), establishing decision rules for judging the adequacy of response to instruction, demonstrating that teachers could routinely employ the procedures, testing the consequential validity of implementing the CBM decision-making process—but the signature features of what proved to be a revolutionary concept of assessment-guided instruction had emerged.

Programmatic Research on CBM

Toward this end, a program of research on CBM ensued. Substantiating the tenability of a CBM measure so it can be used not only to describe competence at a given time but also to track growth in competence and to design instructional programs involves three research stages (see Fuchs, 2004). Investigation of the technical features of the *static score* (i.e., performance level at one point in time) constitutes stage 1. In stage 2, technical features of *slope* are assessed to determine whether increasing CBM scores (or slope) are in fact associated with improvement in overall competence in the academic domain (e.g., Fuchs, Fuchs, Hamlett, Walz, and Germann, 1993). Stage 3 concerns *instructional utility*. This is where studies are conducted to determine whether practitioners can use the CBM information to improve instructional decisions and student achievement (e.g., Fuchs, Deno, and Mirkin, 1984; Fuchs, Fuchs, Hamlett, and Stecker, 1991). It is interesting to consider whether supportive research at each of these stages is required prior to broad field-based application of a CBM measure. It is possible, for example, that a combination of stage 1 and 2 evidence constitutes adequacy for indexing a student's progress and overall responsiveness to instruction, whereas stage 3 evidence is required before a progress-monitoring tool can be considered scientifically validated for formatively designing a student's instructional program.

In any case, over the past thirty-five years, an impressive body of research has accumulated focusing on all three CBM research stages, using both dynamic and curriculum sampling approaches to design CBM tasks. In 2004, the Research Institute on Progress Monitoring (Espin and Wallace) identified 585 CBM research reports, 307 of which were published in journals (121 were unpublished documents, 131 were dissertations, 26 were unclassified). Among the 307 publications, 141 reported empirical studies addressing questions of technical adequacy, instructional utility, and the logistics of implementation in reading, writing, spelling, and math. This literature documented how CBM had expanded its initial focus on special education progress monitoring to include universal screening, general education progress monitoring, and learning disability classification within a Response to Intervention eligibility framework.

At the same time, an analysis of the CBM research base suggests a disproportionate focus on stage 1, where technical features of the static score are examined. Such interest may reside with CBM's increasing popularity as a universal screener, where questions about the static score's relation to predictive criterion measures are essential. Yet universal screening can be accomplished with a wide range of tools, whereas CBM's unique contribution resides in its capacity to model learning over time and to inform instruction. Although a focus on the static CBM score (stage 1) is an important first step in validating CBM for modeling learning over time and informing instruction, it is insufficient. It is not surprising that stage 1 research has captured so much attention because questions about reliability and validity of the static score represent traditional psychometrics, a set of methods and concepts with which most researchers are familiar and comfortable. Also, systematic exploration of stages 2 and 3 is more laborious, requiring ongoing data collection for stage 2 and additionally necessitating practitioners' data utilization for stage 3. Yet to advance the literature on CBM in important ways that capitalize on CBM's unique contribution for modeling progress and enhancing instruction, additional attention to stages 2 and 3 is required.

CBM's Continuing Potential

As a simple, quick, overall indicator of academic competence, CBM has the potential to exert a major impact on the practice of education and student outcomes. In this vein, it is interesting to consider how the Apgar score, another simple indicator of outcome, impacted the obstetricians' practice and the health of newborns. In *Better* (2007), Atul Gawande described the history of obstetrics, which suffered from a mortality rate of one in thirty newborns as recently as the mid-1930s, a statistic that had not substantially improved over the previous century. In 1953, however, Virginia Apgar set the stage for revolutionizing the practice of obstetrics with the publication of a "ridiculously simple" and "revolutionary" idea (p. 185): rating the general health of newborns on a ten-point scale. Babies received two points for being pink all over, two for crying, two for taking vigorous breaths, two for moving all four limbs, and two for having a heart rate that exceeded one hundred. This simple score turned "an intangible and impressionistic clinical concept, the condition of newborn babies, into numbers that people could collect and compare" (p. 187). This quick, general indicator of health permitted obstetricians to experiment with their own strategies and procedures, using their Apgar scores as the dependent variable to determine if outcomes improved. Essentially, it permitted them to formatively evaluate the choices they made about the conduct of their own practice. Additionally, however, the Apgar score allowed hospitals to aggregate data over many obstetricians to evaluate which practices resulted in better outcomes, thereby permitting administrators to standardize practice in ways that further decreased death rates. According to Gawande, the Apgar score "changed everything" (p. 190), producing dramatic improvements in the practice of obstetrics and reducing the 1930s death rate from one in thirty to today's rate of one in five hundred. Gawande concludes, "All patients deserve a simple measure that indicates how well or badly they have [responded to medical intervention] . . . and that pushes the rest of us to innovate" (p. 199).

The analogy between the Apgar score and CBM is not a perfect one. The Apgar is collected only twice with a given baby. The measurement taken immediately upon birth provides guidance to the doctor about whether and if so how to intervene with the child. The measurement collected five minutes after birth serves as the predictor of developmental trajectory. By contrast, although a single CBM, as used in screening, can be used to index "academic health" and to help determine whether intervention may be warranted, a single measurement cannot be used to project developmental trajectory or to determine how to design that intervention, as the Apgar score does. Instead, to estimate developmental trajectory and inform instructional decision making, it is necessary to collect CBM on an ongoing basis, usually weekly, with the resulting trajectory serving to predict future outcome and inform instructional design.

Even given these differences, however, CBM, as a simple indicator of overall academic competence, has the potential to transform an impressionistic clinical concept about academic competence into a score that educators can collect and compare. As the Apgar score transformed obstetrics, the CBM score permits educators to experiment with their own strategies and procedures, using their CBM scores as the dependent variable to determine what produces superior outcomes. In this way, CBM allows teachers to formatively evaluate the choices they make about the conduct of their own education practice, and it permits schools, districts, and states to aggregate data over many teachers to evaluate which practices enhance outcomes, thereby permitting administrators to standardize effective practice. In fact, CBM has the potential to "change everything" (p. 190), as did the Apgar score: to give the education system the tool to formatively enhance services to an individual student and to formatively build knowledge about effective practice. Interestingly, the Apgar score represented an alternative to randomized control trials for building scientific knowledge about what works. As an essentially correlational method answering the question, what practices are associated with better outcomes, practitioners build knowledge by evaluating their outcomes.

The Legacy

Has CBM achieved the impact that the Apgar score exerted on obstetrics? The answer to this question is a definite no. Over the past three decades, CBM screening and progress monitoring has become a widely used tool with important benefits. But recent applications of CBM have been overweighted on the screening end, whereby teachers use CBM to identify students who may require additional intervention. This impact is important; it sensitizes teachers and schools to the need for prevention services for students who are at risk for poor learning outcomes. But this impact is limited, and it fails to achieve the promise of Stanley Deno's revolutionary idea. It fails to achieve the full promise of what CBM offers. Instead, practitioners need to adopt a scientific perspective on the practice of education, whereby they use CBM to evaluate the effects of their instruction—not only to formatively build effective programs and to effect positive outcomes for individual students but also to distinguish generally effective from ineffective practices, thereby providing the basis for data-based education reform. To achieve this promise, educators will require deeper understanding about what the CBM score represents and better understanding about why they engage in progress monitoring. Improving such understanding is an important goal for preservice and inservice professional development because as Gawande concluded, "All . . . [students] deserve a simple measure that indicates how well or badly they have [responded to education intervention] . . . and that pushes the . . . [field] to innovate" (p. 199). This is the promise of Stanley Deno's revolutionary idea; it's the promise of CBM, which should be pursued.

Even so, there are few figures in the history of special education whose scholarship has had such a large impact on advancing thinking in learning disabilities in general and in academic assessment in particular. Deno's conceptualization of CBM is not only universally recognized as a best practice, infused in preparation programs for special education teachers and school psychologists, and employed by practitioners in both fields but also continues to generate research questions that otherwise would not have been raised and prompted the field to think in altogether new ways about the measurement of academic ability. A few examples of such questions follow. How rapidly (days, weeks, months) does general proficiency develop in reading, writing, and math, and which measures are most sensitive to this growth? How often (e.g., semiweekly, weekly, bimonthly) and how many times (e.g., twice, thrice, or more) must we measure to obtain a reliable and valid estimate of growth for purposes of instructional decision making? Do robust indicators of proficiency exist in all academic subjects and skills? Are there other reading indicators besides RAFT and maze? Are dynamic indicators equally valid across vastly different levels of proficiency (e.g., is RAFT an equally valid measure of reading proficiency throughout the range of reading skill?)? Is it possible to improve instructional decision making by supplementing reading and writing CBM with skills analysis in the same way that skills analysis supplements math CBM? Can CBM tasks be refined to reduce measurement error (i.e., to better detect a clear signal of growth amid the noise)? Are there reading CBMs that can reduce false negatives and that better distinguish between students whose oral reading of text is relatively strong but whose comprehension is poor?

Assigning Credit

How much credit does Stanley Deno deserve for this breakthrough idea? In his recent book *Outliers*, Malcom Gladwell argues that when we regard individuals whose achievements mark them as truly exceptional (i.e., outliers) in their field of endeavor (think Bill Gates in technology, the Beatles in music, Oprah Winfrey in entertainment), we mistakenly conflate the person's accomplishments with the person's talents—assigning too much credit to the latter. Gladwell acknowledges that outliers obviously have an abundance of talent, but he reminds us that other factors (e.g., opportunity, social and political context, timing, and luck) may be even more responsible for an individual's achievement of outlier status. We can imagine Gladwell interpreting Deno's achievement of outlier status as the result of the happy intersection of the following: (1) timely government intervention into graduate education that plucked him from public school teaching and allowed him to pursue a doctorate in educational psychology; (2) the opportunity for training in behavioral psychology and educational measurement at the University of Minnesota; (3) exposure to Precision Teaching, an important advance in measurement technology; (4) a laboratory school in which to work; (5) social and legislative forces that gave priority to measuring academic growth toward short and long-term goals; (6) generous research support; and (7) a collection of talented and hardworking colleagues and graduate students, the likes of which occur far too rarely in academia. Gladwell would point to these conditions as instances of social support, political context, opportunity, and auspicious timing. The philosopher-sociologist Michel Foucault (1972) would have had a similar take, although expressed in different terms—it hasn't been Deno speaking and acting, rather Deno was "spoken" by events.

Although there are certainly elements of truth to the environment-weighted analyses of Gladwell and Foucault, we favor a more balanced person-environment attribution. Adaptive expertise (Hatano and Inagaki, 1986) and flexibility (Schwartz, Bransford, and Sears, 2005) allowed Deno to think in innovative ways and adapt and transfer the Precision Teaching problem-solving framework to new contexts. His habits of mind (Costa and Kallick, 2000) including an ability to sustain attention, think and communicate clearly, and persist over the long term were key to this endeavor. Finally, his leadership qualities and capacity for working constructively with colleagues and research teams allowed him to take advantage of university and government resources. Deno's contribution to research and practice has been enormous. He has left us with much to think about and plenty of work ahead.

Note

Both authors contributed equally to this chapter. Order of authorship was determined by the toss of a coin.

References

Bransford, J. D., Brown, A. L., & Cocking, R. R. (2000). *How people learn: Brain, mind, experience, and school* (Expanded ed.). Washington, DC: National Academies Press.

Costa, A., & Kallick, B. (2000). *Habits of mind: A developmental series*. Alexandria, VA: Association for Supervision and Curriculum Development.

Deno, S. L. (1985). Curriculum-based measurement: The emerging alternative. *Exceptional Children, 52*, 219–232.

Deno, S. L., & Jenkins, J. R. (1969). On the "behaviorality" of behavioral objectives. *Psychology in the Schools, 6*(1), 18–24.

Deno, S. L., & Mirkin, P. (1977). *Data-Based Program Modification: A manual*. Reston, VA: Council for Exceptional Children.

Deno, S. L., Mirkin, P. K., & Chiang, B. (1982). Identifying a valid measure of reading. *Exceptional Children, 49*, 36–45.

Espin, C. A., & Wallace, T. (2004). *Descriptive analysis of Curriculum-Based Measurement literature*. Working document. University of Minnesota Institute for Research on Progress Monitoring.

Foucault, M. (1972). *The archaeology of knowledge*. New York, NY: Pantheon.

Fuchs, L. S. (2004). The past, present, and future of Curriculum-Based Measurement research. *School Psychology Review, 33*, 188–192.

Fuchs, L. S., & Deno, S. L. (1991). Paradigmatic distinctions between instructionally relevant measurement models. *Exceptional Children, 57*, 488–501.

Fuchs, L. S., & Deno, S. L. (1992). Effects of curriculum within Curriculum-Based Measurement. *Exceptional Children, 58*, 232–243.

Fuchs, L. S., Deno, S. L., & Mirkin, P. K. (1984). The effects of frequent Curriculum-Based Measurement and evaluation on pedagogy, student achievement, and student awareness of learning. *American Educational Research Journal, 21*, 449–460.

Fuchs, L. S., Fuchs, D., Hamlett, C. L., & Allinder, R. M. (1991). The contribution of skills analysis to Curriculum-Based Measurement in spelling. *Exceptional Children, 57*, 443–452.

Fuchs, L. S., Fuchs, D., Hamlett, C. L., Phillips, N. B., Karns, K., & Dutka, S. (1997). Enhancing students' helping behavior during peer-mediated instruction with conceptual mathematical explanations. *Elementary School Journal, 97*, 223–250.

Fuchs, L. S., Fuchs, D., Hamlett, C. L., & Stecker, P. M. (1990). The role of skills analysis in Curriculum-Based Measurement in math. *School Psychology Review, 19*, 6–22.

Fuchs, L. S., Fuchs, D., Hamlett, C. L., & Stecker, P. M. (1991). Effects of Curriculum-Based Measurement and consultation on teacher planning and student achievement in mathematics operations. *American Educational Research Journal, 28*, 617–641.

Fuchs, L. S., Fuchs, D., Hamlett, C. L., Walz, L., & Germann, G. (1993). Formative evaluation of academic progress: How much growth can we expect? *School Psychology Review, 22*, 27–48.

Fuchs, L. S., Fuchs, D., Hosp, M., & Jenkins, J. R. (2001). Oral reading fluency as an indicator of reading competence: A theoretical, empirical, and historical analysis. *Scientific Studies of Reading, 5*, 239–256.

Gawande, A. (2007). *Better*. New York, NY: Picador.

Gladwell, M. (2008). *Outliers*. New York, NY: Little, Brown.

Hatano, G., & Inagaki, K. (1986). Two courses of expertise. In H. Stevenson, H. Azuma, & K. Hakuta (Eds.), *Child development and education in Japan* (pp. 262–272). New York, NY: Freeman.

Hosp, M. K., & Fuchs, L. S. (2005). Using CBM as an indicator of decoding, word reading, and comprehension: Do the relations change with grade? *School Psychology Review, 34*, 9–26.

Jenkins, J. R., & Deno, S. L. (1968). On the critical components of behavioral objectives. *Psychology in the Schools, 5*, 296–302.

Lovitt, T. C., Schaaf, M. E., & Sayre, E. (1970). The use of direct and continuous measurement to evaluate reading materials and pupil performance. *Focus on Exceptional Children, 2*, 1–11.

Lovitt, T. C. (1975a). Applied behavior analysis and learning disabilities—Part I: Characteristics of ABA, general recommendations, and methodological limitations. *Journal of Learning Disabilities, 8*, 432–443.

Lovitt, T. C. (1975b). Applied behavior analysis and learning disabilities—Part II: Specific research recommendations and suggestions for practitioners. *Journal of Learning Disabilities, 8*, 504–518.

Marston, D. (1989). A curriculum-based approach to assessing academic performance: What is it and why do it? In M. R. Shinn (Ed.), *Curriculum-based measurement: Assessing special children* (pp. 18–78). New York, NY: Guilford Press.

Neisworth, J. T., Deno, S. L., & Jenkins, J. R. (1969). *Student motivation and classroom management.* Lemont, PA: Behavior Technics Press.

Schwartz, D. L., Bransford, J. D., & Sears, D. (2005). Efficiency and innovation in transfer. In J. P. Mestre (Ed.), *Transfer of learning from a modern multidisciplinary perspective* (pp. 1–51). Greenwich, CT: Information Age.

Wayman, M. M., Wallace, T., Wiley, H. I., Tichá, R., & Espin, C. A. (2007). Literature synthesis on Curriculum-Based Measurement in reading. *Journal of Special Education, 41*, 85–120.

I

Contributions to Educational Policy and Practice

2

A Review of Deno and Mirkin's Special Education Resource Teacher (SERT) Model

An Early Effort to Reconcile the Right to Social Integration with a Need for Effective Instruction

Douglas Fuchs and Renee Bradley

In this chapter, we focus on Deno and Mirkin's (1977) well-known Data-Based Program Modification manual. Despite its title, the manual's main purpose is to detail an innovative and ambitious model of service delivery (Special Education Resource Teacher, or SERT) by which special educators' roles would change to ensure an appropriate education for students with disabilities. Although formulated more than three decades ago, this SERT model addresses important issues and problems that resonate today. Our review serves in part as an example of the sometimes cyclical nature of educational policy discussions. It also illustrates the informed, innovative, and practical thinking that has often been demonstrated by the special education community.

To explain the Deno-Mirkin SERT model and its continuing relevance, we begin with the forward to their Data-Based Program Modification manual. It was written by Maynard Reynolds, who explains that the manual's production and dissemination was supported by the Leadership Training Institute and awarded by the U.S. Department of Education to the University of Minnesota, which Reynolds directed in the 1970s. A major purpose of the Leadership Training Institute, he writes, is to support projects helping educators implement Public Law 94-142 (1975), the groundbreaking disability law that, just two years before, had been passed by the U.S. Congress. A related and more specific purpose of the Leadership Training Institute is to "enlarg[e] the capabilities of both regular and special educators to serve handicapped children within as normal environments as possible" (p. iii).

The Leadership Training Institute's twin focus on special educators and general educators was foreshadowed, if not directed, by a basic, important, and often unrecognized aspect of Public Law 94-142. By promoting both the social integration of children and youth with disabilities and their appropriate academic instruction, the architects of the federal law created a dilemma for those responsible for implementing it. Whereas virtually all agreed that a regular class placement was necessary (if not sufficient) to achieve social integration, there was little agreement about where a special-needs student would get the academic instruction she or he needed. To help educators think broadly about this, the U.S. Department of Education described a continuum of placements and services in the regulations accompanying the federal law. This continuum included resource rooms, self-contained classes, special day schools, and residential facilities in addition to the regular classroom. But the establishment of a continuum of special placements and services still raised the issue of how to maximize the joint probability of providing both integration and effective instruction to every special-needs child. This is the pivotal issue that shaped the work of Reynolds's Leadership Training Institute and Deno and Mirkin's SERT model—how, in other words, to reconcile the tension between addressing the necessities of social integration and academic preparation.

Social Integration versus Academic Instruction

Social Integration

Deno and Mirkin's SERT model reflects strong support for the importance of social integration. In describing and affirming the Normalization Principle, the two authors write the following:

> The assumption is that unless a sufficient case can be made for an alternative educational setting, the least restrictive environment for the individual and, therefore, the one in which he belongs, is the modal educational program. For the large majority of handicapped children this modal program is the regular classroom—the mainstream. (p. 18)

In the 1970s and 1980s, additional faculty in the University of Minnesota's Department of Psycho-Educational Studies (now Educational Psychology) supported social integration. Many actively challenged the still-prevailing practice of separating all or most children and adults with disabilities from those without disabilities. For example, Bruce Balow closed the department's reading clinic, which he directed, believing it was more appropriate for the local schools than the university to provide reading services (personal communication). He worked with local educators to establish the Minneapolis Public Schools' Basic Skills Reading Center (see Balow, Fuchs, and Kasbohm, 1978). Don Moores promoted Total Communication for children with hearing impairments because he believed it would promote greater skill development and integration than conventional, aural-oral methods of communication. Bob Bruininks (former president of the University of Minnesota) founded the Institute on Community Integration, which, then as now, aims to improve policies and practices to ensure that all children, youth, and adults with disabilities contribute to their communities of choice. And Maynard Reynolds, through the Leadership Training Institute and other federally funded and state-funded projects, was perhaps the department's most articulate, passionate, and visible advocate of social integration.

Academic Instruction

Yet in their Data-Based Program Modification manual, Deno and Mirkin also express strong skepticism that the regular classroom can accommodate all children. They write the following:

> The problem [remaining] . . . is to create educational programs
> that . . . produce the greater inclusion of persons into the mainstream
> of our society. [Such] effective programs are defined not in terms
> of their procedures but, rather, of their outcomes. Placing students
> with skill deficiencies in more normal settings means nothing unless
> the placement enhances their development . . . [T]he reality is that
> general educational programs, regardless of attempts to individualize
> them, will always be unable to provide an appropriate education for
> some proportion of children. (p. 21)

These last quotations indicate Deno and Mirkin's support of the concept of mainstreaming (pp. 22–25) and the continuum of special education placements and services. The mainstreaming concept and special education continuum bespoke fundamental beliefs that (a) the needs of students with disabilities must be served in the regular class whenever possible (p. 21), and (b) the regular class placement was not going to meet the necessities of all special-needs children.

At the same time, Deno and Mirkin—and much policymaking in the 1970s (see section VIII of the bylaws of the Council for Exceptional Children [CEC])—held that if a student's designated least restrictive environment was not the regular classroom, an important educational objective was to prepare him or her for transition to a setting closer to the regular classroom, if not the mainstream itself. Thus, according to the CEC policy, no placement was viewed as permanent. Rather, self-contained classes, resource rooms, and the like were conceptualized as stopovers en route to the eventual destination of the mainstream classroom. This training-for-the-next-setting concept (e.g., Cardin-Smith and Fowler, 1983; Vincent, Salisbury, Walter, Brown, Gruenwald, and Powers, 1980) did not mean that sooner or later all students with disabilities would be educated in the regular classroom. It did mean that teachers and administrators should judge their success, at least in part, in terms of how far they advanced their students up the continuum toward regular classrooms.

The SERT Model

Deno and Mirkin write the following:

> The SERT is a school-based (rather than itinerant) teacher/consultant who is the first person to whom the regular class teacher turns when [she or he] recognizes that the modal program is not optimum for a child's continued personal-social or academic development. The SERT is a specialist . . . capable of organizing and managing individual program modifications that . . . meet the requirements of due process and [advance] individual development . . . through . . . continuous objective evaluation of programs and their impacts on individual children. (p. 26)

Instructional Role

The SERT's instructional role was heavily influenced by Data-Based Instruction, or experimental teaching (see Deno, 1985; Deno and Mirkin, 1977; Fuchs, Deno, and Mirkin, 1984). Data-Based Instruction requires a trained clinician-researcher to work individually with children or with small groups of children to determine effective instruction by both systematically applying various teaching strategies and continually measuring the child's academic response. It requires patience, perseverance, ingenuity, and tolerance of ambiguity, as well as deep knowledge of assessment and instruction. Whereas the SERT model was largely based on Data-Based Instruction, this instruction, in turn, is based on several key assumptions, expressed by Deno and Mirkin as follows:

- Assumption 1: At the present time we are unable to prescribe specific and effective changes in instruction for individual pupils with certainty. Therefore, changes in instructional programs which are arranged for an individual child can be treated only as hypotheses which must be empirically tested before a decision can be made on whether they are effective for that child. (p. 22)
- Assumption 2: Time series research designs are uniquely appropriate for testing instructional reforms (hypotheses) which are intended to improve individual performance. (p. 22)
- Assumption 3: Special education is an intervention system, created to produce reforms in the educational programs of selected individuals, which can (and, now with due process requirements, must) be empirically tested. (p. 24)

Deno and Mirkin write the following:

The arguments supporting assumptions #1 and #2 establish that we cannot know in advance whether a specific reform will . . . benefit a child, and that the best methodology . . . for empirically verifying instructional hypotheses is the time series design. The implication we draw . . . is that we [must] . . . apply time series research designs to evaluate the effects of special education services provided for every pupil. (p. 24)

Indeed, research (e.g., Fuchs and Fuchs, 1984) has demonstrated that Data-Based Instruction helps knowledgeable practitioners develop instructional programs that accelerate the academic progress of students with disabilities. As advocates of mainstreaming, Deno and Mirkin's (1977) hope and expectation was that this acceleration of academic progress would increase the likelihood that more special-needs children would move up the special education continuum of placements toward regular classrooms. In short, Data-Based Instruction (including use of Curriculum-Based

Measurement—or progress monitoring or formative assessment) was viewed as both strengthening students' academic performance and preparing them to move into settings closer to typically developing peers.

The Need for Cross-Training

Despite its effectiveness and importance, Data-Based Instruction, by itself, was viewed by Deno and Mirkin as insufficient to achieve social integration. SERTs, therefore, were cross-trained to do much more. The SERT model emphasized "interpersonal and resource management skills" (p. 26). SERTs were called on to coordinate the comprehensive assessments of student problems. Thus they required knowledge of medical, psychological, and educational diagnostic procedures and training to prepare them as effective and efficient managers and communicators. They were responsible for ongoing collaborative decision making; they coordinated all changes to a child's program with the classroom teachers and led building-based reviews of program modifications that necessitated the separation of a child from his or her regular class. These responsibilities meant they had less time for direct instruction. So they were prepared to conduct direct instruction primarily during initial assessment and program development. They were trained to turn over instruction and program management to the child's regular classroom teacher, peer, or paraprofessional. In this way, they had the opportunity to individualize instruction for more children rather than be restricted to a case load (p. 27). Finally, they were responsible for the review of all special-needs students in the building, irrespective of who was providing the instruction.

The Postmainstreaming Era: The Case against Mainstreaming

For the past fifteen years or so, we have been in a "postmainstreaming" era. Like the term *postmodern*, postmainstreaming connotes rejection; in this case, rejection of an approach to integration that, as described, was promoted in Public Law 94-142 and proceduralized by Deno and Mirkin in their Data-Based Program Modification manual. Many today would dismiss the SERT model on grounds that it doesn't take inclusion far enough. Some might even suggest that the model is exclusionary, not inclusionary. Mainstreaming is rejected by many today because it requires that disability should first be attenuated—that is, academic weaknesses must be strengthened; inappropriate behaviors should be made more appropriate, before children are moved from special education to regular education (or from a placement further away from the mainstream to a setting closer to it). In other words, mainstreaming requires special educators and other school personnel to *change the child* before placing her or him closer to or into the regular class. According to mainstreaming critics, this places an unfair burden on children and youth with special needs. The burden, say the critics, should be on the educators; it is their responsibility to *change the regular classroom* to accommodate all.

The legitimacy of this postmainstreaming position rests partly on the fact that over the years many special education placements have failed to provide appropriate instruction. As a result, numerous students with disabilities remained separated in settings that did not provide educational benefit. Years ago, Fuchs, Fuchs, and Fernstrom (1993) asked the following:

> If all special educators in a given district viewed the cascade [continuum of special education placements and services] as a dynamic concatenated system, and regularly trained students for the next setting, what might we see? Teachers and administrators from hospital and residential placements to part-time resource rooms would work in synchrony, tuning activity in their respective settings to that of adjacent settings. This would demand frequent communication, visitations, and development of inclusionary and exclusionary criteria for guiding student movement into and out of the different levels of the special education system. As a result, many children would move "up" the cascade. Teachers of resource and self-contained classes would work with regular educators to reintegrate students with disabilities into mainstream classrooms where more than a few might be decertified as disabled. An ultimate effect might be a leveling off of, if not a reduction in, special education enrollment and costs to local and state governments. (pp. 151–152)

"In fact," Fuchs et al. (1993) wrote,

> special education enrollment increased by 93,090 students in 1988–89, raising the number of students served nationwide to 4,587,370, a 23.7% increase over the number reported in 1976–77 (Annual Report to Congress, 1990, table 1.1, pp. 5–6). Whereas special education students in some school districts make impressive academic gains (e.g., Marston, 1987–1988) and indeed move up the cascade and into

the mainstream where some are decertified as disabled (e.g., Osborne, Schulte, & McKinney, 1991; Walker et al., 1988), national data on special education enrollment and cost suggest these districts are the exception, not the rule. In many school systems the cascade of services may be characterized more accurately as a turgid backwater than as a swiftly flowing current carrying students toward the mainstream. (p. 152)

"Inclusive Education"

In the current postmainstreaming era, general and special educators, advocates, and policymakers have all placed their hopes on teacher consultants, cooperative learning, coteaching, accommodating the curriculum, and problem solving. Each of these professional roles, best practices, and policies has attempted to expand the resources and capacity of general education by drawing on resources from other programs, including special education. Indeed, the Regular Education Initiative in the 1980s, the Full-Inclusion movement of the 1990s, and the current Responsiveness-to-Intervention/Instruction approaches have all been based on the assumption that general education can and should be better resourced and made more capable of accommodating all or virtually all children's academic and social needs. Whereas these initiatives, movements, and approaches have no doubt helped some—perhaps many—children with disabilities, they have not helped many others (see Fuchs and Deshler, 2007). And the reason for this is clear. They have not been intensive enough—which is to say, they have not been individualized, data based, or systematic. They have not involved educators trained in assessment, instruction, and applied behavior analysis, as Deno and Mirkin's (1977) SERTs. These instructional and instructor characteristics are what students at the bottom 5 percent to 10 percent of the achievement continuum require.

"Inclusive education" is not inclusive for hundreds of thousands of children and youth with severe learning or behavioral problems who may be called *learning disabled, behavior disordered, language impaired,* or *intellectually disabled.* Some would object to this assertion. They might characterize it as unduly pessimistic, insufficiently documented, or politically motivated. Whereas we would disagree with these characterizations, pointing, for example, to the National Longitudinal Transition Study database (Wagner, Newman, Cameto, Levine, and Marder, 2003), we would accept that it is probably politically incorrect to suggest that inclusive education has not worked for many special-needs students. Politically incorrect or not, it is past time to acknowledge the fact. Rather than pointing a finger of blame at this person or that group for contributing to the unacceptably low performance of so many special-needs children, it is time for serious reflection, for dialogue between groups within the disability community on the conundrum of reconciling the importance of social integration with the importance of effective instruction.

Deno and Mirkin's prointegration orientation and skeptical view of general education's capacity to accommodate all students with disabilities represents not really a contradiction or inconsistency but a view that combines principle and reality, an important ideal whereby all students are schooled effectively and together and an indisputable fact that, despite best intentions all around, regular education as currently conceived doesn't often have the will or way to make this happen. It is this disjunction—between what we wish for and what is—that creates cracks in service delivery into which many of our children fall and fail, resulting in disappointment and discord among service providers, advocates, professional organizations, and others. Deno and Mirkin attempted to resolve the discord by creating a role for special educators that balanced integration with instruction—much like the balance reflected in the least restrictive principle in PL 94-142. Although they created a service delivery model that many today would not support, their effort was detailed, reasonable, innovative, and largely data based. It could serve as a starting point for rethinking how to educate many special-needs children and youth in the new century.

Note

Renee Bradley participated in the preparation of this manuscript as a former teacher, consultant, clinical professor, and professional colleague. Opinions expressed herein are those of the authors and do not necessarily reflect the position of the U.S. Department of Education, Office of Special Education Programs, and no official endorsement should be inferred.

References

Annual Report to Congress. (1990). *Twelfth annual report to Congress on the implementation of the Education of the Handicapped Act.* Washington, DC: U.S. Department of Education.

Balow, B., Fuchs, D., & Kasbohm, M. (1978). Teaching non-readers to read: An evaluation of the Basic Skill Centers in Minneapolis. *Journal of Learning Disabilities, 11,* 351–354.

Cardin-Smith, L. K., & Fowler, S. A. (1983). An assessment of student and teacher behavior in treatment and mainstream classrooms for preschool and kindergarten. *Analysis and Interpretation in Developmental Disabilities, 3,* 35–37.

Deno, S. L. (1985). Curriculum-based measurement: The emerging alternative. *Exceptional Children, 52,* 219–232.

Deno, S. L., & Mirkin, P. K. (1977). *Data-Based Program Modification: A manual.* Minneapolis: Leadership Training Institute, University of Minnesota. (Also, Reston, VA: The Council for Exceptional Children.)

Fuchs, D., & Deshler, D. (2007). What we need to know about Responsiveness to Intervention (and shouldn't be afraid to ask). *Learning Disabilities Research and Practice, 22,* 119–128.

Fuchs, D., Fuchs, L. S., & Fernstrom, P. (1993). A conservative approach to special education reform: Mainstreaming through transenvironmental programming and Curriculum-Based Measurement. *American Educational Research Journal, 30,* 149–177.

Fuchs, L. S., Deno, S. L., & Mirkin, P. K. (1984). The effects of frequent Curriculum-Based Measurement and evaluation on pedagogy, student achievement, and student awareness. *American Educational Research Journal, 21,* 449–460.

Fuchs, L. S., & Fuchs, D. (1984). Effects of systematic formative evaluation: A meta-analysis. *Exceptional Children, 53,* 199–208.

Marston, D. (1987–1988). The effectiveness of special education: A time-series analysis of reading performance in regular and special education settings. *Journal of Special Education, 21,* 13–26.

Osborne, S. S., Schulte, A. C., & McKinney, J. D. (1991). A longitudinal study of students with learning disabilities in mainstream and resource programs. *Exceptionality, 2,* 81–95.

Vincent, L. J., Salisbury, C., Walter, G., Brown, P., Gruenwald, I. J., & Powers, M. (1980). Program evaluation and curriculum development in early childhood special education: Criteria of the next environment. In W. Sailor, B. Wilcox, & L. Brown (Eds.), *Methods of instruction for severely handicapped students* (pp. 303–338). Baltimore, MD: Brooks.

Wagner, M., Newman, L., Cameto, R., Levine, P., & Marder, C. (2003). Going to school: Instructional contexts, programs, and participation of secondary school students with disabilities. *A report of the National Longitudinal Transition Study-2 (NLTS2).* Menlo Park, CA: SRI International. Available at http://www.nlts2.org/reports/2003_12/nlts2_report_2003_12_complete.pdf

Walker, D. K., Singer, J. D., Palfrey, J. S., Orza, M., Wenger, M., & Butler, J. A. (1988). Who leaves and who stays in special education: A 2-year follow-up study. *Exceptional Children, 54,* 393–402.

3
_____

Using Curriculum-Based Measurement to Develop Educationally Meaningful and Legally Sound Individualized Education Programs (IEPs)

Mitchell L. Yell and Todd W. Busch

In 1977, the Council for Exceptional Children published *Data-Based Program Modification: A Manual*, written by Stan Deno and Phyllis Mirkin. Deno and Mirkin developed Data-Based Program Modification to provide teachers with a set of behaviorally based procedures for evaluating and improving the educational programs of students with learning problems. The basic process of data-based program modification consisted of (a) assessing a student's performance discrepancies, (b) specifying the student's educational program goals and objectives, and (c) measuring the student's progress and performance. Data-Based Program Modification served as a precursor to Curriculum-Based Measurement (CBM).

Interestingly enough, 1977 was also the year that the regulations implementing the Education for All Handicapped Children Act (EAHCA), sometimes called PL 94-142, took effect. The purpose of the law was to require that states provide a free appropriate public education (FAPE) to students with disabilities. Although the EAHCA and the implementing regulations were complex, the purpose of the law was elegant and relatively straightforward: School district personnel were required to locate students with disabilities who were failing to learn in general education classrooms and then to convene collaborative teams to plan and deliver a program of special education services based on students' unique educational needs. The keystone of the FAPE requirement was that all eligible students with disabilities would receive a special education provided in conformity with his or her Individualized Education Program (IEP).

The purposes of the IEP were remarkably similar to Deno and Mirkin's purposes in developing Data-Based Program Modification. That is, an individualized assessment of the student was conducted to determine his or her educational needs. Based on this assessment a program consisting of measurable goals and special education services was developed to address the student's needs. The success of the student in the program was then monitored, and teachers used the resulting data to make important educational decisions regarding the student's program. Although the scope and empirical research on CBM has expanded over the past thirty-four years from core academic skills to also include preacademic skills areas and content-area learning for older secondary students (Espin, Shin, and Busch, 2005; Greenwood, Dunn, Ward, and Luze, 2003; Kaminski and Good, 1996, 1998; Lembke, Foegen, Whittaker, and Hampton, 2008; McConnell, McEvoy, and Priest, 2002), the tenants on which CBM was founded remain. CBM measures must be technically adequate, allow for frequent administrations, be sensitive to small changes in student growth, and be time efficient (Deno, 1985, 1992). These characteristics of CBM and the ability of the measures to index student growth make it a viable tool for monitoring students' progress on goals and objectives written into their IEPs.

Our purpose in this chapter is to examine how CBM can be used in developing, implementing, and monitoring students' IEPs. We first examine the procedural and substantive aspects of IEP development. We then explain how CBM can be used when developing IEPs. It is our contention that by using CBM as a basis to develop students' IEPs, teachers and other members of the team can ensure that their IEPs are both educationally meaningful and legally sound. In fact, we believe by using CBM to develop students' IEPs, monitor student progress, and react appropriately to the data, school-based teams will have IEPs that are virtually legally unassailable.

Background on IEPs

In 1975, the EAHCA was enacted to guarantee that eligible students with disabilities received an education suited to their unique needs. In this law, Congress granted every eligible student with a disability the right to receive a FAPE. Congress believed that this goal was best accomplished by individualizing a student's education. The vehicle by which Congress attempted to ensure that students with disabilities would receive an individualized and appropriate education was the IEP. The purpose of the IEP process was to develop an *individualized and meaningful* educational program for eligible students with disabilities. In the IEP process, school-based teams (a) conduct relevant assessments of students' educational needs, (b) develop meaning-ful goals and objectives based on the assessment, (c) determine the special education and related services that will be provided to the student, and (d) establish evaluation and measurement criteria by which a student's progress toward his or her goals will be monitored. The IEP, therefore, is of critical importance to educators, parents, and students. It is the process by which school-based teams determine the content of a student's program of special education and a written document that is the blueprint of the student's FAPE. Because of the legal and educational importance of the IEP, it is imperative that school-based teams develop IEPs that are both educationally meaning-ful and legally sound.

Although IEPs have been the soul of the individual students' special education programs for thirty-five years, they have not yet met the expecta-tions that Congress originally intended when it mandated IEPs. Frequently, IEPs are fraught with legal errors (Huefner, 2008), and far too often IEPs are neither individualized nor educationally meaningful (Drasgow, Yell, and Robinson, 2001). Moreover, often (a) assessments are not aligned with the annual goals in an IEP (Bateman, 2007; Yell and Stecker, 2003); (b) goals that are written are not measurable (Bateman, 2007; Drasgow et al., 2001); and (c) data are not collected to monitor student progress (Bateman and Linden, 2006; Yell and Stecker, 2003). The problems that school-based teams have with IEP development led Bateman and Linden (2006) to ob-serve the following:

> Sadly, most IEPs are horrendously burdensome to teachers and
> nearly useless to parents and children. Far from being a creative,
> flexible, data-based, and individualized application of the best edu-
> cational interventions to a child, the typical IEP is empty . . . many, if
> not most goals and objectives couldn't be measured if one tried, and
> all too often no effort is made to actually assess the child's progress
> toward the goal. (p. 63)

Clearly, to meet the requirements of the Individuals with Disabilities Education Improvement Act (IDEA; 2004) and to develop special educa-tion programs that confer meaningful benefit, special educators and school-based teams must have the skills to develop educationally meaningful and legally sound IEPs. Unfortunately, as Bradley and Danielson (2004) observe, many school personnel and parents lack the resources, training, and supports necessary to craft meaningful and legally sound IEPs.

Procedural and Substantive Aspects of IEP Development

An additional challenge faced by IEP teams is that properly crafted IEPs must address two sets of requirements: procedural and substantive. These requirements guide the development and implementation of a student's FAPE (Drasgow et al., 2001). *Procedural requirements* refer to those aspects of the IDEA that compel schools to follow the strictures of the law when developing an IEP (e.g., timelines, IEP membership). Adherence to these requirements is necessary because major procedural errors on the part of a school district may render an IEP inappropriate in the eyes of a hearing officer or court (Bateman and Linden, 2006; Huefner, 2008; Yell and Drasgow, 2000). It is important, therefore, that school district personnel understand their procedural responsibilities when planning, developing, and reviewing the IEP. The most serious procedural error that IEP teams can make is to fail to involve a student's parents in a meaningful collaboration when developing an IEP. In fact, this error may be the most likely to result in a hearing officer or judge invalidating an IEP.

Developing educationally meaningful and legally sound IEPs, however, is not just about following procedures; it is also about crafting and implementing special education programs that lead to meaningful educational benefit for students. Unfortunately, as the President's Commission on Excellence in Special Education notes, educators often place "process above results, and bureaucratic compliance above student achievement, excellence, and outcomes" (U.S. Department of Education, 2002, p. 3). It is important to understand, however, that procedurally correct IEPs will not meet legal standards if the student's educational program does not result in his or her achieving meaningful educational benefit (Bateman and Linden, 2006). It is crucial that IEPs also meet the substantive standards of the IDEA. In fact, this is so important that in 2004 Congress included the following language in the reauthorized IDEA: "A hearing officer's determination of whether a child received FAPE must be based on substantive grounds" (34 C.F.R. § 513(a)(1)).

Substantive requirements refer to the content of a student's special education program and compel schools to provide an education that confers meaningful educational benefit to a student. According to Drasgow et al. (2001), the crucial determinant in hearings or cases involving the substantive standard of the IDEA is whether the student makes educational progress. Regrettably, schools often seem to have a difficult time with the substantive requirements for developing and implementing IEPs. In fact, there is probably less compliance with the mandate that students show educational progress than any other IDEA-related obligation (Bateman and Linden, 2006).

Meeting the Substantive Requirements of the IDEA

Because of the crucial nature of the IEP to all students with disabilities, and the requirement that IEPs confer meaningful educational benefit, it may be logical to assume that special education teachers are prepared to meet both the procedural and substantive requirements of the IDEA when they take part in developing IEPs. Unfortunately, this is frequently not the case. Too often the preservice and inservice education of special education teachers stress the procedural requirements of IEPs but do not include professional development in the substantive development of IEPs. The problem with such a focus is that an IEP team may develop a procedurally impeccable IEP that is substantively worthless. That is, just because an IEP has passed the procedural litmus test does not mean that the IEP will confer meaningful educational benefit. To ensure that students' IEPs meet the substantive requirement of the IDEA, it is crucial that IEP teams understand the importance of assessment, research-based educational programming, and progress monitoring.

Using Curriculum-Based Measurement to Develop
Educationally Meaningful and Legally Sound IEPs

To ensure that IEPs confer meaningful educational benefit, and thus provide a FAPE, IEP teams must develop IEPs that meet the procedural and substantive requirements of the IDEA. The procedural requirements are seemingly easily met as long as a student's parents are meaningfully involved in the IEP process and the IEP team includes the required members. Developing IEPs that meet the substantive requirements of the IDEA poses a greater challenge to IEP teams. Meeting these requirements requires that assessment, programming, and progress monitoring be aligned and that the IEP confers meaningful educational benefit. This can only be ensured if IEP teams (a) conduct educationally meaningful assessments, (b) develop measurable annual goals, (c) implement appropriate special education services based on peer-reviewed research, and (d) adopt a data-based progress monitoring system that is implemented systematically and frequently and is used to guide decision making.

CBM presents IEP teams with a research-validated assessment tool that can be used to monitor student progress (Deno, 1985). Most importantly for IEP development, the results of CBMs can be used to develop the present levels of academic achievement and functional performance (PLAAFP) statements, measurable annual goals, and formatively assess a student's progress toward achieving his or her goals. Because CBM is a measure of global achievement and not just a measure of mastery of curriculum objectives, it yields important information that allows teachers and IEP teams to assess student progress toward long-term goals. CBM data are collected on a frequent and systematic basis; therefore, teachers have the information necessary to make instructional decisions regarding the effectiveness of a student's special education program and to adjust the student's instructional program when necessary. Thus CBM is an excellent tool for ensuring that students' IEPs confer meaningful educational benefit.

Writing PLAAFP Statements Using CBM

The first step in developing an IEP that meets the substantive requirements of the IDEA is developing a PLAAFP statement that is based on an instructionally relevant assessment. The information gathered from the assessment and reported in the PLAAFP statement is, in essence, the baseline information from which annual goals are written, special education services are determined, and educational progress is measured. A U.S. district court judge directly addressed the importance of the PLAAFP when he ruled that a school district had denied a student a FAPE because the school's IEP was based on an inadequate assessment. In his opinion, the judge wrote the following:

> This deficiency goes to the heart of the IEP; the child's level of academic achievement and functional performance is the foundation on which the IEP must be built. Without a clear identification of [the child's] present levels, the IEP cannot set measurable goals, evaluate the child's progress and determine which educational and related services are needed. (*Kirby v. Cabell County Board of Education*, 2006, p. 694)

When a student has deficits in basic academic skill areas, writing a PLAAFP statement using CBM meets the requirements of the IDEA. To explain how CBM may be used to develop the PLAAFP statement, Yell and Stecker (2003) provide the example of Sally, a fourth-grade student with learning disabilities. Sally had a serious reading problem. Her teacher administered several randomly selected reading passages from the fourth-grade reading curriculum. (Note that although Sally was in fourth grade, she was being taught in the third-grade reading textbook and assessed in the fourth-grade reading textbook. All CBM reading passages were selected from the fourth-grade book.) After three administrations, the teacher calculated the median of forty words read correctly per minute. The median was entered as the baseline on a graph. This represented the beginning point for Sally's special education program. The fourth-grade teachers had collected information on the words read per minute for all fourth-grade students, so Sally's teacher was able to use this information when writing her PLAAFP statement.

The PLAAFP statement reads as follows:

> Sally's learning disability affects her performance in reading. When Sally is given randomly selected passages from the fourth-grade reading textbook she reads 40 words correctly per minute. Her same age peers read the same material at an average of 100 correct words per minute. Sally's learning disability makes it very difficult for her to progress in classes in which extensive reading is required. (p. 82)

Recall that legally sound PLAAFP statements must (a) describe the effects of a student's disability on his or her performance in all areas that are affected by his or her disability (e.g., reading, mathematics, behavior), (b) be written in objective and measurable terms that are easily understood by all members of the team, and (c) describe how a student's disability affects his or her involvement and progress in the general curriculum. Sally's PLAAFP statement satisfies the requirements in the IDEA for the PLAAFP statement.

Following development of the PLAAFP and a discussion of a student's educational needs, the IEP team must develop a student's special education program. This consists of two tasks: (a) writing the measurable annual goals and (b) determining the special education services that will be needed in order to meet the student's needs.

Writing Measurable Annual Goals Using CBM

The purpose of the annual goals is to measure the progress a student makes in his or her special education program. The Individuals with Disabilities Education Act Amendments of 1997 added the requirements that annual goals be written in measurable terms and that an IEP must also include a statement about how a student's progress toward the goals will be measured. All IEPs must include objectively measurable annual goals. A critical requirement that must be included in all IEPs is a method for measuring a student's progress toward his or her goals. This means that the goals must actually be measurable. In fact, failing to measure a student's progress most likely would result in a hearing officer or judge invalidating the IEP and determining that FAPE had been denied if the IEP was challenged in a due process hearing or court case (Bateman and Linden, 2006). If IEP members do not develop measurable goals and do not measure a student's progress toward them, the IEP goals become meaningless and useless (Bateman, 2007). A due process hearing officer in Rio Rancho Public Schools (2003) summarized the importance of including measurable goals when he ruled the following:

> The purpose of measurable goals is to enable the child's teacher(s), parents, and others to gauge how well the child is progressing toward achieving the goal . . . This information allows the IEP team to determine whether a child is making adequate progress, and, if not, to revise the child's program accordingly. (p. 140)

In his decision he also noted, "Measurable goals are critical to planning and implementing an IEP" (Rio Rancho, p. 140).

Unfortunately the annual goals written in many IEPs are not measurable. Bateman and Linden (2006) asserted that IEP goals that were not measurable would very likely invalidate the IEP in the eyes of a hearing officer or judge. Goals are too often not aligned with the PLAAFP statement and frequently lack measurable outcomes. Neither the IDEA nor the regulations implementing the IDEA indicate the specific form that goals are to take, beyond requiring that they be measurable. One method that can be used is the model first proposed by Mager in 1962. Mager suggests that to be measurable, goals (which Mager referred to as instructional objectives) need to have three components. These components are (a) a target behavior, (b) the conditions under which the goal was to be measured, and (c) a criterion for acceptable performance.

CBM is an excellent tool for writing annual goals. To set an annual goal, Sally's teacher uses the baseline measure of Sally's reading performance, the number of weeks until the end of the school year, and an ambitious but reasonable target of words gained per week. These data are used to predict the number of words that Sally will be able to read correctly in one minute at the end of the school year.

Sally's measurable annual goal was as follows:

> By the end of the school year, when presented with a passage from the fourth-grade reading textbook, Sally will correctly read aloud 100 words per minute. (p. 83)

This CBM goal contains the three components that Mager (1962) suggests are needed to write measurable goals: (a) the target behavior (i.e., read aloud), (b) the conditions of measurement (i.e., by the end of the school year, when presented with a passage from the fourth-grade reading textbook), and (c) the criterion for acceptable performance (i.e., one hundred words read correctly per minute).

Monitoring Students' Progress Using CBM

Progress monitoring is essential to evaluating the appropriateness of a student's IEP (Etscheidt, 2006). Additionally, all IEPs must also include a description of how and when a student's progress will be measured. Thus school-based teams must develop and implement progress-monitoring procedures, which result in the collection of meaningful data, in every student's IEP. A student's progress toward his or her IEP goals must be reported to his or her parents as often as the parents of nondisabled children receive progress reports or report cards, usually every six to nine weeks. The purpose of the progress monitoring requirement of the IDEA was aptly stated by a state review panel in the Escambia Public School System (2004) when they held that "frequent reviews of progress toward the goals provides the student's teacher with supportive data needed to make a determination of the success of the services provided. Without such data these critical decisions cannot be made" (Escambia, p. 254). Unfortunately, there is less compliance with this required component of the IEP than almost any other legal requirement (Bateman, 2007; Etscheidt, 2006; Yell,

2009). Moreover, when progress-monitoring procedures are actually included in IEPs, they are often the types of procedures that will not produce meaningful data (Pemberton, 2003; Yell, 2009).

Administrative and judicial decisions have shown that there are four critical mistakes IEP teams make with respect to monitoring students' progress. These mistakes are failing to (a) include any method for progress monitoring in IEPs, (b) delegate the task of collecting the progress-monitoring data to anyone on the team, (c) collect progress-monitoring data frequently enough to meet the requirements of the data, and (d) collect meaningful data that can actually provide valid information regarding a student's progress. An important consideration in determining how progress will be monitored, therefore, is that the measures must be objective and meaningful. That is, subjective or anecdotal data are not sufficient. If the data show that the student is not progressing, something in his or her program must be changed. Yell and Stecker (2003) asserted that IEP teams must continually collect meaningful data to document student progress and, thus, to demonstrate the effectiveness of the special education program. Students' IEP teams can meet these requirements of the IDEA by using appropriate data-collection procedures and using the data to guide instructional decision making.

CBM allows the IEP team and special education teacher to collect meaningful data on a student's progress. These data are information that a teacher can use to make decisions about the effectiveness of a student's program. Moreover, this information can be reported to a student's parents. Because CBM data are graphed, the information is easily understood. In Yell and Stecker's example, Sally's teacher collected CBM reading data twice a week and plotted the data on Sally's graph. When the teacher had seven or more data points, he would apply data-based decision rules to determine if Sally was making sufficient progress to allow her to reach her long-term goal by the end of the year. Sally's teacher used this formative data to develop a maximally effective reading program, thus increasing the likelihood of conferring meaningful benefit and meeting the substantive requirements of the IDEA.

Summary: Using CBM to Develop IEPs

The FAPE requirements of the IDEA compel school-based teams to develop IEPs that meet the procedural and substantive requirements of the law. That is, IEP team members need a thorough understanding of the legal strictures that they must follow when developing a student's IEP. It is more important, from a legal and educational standpoint, that teams develop and implement IEPs that result in meaningful educational benefit, thus meeting the substantive requirements of the IDEA. The development of CBM by Deno and his colleagues allows for teachers to empirically test on an ongoing basis whether students are deriving meaningful educational benefit from the instruction being delivered and to adjust the instruction if gains toward the IEP goals and objectives are not being realized. By using CBM, teachers and IEP teams can ensure that their IEPs are educational meaningful and legally sound.

References

Amanda J. v. Clark County Sch. Dist., 260 F.3d 1106 (9th Cir. 2001).

Bateman, B. D. (2007). *From gobbledygook to clearly written annual IEP goals.* Verona, WI: Attainment/IEP Resources.

Bateman, B. D., & Linden, M.A. (2006). *Better IEPs: How to develop legally correct and educationally useful IEPs* (4th ed.). Verona, WI: Attainment/IEP Resources.

Board of Education v. Rowley, 458 U.S. 176 (1982).

Bradley, M. R., & Danielson, L. (2004). The Office of Special Education Programs LD initiative: A context for inquiry and consensus. *Journal of Learning Disabilities, 27*, 186–194.

Deno, S. L. (1985). Curriculum-based measurement: The emerging alternative. *Exceptional Children, 52*, 219–232.

Deno, S. L. (1992). The nature and development of Curriculum-Based Measurement. *Preventing School Failure, 36*(2), 5–10.

Deno, S. L., & Mirkin, P. K. (1977). *Data-Based Program Modification: A manual.* Reston, VA: The Council for Exceptional Children.

Drasgow, E., Yell, M. L., & Robinson, T. R. (2001). Developing legally and educationally appropriate IEPs: Federal law and lessons learned from the Lovaas hearings and cases. *Remedial and Special Education, 22*, 359–373.

Escambia County Public School System, 42 IDELR 248 (SEA AL 2004).

Espin, C. A., Busch, T., Shin, J., & Kruschwitz, R. (2001). Curriculum-based measures in the content areas: Validity of vocabulary-matching measures as indicators of performance in social studies. *Learning Disabilities Research and Practice, 16*, 142–151.

Espin, C. A., Shin, J., & Busch, T. W. (2005). Curriculum-based measurement in the content areas: Vocabulary-matching as an indicator of social studies learning. *Journal of Learning Disabilities, 38*, 353–363.

Etscheidt, S. K. (2006). Progress monitoring: Legal issues and recommendations for IEP teams. *Teaching Exceptional Children, 39*(3), 56–60.

Foegen, A., Olson, J. R., & Impecoven-Lind, L. (2008). Developing progress monitoring measures for secondary mathematics: An illustration in algebra. *Assessment for Effective Instruction, 33,* 240–249.

Greenwood, C. R., Dunn, S., Ward, S. M., & Luze, G. J. (2003). The Early Communication Indicator (ECI) for infants and toddlers: What it is, where it's been, and where it needs to go. *The Behavior Analyst Today, 3,* 383–388.

Huefner, D. S. (2008). Updating the FAPE standard under IDEA. *Journal of Law and Education, 37,* 381–392.

Individuals with Disabilities Education Act, 20 U.S.C § 1400 *et seq.*

Individuals with Disabilities Education Act Regulations, 34 C.F.R. § 300 *et seq.*

Kaminski, R. A., & Good, R. H. (1996). Towards a technology for assessing basic early literacy skills. *School Psychology Review, 25,* 215–227.

Kaminski, R. A., & Good, R. H. (1998). Assessing early literacy skills in a problem-solving model: Dynamic indicators of basic early literacy skills. In M. R. Shinn (Ed.), *Advanced applications of Curriculum-Based Measurement* (pp. 113–142). New York, NY: Guilford Press.

Kirby v. Cabell County Bd. of Educ., 46 IDELR § 156 (S.D. W.Va. 2006).

Lembke, E. S., Foegen, A., Whittaker, T. A., & Hampton, D. (2008). Establishing technically adequate measures of progress in early numeracy. *Assessment for Effective Intervention, 33,* 206–214.

Mager, R. F. (1962). *Preparing instructional objectives.* Palo Alto, CA: Fearon. (This book is now published by the Center for Effective Performance in Atlanta, Georgia.)

McConnell, S. R., McEvoy, M. A., & Priest, J. S. (2002). "Growing" measures for monitoring progress in early childhood education: A research and development proves for individual growth and development indicators. *Assessment for Effective Intervention, 27,* 3–14.

Pemberton, J. B. (2003). Communicating academic progress as an integral part of assessment. *Teaching Exceptional Children, 35*(4), 16–20.

President's Commission on Excellence in Special Education. (2002). A new era: Revitalizing special education for children and their families. Washington, DC: U.S. Department of Education. Retrieved March 21, 2005, from http://www.ed.gov/inits/commissionsboards/whspecialeducation/reports/index.html

Rio Rancho Public Schools, 40 IDELR 140 (SEA NM 2003).

Yell, M. L. (2009). Developing educationally meaningful and legally sound individualized education programs. In M. L. Yell, N. B. Meadows, E. Drasgow, & J. G. Shriner (Eds.), *Evidenced-based practices for educating students with emotional and behavioral disorders* (pp. 3–21). Upper Saddle River, NJ: Pearson/Merrill Education.

Yell, M. L., & Drasgow, E. (2000). Litigating a free appropriate public education: The Lovaas hearings and cases. *Journal of Special Education, 33,* 206–215.

Yell, M. L., & Stecker, P. M. (2003). Developing legally correct and educationally meaningful IEPs using Curriculum-Based Measurement. *Assessment for Effective Intervention, 28,* 73–88.

4

When the "Emerging Alternative" Becomes the Standard

John L. Hosp and Michelle K. Hosp

In the past, for many educators and parents, the collection and interpretation of academic assessment data meant relying on school psychologists, speech language pathologists, or other specialists with degrees and licenses to administer and interpret high-stakes tests. While there is merit in having trained specialists administer and interpret such assessments, it also leaves teachers and parents, who typically work most closely with students, in a passive role. This role involves being a recipient of information rather than an active collaborator, which can foster a disconnect between assessment and instruction because the individuals doing the assessment are not providing the instruction. It also can facilitate an aura of mysticism about what the tests mean and can do—especially when coupled with the necessity of test security rules and copyright laws (American Educational Research Association, American Psychological Association, and National Council on Measurement in Education, 1999). Add in the use of often confusing and unintuitive metrics and it is clear how this disconnect could persist.

While public education has strived to build collaborative relationships by including teachers, parents, and students in planning and providing education, the gap that has existed between assessment and instruction has often inhibited such active roles. The work of Stanley Deno with his colleagues and students (and subsequently his students' colleagues and students) to develop Curriculum-Based Measurement (CBM) has been instrumental in bridging that gap and opening a whole new realm of data-based decision making. Two main avenues that we have seen bridge the gap are demystification of assessment data and facilitation of collaboration.

Demystification of Assessment Data

As accountability has become increasingly popular and ingrained as an important aspect of education (Sleeter, 2007), assessment data have become increasingly plentiful. Numerous types and quantities of data are collected about every student, teacher, school, and district in the United States. In addition, the methods used to develop and validate assessment tools have undergone numerous advances including the use of Item Response Theory (IRT; de Ayala, 2009) and Generalizability Theory (G Theory; Cardinet, 2009) and their resultant methods rather than Classical Test Theory (CTT) as the framework for test development. As such, over the past thirty years it has become increasingly important, yet difficult, to sift through the cacophony of scales, metrics, and measures to use assessment data to make important decisions about student progress. As other measures have been developed to be technically adequate, some have been criticized as having a focus on marketability or cash validity rather than utility for practitioners. Deno's work on CBM has focused on technical adequacy *and* utility—producing measures that are useful for educators, parents, and students to make consistent and valid decisions about a student's progress. The hundreds of studies, reports, and dissertations examining the reliability and validity of CBM (e.g., MacArthur and Ferretti, 2007) demonstrate the importance of technical adequacy.

With CBM, the representation of performance is not mysteriously hidden in some magic number on a test as parents and teachers have referred to standard scores to us. Rather, the score reported is a number that is directly related to a task that is clearly observable and measurable as well as measured within the context of expected performance. For example, the number of words read correctly in a minute can be observed and measured with high interrater reliability (Tindal, Marston, and Deno, 1983; also see Wayman, Wallace, Wiley, Tichá, and Espin, 2007, for a review of relevant studies). It can be consistently observed and measured by a teacher, paraprofessional, parent, or student (see Owens, 2001; Sevcik, 1983). Use of these intuitive metrics and visual representations of progress over time through line graphs makes interpretation of performance much easier than most standard scores (Eckert, Shapiro, and Lutz, 1995). This ease of interpretation, as well as the ease of administration, makes CBM appealing to educators, parents, and students. Eliminating the mystery around confidential protocols and allowing all participants to see, have, and share a copy of the student's graph also allows progress monitoring and CBM to facilitate collaboration and consensus building.

Facilitation of Collaboration

Collaboration is a key ingredient to successful provision of education services (Sabatino, 2009). Because CBM is directly tied to the curriculum and assesses skills that are taught in school, it facilitates communication among teachers, parents, and students. The information collected using CBM is not unlike what the teacher is teaching, the student is learning, and the parents see sent home. In addition, because of CBM's demystification, the data are easy to interpret (Shinn, Habedank, and Good, 1993). This may be attributed to the use of the line graph including standards such as a goal line for comparison between current and expected performance. This ease of interpretation makes it more likely for teachers, parents, and students to reach similar conclusions when interpreting the graph (Fuchs, Deno, and Mirkin, 1984). This common core of information facilitates productive discussion, thereby increasing the likelihood of building consensus.

CBM has also been successful in facilitating collaboration between general education and special education teachers (see Deno, 2003, for a review). Assessments used in special education have often remained out of reach and mysterious to general educators. General and special educators often use assessments they feel are only related to general or special education purposes—often times using different measures for similar purposes. CBM bridges that gap because it is derived from the curriculum all students are expected to learn. In addition, CBM was designed to be efficient to administer and score so that it could be used more widely and more often. The scores are easy to interpret and do not just align with one population, be that general or special education students, but rather to a standard that is appropriate for *all* students to achieve. These universal standards make reading and interpreting the data easier and lead to similar conclusions—making CBM the common language of assessment that both general and special education teachers can use to build consensus for the common good of all students (Deno, 2003).

Personal Examples and Reflections

Not only has CBM been successful at building consensus and demystifying assessment at an individual level among teachers, parents, and students, but we have also seen the positive influence of using CBM data to make decisions at the school, district, and state levels. This section includes some examples of the considerable contribution we have witnessed progress monitoring and CBM have on the lives of individuals and organizations at every level of education.

Individuals: Parent

When I (Michelle) was working as a school psychologist, I worked with a fifth grader who was moving up to the middle school the following school year. During his fifth grade year, CBM reading data were collected weekly, and the student graphed his own progress. The teacher, parent, and student met often to look at the student's CBM graph. They used the data on the graph to have conversations about how he was progressing and what skills could be worked on at school as well as at home. The teacher reported feeling very supported by the parent, the parent reported feeling she was really part of her child's educational decisions, and the student reported being able to see (by looking at the graph) that he was getting better at reading. This degree of communication and collaboration would not have been possible without the use of CBM. The parent and student liked using CBM so much that I trained the parent to administer and score CBM reading probes so that she could continue to monitor her son over the summer. The parent then planned to bring her son's graph to the start of school the following year as a way to collaborate with his new teacher.

Individuals: Teacher

At the same time (the mid-1990s) as the example Michelle provided, I (John) was working in a different elementary school as a school psychologist. It was a brand new school, and we were developing our process and procedures for a student intervention team (SIT). I was advocating for the use of CBM school-wide, but it was something with which the SIT leader (a first-grade general education teacher) was not familiar. She decided she would need to read the research and try using CBM before recommending that others use it. A student in her class was having difficulty, so after being trained by me, she started administering weekly CBM reading passages to him. After two months, she brought his graph to the SIT meeting and discussed what she had been doing to the other members. She displayed the fervor of the converted, raving about the ease of use and simplicity of interpretation. By the end of the school year, every teacher in the school was using CBM with their students who were struggling, and a few were screening their entire classes to compare their performance to the district norms.

School

In one school with which we both consulted, CBM had been nonexistent until it was awarded a Reading First grant. Rather than bristle at the additional requirement, the principal and faculty in this school embraced CBM and the possibilities from using the data. In addition to individual teachers and reading coaches using the data to make decisions about individual students, the data were being used school-wide. One of us (Michelle) arrived for a site visit and on entering the principal's office noticed the results from the CBM screening assessments covering an entire wall of his office. Post-it notes for each student were color coded for different levels of proficiency to allow for grouping and regrouping students based on their needs and their rates of progress. When asked about why he had them displayed so prominently, he commented, "Out of sight, out of mind," and said how much more impact it had when he and the teachers had to look at the data each day as a reminder of the work they still had to do.

District

Both of us consulted with another school district that was benchmarking all students in grades one through three using oral reading fluency (ORF) as part of their Reading First project. While the data were primarily being used by classroom teachers and reading coaches to make decisions about individual students, the Reading First coordinator for the district and the reading coaches decided to use the aggregated data to evaluate the instructional programs they were using to implement the curriculum. Overall, the students were showing good progress in word reading (as measured by Nonsense Word Fluency [NWF], a CBM derivative) and in comprehension (as demonstrated on the state test) but much less progress on ORF. The students' unexpectedly low ORF performance was somewhat confusing because ORF, being a General Outcome Measure, is designed to reflect performance of decoding, comprehension, and other areas of fluent and competent reading; however, the state test is solely a power test, whereas ORF incorporates rate or fluency. The students' performance triggered the team to look at their basal reading program to evaluate its coverage of the five areas of good reading instruction (phonological awareness, alphabetic knowledge, fluency, vocabulary, and comprehension). As they examined the materials, they noticed that there was little time devoted to practice of text reading or fluency. They surmised that reading at-rate had not been stressed but that prosody had been, and although students were able to comprehend what they read, they were not practicing reading at an appropriate pace. With the thought that not practicing reading at an appropriate pace might be problematic for students in later grades (when they would be required to read greater amounts of text while still comprehending), they began the search for a fluency program that could be used school-wide as a supplement to the basal to fill in the gap that had been identified from their CBM data.

State

In August of 2002, we arrived at the University of Utah. In order to get to know education in Utah and make some connections, we spent several months meeting special education directors, state office of education personnel, principals, teachers, and school psychologists. We always asked whether or not they used CBM. Many responded with the same question, "What is CBM?" Others were familiar with it or had heard about it but were not using it in their classrooms or schools. Attempts at monitoring student progress were typically informal and not coordinated across a school or district. By the 2005–6 school year, every school we were in contact with in the forty districts in the state was using CBM not only for individual progress monitoring but also for periodic screening (i.e., benchmarking). There were certainly political and policy considerations for the widespread adoption of CBM across Utah, but most educators were fully embracing the use of CBM rather than considering it just another fad. For the first time in our careers as educators we were consistently hearing general educators talk about using data. They were talking with special educators, school psychologists, and administrators—all using the same data and making similar inferences. Because assessment data had been demystified and made accessible to all, in a consistent and technically adequate format, collaboration appeared to be facilitated in ways that it had not before.

Conclusions

Curriculum-Based Measurement and Stanley Deno and his colleagues' work from the late 1970s up to the present have made significant changes in how educators collect and use data to make decisions for students. Nowhere has this been more striking than with the elementary population, most likely because the majority of Deno's work has focused on these grades, and also because elementary grades are a time when the majority of students with disabilities are first assessed and identified. Therefore, it stands to reason that there has been great progress in how elementary educators use data to help inform their decisions. With the increased use of CBM from the individual to the district level, we have seen how it has increased data-based decision making by demystifying the use of assessment data and facilitating collaboration and consensus building among educators, parents, and teachers. Without CBM and the work of Stanley Deno, there would still be a large gap between general and special education. With CBM, all students can now be assessed the same way with the same general outcomes in mind.

References

American Educational Research Association, American Psychological Association, & National Council on Measurement in Education. (1999). *Standards for educational and psychological testing.* Washington, DC: American Educational Research Association.

Cardinet, J., Johnson, S., & Pini, G. (2009). *Applying generalizability theory using EduG.* London, UK: Taylor and Francis.

de Ayala, R. J. (2009). *The theory and practice of item response theory.* New York, NY: Guilford Press.

Deno, S. L. (2003). Developments in Curriculum-Based Measurement. *Journal of Special Education, 37,* 184–192.

Eckert, T., Shapiro, E., & Lutz, J. (1995). Teachers' ratings of the acceptability of curriculum-based assessment methods. *School Psychology Review, 24,* 497–511.

Fuchs, L. S., Deno, S. L., & Mirkin, P. (1984). Effects of frequent Curriculum-Based Measurement and evaluation on pedagogy, student achievement, and student awareness of learning. *American Educational Research Journal, 21,* 449–460.

MacAuthur, C. A., & Ferretti, R. P. (Eds.). (2007). Special series: Curriculum-based measurement [Special issue]. *Journal of Special Education, 41*(2), 65–140.

Owens, S. H. (2001). *Validated practices in spelling for students with learning disabilities.* Unpublished doctoral dissertation, Georgia State University, Atlanta.

Sabatino, C. A. (2009). Collaboration and consultation: Professional partnerships for serving children, youths, families, and schools. In C. Massat, C. Rippey, R. Constable, S. McDonald, & J. Flynn (Eds.), *School social work: Practice, policy, and research* (7th ed., pp. 376–402). Chicago, IL: Lyceum Books.

Sevcik, B., Skiba, R., Tindal, G., King, R., Wesson, C., Mirkin, P., & Deno, S. (1983). *Communication of IEP goals and student progress among parents, regular classroom teachers, and administrators using systematic formative evaluation* (Research Report No. 114). Minneapolis: University of Minnesota, Institute for Research on Learning Disabilities.

Shinn, M. R., Habedank, L., & Good, R. H. (1993). The effects of classroom reading performance data on general education teachers' and parents' attitudes about reintegration. *Exceptionality, 4,* 205–228.

Sleeter, C. E. (Ed.). (2007). *Facing accountability in education: Democracy & equity at risk.* New York, NY: Teachers College Press.

Tindal, G., Marston, D., & Deno, S. (1983). *The reliability of direct and repeated measurement* (Research Report No. 109). Minneapolis: University of Minnesota, Institute for Research on Learning Disabilities.

Wayman, M. M., Wallace, T., Wiley, H. I., Tichá, R., & Espin, C. (2007). Literature synthesis on Curriculum-Based Measurement in reading. *Journal of Special Education, 41,* 85–120.

II

School-Based and
District-Wide Applications

5

School- and District-Wide Implementation of Curriculum-Based Measurement in the Minneapolis Public Schools

Doug Marston

The collaboration of Dr. Stanley Deno and the Minneapolis Public Schools (MPS) can be traced to 1971 when Deno initiated the Seward-University Project, a cooperative effort between MPS and the University of Minnesota. In writing a chapter for a book titled *Instructional Alternatives for Exceptional Children*, he observes that traditional assessments fell short on measuring student performance and that better evaluation techniques were necessary for making accurate judgments about student needs and progress (Deno and Gross, 1973).

> Without such measures, communication among interested persons on objectives and evaluations of progress can become mired in personal subjective judgments and disagreements. Quantitative representations give the teacher a firmer grasp of the problem and provide a basis for all subsequent decisions on the success of an intervention . . . it can be used repeatedly for assessing and representing a child's progress, setting objectives, and evaluating interventions. (pp. 115–116)

An extension of his ideas on data-based decision making and progress monitoring, not yet named Curriculum-Based Measurement (CBM), was clearly evident later in *Data-Based Program Modification: A Manual* (Deno and Mirkin, 1977). This book, published by the Council for Exceptional Children, had a significant impact on practice in our district and also received national attention. Data-Based Program Modification (DBPM) was a blueprint for future CBM procedures, the Problem-Solving Model, and Response to Intervention. In that document, he outlines a framework for decision making and providing services to low-performing students that was data based. DBPM describes how to analyze student growth and use these data to examine the effectiveness of instruction.

Collaboration with MPS on progress monitoring continued in the late 1970s when Deno and his research team from the Institute for Research on Learning Disabilities (IRLD) at the University of Minnesota conducted some of the initial CBM validity studies in MPS (Deno, 1985; Deno et al., 1980; Deno, Mirkin, and Chiang, 1982; Deno, Marston, and Mirkin, 1982). It was in 1982 when formal use of CBM began in MPS and the research of Deno (1985) and his colleagues was soon adopted by the Special Education Department as policy in the district (Marston and Magnusson, 1985). Since that time, CBM has significantly contributed to data-based decision making in a variety of ways. The applications of CBM within special education can be grouped into the educational decision areas identified by Salvia and Ysseldyke (1985): screening, eligibility, instructional planning, progress monitoring, and program evaluation. In general education, the uses of CBM expanded to the Cooperative Teaching Project, the Problem-Solving Model, Tests of Accountability, and School Improvement Planning and has been an integral part of the district electronic student data warehouse and a major role in the Demonstration of Response to Intervention (RTI) Project. This chapter provides a brief description of the role of CBM in our district's implementation of these educational decision-making areas.

Screening

Early in our use of CBM, MPS staff developed procedures for screening students with academic difficulties and produced norms for decision-making criteria. Marston and Magnusson (1985) described how CBM reading procedures were created using the district's basal reading series and probes written for spelling, math, and written expression. In reading, 8,460 randomly selected students were administered three grade-level passages, and the median number of words read correctly and incorrectly was determined for the fall, winter, and spring. The district-wide means and standard deviations for reading reported by Marston and Magnusson (1985) are presented in Table 5.1. MPS staff used these data for screening to determine those students most discrepant from their peers. At the time, our district used Deno and Mirkin's (1977) two-times-discrepant criteria for identifying students needing more assistance. However, after analyzing the impact of this approach, the district changed to percentile ranks based on the large normative samples collected in the fall, winter, and spring. Further, it was evident to staff that significant growth occurred between these testing sessions, which highlighted the importance of having norms linked to the time of year that a student's performance was measured. In first grade, for example, the average student improved from reading fifteen words correctly in the fall to almost sixty-nine words correctly in the spring. Consequently, monthly percentile ranks were developed, and they have played a significant role in making screening decisions throughout the academic year in our district.

Eligibility

In the area of special education eligibility, CBM measures have been used as one of several sources of assessment information (Marston, Mirkin, and Deno, 1984; Deno, Marston, and Tindal, 1986). MPS adopted procedures that assisted staff in determining the number of years behind a student was when compared to grade-level peers. Marston and Magnusson (1988) described the *sampling back procedure* where students in the special education evaluation process were first measured in grade-level materials and then administered reading passages at successively easier levels. This process, known as *survey level assessment*, provided an approximate indicator

TABLE 5.1.

Typical CBM performance of first through sixth graders in regular education

GRADE	FALL MEAN	S.D.	WINTER MEAN	S.D.	SPRING MEAN	S.D.
1	14.7	31.6	36.7	39.9	68.5	40.8
2	53.0	44.8	83.0	47.8	98.4	46.8
3	81.3	39.7	100.6	41.9	119.9	39.5
4	91.5	39.0	108.3	39.0	114.9	38.4
5	103.3	40.0	116.6	39.1	124.1	39.7
6	129.8	38.8	138.0	38.1	143.4	39.8

From Marston and Magnusson (1985). Reproduced with permission, copyright 1985 by the Council for Exceptional Children, Inc., http://www.cec.sped.org. All rights reserved.

of the student's functioning grade level and is illustrated in Figure 5.1 (from Marston and Magnusson, 1988). In the chart, typical reading performance at each grade level is represented by the range of "plus and minus one standard deviation from the district mean" (p. 152). In this example, a sixth-grade student reads only twelve words correctly in grade-level material and is very discrepant from general education peers. The sampling back process used during eligibility determination shows the student reads twenty-one words correctly on fifth-grade passages, fifty-one words correctly on fourth-grade passages, and sixty-four words correctly on third-grade passages. This last CBM score falls into the typical range of third-grade students, which is interpreted as approximately three years behind peers.

Several validation studies related to eligibility, and conducted in MPS, provide evidence of CBM as a valid assessment for this purpose. In grades one to three, Marston and Magnusson (1985) showed differences on words read correctly for students in regular education, Title I, and special education. Shinn and Marston (1985) replicated these results for grades four to six. Both studies suggest the differences among these groups inform our

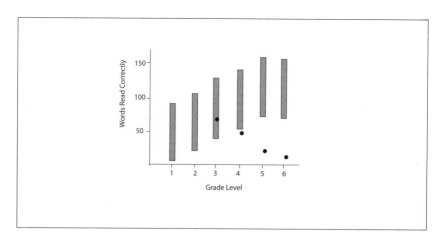

Figure 5.1. Example of using CBM Survey Level Assessment for eligibility. From Marston and Magnusson (1988). Curriculum-based Measurement: District level implementation. In J. Graden, J. Zins, & M. Curtis (Eds.), Alternative educational delivery systems: Enhancing options for all students *(pp. 137–172). Kent, Ohio: National Association for School Psychologists. Copyright 1988 by the National Association of School Psychologists. Washington, DC. Reprinted with permission of the publisher. www.nasponline.org.*

decisions related to program eligibility, as shown in Figure 5.2. For example, the average second-grade student in general education reads almost ninety words correctly while the average special education student in that grade reads only twenty words correctly. These studies demonstrated that CBM possessed discriminant validity and could significantly contribute to the eligibility decision-making process.

Instructional Planning

Maynard Reynolds (1982) of the University of Minnesota wrote often about the importance of assessment in the delivery of effective special education services. He observed, "In general, assessment processes in the schools should be oriented to instructional decisions: that is, the assessments should help to design appropriate instructional programs for students" (p. 104). Given the concerns of many that assessment and instruction are not linked, CBM provides a connection. One of the original purposes of developing CBM procedures was to tie assessment to instruction and improve instructional decision

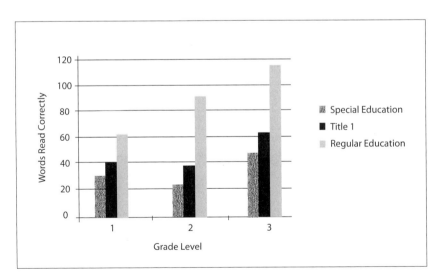

Figure 5.2. Comparison of regular education, Title I, and special education students for grades one to three. Figure created from data presented in Marston and Magnusson (1985) Reproduced with permission, copyright 1985 by the Council for Exceptional Children, Inc., http://www.cec.sped.org. All rights reserved.

making through the process of writing Individualized Education Program (IEP) goals, objectives, and monitoring growth. Deno and Mirkin (1977) remarked such a system that required the Special Education Resource Teacher (SERT) to test hypotheses "about what might help the student improve his performance, and to make instructional decisions on the basis of objectively determined effects rather than subjectively formed speculations" (p. 33). Our district implemented procedures outlined by Deno, Mirkin, and Wesson (1984) for setting annual IEP goals, writing short-term objectives, and developing an instructional plan for the student that specified curriculum materials, specific instructional strategies, allocated time, size of group, motivational strategies, and a progress-monitoring plan. This plan, driven by the measurement of student progress, informed the instructional planning process. Fuchs, Deno, and Mirkin (1984) documented that instructional decision making was significantly improved when student instruction was guided by CBM data. Marston and Magnusson (1988) shared an example where an annual IEP goal of reading seventy words correctly had been set for a student with mild disabilities and noted that measuring the student's progress toward that goal informed the teacher of the effectiveness of the instructional plan.

Progress Monitoring

While CBM was used for screening and eligibility purposes early in its implementation in MPS, it was the progress monitoring aspect of the model that was at the core of its use and is a critical link to effective instructional planning for the student's IEP. As described in the previous section, all K–6 SERTs were trained to write IEP goals and objectives with CBM procedures (Marston and Magnusson, 1988). The next step in implementation of data-based decision making was to begin progress monitoring on these IEP goals. To start a progress-monitoring chart, teachers were trained to establish the level of progress monitoring by using survey level assessment data, collecting initial baseline data, using average weekly gain criteria to establish an annual IEP goal, generating the student's goal line (which connected the baseline and goal), and beginning frequent measurement. Marston and Magnusson (1988) reviewed several hundred IEP progress-monitoring graphs and reported average growth rates for special education students of 1.0 to 1.5 correct words per week.

Two approaches to interpreting the progress-monitoring data, referred to as *data-utilization strategies*, were used by MPS teachers. In the treatment-oriented approach, reading data were collected two to three times per week, and trend lines based on nine to twelve data points, using White and Haring's (1980) quarter-intersect method, were generated. The slope of the trend line was then compared to the slope calculated for the prior instructional phase. A second approach to data utilization evolved in our effort to make the progress-monitoring system more efficient. In the goal-oriented approach, the frequency of measurement was changed to collecting reading data on three passages once per week and plotting a weekly median. The medians were then compared to the student's goal line, and teachers made instructional changes when data fell below the goal line for three consecutive weeks. An example of this is shown in Figure 5.3.

In addition to implementing the progress-monitoring procedures developed by Deno and associates from the IRLD, our district conducted several validity studies providing evidence that CBM progress monitoring was sensitive to student growth. Marston, Fuchs, and Deno (1986) demonstrated that slopes for words read correctly over a sixteen-week period correlated with teacher judgment of growth and that these coefficients were considerably higher than correlations between growth measures from standardized tests of reading and teacher judgment of reading growth.

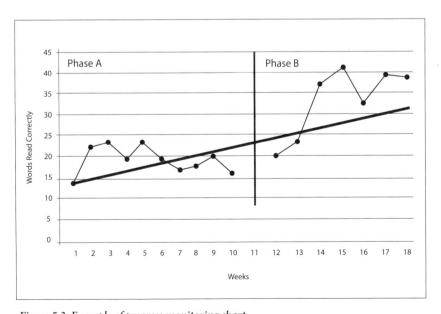

Figure 5.3. Example of progress monitoring chart

Program Evaluation

CBM has been used in MPS as a dependent measure in program evaluation, including the following topics: effectiveness of math interventions, special education effectiveness, noncategorical delivery of special education services, pull-out versus inclusion, and a study of six reading interventions. In the area of evaluation of math programs, CBM math data were used to evaluate the effectiveness of math interventions by reviewing the growth of students with mild disabilities across grades one to six. Faced with evidence of little progress at grades two and three, special education educators increased funding for professional development in math. Marston and Magnusson (1988) concluded, "Databases such as these can be compared across years, academic areas, and schools, providing the administrator with valuable information regarding severity of student needs, in-service training priorities, and allocation of resources to schools" (p. 160).

The topic of effectiveness of special education was addressed in MPS by using CBM slope data as a dependent measure. In a quasi-A-B-A design, CBM reading slopes based on weekly progress-monitoring data of students before entering special education (average slope = 0.60 correct words) were compared with CBM slopes of the same students while being served in special education (average slope = 1.15 correct words). These data demonstrated greater improvement for the students after being found eligible for special education and receiving specialized instruction, which indicated that special education was an effective program placement for these students (Marston, 1988).

Another program evaluation application utilizing CBM as the dependent measure was the analysis of the effectiveness of noncategorical service delivery (Marston, 1987). In this study, the researcher was able to contrast the progress of learning disabled (LD) and educable mentally retarded (EMR) students who were taught by a LD-licensed teacher with the progress of LD and EMR students who were instructed by an EMR-licensed teacher. These data indicated that LD and EMR student progress was the same regardless of the teaching license of the teacher, which suggested students with mild academic disabilities could be instructed within a noncategorical service delivery model.

CBM growth indicators were used to study special education service models in MPS for students with mild disabilities. Because a variety of service models were available in MPS, it was possible to study three models:

(1) the *inclusion only* model where all special education services were provided in general education, (2) the *pull-out only* model where special education services were provided in a resource room, and (3) the *combined service* model, which utilized both services in general education and in the resource room. An analysis of CBM growth data for these students demonstrated that the *combined service* model was the most effective approach to providing services (Marston, 1996).

In an Office of Special Education Programs (OSEP)-funded Model Demonstration project, CBM played a critical role in the evaluation of six reading interventions implemented with 176 students with mild disabilities. The interventions included reciprocal teaching, peer tutoring, computer-assisted instruction, a reading intervention based on research-based instruction components, and two direct instruction approaches. CBM reading procedures were used as the dependent measures in the analysis of covariance (ANCOVA) design, which identified the greatest gains in reciprocal teaching, computer-assisted instruction, and one of the direct instruction groups (Marston, Deno, Kim, Diment, and Rogers, 1995).

Cooperative Teaching

The Cooperative Teaching Project at Hiawatha School was a forerunner of the Problem Solving and RTI models and demonstrated how weekly CBM data could be used by building teams to evaluate student response in small group reading intervention settings (Self, Marston, Benning, and Magnusson, 1991). In the project, regular education teachers had responsibility for meeting the instructional needs of all students in their class; however, Title I, compensatory education, and special education teachers provided daily supplemental, small group reading instruction in the general education classroom to lower-performing students. CBM screening and progress-monitoring data were used to create groups with similar instructional needs. The progress of these students was measured weekly and reviewed by the grade-level team of teachers once a month. These data were used to move students in and out of supplemental groups and coordinate instructional plans. Lesson plans were exchanged, and the teachers used this time to review specific reading objectives for students and talk about their instructional strategies. Staff attitudes toward Cooperative Teaching were positive, with over 80 percent agreeing that the model led to effective instructional planning, coordinated instruction among team members, and that progress monitoring led to accurate identification and placement of at-risk students. These authors also reported a significant decrease in students identified as needing special education services.

Problem-Solving Model

MPS formally began using the Problem-Solving Model (PSM) as an alternative special education eligibility model in 1993. At that time, new state criteria for the mild disability areas required the use of intelligence tests for special education identification. MPS staff were concerned about the use of IQ tests for this purpose given the many diverse learners in the district. In response, the MPS special education department received a waiver from these rules and was allowed by the State Board of Education to pursue the implementation of the PSM as an alternate eligibility approach (Marston, 2002). The key components to PSM are (1) identifying the student problem, (2) selecting a regular education intervention to address the student's needs, (3) monitoring the progress of the student and response to the intervention, and (4) repeating this sequence if the intervention is not effective. The PSM steps are implemented at three levels: stage 1, which is an intervention tried by the classroom teacher; stage 2, which is an intervention selected by the school problem-solving team and implemented in the general education setting; and stage 3, which is the formal special education evaluation that includes a review of the data and interventions implemented at stages 1 and 2. A primary tenet of the model is measuring student growth to determine if the student is responding to the intervention and using these data to move students through stages 1, 2, and 3 of the PSM model. A second major purpose of PSM implementation is to reduce the stigma of special education disability labels. Students found eligible for special education services using the PSM are referred to as Students Needing Alternative Programming (SNAP) and not labeled "learning disabled" or "mild mental impairment."

In 1998, our district entered into a voluntary compliance agreement with the Office of Civil Rights (OCR) to address disproportion for students of color referred and identified for special education. A major assumption of the agreement was that referral of general education students for special education evaluations would be improved by implementing a PSM approach, which at that time was only partially implemented in the district. The framework adopted by the district used a screening process to determine which students needed help in behavior and academics, provided extra interventions in general education, and monitored the progress of students in these interventions. As a result, district staff used CBM within the PSM model, in addition to other achievement and behavior measures, to identify the students needing supplemental interventions and progress monitoring.

Marston, Muyskens, Lau, and Canter (2003) reported on several outcomes of the PSM implementation. Noting there was concern the alternate model would increase the number of students identified as needing special education services, these researchers found the number of students with mild academic disabilities did not increase in comparison to years prior to the PSM implementation and was stable across a seven-year period during implementation. The reading gains of the students within the PSM were also a function of the student level of intervention. As shown in Figure 5.4, general education students in grades one to six had the greatest growth with average gains of 1.0–1.6 correct words per week (excluding grade six), gains of 0.9–1.2 correct words per week for stage 1, gains of 0.8–1.1 correct words per week for stage 2, and weekly gains of 0–0.9 correct words for stage 3. With respect to the district OCR plan for disproportion, these researchers found that district-wide screening and implementation of the PSM was associated with a 20 percent reduction in the percentage of African American students declared eligible for special education. A survey of parents of students found eligible for special education through the PSM established 91 percent were satisfied the labels "learning disabled" and "mild mental impairment" were not used with their child (Marston, 2002). Other evaluators of the PSM found that prereferral interventions with the PSM were superior to the interventions tried in more traditional referral models, that special education students received services earlier, and that staff attitudes and beliefs toward the PSM were positive (Reschly and Starkweather, 1997). MPS was one of four large-scale RTI models that was studied in a meta-analysis conducted by Burns, Appleton, and Stehouwer (2005). These investigators found significant effect sizes for student achievement and systemic outcomes.

The roles of school staff have also been changed by using data-based decision making, CBM, and the PSM (Lau et al., 2006). For the school psychologist, the "PSM expands this role from one of gate-keeping psychometrician to data-based problem solver" (Lau et al., p. 122) and allows them to focus on the instructional or environmental conditions that may lead to improved student academic and behavior skills. Marston and colleagues (2003) reported that school psychologists reduced their time administering tests from 58 percent to 35 percent, which increased their availability for direct intervention with students and consultation with staff. For the

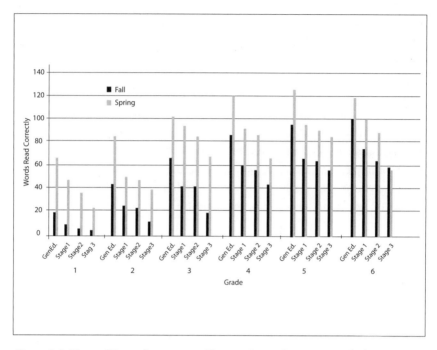

Figure 5.4. Means, SDs, and average weekly gains for students in general education, stage 1, stage 2, and stage 3 of PSM. Figure created from data presented in Marston, Muyskens, Lau, and Canter (2003). Copyright 2003 by John Wiley & Sons, Inc.

special education teacher, the PSM led to increased collaboration with general education staff and provided improved instructional planning information for the IEP since documented interventions and RTI data were more relevant to instruction. In the PSM, the principal became a change agent supporting the use of evidenced-based interventions, frequent progress monitoring, and data review teams that attended to the unique needs of students not making benchmarks and creating the conditions within the school for successful implementation.

Accountability Testing and No Child Left Behind

With the advent of state accountability tests in the mid-1990s, schools had a need to monitor whether students were on track or not on track to be proficient on these assessments. CBM procedures provided data that informed school staff throughout the school year. Fuchs, Deno, and Marston (1997) showed CBM reading procedures were highly correlated with the Minnesota Basic Standards Test (MBST) and were excellent predictors of students passing or failing the MBST. The Minnesota accountability tests eventually evolved to a succession of grade-level accountability tests in reading, the Minnesota Comprehensive Assessments (MCA), that are administered in grades three through eight and grade ten. Deno and Marston (2006) reported analyses showing the CBM procedures significantly differentiated students who were proficient and not proficient on the MCA. Figure 5.5 shows the performance of a third-grade cohort while in grades one, two, and three and the average words read correctly for those students who were proficient and not proficient. For example, for third-grade students who were proficient on the MCA, the average words read correctly in the spring was about 121. For students who were not proficient, the average number of words read correctly in the spring of third grade was approximately 78. The differences can be detected as early as the fall of first grade. The average number of words read correctly by first grade students who were proficient two years later was over 45, and the mean number of words read correctly for students who were not proficient was almost 20. By examining several thousand students, Minneapolis staff were able to establish fall, winter, and spring CBM benchmarks to be used in tracking the progress of all students toward proficiency on the MCA. For example, in the spring of second grade, students at or above 84 words read correctly are on track to be proficient on the third-grade reading MCA. Additional benchmarks were developed for predicting partial proficiency on the MCA. The current benchmarks, published by MPS, can be found in Figure 5.6. The benchmarks play a key role in helping school staff make decisions about students needing more intensive reading interventions within the RTI framework.

One issue affecting the measurement of progress toward proficiency on tests of accountability is the lack of early literacy measures. Marston and colleagues (2007) addressed this concern by developing CBM-type measures of early literacy including Letter Sound Identification, Onset Phonemes, and Phoneme Segmentation. Procedures were developed for beginning and end of kindergarten assessments and used to predict later reading success. All three measures administered in the spring of kindergarten had moderate to high validity coefficients in predicting end of grade one oral reading on CBM passages. Heistad, Pickart, and Chan (2009) linked these measures to the third-grade reading MCA.

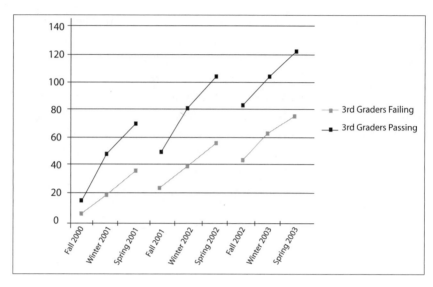

Figure 5.5. Comparison of proficient and nonproficient students on CBM reading measures. From Deno and Marston (2006). Curriculum-based measurement of oral reading: An indicator of growth in fluency (Chapter 9). In S. J. Samuels & A. E. Farstrup (Eds.), What research has to say about fluency instruction *(pp. 179–203). Newark, DE: International Reading Association. Reproduced with permission, copyright 2006 by the International Reading Association (http://www.reading.org).*

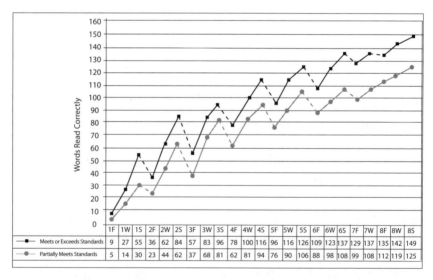

Figure 5.6. CBM benchmarks for predicting "proficiency" and "partial proficiency" on MCAs. From Minneapolis Public Schools (2009). Reproduced with permission, copyright 2009 by the Minneapolis Public Schools.

Student Data Warehouse

The format for implementation of the initial PSM and OCR procedures, including the use of CBM, was paper and pencil. These procedures, however, were time consuming, and staff requested alternatives that would be more time efficient. Consequently, the district developed a web-based student data system that provided all MPS staff with electronic implementation of the major components of the Problem-Solving Model, including screening, documentation of interventions, and progress monitoring. The data system, known as the district's OCR website, described by Marston, Lau, and Muyskens (2007), has over five thousand users and includes additional reports for district and state assessments, attendance, suspensions, school mobility, and other essential family and demographic information necessary for improved decision making for the student. The website contains "drill down" capabilities providing the user with data analysis at the district, school, grade, classroom, and student levels. In addition to reports and data tables, student data are often presented in graphs or charts, which contributes to improved data-based decision making. The website can also be used to document interventions implemented with students, which provides staff with a current and historical record of strategies and instructional materials used. An example of a Problem-Solving Model Classroom Intervention Worksheet is shown in Figure 5.7. The electronic form includes a download of student performance data, a menu for evidenced-based interventions, and the opportunity to document input from the student, parents, and staff.

OSEP-Funded Demonstration of Progress-Monitoring Project and RTI

The principles of CBM, the PSM, and the electronic data system have been applied to an Office of Special Education Programs–funded Demonstration of Progress-Monitoring Project in MPS (Marston, 2009). During three years of implementation, three schools utilized these concepts to create an RTI framework to address the instructional needs of low-performing readers. Each school conducted fall screening of students, identified Tier 2 and Tier 3 interventions for students below benchmarks, and measured the progress of these students weekly. School grade-level teams were formed, and the progress of students was reviewed at monthly meetings using the CBM benchmarks described earlier in the accountability section. Wallace, Marston, Tichá, Lau, and Muyskens (2011) examined the outcomes at one of

CLASSROOM INTERVENTION WORKSHEET

For students with Below Grade Level Standard selected above, continue on with the classroom intervention worksheet

FORM DATES:	Date Started: (mm/dd/yy) [ ]	Date Finished: (mm/dd/yy) [ ]

Areas Addressed By Worksheet (Multiple worksheets no longer necessary)

READING	☐ Math	☐ Behavior	☐ Writing
☐ Speech	☐ Other		
	Description [ ]		

RELEVANT SCHOOL HISTORY: [ ]

INPUT FROM OTHER STAFF: [ ]

INPUT FROM STUDENT: [ ]

RELEVANT HEALTH INFORMATION: [ ]

Click Here to see Possible Interventions and Their Description

FIRST INTERVENTION/RESULTS:
- Select Reading ▼
- Select Math ▼
- Select Behavior ▼

Start Date Int 1: (mm/dd/yyyy) [ ]   Follow up Date Int 1: (mm/dd/yyyy) [ ]

SECOND INTERVENTION/RESULTS:
- Select Reading ▼
- Select Math ▼
- Select Behavior ▼

Start Date Int 2: (mm/dd/yyyy) [ ]   Follow up Date Int 2: (mm/dd/yyyy) [ ]

Figure 5.7. PSM Classroom Intervention Worksheet on electronic student data system. From Minneapolis Public Schools Office of Civil Rights website. Reproduced with permission from the Minneapolis Public Schools.

these schools and found higher rates of student engaged time in Tier 2 versus Tier 1 instruction, increases in scores on state tests of accountability, and special education eligibility rates during the last two years of implementation that were lower than the district average.

Summary

As educators, we have a responsibility for providing effective educational practices that promote student development in academic and behavior areas. The success of our endeavor depends greatly on our ability to make data-based decisions in choosing educational programs for the diverse students we serve. Valid and reliable evaluation tools, such as those developed by Stanley Deno, contribute to improved decision making at the student, classroom, school, and district levels. Deno (2005) points out the following:

> CBM exists as one technically adequate approach for taking a more functional problem-solving approach to the prevention and solution of educational problems. Evidence exists that professional educators can increase their problem-solving effectiveness through the use of progress monitoring of student development and by systematic responding to those data as they reflect student growth. (p. 36)

Implementation of Deno's work in our district supports his conclusion. For over thirty years, his research and development at the University of Minnesota on CBM has inspired the implementation of data-based decision making in screening, eligibility, instructional planning, progress monitoring, program evaluation, school improvement planning, problem solving, and Response to Intervention. The work of Deno has indeed had a profound effect on the Minneapolis Public Schools and improved our ability to make informed educational decisions for our students.

References

Burns, M. K., Appleton, J. J., & Stehouwer, J. D. (2005). Meta-analytic review of responsiveness-to-intervention research: Examining field-based and research-implemented models. *Journal of Psychoeducational Assessment, 23*, 381–394.

Deno, S. L. (1985). Curriculum-Based Measurement: The emerging alternative. *Exceptional Children, 52*, 219–232.

Deno, S. L. (2005). Problem-solving assessment. In R. Brown-Chidsey (Ed.), *Assessment for intervention: A problem-solving approach*. New York, NY: Guilford Press.

Deno, S. L., & Gross, J. (1973). The Seward-University Project: A collaborative effort to improve school services and university training. In E. N. Deno (Ed.), *Instructional alternatives for exceptional children* (pp. 135–149). Arlington, VA: Council for Exceptional Children.

Deno, S. L., & Marston, D. (2006). Curriculum-Based Measurement of oral reading: An indicator of growth in fluency. In S. J. Samuels & A. E. Farstrup (Eds.), *What research has to say about fluency instruction* (pp. 179–203). Newark, NJ: International Reading Association.

Deno, S. L., Marston, D., & Mirkin, P. K. (1982). Valid measurement procedures for continuous evaluation of written expression. *Exceptional Children, 48,* 368–371.

Deno, S. L., Marston, D., & Tindal, G. (1986). Direct and frequent Curriculum-Based Measurement: An alternative for educational decision-making. *Special Services in the Schools, 2*(2/3), 5–28.

Deno, S. L., & Mirkin, P. (1977). *Data-Based Program Modification: A manual*. Reston, VA: Council for Exceptional Children.

Deno, S. L., Mirkin, P., & Chiang, B. (1982). Identifying valid measures of reading. *Exceptional Children, 49,* 36–45.

Deno, S., Mirkin, P., Chiang, B., Kuehnle, K., Lowry, L., Marston, D., & Tindal, G. (1980). Current status of research on the development of a formative evaluation system for learning disability programs. In W. C. Cruickshank (Ed.), *The best of ACLD* (pp. 125–147). Syracuse, NY: Syracuse University Press.

Deno, S. L., Mirkin, P. K., & Wesson, C. (1984). How to write effective data-based IEPs. *Teaching Exceptional Children, 16,* 99–104.

Fuchs, L., Deno, S., & Marston, D. (1997, February). *Alternative measures of student progress and state standards testing*. Paper presented at the annual Pacific Coast Research Conference.

Fuchs, L. S., Deno, S. L., & Mirkin, P. (1984). The effects of frequent Curriculum-Based Measurement and evaluation on pedagogy, student achievement, and student awareness of learning. *American Educational Research Journal, 21,* 449–460.

Heistad, D., Pickart, M., & Chan, C. K. (2009). *Linking early literacy assessments to reading MCA-II performance*. Presentation at Minnesota Assessment Conference, St. Paul, MN.

Lau, M. Y., Sieler, J. D., Muyskens, P., Canter, A., Vankeuren, B., & Marston, D. (2006). Perspectives on the use of the Problem Solving Model from the viewpoint of a school psychologist, administrator, and teacher from a large Midwest urban school district. *Psychology in the Schools, 43*(1), 117–127.

Marston, D. (1987). Does categorical teacher certification benefit the mildly handicapped child? *Exceptional Children, 63,* 423–431.

Marston, D. (1988). The effectiveness of special education: A time series analysis of reading performance in regular and special education. *Journal of Special Education, 21*, 13–26.

Marston, D. (1996). A comparison of inclusion only, pull-out only, and combined service models for students with mild disabilities. *Journal of Special Education, 30*, 121–132.

Marston, D. (2002). A functional and intervention-based assessment approach to establishing discrepancy for students with learning disabilities. In R. Bradley, L. Danielson, & D. P. Hallahan (Eds.), *Identification of learning disabilities: Research to practice* (pp. 437–447). Mahwah, NJ: Lawrence Erlbaum Associates.

Marston, D. (2009, July). *Outcomes from the Minnesota Demonstration of Progress Monitoring (DPM) Project.* Paper presented at the Office of Special Education Project Directors Meeting, Washington, DC.

Marston, D., Deno, S. L., Kim, D., Diment, K., & Rogers, D. (1995). Comparison of reading intervention approaches for students with mild disabilities. *Exceptional Children, 62*, 20–37.

Marston, D., Fuchs, L., & Deno, S. L. (1986). Measuring pupil progress: A comparison of standardized achievement tests and curriculum-related measures. *Diagnostique, 11*(2), 77–90.

Marston, D., Lau, M., & Muyskens, P. (2007). Implementation of the Problem-Solving Model in the Minneapolis public schools. In S. R. Jimerson, M. K. Burns, & A. M. Van Der Heyden (Eds.), *Handbook of Response to Intervention: The science and practice of assessment and intervention* (pp. 279–287). New York, NY: Springer Publishing.

Marston, D., & Magnusson, D. (1985). Implementing Curriculum-Based Measurement in special and regular education settings. *Exceptional Children, 52*, 266–276.

Marston, D., & Magnusson, D. (1988). Curriculum-based Measurement: District level implementation. In J. Graden, J. Zins, & M. Curtis (Eds.), *Alternative educational delivery systems: Enhancing options for all students* (pp. 137–172). Kent, OH: National Association for School Psychologists.

Marston, D., Mirkin, P. K., & Deno, S. L. (1984). Curriculum-based measurement of academic skills: An alternative to traditional screening, referral, and identification of learning disabled students. *Journal of Special Education, 18*, 109–118.

Marston, D., Muyskens, P., Lau, M., & Canter, A. (2003). Problem-Solving Model for decision-making with high-incidence disabilities: The Minneapolis experience. *Learning Disabilities Research and Practice, 18*, 187–200.

Marston, D., Pickart, M., Reschly, A., Heistad, D., Muyskens, P., & Tindal, G. (2007). Early literacy measures for improving student reading achievement: Translation research into practice. *Exceptionality, 15*, 97–118.

Minneapolis Public Schools. (2009). *Performance assessment manual for reading.* Minneapolis, MN: Minneapolis Public Schools.

Reschly, D. J., & Starkweather, A. R. (1997). *Evaluation of an alternative special education assessment and classification program in the Minneapolis Public Schools.* Ames: Iowa State University.

Reynolds, M. C. (1982). The rights of children: A challenge to school psychologists. In T. R. Krotochwill (Ed.), *Advances in school psychology* (Vol. 2, pp. 97–118). Hillsdale, NJ: Lawrence Erlbaum Associates.

Salvia, J., & Ysseldyke, J. (1985). *Assessment in special and remedial education.* Boston, MA: Houghton Mifflin.

Self, H., Benning, A., Marston, D., & Magnusson, D. (1991). Cooperative Teaching Project: A model for students at risk. *Exceptional Children, 58,* 26–34.

Shinn, M., & Marston, D. (1985). Differentiating mildly handicapped, low achieving, and regular education student using Curriculum-Based Assessment procedures. *Remedial and Special Education, 6,* 31–38.

Wallace T., Marston, D., Tichá, R., Lau, M., & Muyskens, P. (2011). Evaluation of implementation. In E. S. Shapiro, N. Zigmond, T. Wallace, & D. Marston (Eds.), *Models of response-to-intervention implementation: Tools, outcomes, and implications* (pp. 246–268). New York, NY: Guilford Press.

White, O. R., & Haring, N. G. (1980). *Exceptional teaching* (2nd ed.). Columbus, OH: Merrill.

6

Implementing Data-Based Program Modification Big Ideas

Gary Germann

I will begin this chapter with a parable. The parable is relevant for a book in honor of Stanley Deno's contribution (originally and foundationally with Phyllis Mirkin) to the field of education.

The king woke up one morning and told the queen that he wanted a kite made for him. The kite had to be fit for a king, so the queen called her most loyal craftsman to her.

"This has to be a kite like no other," she said. "The king told me that he wanted it made out of gold instead of wood."

The craftsman went home and began to make the kite. He made its frame out of solid gold, and then he tied a red, satin sail to it. Next, he fashioned a tail for the kite out of velvet and, following the queen's strict instructions, he sewed precious gems onto it. When the kite was complete, it was a sight to behold, but it weighed as much as an elephant.

"The wind will never pick this contraption up," the craftsman sadly told his wife. "I'll lose the king's favor and we'll be cast out of the kingdom."

As he said this, his son, Stanley, ran laughing into the kitchen with the kite he'd made him for his birthday. This kite was not made out of gold and satin but wood and cotton. His wife had made a colorful tail for it using scraps from her rag pile. When Stanley flew it in the field behind their cottage, it dove like a hawk and soared like an eagle.

The king was happy to see his new kite the next day. He held it up for the young princes and princesses to admire, but he wouldn't let them touch it.

"You might smudge the gold," he told them.

A formal procession followed the king out into the royal meadow to watch him fly it. The craftsman trailed behind them with his son, Stanley. It was a windy day, but not even a tornado would have picked up the king's magnificent kite.

"I can't understand it," said the king. "This kite is made out of the finest materials. It should dive like a hawk and soar like an eagle."

Stanley approached the king. "Sometimes the most expensive isn't the best," he told him. And from that moment on, Stanley devoted his life to creating things that were simple but functional and purchasing things that were the least expensive.

One can envision Stanley Deno studying special education psychometric assessment practices (the king) as defined and built by academics and publishing companies (craftsmen building kites made of gold); questioning the assumptions on which they are based (identifying the disability because that is the problem); worrying about their complexities, relevance, and functionality (do they really identify the problem the teacher is concerned about?); and challenging their technical adequacy and fussing over their expense.

Just as kites made of gold fail to fly, traditional psychometric practices fail to identify educational problems or provide a means to measure and monitor the problem's instructional solution. Depending on cash validity as a measure of a test's adequacy was contrary to Deno's training as a scientist and his nature as a frugal person.

A Brief History

In 1975, the Education for All Handicapped Children Act (EAHCA; PL 94-142) was enacted. This landmark legislation represented the original federal special education law and guaranteed the right to a free appropriate public education (FAPE) in the least restrictive environment (LRE) to all children with disabilities. This law, based on eligibility by deviant status, has had devastating effects on how, why, where, and who is served by special education.

At this time I was a young director of special education in the Pine County Special Education Cooperative (now the St. Croix River Education District or SCRED), with just three years of experience. I joined a growing legion of energized special educators who vigorously advocated for students whose achievement and behavior problems required specially designed instructional modifications. Working with young, newly trained, and dedicated teachers, inspired by the good intentions of parent advocate groups and enabled by concerned policymakers, we championed the special education cause and dramatically increased the number and kinds of services and students. These were times of unprecedented expansion of services resulting in new educational opportunities for millions of students. New special education teachers taught in special places to special kids using special materials.

No one questions the promise or intent of EAHCA, nor can the motivations of those who struggled to implement it in those early years, or now, be characterized as anything but well intended. However, the foundational beliefs on which that law was written has had a profound, and often negative, influence on special education over the last thirty-three years in terms of research, training, and practice.

What should have heralded a revolution of innovation resulting in improved instruction and increased achievement instead turned into a quagmire of rules, processes, testing, and regulation focused on controlling entitlement, not improving instruction. Unfortunately, federal law based on a deviant status classification system resulted in the wrong labels, identified with the wrong instruments, and given for the wrong purposes by people trained in the wrong methodology and implementing the wrong interventions. It created an administrative bureaucracy (i.e., special education) separate from the general education system in terms of its funding, administration, staffing, licensing, rules, curriculum, locations, language, and so on. It focused attention on process, not progress, to the detriment of all. It perpetuated a model that blames the child for instructional failure, with the unintended consequence of delaying instructional improvements in the general education programs.

It is easy to understand why this deviant status disability model became so popular. A service model that blames the child's achievement and behavior failures on the child's disability and allows adults to abdicate their instructional responsibility is one that is easy to embrace. Couple this with the user friendliness of the system to general education (i.e., the problem is the disability, not the instruction; we refer them, you serve them; we are not a part of the problem, we are apart from the problem; don't ask us to change a system that serves us so well and you—special education—championed for so many years; and if you want us to serve them, give us the money).

In the 1970s, Deno and Mirkin envisioned and articulated a different delivery model, one predicated on the assumption that the disability is never the problem. The problem, from their perspective, was always a discrepancy between the child's actual progress and his or her expected progress. This was a radical shift in thinking and posed a completely different set of assumptions to both special and general educators: (a) the problem is the academic/behavior discrepancy; (b) the child's lack of progress has its solution in modification of the instructional program; (c) a modification may or may not work; (d) you need to frequently, directly, and continually monitor the effects of the modification; (e) you may have to modify the instructional program again if it is not successful; (f) you begin this process in the general education classroom; and (g) you intervene early in an effort to prevent referral to special education. This model was not nearly so user friendly and was easy for special and general education to resist and reject (Germann, 2009).

From Cursing the Darkness to Lighting a Candle

I first met Stanley Deno in the winter of 1979. I was introduced to him via his and Phyllis Mirkin's *Data-Based Program Modification: A Manual* (Deno and Mirkin, 1977). Suddenly, I realized there was a path less taken. This path was clearly marked and led me from the darkness of thoughts, theories, and dreams into a new world informed by science.

From that initial meeting until my retirement as director of SCRED in 2000 and later as the president and CEO of Edformation, Inc. (AIMSweb), I attempted to implement into practice and provide others a working model based on Deno and Mirkin's Data-Based Program Modification (DBPM) big ideas.

DBPM Big Ideas

Implementation of a comprehensive problem-solving model requires adherence to at least five general DBPM big ideas. First, special education service entitlement is not contingent on the identification of a medical disability but rather based on an academic or behavior discrepancy that is situation dependent. Second, the purpose of assessment refocuses from identifying a disability to determining the extent of the discrepancy in academic/behavior progress and the instructional factors that may be contributing to its existence and continuation. Third, progress monitoring is direct, frequent, and continuous (formative, not summative). Fourth, Curriculum-Based Measurement (CBM) methodology provides the dependent variable necessary for formative evaluation, and finally, problem solving is guided by a systematic, defined, and structured process. A brief discussion of each of these big ideas follows.

Big Idea 1: The problem is never the disability. The problem is always the discrepancy between the student's actual progress and his or her expected progress.

The foundational idea of DBPM, from my perspective, is the disability is *never* the problem. The handicap or problem is *always* the discrepancy between the student's actual progress and the expected progress. It is this discrepancy that provides the basis of the teacher's referral and concern. It is this discrepancy the referrer is requesting to be assessed. It is this discrepancy the referrer wants targeted for reduction or elimination in the Individualized Education Program (IEP). It is the reduction of this discrepancy that is periodically reviewed, and ultimately, it is the elimination or reduction of this discrepancy that certifies the referring problem's solution.

The problem, from a DBPM perspective, is always the discrepancy between a set of expectations for progress/performance and the child's actual progress/performance. The purpose of assessment is to identify this discrepancy as the problem, measure and quantify it, and monitor the response to instruction intended to reduce or eliminate the discrepancy. Within a DBPM model, the purpose of assessment is not to measure child *defectiveness* but rather to measure instructional *effectiveness*.

Big Idea 2: The purpose of assessment is to quantify and measure the student's actual progress, the student's expected progress, and the discrepancy between the two.

In DBPM, the purpose of assessment is not to determine the cause of the variance (identify the disability and search for pathology); it is to determine the extent of the discrepancy and the instructional factors that may be contributing to its existence. Assessment becomes a formative process whereby a database of student progress establishes the basis to form and direct instruction. Instruction is modified a posteriori (dependent on experience) the process of assessing as opposed to attempting to predict a priori (independent of experience) the instructional modifications that may be effective.

Big Idea 3: Program modifications directed at reducing or eliminating a problem must be directly, frequently, and continuously monitored to determine their effects.

In a DBPM system, development of an IEP does not mark the *end* of the assessment process but rather signals the *intensification* of a continuous assessment process. The IEP does not define the instructional modification plan that will solve the student's problem; rather, it establishes a "best guess" at the beginning of the problem-solving effort as to a possible successful intervention. In a DBPM system, periodic reviews of program effects are necessary far more frequently than annually or semiannually. In fact, several reviews each week are often required to maximize intervention effectiveness.

Big Idea 4: Curriculum-Based Measures are valid and reliable indicators of students' progress.

Medicine measures height, weight, temperature, and blood pressure; the Federal Reserve Board measures the consumer price index; Wall Street measures the Dow-Jones Industrial Average; companies report earnings per share; and even McDonald's measures how many hamburgers they sell. What do these measures have in common? They all assess general outcomes, so decisions are data based and timely.

Although these measures do not assess all health, economic, stock market, business, or even fast-food sales behavior, they are indicators considered so important to outcomes that they are routine. These measures are simple, accurate, and reasonably inexpensive in terms of time and materials. They are collected on an ongoing basis over time. They shape a variety of important decisions.

Big Idea 5: Problem solving is most effective and efficient when conducted within an orderly and defined problem-solving model.

DBPM suggests a program evaluation model consisting of five decision areas, each requiring the answer to a decision question. Figure 6.1 describes the model.

This evaluation model directs team decision making throughout the problem-solving effort. The forms (paperwork) developed to document the process give evidence to its proper implementation.

Decision Areas	Decision Question
Problem Selection	What are the problem(s) requiring program modification?
Program Selection	What plan is likely to be least restrictive and yet effective in solving the problem?
Program Operationalization	Is the agreed-upon program modification being implemented as planned?
Program Improvement	Does the program modification as implemented appear to be solving the problem?
Program Certification	Should the program as presently planned and implemented be terminated?

Figure 6.1. DBPM decision areas and questions. Adapted from Deno & Mirkin (1977).

The Pine County Special Education DBPM Model (Later the St. Croix River Education RTI Model)—CBM to General Outcome Measurement (GOM)

In the beginning, the purpose of CBM was to monitor a student's IEP goal attainment. CBM was implemented *after* a traditional special education assessment process determined the existence of a disability and after placement into special education. The assessment probes were taken from the student's actual curriculum (Curriculum-Based Measurement). Discrepancies in progress were determined by assessing the referred child's reading performance using CBM and comparing that performance to the performance of a randomly sampled group of classmates (e.g., five peers). The resultant data were managed, graphed, analyzed, and reported by teachers via hand-drawn charts.

Originally, CBM was designed to assess growth and development in students' specific curricula. In reading and spelling, teachers would create their own individual set of CBM reading passages or spelling lists based on what they were teaching and would use the information to determine students' rates of progress and make changes in instruction as needed. This tie to curriculum had high instructional validity but lacked the necessary other technical features of reliable and valid measurement.

In 1981, the Pine County Special Education Cooperative conducted its first fall, winter, and spring benchmarking of all students in all of its districts using CBM. It soon became apparent that the positive effects of testing from materials selected from an individual teacher's curriculum were offset by the lack of standard information about students' progress. Some teachers had no curriculum; the curriculum would change year to year; and the differences between schools, between teachers within schools, and so on made accurate decisions about students' progress very difficult. Furthermore, teachers were too often burdened by the task of creating their own testing materials. In addition to being more time consuming, the variability in assessment practices was a concern.

After considerable research, it has been demonstrated that a perfect correspondence between what CBM assesses and students' specific curricula is not necessary. In fact, by using standard assessment materials, the same judgments about students' level of reading or spelling skill and spelling progress can still be made accurately, as well as provide appropriate standards of growth and development across varied curricula, teachers, schools, and school districts.

What emerged from this school-based research was the following conclusion: Achievement can be improved by testing students (1) using standard, valid tests (2) that measure something important (3) on tasks of about equal difficulty, tied to general curriculum (4) over time. CBM provides the assessment procedures to be able to do numbers 1, 2, and 4. By developing graded and equivalent assessment materials of about equal difficulty that are tied to general curriculum (number 3), General Outcome Measures evolved. Thus the assessment procedures known as CBM are used in an assessment approach called General Outcome Measurement (GOM).

Beginning in 1985, the Pine County Special Education Cooperative's problem-solving system was characterized by the use of *standard* and *near equivalent* (curriculum *benign*) GOMs based on CBM assessment methodology; systematic, standardized, and universal screening of all students three times each year; early response to all discrepancies with high-quality and evidence-based interventions; team decision making based on and matched to individual student needs; frequent, direct, and continual assessment of progress within a formative evaluation model; and the utilization of data-monitoring software that allows users to input, manage, view, report, graphically display, evaluate, and analyze student-, classroom-, building-, or district-level student progress and instructional effectiveness.

Later, after my retirement in 2000, I developed a web-based data management and reporting program called AIMSweb. AIMSweb was the culmination of more than two decades of work in implementing DBPM.

Summary

In 1979, special education delivery was crisis oriented, focused on pathology, based on flawed assumptions, overburdened by process, separate from general education, primitive in evaluation, void of accountability, and often ineffective as a service mechanism. Eighty percent of the students receiving special education had reading problems, and yet the measurement of the skill was confusing and derived from multiple sources, with multiple metrics reported but not trusted even by the examiners themselves. IEPs were most often meaningless, seldom helpful, rarely measured, and using them to monitor change in an individual student's reading behavior (or any other skill) was unheard of.

As best as I can remember, this was the situation in 1979. It is not the situation that exists today, at least in an increasing number of schools focused on formative assessment, instructional improvement, academic gains, and data management and reporting. Special education instruction now exists within the same universe as that provided by general education. The field of special education, as distinct from the field of general education itself, is increasingly difficult to differentiate. Indeed, the term "special" is slowly passing from our technical vocabulary.

Learning disabilities and other equally hypothetical mental constructs are destined for disposal with other psychological relics. Old "laws" of disability and eligibility have lost their allure and the search for pathology attracts fewer volunteers.

Where and when did the movement begin that made possible the changes between 1979 and now? Others will have opinions, but based on my own personal before-and-after experiences, I suggest it all began at the University of Minnesota in the early 1970s in the teaching, writing, and experimental efforts of Stanley Deno.

Acknowledgement

As Deno likes to say, "There is no right way to do a wrong thing!" It would be wrong to not recognize the contributions of Phyllis Mirkin (deceased May 1982). Deno and Mirkin were partners in the development of DBPM, and she was instrumental in its implementation in Pine County. Deno may have built the original kite, and many including myself have attempted to fly it, but Mirkin was the one that provided the guiding wind that first lifted it into the air.

References

Deno, S. L., & Mirkin, P. (1977). *Data-based program modification: A manual.* Reston, VA: Council for Exceptional Children.

Germann, G. A. (2009). Thinking of yellow-brick roads, emerald cities and wizards. In M. R. Shinn & H. M. Walker (Eds.), *Interventions for achievement and behavior problems in a three-tier model including RTI* (pp. 1–23). Bethesda, MD: National Association of School Psychologists.

7

The Contribution of Curriculum-Based Measurement to Response to Intervention

Research, Policy, and School Practice

Kim Gibbons and Ann Casey

At the Institute for Research on Learning Disabilities (IRLD) at the University of Minnesota, Dr. Stanley Deno, as coprincipal investigator, began his quest to find a practical tool for educators to use for the purpose of frequently monitoring students' progress. One of the driving concerns in developing such a tool was the need for educators to know early in their instruction whether students were progressing. If progress was not satisfactory, changes in instruction could be made in a timely fashion to improve the student's trajectory.

In the 1970s, the main assessment tools available to educators were standardized norm-referenced measures that were developed for a different purpose—to compare an individual's performance to a normative group. These kinds of tools were not designed to be measures of progress as they only provided information on a student's relative standing compared to his or her peers. Although other informal measures were available to teachers, these measures often focused on whether a student had mastered units of instruction rather than on growth in a general academic area, such as reading proficiency. Deno's idea of frequent progress measurement on tasks reflective of general academic proficiency was new and innovative and helped to change the way educators viewed educational measurement.

In the twenty-first century, measurement of student performance and progress has become more important than ever. States are required to implement high-stakes assessments as a part of state accountability measures required by the No Child Left Behind Act (NCLB, 2001), and many districts are implementing a Response to Intervention (RTI) framework to address the needs of students with learning and behavioral disabilities.

Unfortunately, there is considerable confusion in schools about assessment and measurement, and districts often struggle to determine which assessments will be used in their district, as well as how many assessments should be given. A useful framework for assisting in this process is one suggested by Salvia and Ysseldyke (1985). Typically, assessment tools can be categorized by one of four purposes. Some tools meet more than one purpose, which further confuses the issue. However, schools need tools that meet all four of these purposes. The first one is a given—we are required to use high-stakes measures by the federal government. One could also refer to such tools as summative or outcome measures. In addition to state-required tests, some districts have their own outcome measures that are used to report to the public. A second purpose of assessment is screening. Schools need tools that assist in identifying students who may be at risk. Screening needs to be universal, meaning that all students are screened. Screening tools are not intended to be diagnostic tools and need to be quick and easy to administer, otherwise the screening process would take too much time. Vision and hearing screenings have been used in schools for years and are good examples for academic and behavioral screening tools. These tools simply tell us this student didn't do well, and we need to take a closer look to see if he or she really can see well (read well, etc.). Thus more diagnostic assessment is typically needed to determine if a student would need additional supports. The third purpose of assessment tools is progress monitoring. When screening measures indicate that a student is at risk, we need to monitor that student's progress more frequently. We don't want these students to fall through the cracks, and we can't wait until the next high-stakes test is given to determine if our additional supports were effective. Yearly tests don't help us at all in this regard—other than to tell us we may have wasted an entire academic year by providing an ineffective intervention, one that was not well matched to the student's needs. We need to know sooner so we can address the needs of struggling learners in a much timelier manner. Finally, we need instructional planning tools, sometimes referred to as diagnostic assessments; informal assessments of particular skills; or mastery monitoring. Instructional planning information is very important in an RTI framework as it helps in matching evidenced-based instructional practices to students' needs. However, planning tools are not meant for monitoring progress toward high-stakes achievement outcomes as they have no predictive validity for this purpose. To reiterate, schools need assessment tools that meet all four purposes, but tools such as

Curriculum-Based Measurement (CBM; Deno, 1985) offer a unique ability to help us determine which students are on track and which are not.

Translating Dr. Deno's Research into Practice: One Education District's Perspective

The St. Croix River Education District (SCRED) has worked with Dr. Deno over the past thirty years to develop and implement a problem-solving process. SCRED worked with the IRLD in the early 1980s to field-test CBMs. When SCRED began using generic CBM probes, often referred to as General Outcome Measures (GOMs), in the early 1980s, the measures were used primarily as a progress-monitoring tool to assist teachers in determining whether instruction was successful or whether additional intervention was warranted for at-risk students. However, as the accountability movement gained momentum, and with the passage of NCLB (2001), SCRED began to use GOMs within an RTI framework to accomplish three primary purposes. First, the measures are used to screen all students regularly for achievement difficulties three times per year. This practice recently has been referred to as Benchmark Assessment. Second, students who are identified as below target or at risk are monitored more frequently to assist teachers in determining whether supplemental interventions are successful. Finally, our schools use GOMs as a way to evaluate systems.

In recent years, much emphasis has been placed on a three-tier model (Sugai, Horner, and Gresham, 2002) and/or a school-wide model (Simmons et al., 2002) within an RTI framework. As a result, our schools analyze data at the classroom, grade, building, and district levels to evaluate core, supplemental, and intensive instructional supports and services. The remainder of this chapter will focus on how GOMs have been used to support the implementation of a multitiered service delivery model within an RTI framework. We will discuss how GOMs are used at each of the three service-delivery tiers.

Tier 1: Quality Instruction for All Students

Our schools administer GOMs to all students three times per year: fall, winter, and spring. This type of assessment is frequently referred to as Benchmark Assessment. Benchmark Assessment serves a number of purposes for our districts. First, it is a screening tool to monitor the progress of every student, calling attention to any student who is having difficulty and might have escaped the attention of the school staff. This signals the need to monitor the student more often. Second, it establishes school norms that can be used to set goals. Third, benchmark data may be used to evaluate the effectiveness of the school's basic skills programs.

When school districts use GOMs as screening measures, they need to have some type of criterion for success on which to evaluate student performance. As the use of GOMs at the system level grew, either local (Deno, 1985) or national (Hasbrouk and Tindal, 1992) norms were suggested as tools to help determine desired outcomes on GOM assessments. However, with the advent of NCLB and high-stakes assessments, a criterion for success has been established in every state in the form of a specific score on the annual statewide assessment. These criterion scores on statewide assessments are dynamic rather than static, requiring districts to make progressive improvement over time. The criterion is generally summative in nature and is not measured until third grade. GOMs allow practitioners the flexibility to continue to measure formatively within and across school years, to begin measurement in early childhood or kindergarten, and to establish criteria for success along the way that will accurately predict whether a child is also likely to be successful on the statewide assessment. In addition, as statewide assessments change, or as concerns in their utility are raised, GOMs provide a trustworthy and proven alternative for effective data-driven decision making. Thus common practice now involves linking scores on GOMs to scores on statewide assessments such that a criterion for success is established at each grade level and time point of system-wide GOM assessment. Many advanced statistical procedures have emerged over the years to assist districts in conducting these analyses, including logistic regression procedures. The end result is a series of target scores at each of the fall, winter, and spring benchmark periods that are linked to proficiency on the statewide accountability tests.

Once districts have target scores established, they can begin examining their data and determining the percentage of students who are at or above, somewhat below, or significantly below target. Most districts implementing an RTI framework strive to have at least 80 percent of their students at or above proficient levels. If a large percentage of students are not reaching the target score, there may be concerns with the curriculum and instructional practices used at tier 1, as the growth rates of students in this tier are not keeping pace with the growth necessary to remain on track for success. Conversely, if students who were in tier 1 in the fall remain above target throughout the year, it indicates that growth rates for these students have been sufficient enough to remain on track for success. GOM data need to be analyzed and displayed in useful ways to assist school staff in decision making.

Reporting Benchmark Data

School staff use a variety of charts to display benchmark assessment data. Grade-level teams often use a top-to-bottom listing of every student in the grade. By comparing these data to the target or expected scores for that norm period, teachers see at a glance who is succeeding and who is not. Examining the entire grade level of students allows teachers to determine how to most effectively use valuable, yet scarce, resources and often use these data to aid in flexible grouping procedures.

Our schools also use these data for program evaluation. Data can be displayed in a box-and-whiskers chart for every class in a school for each norming period to provide a quick analysis of how each grade level is performing relative to the target score. Another useful report is a chart showing the percentage of students at each grade level who met the target score for that benchmark period. This is an excellent report for grade-level teams and schools to use to set grade-level or school improvement goals. If large numbers of students are below target, this indicates a need to intervene at tier 1 and examine whether appropriate curriculum and instructional strategies are being used. Schools can also examine the percentage of students who are somewhat below target (tier 2) and well below target (tier 3) at each norming period to evaluate whether supplemental and intensive interventions are effective.

Using Benchmark Data

Once data are collected and analyzed, schools must be organized in such a way that teachers and support staff *use* the data to aid in instructional decision making. Schools must be organized to support collaboration and teamwork within each of the grade levels. Our schools have supported collaboration and teamwork by establishing grade-level teams that meet regularly to examine student achievement data. Meetings occur at a minimum of three times per year following the collection of benchmark data or, more desirably, monthly. These meetings are collaborative and include all staff members (both general and special education) who serve students at a particular grade level. Rather than considering students in each particular classroom to be the primary responsibility of the teacher of that class, the grade-level staff members can collectively consider all students as one group to be supported together. These teams review benchmark assessment data and help develop standard treatment protocol interventions for groups of students who are below target.

Tier 2: Supplemental Instruction for Some Students

Once data are collected and analyzed, our schools need to identify the acceptable percentage of students who will need supplemental instruction and intervention. The literature provides some direction that no more than 15 percent of students should be in need of supplemental instruction (e.g., Caplan and Grunebaum, 1967; Simeonsson, 1994); however, that number was not empirically derived. Rather, from a resource standpoint, schools often do not have the time, money, or expertise to provide supplemental instruction to large numbers of students. Thus many of our schools have used 15 percent as a target goal.

Next, schools must determine performance indicators of student performance. We have continued to use the same performance indicators across all three tiers to ensure a common measure is used in decision making. At tier 2, we recommend using strategic monitoring procedures once per month for all students at this tier. Strategic monitoring serves several purposes. First, it provides a basis for evaluation of instructional programming for individual students with difficulties. Second, it provides information to help teachers make decisions about goals, materials, levels, and groups. Third, the graphically displayed data aids communication with parents and other professionals. Many schools that we work with provide a copy of students' graphs to parents during parent-teacher conferences. Parents have reported that they appreciate being able to see how their children perform relative to other students in the same grade.

The criterion for success at tier 2 is, ultimately, to move into the tier 1 range. Our schools set target scores for tier 1 and tier 2. Students who score at the tier 1 target have an 80 percent probability of passing the high-stakes test. Students who score at or below the tier 2 target have a 30 percent probability of success. These targets can be flexibly determined based on the probability curve and the school's available resources and desired goals. Based on diagnostic accuracy of these target scores and on the individual school's performance and available resources, both of these targets can be adjusted upward when deemed appropriate.

While progress-monitoring data allows for evaluation of success at the individual level, regular benchmark assessments provide an opportunity for evaluation at the system level to evaluate tier 2 services. Keeping the goal of 15 percent in mind, we examine the percentage of students who fall into the tier 2 range on the fall, winter, and spring GOM assessments. We continue to remember that a rising percentage could be due to highly effective tier 3 services (or ineffective tier 1 services) rather than to inadequate services at tier 2. Similarly, a falling percentage is not an indicator of strong tier 2 services if the percentage of students at tier 3 is growing. In addition to the percentages of students in each tier, we examine the number of students in tier 2 who move up to tier 1, down to tier 3, and remain in tier 2.

Tier 3: Intensive Instruction

Similar to tiers 1 and 2, our schools have developed a clearly defined goal of the percentage of students who will be in need of intensive instruction. If school districts use the 80 percent (core), 15 percent (supplemental) goals recommended in the literature (e.g., Caplan and Grunebaum, 1967; Simeonsson, 1994), then that leaves 5 percent of students who may be in need of the most intensive instruction and support. Again, similar to tier 2, the goals that are set are aligned with the existing resources within a school.

Once goals are set, we continue to use GOMs at tier 3. We use intensive monitoring procedures (Shinn, Walker, and Stoner, 2002), which involve monitoring student progress on at least a weekly basis. For students who receive special education services and support, these measures can be used to write Individualized Education Program (IEP) goals and evaluate progress toward goals. The criterion for success at tier 3 is examining data to determine the percentage of students at tier 3. Thus the goal for students in tier 3 is initially to reach the GOM score associated with the bottom of the tier 2 range for the upcoming benchmark period (i.e., students in tier 3 in the fall should aim for reaching tier 2 in winter or spring, depending on the severity of the discrepancy). Once this intermediate goal is achieved, the ultimate goal of reaching grade-level proficiency can be reasonably set.

To support collaboration and teamwork at tier 3, our schools have established problem-solving teams. It would be surprising to find any public school in the United States that does not host some sort of team of teachers who meet regularly to discuss the needs of students experiencing difficulty and to consider possible supports for these students. These teams have a wide variety of names (e.g., teacher assistance teams, student assistance teams, student support teams, student success teams), as well as a wide variety of behavioral norms and activities completed. We have found it useful for problem-solving teams to work in conjunction with grade-level teams to help identify appropriate interventions for students when the knowledge and resources of the grade-level teams have been exhausted. We use a four-step problem-solving process including problem identification, problem analysis, plan development and implementation, and plan evaluation. This is a continuous improvement process, as the evaluation data inform the team about whether further identification or analysis should be done.

For some students at tier 3, problem-solving teams may determine that a special education evaluation is warranted. With the 2004 reauthorization of Individuals with Disabilities Act (IDEA), districts may use a process that determines whether a child responds to scientifically based instruction as part of the evaluation criteria. SCRED uses GOM data to assist in making entitlement decisions. We ensure that a problem-solving framework was implemented with integrity to identify and analyze problems, select appropriate interventions, implement interventions with integrity, and evaluate intervention effectiveness. Next, we use GOM data to identify students with extremely low achievement and low rates of academic progress. Thus students who are identified as needing special education resources are those students with high levels of instructional needs, low rates of progress, and who are extremely discrepant from local expectations.

In closing, RTI is not a program, curriculum, or instructional strategy. It is a framework for schools to organize their work in meeting all students' academic and social/behavioral needs. An important component of RTI is a strong measurement system for universal screening and for monitoring progress of those identified as at-risk in the screening. Dr. Deno's work is invaluable in this aspect. While more than thirty years have transpired since the development of this system of measurement, we continue to have few other tools that have the same predictive capabilities of identifying students who may need something more or different in order to make progress. This is an integral part of RTI. While many schools say they are focused on meeting all students' needs, few schools have actually done so. RTI has been a long time in the making, but Dr. Deno's seminal work in screening and progress monitoring, along with the emphasis on evidence-based practices in all tiers of instruction, has made this goal achievable. Most importantly, countless students have achieved positive educational outcomes as a result of having their progress monitored frequently and changes made to their instructional programs when progress was insufficient.

References

Caplan, G., & Grunebaum, H. (1967). Perspectives on primary prevention: A review. *Archives General Psychiatry, 17*, 331–346.

Deno, S. L. (1985). Curriculum-based measurement: The emerging alternative. *Exceptional Children, 52*, 219–232.

Hasbrouck, J. E., & Tindal, G. (1992). Curriculum-based oral reading fluency norms for students in grades 2 through 5. *Teaching Exceptional Children, 24*(3), 41–44.

Salvia, J., & Ysseldyke, J. (1985). *Assessment in special and remedial education*. Boston, MA: Houghton Mifflin.

Shinn, M., Walker, H., & Stoner, G. (2002). *Interventions for academic and behavior problems II: Preventions and remedial approaches*. Silver Spring, MD: National Association of School Psychologists.

Simeonsson, R. J. (1994). *Risk, resilience, & prevention: Promoting the well-being of all children*. Baltimore, MD: Paul H. Brookes.

Simmons, D., Kame'enui, E., Good, R., III, Harn, B., Cole, C., & Braun, D. (2002). Building, implementing, and sustaining a beginning reading improvement model: Lessons learned school by school. In M. Shinn, H. Walker, & G. Stoner (Eds.), *Interventions for academic and behavior problems II: Preventions and remedial approaches* (pp. 200–236). Silver Spring, MD: National Association of School Psychologists.

Sugai, G., Horner, R. H., & Gresham, F. (2002). Behaviorally effective school environments. In M. Shinn, H. Walker, & G. Stoner (Eds.), *Interventions for academic and behavior problems: Preventive and remedial approaches* (pp. 315–350). Silver Spring, MD: National Association of School Psychologists.

III

Applications in Elementary Education

8

How Curriculum-Based Measures Help Us Detect Word Recognition Problems in First Graders

Éric Dion, Isabelle Dubé, Catherine Roux,
Danika Landry, and Laurence Bergeron

For reasons that remain poorly understood, learning to recognize written words constitutes a formidable challenge for some first graders. Figuring out which word is represented by a sequence of letters sometimes seems almost impossible for these students, even when they receive help (e.g., Torgesen et al., 1999). Word-recognition difficulties are serious and should be prevented or addressed through remediation as early as possible and in the most efficient manner available, if only to avoid students developing a deep aversion for reading.

Well-implemented, evidence-based, class-wide interventions represent a critical first-line prevention effort (Al Otaiba and Fuchs, 2006; Dion, Brodeur, Gosselin, Campeau, and Fuchs, 2010; Fuchs et al., 2001). However, because of their low intensity, interventions of this kind will not help all students (McMaster, Fuchs, Fuchs, and Compton, 2005). Such students, the so-called nonresponders, have to be targeted for more individualized and intensive interventions, and Curriculum-Based Measures (CBMs) are ideally suited to this end (Deno, 2003). In this chapter, we review studies that have examined how these measures can be used to monitor first graders' progress, or lack thereof, toward competent word recognition.

The Challenges of Progress Monitoring in First Grade

It is not rare for students to begin first grade with only a rudimentary knowledge of letter shapes and sounds and to still proceed to become competent readers over the course of the school year. In fact, the progress sometimes accomplished during this period is often impressive. Also impressive, however, are the differences in ability levels at the beginning of first grade and in the pace at which word recognition is mastered (e.g., Mathes, Howard, Allen, and Fuchs, 1998). While some students make remarkably good progress, others stagnate, creating an accentuation of individual differences described by statisticians as *spanning* (Rogosa, 1995). First graders' progress in learning to read represents what is perhaps the clearest example of this kind of phenomenon.

Such diversity makes progress monitoring important but also raises measurement problems. To be useful for progress monitoring, a measure must present specific characteristics. Specifically, it must be available in alternate versions of a uniform level of difficulty, and its score has to be free of floor or ceiling effects (Dion, Roux, and Dupéré, in press). This means that the unchanging assessment procedure must remain relevant throughout the assessment period (i.e., the school year). If the procedure is too difficult, scores will not reflect students' emerging skills. If it is too easy, scores will stop reflecting progress after a while. Finally, a change in the assessment procedure will make it impossible to determine whether scores vary because of this change or because real progress has been made.

How, then, should we monitor progress during first grade? For the most part, efforts to develop measures of reading progress have focused on students in second and higher grades (Wayman, Wallace, Wiley, Tichá, and Espin, 2007). In these studies, students are typically asked to read from a text, and the number of words read correctly per minute is scored (e.g., Fuchs, Fuchs, and Maxwell, 1988). Although this approach works well for students who have at least partially mastered word recognition, it is too difficult for many beginning readers and, hence, subject to floor effects until the middle of first grade and possibly later. For instance, in Silberglitt and Hintze's (2005) longitudinal study, students were asked to read aloud from a text for one minute, two or three times a year, from winter of first grade to spring of third grade. It is only in winter of second grade that numbers of words read correctly began to be appropriately distributed. Before, score distributions were positively skewed because a large number of students were able to read only a very limited number of words (see also Schatschneider, Wagner, and Crawford, 2008). It is evidently too much to ask of many first graders to try to read a whole text at the beginning of the school year. Easier tasks need to be considered for monitoring their progress.

Potential Candidates

As noted by Wayman and colleagues (2007), word selection is difficult to control with text because of the requirement of creating coherent stories. Text thus inevitably includes words that first graders are unable to read without help. To circumvent this problem, researchers have selected words considered of appropriate difficulty and presented these words in randomly ordered lists (Deno, Mirkin, and Chiang, 1982). First graders have one minute to read as many words as they can and, once again, the number of word read correctly per minute is scored. Only words pronounced completely correctly are counted as correct. At the beginning of first grade, scores based on lists of words are less subject to floor effects than scores based on text, even if a minority of students is not yet able to recognize any word from the lists at this point (Daly, Wright, Kelly, and Martens, 1997). Interestingly, presenting words in a list, out of context, does not prevent a valid assessment of reading skills. Strong positive correlations indicate that students who quickly and accurately recognize words in a list also read text fluently and with understanding at the end of first grade (Fuchs, Fuchs, and Compton, 2004).

A difficulty with lists of words concerns the selection of words, a topic on which there has been almost no research. In fact, there are at present no explicit guidelines, empirically based or otherwise, for selecting words. This is problematic because the limited evidence available suggests that word selection can have a substantial effect on scores. In the Fuchs, Tindal, and Deno (1981) study, second- to fourth-graders participated in a word-recognition intervention. Their progress was assessed with lists generated from three sets of different sizes: instructed words only, words from the grade-level material, and across-grade-level words (preprimer to fourth-grade material). Progress was more than two times as great on the lists of instructed words than on the lists of grade-level words, and it was undetectable on the lists of across-grade-level words. Progress thus appears slower with more difficult lists. On the other hand, progress was more linear or orderly on the lists of grade-level words, suggesting that these lists measured progress more reliably than the other ones (see Dion et al., in press). No comparable study has been conducted with first graders, but the optimal set of words probably lies between the two extremes. On the one hand, generating lists from a small set comprising only short, familiar, and orthographically regular words could help avoid floor effects but may also limit validity, because being able to read words like "red" or "milk" might be a good start, but little more than that.

On the other hand, generating lists from a large and heterogeneous set that includes challenging words could create floor effects severe enough to limit validity (variance restriction negatively affects validity coefficients).

Another approach, inspired by measures of "word-attack" (Torgesen, Wagner, and Rashotte, 1997), has also been tried. First graders are presented with a list of orthographically correct but "nonsense" consonant-vowel (e.g., "bu") or consonant-vowel-consonant words (e.g., "tob"), and they have to read as many of these nonsense words as possible in one minute (Good, Simmons, and Kame'enui, 2001). Scoring is based on the number of correctly pronounced letter sounds. Credit is thereby given for partially correct pronunciation of nonsense words, probably to compensate for first graders' proneness to minor pronunciation mistakes. Available results nevertheless indicate the presence of rather strong floor effects up until the middle of first grade (Fien et al., 2008). From a theoretical standpoint, lists of nonsense words are potentially interesting because they directly assess the ability to decode or sound out unfamiliar words based on their orthography, an ability considered the foundation of word recognition (Share, 1995). In practice, however, numbers of correctly pronounced letter sounds in lists of nonsense words are only moderately correlated with end-of-first-grade outcomes, raising doubts about the usefulness of the approach with first graders (Fuchs et al., 2004; Riedel, 2007).

What could explain these mitigated results? Assessing progress with lists of nonsense words means postulating that to become competent readers, first graders must learn to accurately decode unfamiliar words (nonsense or otherwise), letter by letter, with increasing speed. This is a postulate of undemonstrated validity. As we have argued elsewhere, the fact that most students can, at some point, quickly pronounce nonsense words does not mean that it is this specific skill that drives the acquisition of the ability to recognize words (Dion et al., 2009). The speed with which unfamiliar words are decoded may not be important. Rather, what is perhaps critical for beginning readers is to carefully decode unfamiliar words when these words are first encountered and then to be able to use one strategy or another to automatize (i.e., speed up) the recognition of these words for subsequent encounters. If this is correct, there is more to competent word recognition than quick and accurate decoding, and this may explain why scores on lists of nonsense words are only moderately correlated with reading outcomes.

Our team has recently adapted an approach developed originally for kindergarteners. During kindergarten, progress can be monitored by simply presenting students with randomly ordered lists of letters and asking them to pronounce the sound of these letters (Elliott, Lee, and Tollefson, 2001; Fuchs et al., 2001). Only single letters are used and any sounds associated with these letters are accepted as good answers. We have modified this approach to make it more difficult and, hence, suitable for first graders (Dion, Roux, and Dupéré, in press). In our study, French-speaking first graders were presented lists of frequently encountered words with, underlined in each word, a letter or group of letters representing a single sound (e.g., "mat<u>ch</u>"). Students were asked to pronounce only the underlined letter or group of letters, the way it should be pronounced in the word. Although students did not have to pronounce the whole word, they had to figure out what it was in order to make distinctions between, for instance, "s" pronounced as /z/ rather than /s/. Of course, they also needed to know the multiple sounds associated with letters and groups of letters. Our participants were asked to pronounce as many sounds as possible in one minute. Even though students at risk of reading problems were overrepresented in our sample, floor effects at the beginning of first grade were minimal. At the end of first grade, scores on our sounds-in-words measure were correlated strongly with decoding and word recognition and moderately with comprehension.

In sum, three candidates have been identified for monitoring progress during first grade: lists of words, nonsense words, and sounds-in-words. Floor effects are less pronounced for these lists than for text, even if they appear nonnegligible for lists of nonsense words. For lists of words, sounds-in-words, and to a lesser degree, nonsense words, scores at one point in time are correlated with end-of-first-grade outcomes and thus exhibit at least some degree of predictive validity. However, such correlations are necessary but insufficient to demonstrate that a measure can reliably and validly assess progress (Dion, Roux, and Dupéré, in press; Wayman et al., 2007). This capacity must be directly examined, something that has been done in only a few studies. We now examine the available evidence, focusing on studies in which progress has been monitored for a substantial part of the first grade year, and information on the psychometric properties of the measures is presented.

Studies of Progress Monitoring in First Grade

Good, Baker, and Peyton (2009) have analyzed progress-monitoring data collected by schools using lists of nonsense words. Their goal was to determine whether it is necessary to monitor progress or if it is enough to conduct a single assessment at the beginning of the school year. To answer this question, Good and colleagues tried to predict end-of-first-grade text-reading fluency with the rate of progress on the nonsense words measure, after controlling for the student's initial score on the same measure. Reasonably complete information was available for only one of the samples ("Oregon Reading First progress monitoring subsample"), and we focus here on results for this group of students. These students were assessed once or twice a month during the first semester of first grade because they were considered "at risk" or "at some risk" of reading problems. Both groups showed limited reading skills at the beginning of first grade, and their initial score on the lists of nonsense words had almost no predictive power, perhaps because of a restriction of variance on this score. Some students nevertheless made substantial progress the following months. On average, students correctly pronounced 1.4 more sounds per week over the fall semester, with important individual differences. At-risk students' weekly rates of progress explained 54 percent of the variance of their end-of-first-grade text-reading fluency scores, as compared to only 11 percent for students "at some risk." Monitoring progress thus appears important, at least for the students who are most at risk of reading problems. Lists of nonsense words may not be the most appropriate measure to do so, however.

Fuchs and colleagues (2004) conducted a study to compare the predictive power and validity of monitoring data obtained with lists of words or nonsense words. For the most part of the first-grade school year, students at risk of reading problems were assessed on these two measures, at least twice a month. A complete assessment of their reading skills was also conducted at the end of the school year. Progress slowed slightly from the fall (1.9 more sounds per week) to the winter semester (1.5 more sounds per week) on lists of nonsense words but somewhat accelerated on the lists of words (0.9 vs. 1.3 more words per week). To examine correlates of progress, weekly rates of progress over the school year as a whole were calculated. Weekly rates of progress on lists of words proved to be strongly predictive of end-of-first-grade reading skills: Students who made the most progress on this measure were the ones who were decoding with the greatest ease and who were reading text with the greatest fluency and understanding at the end of first grade. The predictive power of weekly rates of progress on lists of nonsense words was significantly less strong, even when it came to predicting end-of-first-grade decoding skills, with correlations in the low to moderate range.

We have examined the usefulness of lists of sounds-in-words to monitor progress in the context of an intervention study (Dion, Roux, Landry et al., 2011). Intact groups of French-speaking first graders were randomly assigned to a control condition or to one of two conditions in which teachers implemented peer-mediated activities for the most part of the school year. In each group, students at risk of reading problems were assessed, along with some of their average peers. Twice a month, from October to March, students were asked to read a list of sounds-in-words. At the end of the school year, a thorough assessment of their reading skills was conducted. Until the middle of the second semester, students made rapid progress on the lists of sounds-in-words, but their progress started slowing down after this point. To illustrate, at-risk students, who were initially able to pronounce five sounds, learned to pronounce two more sounds per week in October, but only one more sound every two weeks in March. Average students initially pronounced a greater number of sounds, but their progress followed a similar pattern. Here also, individual differences were apparent. At-risk and average students who made faster progress during the first semester became better decoders and were able to read text with greater fluency and understanding at the end of the school year. Finally, compared with their peers in the control condition, at-risk and average students assigned to the intervention condition made more progress on the lists of sounds-in-words. This indicates that our measure is sensitive to the quality of instruction.

Implications and Unresolved Issues

The studies reviewed here have demonstrated that by frequently assessing at-risk first graders, rates of progress can be estimated in a reliable and valid manner. Accordingly, it appears feasible to determine which at-risk students are not making sufficient progress and to offer them help with minimal delay (Dion, Morgan, Fuchs, and Fuchs, 2004; McMaster et al., 2005).

Progress monitoring with lists of words is the approach with the strongest empirical support, but important issues remain unresolved. It is notably crucial to determine the extent to which first graders' scores are influenced by word selection (see Fuchs et al., 1981) and to develop guidelines for word selection. In a related manner, because the influence of word selection has not been explored, norms regarding the amount of progress to be expected cannot be specified (Fuchs, Fuchs, Hamlett, Walz, and Germann, 1993; Silberglitt and Hintze, 2007). In the absence of such norms, it is difficult to determine whether a student is making enough progress or not. Furthermore, word recognition requires the coordination of multiple component skills (e.g., Lovett et al., 2000), and difficulties in learning to recognize words could be caused by problems involving any of these skills. Identifying the skills that cause difficulties for a student would help tailor the intervention to the student's specific needs. Although the relevance of diagnostic analysis of responses to progress monitoring measures is well documented in mathematics, this kind of analysis has only been tried recently in reading and never with beginning readers (Fuchs, Fuchs, and Hamlett, 2007). One simple way to diagnose at-risk first graders' word-recognition difficulties would be to monitor their progress with lists generated from different sets of words (e.g., frequent but orthographically irregular words, short orthographically regular words, or multisyllabic words). In this manner, difficulties could be diagnosed by identifying the kind of words that pose problems for a student. Apart from lists of words, lists of sounds-in-words and perhaps lists of nonsense words could be useful additions to a diagnostic battery.

Finally, it has become customary to generate lists in which words or other stimuli are presented in random order. If the set from which words are sampled include words of diverse degrees of difficulty, some challenging words will inevitably be presented at the beginning of the lists. It is our impression that many at-risk students will stop making efforts after encountering two or three difficult words and will thereby not read easier words further in the list. The number of words a student read per minute in a list could thus be a function of the difficulty of the words sampled for this particular list and of the order in which they are listed. One way to reduce the error variance created by the order of presentation would be to list sampled words in a rough order of increasing difficulty (e.g., as a function of their length). It is also our impression that practitioners would find such lists more acceptable and hence would be more inclined to use them for monitoring purposes.

Since their creation by Stanley Deno and his former students and collaborators, progress monitoring measures have mostly been used to guide remediation efforts with students presenting diagnosed difficulties (Stecker, Fuchs, and Fuchs, 2005). As we have seen in this chapter, such measures could also play a crucial role in prevention efforts targeting younger students.

References

Al Otaiba, S., & Fuchs, D. (2006). Who are the young children for whom best practices in reading are ineffective? An experimental and longitudinal study. *Journal of Learning Disabilities, 39*, 414–431.

Daly, E. J., Wright, J. A., Kelly, S. Q., & Martens, B. K. (1997). Measures of early academic skills: Reliability and validity with a first grade sample. *School Psychology Quarterly, 12*, 268–280.

Deno, S. L. (2003). Curriculum-Based Measures: Development and perspectives. *Assessment for Effective Intervention, 28*, 3–12.

Deno, S. L., Mirkin, P. K., & Chiang, B. (1982). Identifying valid measures of reading. *Exceptional Children, 49*, 36–45.

Dion, É., Brodeur, M., Gosselin, C., Campeau, M.-È., & Fuchs, D. (2010). Implementing research-based instruction to prevent reading problems among low SES students: Is earlier better? *Learning Disabilities Research and Practice, 25*, 87–96.

Dion, É., Morgan, P. L., Fuchs, D., & Fuchs, L. S. (2004). The promise and limitations of reading instruction in the mainstream: The need for a multi-level approach. *Exceptionality, 12*, 163–173.

Dion, É., Roux, C., & Dupéré, V. (in press). Utilisation et développement des mesures de progrès en lecture [Use and development of progress monitoring reading measures]. In M. J. Berger & A. Desrochers (Eds.), *L'évaluation de la littératie*. Ottawa, ON: Presses de l'Université d'Ottawa.

Dion, É., Roux, C., Landry, D., Fuchs, D., Wehby, J., & Dupéré, V. (2011). Improving attention and preventing reading difficulties among low-income first-graders: A randomized study. *Prevention Science, 12*, 70–79.

Dion, É., Roux, C., Lemire-Théberge, L., Guay, M.-H., Bergeron, L., & Brodeur, M. (2009). Teaching reading comprehension to at-risk beginning readers. In G. D. Sideridis & T. A. Citro (Eds.), *Strategies in reading for struggling learners* (pp. 95–109). Weston, MA: Learning Disabilities Worldwide.

Elliott, J., Lee, S. W., & Tollefson, N. (2001). A reliability and validity study of the Dynamic Indicators of Basic Early Literacy Skills—Modified. *School Psychology Review, 30*, 33–49.

Fien, H., Baker, S. K., Smolkowski, K., Smith, J. L. M., Kame'enui, E. J., & Beck, C. T. (2008). Using nonsense word fluency to predict reading proficiency in kindergarten through second grade for English learners and native English speakers. *School Psychology Review, 37*, 391–408.

Fuchs, D., Fuchs, L. S., Thompson, A., Al Otaiba, S., Yen, L., Yang, N. J., Braun, M., & O'Connor, R. (2001). Is reading important in reading-readiness programs? A randomized field trial with teachers as program implementers. *Journal of Educational Psychology, 93*, 251–267.

Fuchs, L. S., Fuchs, D., & Compton, D. L. (2004). Monitoring early reading development in first grade: Word identification fluency versus nonsense word fluency. *Exceptional Children, 71*, 7–21.

Fuchs, L. S., Fuchs, D., & Hamlett, C. L. (2007). Using Curriculum-Based Measurement to inform reading instruction. *Reading and Writing, 20,* 553–567.

Fuchs, L. S., Fuchs, D., Hamlett, C., Walz, L., & Germann, G. (1993). Formative evaluation of academic progress: How much growth can we expect? *School Psychology Review, 22,* 27–48.

Fuchs, L. S., Fuchs, D., & Maxwell, L. (1988). The validity of informal reading comprehension measures. *Remedial and Special Education, 9,* 20–29.

Fuchs, L. S., Tindal, G., & Deno, S. L. (1981). *Effects of varying item domain and sample duration on technical characteristics of daily measures in reading.* Minneapolis: University of Minnesota. (ERIC Document Reproduction Service No. ED211606)

Good, R. H., Baker, S. K., & Peyton, J. A. (2009). Making sense of nonsense word fluency: Determining adequate progress in early first-grade reading. *Reading & Writing Quarterly, 25,* 33–56.

Good, R. H., Simmons, D. C., & Kame'enui, E. J. (2001). The importance and decision-making utility of a continuum of fluency-based indicators of foundational reading skills for third-grade high-stakes outcomes. *Scientific Studies of Reading, 5,* 257–288.

Lovett, M. W., Lacerenza, L., Borden, S. L., Frijters, J. C., Steinbach, K. A., & De Palma, M. (2000). Components of effective remediation for developmental reading disabilities: Combining phonological and strategy-based instruction to improve outcomes. *Journal of Educational Psychology, 92,* 263–283.

Mathes, P. G., Howard, J. K., Allen, S. H., & Fuchs, D. (1998). Peer-assisted learning strategies: Responding to the needs of diverse learners. *Reading Research Quarterly, 33,* 62–94.

McMaster, K. N., Fuchs, D., Fuchs, L. S., & Compton, D. L. (2005). Responding to nonresponders: An experimental field trial of identification and intervention methods. *Exceptional Children, 71,* 445–463.

Riedel, B. W. (2007). The relation between DIBELS, reading comprehension, and vocabulary in urban first-grade students. *Reading Research Quarterly, 42,* 546–567.

Rogosa, D. S. (1995). Myths and methods: "Myths about longitudinal research," plus supplemental questions. In J. M. Gottman (Ed.), *The analysis of change* (pp. 3–65). Hillsdale, NJ: Lawrence Erlbaum Associates.

Schatschneider, C., Wagner, R. K., & Crawford, E. C. (2008). The importance of measuring growth in response to intervention models: Testing a core assumption. *Learning and Individual Differences, 18,* 308–315.

Share, D. L. (1995). Phonological recording and self-teaching: Sine qua non of reading instruction. *Cognition, 55,* 151–218.

Silberglitt, B., & Hintze, J. (2005). Formative assessment using CBM-R cut scores to track progress toward success on state-mandated achievement tests: A comparison of methods. *Journal of Psychoeducational Assessment, 23,* 304–325.

Silberglitt, B., & Hintze, J. M. (2007). How much growth can we expect? A conditional analysis of R-CBM growth rates by level of performance. *Exceptional Children, 74,* 71–84.

Stecker, P. M., Fuchs, L. S., & Fuchs, D. (2005). Using Curriculum-Based Measurement to improve student achievement: Review of research. *Psychology in the Schools, 42,* 795–819.

Torgesen, J. K., Wagner, R. K., & Rashotte, C. A. (1997). *Test of word reading efficiency.* Austin, TX: Pro-Ed.

Torgesen, J. K., Wagner, R. K., Rashotte, C. A., Rose, E., Lindamood, P., Conway, T., & Garvan, C. (1999). Preventing reading failure in young children with phonological processing disabilities: Group and individual responses to instruction. *Journal of Educational Psychology, 91,* 579–593.

Wayman, M. M., Wallace, T., Wiley, H. I., Tichá, R., & Espin, C. A. (2007). Literature synthesis on Curriculum-Based Measurement in reading. *Journal of Special Education, 41,* 85–120.

9

How Progress Monitoring Research Contributed to Early Intervention for and Prevention of Reading Difficulty

Roland H. Good III, Ruth A. Kaminski, Hank Fien,
Kelly A. Powell-Smith, and Kelli D. Cummings

Since the inception of Curriculum-Based Measurement (CBM) in the late 1970s at the University of Minnesota, Stanley Deno's work on CBM and goal-oriented monitoring, data-based decision making, and General Outcome Measurement has provided the foundation for the development of measures to be used for formative evaluation of academic progress (e.g., Deno, 1985; Deno and Fuchs, 1987; Deno and Mirkin, 1977; Fuchs and Deno, 1994). This chapter focuses on three key principles of General Outcome Measurement and data-based decision making that have guided and provided energy for much of our work in early literacy: (a) targeting assessment on *indicators* of basic skills, (b) focusing on student *outcomes*, and (c) combining assessment with targeted interventions in a data-based decision making model for the *prevention* of reading difficulty. In this chapter we will use a recent analysis of Dynamic Indicators of Basic Early Literacy Skills (DIBELS) Nonsense Word Fluency (NWF) data from the DIBELS Data System to illustrate the application of these principles to early literacy and to highlight the importance of formative assessment for the prevention of reading difficulties.

Assessing Indicators of Basic Skills

Curriculum-Based Measures were designed to serve as "vital signs" or *indicators* of basic skills (Deno and Mirkin, 1977, p. 14; Deno, 1985; Shinn and Bamonto, 1998). Such indicators efficiently and economically measure key behaviors that are indicative of a student's performance on a broader array of skills within a domain. For example, oral reading fluency (ORF) provides an indicator of a student's proficiency in reading, including comprehension. Each ORF passage is an alternate form that represents and samples the domain of reading skills for that year. As students learn specific reading skills over time, their ORF improves.

Similarly, NWF was designed to provide an indicator of a student's basic phonics skills. Basic phonics skills enable children to begin to read simple, phonetically regular words. While teachers provide instruction on a variety of skills, including phonemic awareness, specific letter-sound correspondences, and strategies for sounding out words, NWF samples the yearlong domain of skills necessary to read phonetically regular words. As students acquire the phonics skills that provide the foundation for word reading and decoding, their NWF scores improve. An important principle regarding General Outcome Measures as indicators is that "general outcome measurement does not determine instructional content and procedures" (Fuchs and Deno, 1991, p. 496). Thus the use of nonsense words is incidental to the focus on the broader task—use of basic phonics skills to decode phonetically regular unknown words.

Focusing on Student Outcomes

The premise that data should inform decisions that change important student *outcomes* is foundational to Deno's work and writing. After all, "effective programs are defined not in terms of their procedures but, rather, of their outcomes" (Deno and Mirkin, 1977, p. 21). Reschly (2004) has termed this principle the *outcomes criterion*. If our assessment activities do not contribute meaningfully and directly to student outcomes, the value of the time spent assessing has been compromised. Thus assessment should be focused and efficient, and it should assist educators in making decisions that improve outcomes.

A critical aspect of any basic skill indicator is its capacity to inform instructional efforts to improve later outcomes. To address this question with regard to DIBELS NWF, we examined students who participated in the DIBELS Data System (DDS) and who were in kindergarten for the 2003–4 academic year and in first grade for the 2004–5 academic year. We selected $n = 156,777$ students who met the following criteria: (a) complete data on all five DIBELS benchmark NWF assessments in the middle and end of kindergarten and the beginning, middle, and end of first grade and (b) complete data on DIBELS ORF for the end-of-first-grade benchmark assessment. The DDS is an extant database, and the data we report should be interpreted in that context. However, DDS offers the advantage that it represents DIBELS assessments as they are actually implemented.

A comparison data set based only on schools in Hawaii ($n = 1{,}234$) also was examined to provide an indication of findings in a site where all the schools received high-quality professional development on implementation of a school-wide reading model including use of data for instructional decision making. Each school participated in a series of professional development activities that were strategically scheduled throughout the school year. This training focused on (a) learning the essential components of beginning reading and implementing a school-wide early literacy assessment system; (b) linking student performance data to instructional support for students; and (c) summarizing student performance data within grade levels and instructional planning for the subsequent school year (Fien, Kame'enui, and Good, 2009). Within this context, students with complete data on all kindergarten and first-grade NWF benchmark assessments and end-of-first-grade oral reading fluency in the 2001–2 and 2002–3 academic years were selected for analysis.

The contribution of initial skills and progress on NWF to first-grade ORF outcomes was examined with a sequential regression analysis. Earlier skills were considered first, followed by skill gains. The dependent variable was end-of-first-grade reading skill (measured by DIBELS ORF). The results are summarized in Table 9.1. The first step was the DIBELS risk category based on middle-of-kindergarten NWF (see Good and Kaminski, 2002 for a complete description of risk categories). The second step was the student's NWF raw score on the middle-of-kindergarten assessment. The raw score would be expected to add additional information to the risk category depending on whether the student was high or low within their category. Note, however, that if the raw score were entered first, the risk category would not add additional information.

In the third step, the student's progress from middle to end of kindergarten was added to the model as a gain score. Gain was computed as the student's end-of-kindergarten NWF score minus the student's middle-of-kindergarten NWF score. In the fourth step of the model, the student's gain from the end of kindergarten to the beginning of first grade (or loss, often referred to as *summer regression*) was entered. The fifth step was the student's gain from the beginning of first grade to the middle of first grade on NWF, and the sixth and final step was his or her gain from middle of first grade to the end of first grade. Note that the student's middle-of-kindergarten NWF score plus all the subsequent gains would yield the student's end-of-first-grade NWF score. By considering the initial score and subsequent gains in a series of steps, we are able to discretely partition the role of progress in basic phonics skills across kindergarten and first grade.

TABLE 9.1.

Contribution of NWF initial skills and rate of progress across kindergarten and first grade to first-grade oral reading fluency

TRAJECTORY	ADDITIONAL PERCENT OF VARIANCE EXPLAINED	
	DDS SAMPLE ($n = 156,777$)	HI SAMPLE ($n = 1,234$)
Middle kindergarten (K) risk category (low risk, some risk, at risk)	25%	22%
Middle K NWF score	15%	14%
Middle K to end K NWF gain	9%	16%
End K to beginning 1 NWF gain (or summer regression)	7%	7%
Beginning 1 to middle 1 NWF gain	7%	6%
Middle 1 to end 1 NWF gain	5%	7%
Total variance explained	69%	72%

Note: Gain is later score minus earlier score. For example, middle K to end K NWF gain is the end K NWF score minus the middle K NWF score. All percents of variance explained are significantly different from 0, p < .01.

Using this sequential regression approach, we examined the importance and timing of the role of early phonics skills (i.e., alphabetic principle) and students' progress on those skills as measured by NWF for later reading outcomes. In the middle of kindergarten, 36 percent to 40 percent of the variance in end-of-first-grade ORF outcomes was predicted from the one-minute DIBELS NWF assessment. By the end of kindergarten, about 50 percent of the variance in end-of-first-grade ORF was explained by the student's basic phonics skills. Almost 60 percent was explained by the time students began first grade. Their progress in phonics skills over first grade added another 12 percent to 13 percent of explained variance, depending on the sample. Overall, a student's initial skills and progress in basic phonics (from middle of kindergarten to the end of first grade) accounted for an astounding 69 percent to 72 percent of the explained variance in end-of-first-grade reading skills as measured by ORF. Although the results differ by a few percentage points between the two samples, the pattern of results was remarkably similar. This similarity indicates that the NWF measure is robust across differences in implementation.

Identifying Needs and Providing Support to Prevent Reading Difficulty

Perhaps the single most important contribution of Deno's work is the focus on instruction as an active agent to change outcomes for children. It is not enough to assess, identify a student as at risk for poor outcomes, and then do nothing of significance to actively address or attempt to change outcomes for the student. "Educational interventions are intended to improve students' academic and social development . . . designers of individual student program modifications must provide data to document the effectiveness of those modifications" (Deno, 1986, p. 358). Thus, if we are going to assess teachable basic skills, we must be prepared to do something with the results to make a difference.

Vadasy, Sanders, and Peyton (2006) provide an excellent experimental demonstration of utilizing formative assessment data to change important student outcomes. Kindergarten students with low phonological decoding and phonemic awareness skills in the middle of the year were assigned randomly, within schools, to treatment or control groups. The treatment group received explicit instruction integrating phonemic awareness and alphabetic principle skills as well as scaffolded oral reading practice in decodable texts. The intervention was delivered by trained paraeducators during thirty-minute individual tutoring sessions, four days per week for eighteen weeks. The control group only received regular classroom reading instruction with levels of Title I, English as a second language (ESL), and special education services similar to those received by the intervention group.

Outcomes were examined using a number of pre- and posttest measures, as well as growth data from progress monitoring assessments with DIBELS Phoneme Segmentation Fluency (PSF) and NWF. Results from the analysis of both types of data indicated positive intervention effects with respect to reading and spelling skills at the end of kindergarten. Notably, when all other variables were held constant, students in the intervention group had a 5.4-point advantage on NWF scores over students in the control group with respect to growth per test interval. Follow-up data collected at the end of first grade indicated that the students who participated in the kindergarten intervention had significantly higher reading performance than the students in the control group. Such results indicate the power of early intervention targeted toward instructional needs identified through assessment and the sensitivity of the NWF measure to detect differential growth in a context of robust phonics instruction.

The DDS data illustrates both (a) the likely pathways or trajectories of student progress on basic phonics skills and (b) the importance of changing those trajectories with early identification and early intervention. We first examined the importance of middle-of-kindergarten NWF performance for early identification of need for support. The three pathways to literacy for students who were identified as needing benchmark, strategic, and intensive instructional support are presented in Figure 9.1. The outcomes for these three groups of students, including the 22 percent of students who were identified as needing intensive instructional support, are reported in Table 9.2. Their average end-of-first-grade ORF score was thirty-three correct words per minute, and 33 percent achieved the first-grade ORF benchmark goal of forty correct words per minute. Compared to students who were identified as needing either strategic or benchmark support, students identified as needing intensive support displayed ORF outcomes that were relatively low. However, the purpose of screening is to provide intensive support to students who need it and to thereby *change their pathway.*

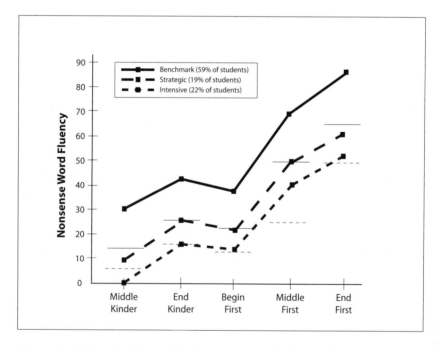

Figure 9.1. Pathways to literacy skills for students identified as needing intensive, strategic, and benchmark support in the middle of kindergarten

TABLE 9.2.

First-grade, end-of-year oral reading fluency outcomes for students on different pathways for the acquisition of basic phonics skills as measured by DIBELS NWF

| | | MIDDLE OF KINDERGARTEN RECOMMENDATION FOR SUPPORT BASED ON NWF | | ALTERNATIVE PATHWAYS FOR STUDENTS IDENTIFIED AS NEEDING INTENSIVE INSTRUCTIONAL SUPPORT IN THE MIDDLE OF KINDERGARTEN ON NWF (n = 34895) | | | | | | | | |
| | | | | ALTERNATE NWF PATHS FOR STUDENTS ON PATH 5 AT THE MIDDLE OF KINDERGARTEN (n = 34895[a]) | | ALTERNATE NWF PATHS FOR STUDENTS ON PATH 5 AT THE END OF KINDERGARTEN (n = 18690[b]) | | ALTERNATE NWF PATHS FOR STUDENTS ON PATH 5 AT THE BEGINNING OF FIRST GRADE (n = 13904[c]) | | ALTERNATE NWF PATHS FOR STUDENTS ON PATH 5 AT THE MIDDLE OF FIRST GRADE (n = 7288[d]) | |
	BENCHMARK	STRATEGIC	INTENSIVE	PATH 1	PATH 5	PATH 2	PATH 5	PATH 3	PATH 5	PATH 4	PATH 5
Count of students	92007	29875	34895	8193	18690	1204	13904	1859	7288	148	6393
Students (%)	59	19	22	23	54	6	74	13	52	2	88
Mean end-of-first-grade ORF	73.16	44.79	32.78	49.6	23.64	43.24	19.67	38.22	11.81	34.67	10.19
Students achieving first-grade ORF goal (%)	84	52	33	61	18	51	12	42	3	36	2

Note: Students who moved from needing intensive support to needing strategic support are not reported here for clarity. For example, 23 percent of students moved from needing intensive support in the middle of kindergarten to needing strategic support at the end of kindergarten. The end-of-first-grade DIBELS ORF goal is forty correct words per minute.
[a] Students who were identified as needing intensive phonics support in the middle of kindergarten.
[b] Students who were identified as needing intensive phonics support in the middle and end of kindergarten.
[c] Students who were identified as needing intensive phonics support in the middle and end of kindergarten and beginning of first grade.
[d] Students who were identified as needing intensive phonics support in the middle and end of kindergarten and beginning and middle of first grade.

Students who were identified as needing intensive support in middle of kindergarten and achieved the end of kindergarten NWF benchmark goal are following Path 1 in Figure 9.2, and their outcomes are reported in the lower part of Table 9.2. Of the students identified as needing intensive support in the middle of kindergarten, 23 percent followed Path 1. Their average end-of-first-grade ORF was fifty correct words per minute, and 61 percent achieved the first-grade ORF benchmark goal. However, most students (54 percent) who were identified as needing intensive support in the middle of kindergarten continued on the pathway of needing intensive support (Path 5 in Figure 9.2 and Table 9.2). The outcomes for students who remain on the needing intensive support pathway experience are worse, with only 18 percent achieving the end-of-first-grade ORF benchmark goal.

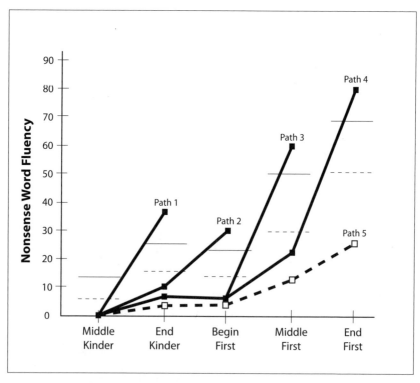

Figure 9.2. Five alternative paths that students who are identified as needing intensive support in the middle of kindergarten might follow. Paths to strategic support levels of skills are not illustrated for clarity.

Of the students who were identified as needing intensive support in both the middle and end of kindergarten (i.e., middle and end of kindergarten on Path 5 in Figure 9.2), 6 percent achieved the benchmark NWF goal for the beginning of first grade (i.e., following Path 2 in Figure 9. 2 and Table 9.2). For students who follow Path 2, 51 percent achieve the first-grade ORF benchmark goal; for students who maintain a trajectory with intensive needs through the beginning of first grade (i.e., following Path 5 at the beginning of first grade), 12 percent achieve the end-of-first-grade ORF benchmark goal. However, even for those students in need of intensive instructional support through the beginning of first grade, achieving the middle-of-first-grade NWF benchmark goal results in an important and meaningful change in outcomes: 42 percent of students whose risk is reduced by meeting the middle-of-first-grade phonics goals (i.e., follow Path 3) achieve the first-grade ORF benchmark goal. Only 3 percent of students who continue to need intensive support in the middle of first grade (i.e., remain on Path 5) achieve the first-grade ORF benchmark goal.

If a student has continued on Path 5 and not made significant progress by the middle of first grade, reaching the end-of-first-grade reading goals is quite difficult. Only 2 percent of students make significant improvements in skills to close the gap in basic phonics skills by the end of first grade (i.e., follow Path 4). However, we again notice an appreciable difference in student outcomes for those students: 36 percent of students who made significant progress on NWF from middle to end of first grade achieved the first-grade ORF benchmark goal compared to only 2 percent of students who continued to be identified as needing intensive instructional support on NWF at the end-of-first-grade benchmark assessment (i.e., Path 5).

Conclusions

The analyses and conclusions using DDS data reported in this chapter were conducted with extant data and are not the result of experimental manipulation of the independent variable. Despite this limitation, the results of our analyses support the importance of early identification, early intervention, and adequate rates of progress in learning basic phonics skills for successful reading outcomes. Students who are achieving benchmark goals in basic phonics skills across kindergarten and first grade are significantly more likely to achieve the first-grade ORF benchmark goal. For students who are identified as at risk of reading difficulty based on DIBELS NWF assessment, providing intensive intervention on the alphabetic principle sufficient to achieve subsequent NWF benchmark goals appears to be essential for achieving successful reading outcomes (e.g., Vadasy et al., 2006).

Earlier intervention reaches more students and has a greater impact than later intervention (e.g., Torgesen, 1998). In our study, the greatest percent of students who changed their trajectories did so between the *middle to end* of kindergarten. Achieving the goal after that time was less likely, and by the middle of first grade, few students were moving from the intensive support path to the NWF benchmark goal. In addition, achieving the NWF benchmark goal by earlier paths appears to have a greater impact on reading outcomes: both average reading outcomes and the percent of students achieving the first-grade ORF benchmark goal decreased with subsequent steps.

Although earlier intervention is better, intensive intervention through grade one still has a substantial impact on reading outcomes. All paths to benchmark status on NWF were associated with increased mean reading skills and greater percentages of students achieving the first-grade ORF benchmark goal. Continuing on Path 5, however, was associated with increasingly poor reading outcomes and lower likelihood of achieving the first-grade ORF goal. With the increasing danger associated with each step on Path 5, it is distressing that more than half of the students at each step continued on this path.

Finally, it is important to note that it is not the DIBELS NWF that it is important for the student to acquire; it is the basic phonics, the alphabetic principle, letter-sound knowledge, and the skill in using those letter sounds to be able to read an unknown or unfamiliar word. DIBELS NWF serves the important role of indicating when students are acquiring these pivotal early literacy skills in time. However, it is not enough to focus only on the NWF goal—if a student achieves the NWF goals but is not able to apply their basic skills and knowledge to accurate and fluent reading of connected text, they also are unlikely to achieve the first-grade benchmark goal.

Our work in extending progress monitoring and an educational decision-making model to early literacy is based on the key principles of General Outcomes Measurement and Data-Based Program Modification originating in the work of Stanley Deno (e.g., Deno and Mirkin, 1977). Monitoring indicators of basic skills gives us the opportunity to observe progress toward important outcomes efficiently and economically. More important, focusing on basic skills that are predictive of meaningful outcomes gives us the ability to change a student's pathway and thereby change the outcome. With targeted assessment and intervention we can prevent reading difficulties for more children than ever before.

References

Deno, S. L. (1985). Curriculum-Based Measurement: The emerging alternative. *Exceptional Children, 52*, 219–232.

Deno, S. L. (1986). Formative evaluation of individual student programs: A new role for school psychologists. *School Psychology Review, 15*, 358–374.

Deno, S. L., & Fuchs, L. S. (1987). Developing Curriculum-Based Measurement systems for data-based special education problem solving. *Focus on Exceptional Children, 19*(8), 1–15.

Deno, S. L., & Mirkin, P. K. (1977). *Data-Based Program Modification: A manual.* Minneapolis, MN: Leadership Training Institute for Special Education, University of Minnesota.

Fien, H., Kame'enui, E. J., & Good, R. H. (2009). Schools engaged in school-wide reading reform: An examination of the school and individual student predictors of kindergarten early reading outcomes. *School Effectiveness and School Improvement, 20*, 1–25.

Fuchs, L. S., & Deno, S. L. (1991). Paradigmatic distinctions between instructionally relevant measurement models. *Exceptional Children, 57*, 488–500.

Fuchs, L. S., & Deno, S. L. (1994). Must instructionally useful performance assessment be based in the curriculum? *Exceptional Children, 61*(1), 15–24.

Good, R. H., III, & Kaminski, R. A. (2002). *Dynamic Indicators of Basic Early Literacy Skills* (6th ed.) [Administration and Scoring Guide]. Eugene, OR: Institute for the Development of Educational Achievement. Available at http://dibels.uoregon.edu

Reschly, D. J. (2004). Paradigm shift, outcomes criteria, and behavioral interventions: Foundations for the future of school psychology. *School Psychology Review, 33*, 408–416.

Shinn, M. R., & Bamonto, S. (1998). Advanced applications of Curriculum-Based Measurement: "Big ideas" and avoiding confusion. In M. R. Shinn (Ed.), *Advanced applications of Curriculum-Based Measurement.* New York, NY: Guilford Press.

Torgesen, J. K. (1998). Catch them before they fall: Identification and assessment to prevent reading failure in young children. *American Educator, 22*, 32–39.

Vadasy, P. F., Sanders, E. A., & Peyton, J. A. (2006). Code-oriented instruction for kindergarten students at risk for reading difficulties: A randomized field trial with paraeducator implementers. *Journal of Educational Psychology, 98*, 508–528.

10

Technological Applications of Curriculum-Based Measurement in Elementary Settings

Curriculum-Based Measurement in the Digital Age

Erica Lembke, Kristen L. McMaster,
and Pamela M. Stecker

When Curriculum-Based Measurement (CBM) research was beginning in the 1970s, members of the University of Minnesota's Institute for Research on Learning Disabilities (IRLD) would probably have scarcely believed that thirty years later, educators and psychologists would be collecting CBM data using handheld devices or laptop computers or that teachers would be sharing and discussing CBM data with their peers online. Yet these and many other technological applications of CBM are becoming increasingly common in today's classrooms. In his seminal article, "Curriculum-Based Measurement: The Emerging Alternative," Stanley Deno (1985) described an assessment system that would be "reliable and valid . . . simple and efficient . . . [and] easily understood" (p. 221). These elements of CBM have continued to evolve through the use of technological applications, and now, more than ever, CBM has the potential to have a significant impact on teachers' instructional decisions and students' academic outcomes.

In this chapter, we trace CBM's technological evolution from early development of software programs designed to enhance teachers' decision making for individual- and classroom-based instruction, to more recent innovations that enable data-based decision making at individual, classroom, school, and even district levels. We illustrate the promise of online collaboration technologies to reduce the barriers of time and distance that often limit teachers' ability to engage in CBM data-sharing and problem-solving discussions with their peers. And we discuss how web-based technologies enable researchers to continue to investigate—in new and innovative ways—the capacity of CBM to inform educational decision making. With the ongoing development of such technological innovations, we predict that CBM will continue to have a significant impact on children's academic progress far into the future.

Enhancing Teachers' Instructional Decisions: Early Technology Developments

CBM was first described by Stanley Deno and Phyllis Mirkin in 1977 as part of "Data-Based Program Modification" or DBPM, an approach to instruction that relies on clearly operationalized, behavioral data to determine when instructional changes are needed. Deno, as coprincipal investigator of the IRLD, concentrated his efforts on helping special educators to use educationally meaningful data for instructional decisions, especially those related to students' goals on their Individualized Education Programs (IEPs). Deno and his colleagues documented the technical adequacy of CBM tools designed to monitor student progress in reading, written expression, spelling, and math (Shinn, 1989), as well as teachers' ability to administer and score measures accurately and to graph data properly. This research indicated that CBM was, indeed, a promising approach for monitoring students' academic progress. Yet the question remained whether teachers would use these data to make effective instructional changes and, ultimately, improve student outcomes.

To address this question, Fuchs, Deno, and Mirkin (1984) conducted an experimental investigation of the impact of teachers' use of CBM data on student achievement. Thirty-nine special education teachers serving students with mild academic disabilities were assigned randomly to DBPM or to a control group. Those in the DBPM group set reading goals for their students, monitored student progress using CBM read-aloud tasks, and made instructional changes using data-based decision rules. Control teachers used their own methods for student evaluation and instructional planning. The results were impressive: DBPM teachers were more responsive to the progress of their students and made more instructional changes, and their students made reliably higher gains in reading compared to controls. However, despite teachers' successful use of CBM data, many reported reluctance to use such an assessment method due to its time-consuming nature (Wesson, King, and Deno, 1984), especially related to developing, administering, and scoring the measures and managing the data.

So researchers began to explore technological applications that would ease the time-consuming burdens teachers had described. Specifically,

Lynn and Douglas Fuchs and their research team at Peabody College of Vanderbilt University initiated a program of research in the late 1980s that focused on computer-based applications for CBM. Deno, along with Joe Jenkins of the University of Washington, consulted on a number of the Fuchs's federally funded grants and helped to design investigations that would build on earlier IRLD work.

One of the first computer applications of CBM was Monitoring Basic Skills Progress (MBSP) developed for reading, spelling, and math by Lynn Fuchs, Carol Hamlett, and Douglas Fuchs and eventually published by ProEd for Apple II computers. These programs started with data-management applications for saving and graphing data and moved quickly to test administration and scoring applications. Teachers reported satisfaction with computerized test administration and data management, and research confirmed that teachers who used these tools were more efficient in their use of CBM (Fuchs, Fuchs, Hamlett, Stecker, and Ferguson, 1988).

Capitalizing on the computer's capabilities and teachers' satisfaction with these programs, the researchers' next step in development centered on providing feedback to teachers about student progress. For example, if student progress was below the goal line, the computer program prompted the teacher to make an instructional change; if progress was above the goal, the teacher was prompted to raise the goal. In addition, item types were coded so that analyses could be provided for the teacher about student mastery of skills being assessed. Teachers were able to use this skill mastery information to devise better instructional modifications for their students and produce greater student achievement in math and spelling (Fuchs, Fuchs, Hamlett, and Allinder, 1991; Fuchs, Fuchs, Hamlett, and Stecker, 1990). Class-wide profiles also were provided, so that teachers could examine levels of mastery for specific skills across students, as well as view average rates of improvement for low-, average-, or high-performing students.

Teachers continued to request assistance with devising appropriate instructional changes, so expert systems and other teacher recommendation systems were developed and evaluated. The addition of these feedback systems had a positive effect on student achievement (Fuchs, Fuchs, Hamlett, and Ferguson, 1992; Fuchs, Fuchs, Hamlett, and Stecker, 1991). As students with disabilities were included more systematically in general education classrooms, teachers monitored progress of all of their students. The MBSP programs incorporated recommendations for class-wide, peer-mediated practice, later known as Peer-Assisted Learning Strategies (http://www.kc.vanderbilt.edu/pals), which enabled teachers to develop important instructional practices that accommodated low-, average-, and high-performing students, including those with disabilities (see Stecker, Fuchs, and Fuchs, 2005, for a review of this research).

In the Classroom and Beyond: Recent Technological Innovations

Today, many of the features described previously have been incorporated into web-based systems that not only summarize student data at the individual and classroom levels but also aggregate student data across classrooms and schools, as well as disaggregate rates of progress by various student demographic variables. Several of these more powerful systems include the Dynamic Indicators of Basic Early Literacy Skills (DIBELS; https://dibels .uoregon.edu), AIMSweb (http://www.aimsweb.com), Edcheckup (http:// www.edcheckup.com), and Yearly ProgressPro (YPP; http://www2.ctb.com/ products_services/ypp/index.html).

One of the earliest web-based systems of CBM was DIBELS (Good and Kaminski, 2002), a system that attracts thousands of users each year. Using web-based technology, administrators can print CBM probes and enter student scores into the system. Following data entry, a variety of graphs and charts can be printed that allow teachers to compare students to national or local norms. Individual progress monitoring graphs and graphs across years can also be accessed.

AIMSweb, a product of Pearson Learning, was originally founded by Gary Germann, a former special education director in Pine County, Minnesota, who had collaborated with Deno and Doug Marston on initial CBM research. AIMSweb continues to provide web-based CBM tools in reading, math, spelling, and written expression. Users can collect student data via handheld technology or on laptop or desktop computers; then, measures are automatically scored and uploaded to student profiles on the web. AIMSweb also provides local and national norms and rates of improvement for each measure so that districts can compare student performance and progress within schools and across districts.

Edcheckup, founded by Deno and Marston, provides a web-based system that users can implement to screen and progress monitor in reading, math, and written expression. Unique features of this system include access to early writing measures and cloze math measures. Electronic scoring and graphing is also provided as part of the Edcheckup system.

Yearly ProgressPro is a McGraw-Hill product that the Fuchs's research team helped to develop. This web-based system enables students to take assessments at the computer, scores tests, gives feedback to students, and saves information for teachers. Teachers may view graphed scores and student/ class skills profiles. Additionally, the system alerts teachers to students whose scores or rate of progress deviate substantially from the class average. Both reading maze and language arts measures are provided for grades two through eight and for grades one through eight in mathematics computation and problem solving.

Web-based systems such as these fill a niche in that national norms are provided that districts can use to compare their own students' performance to that of students nationally. This capability broadly increases the applicability of CBM to students across the nation. For example, many schools are adopting Response to Intervention systems, in which all students in a school are screened, those at risk for academic failure are identified, progress is monitored within general education instruction, and students for whom core instruction is insufficient receive more intensive interventions. Progress monitoring is an essential element of this process, and because of its strong research base (see Fuchs and Fuchs, 2007; Stecker, 2007), many schools and districts have selected CBM for this purpose. As more users have continued to incorporate CBM into their school-wide educational programming, it has become increasingly important to have all data in one place and to be able to efficiently use decision-making rules and document instructional changes. Software programs have met this challenge and are continually being refined to make data collection even more straightforward.

With this array of web-based tools, technical adequacy needs to continue to be at the forefront of schools' consideration for adopting CBM. The National Centers on Student Progress Monitoring (http://www.student progress.org) and Response to Intervention (http://www.rti4success.org) provide users with reviews of screening and progress monitoring tools, many of which would be characterized as CBM. Detailed reviews are conducted by experts in the field on the reliability and validity of measures submitted by vendors. Results are posted indicating the level of evidence that supports each of the measures.

Reducing the Barriers of Time and Distance

In addition to enhancing data collection, management, and summarization capabilities, technological innovations have also opened new doors for teachers, parents, and students to communicate about student progress and make instructional systems. New technologies can be used to provide students, parents, and teachers with feedback about student progress and to provide teachers with a potentially more efficient way to communicate, collaborate, and problem solve.

Researchers at the Research Institute on Progress Monitoring (RIPM) at the University of Minnesota, led by Christine Espin and Teri Wallace, have been exploring new ways of using technology to enhance teachers' use of CBM data. For example, Espin, Deno, McMaster, Pierce, and Yeo (2009) and Espin, Deno, McMaster, Pierce, Yeo et al. (2009) used Moodle (http://moodle.org), a free, web-based virtual learning environment as a venue for teachers to share and discuss student CBM data. One purpose of this web-based environment is to begin to remove barriers of time and distance that make it challenging for teachers to collaborate with peers around instructional decision making. Because little is known about how teachers might use such an environment, Pierce (2009) examined how teachers interacted with each other using Moodle, including the facilitators and barriers to their use of online learning environments to support each other's use of data for instructional decision making. She used a grounded theory approach to analyze the dyadic discussions of thirty-nine urban and rural teachers. From these discussions, she generated a theory of collaborative support, proposing that teachers support each other by offering both constructive support and solidarity and that a lack of response reduces both types of offers. This theory provides the foundation for further work in developing online environments that will eventually be used to enhance teachers' instructional decision making and, hopefully, improve student achievement outcomes.

Technological Applications to Facilitate New and Innovative CBM Research

Thus far, we have illustrated how technological applications can facilitate CBM data collection, management, and use to enhance educators' instructional decision making. Another important benefit of technology is that it enables researchers to study students' academic progress and teachers' instructional behaviors in new and innovative ways. For example, schools' and districts' use of web-based technologies have created vast national databases that allow for large-scale studies that can shed new light on questions about technical characteristics of CBM used for different purposes, such as screening or progress monitoring.

As one example, Wireless Generation has created handheld data systems for reading and mathematics, and the mathematics system has been examined in a series of studies across several years as part of an Institute on Educational Sciences (IES) funded project with coprincipal investigators Herb Ginsburg and Young-Sun Lee from Columbia University Teachers College. Researchers have examined the construct validity of early numeracy measures, such as oral counting, missing number, and next number tasks with over six hundred kindergarten and first-grade students in two different states (Lee, Pappas, Ginsburg, and Lembke, 2008), as well as the capacity of the measures to capture growth across years.

Online applications, such as the Moodle learning environment described previously, also offer new opportunities to observe teachers' instructional decision making, which should enable researchers to find ways to continue to improve this process. For example, in the RIPM project described earlier (Espin, Deno, McMaster, Pierce, and Yeo, 2009; Espin, Deno, McMaster, Pierce, Yeo et al., 2009), data from teachers' participation in the Moodle environment were used not only to examine their interactions with each other but also to answer specific questions about their instructional decision making. Thirty-nine urban and rural special education teachers participated in two related studies. The purpose of study 1 was to determine the effect of reading aloud versus maze CBM data on teachers' instructional decision making and student achievement. The purpose of study 2 was to determine the effect of reading aloud alone versus reading aloud plus computerized diagnostic feedback (using the Subskill Analysis of Reading Fluency [SARF] program developed by Theodore Christ at the University of Minnesota; Scullen, Werde, and Christ, 2006) on teachers' instructional decision making and student achievement outcomes.

In both studies, teachers identified two to six of their lowest performing readers, who were matched on initial oral reading level and assigned randomly to one of two progress-monitoring approaches (reading-aloud CBM alone or reading-aloud CBM plus diagnostic feedback). Teachers monitored student progress weekly using the assigned approach and posted CBM data on Moodle to discuss the students' progress with a peer. Teachers' Moodle discussions were coded based on instructional focus (i.e., phonemic awareness, phonics, fluency, vocabulary, and comprehension); additional categories included word recognition, materials in general, measurement procedure change, and practice reading connected text.

In study 1, a content analysis of teacher discussions using these codes indicated that when teachers monitored student progress with reading-aloud CBM, their instructional discussions focused on word recognition and fluency, whereas when teachers monitored student progress using maze, their instructional discussions focused on vocabulary and comprehension. The type of CBM data used did not, however, have a statistically significant effect on student achievement outcomes. In study 2, a similar content analysis indicated that when teachers monitored student progress with reading-aloud CBM alone, their instructional discussions focused on word recognition and reading errors, whereas when teachers monitored student progress using reading-aloud CBM plus diagnostic feedback, their instructional discussions focused slightly more on comprehension. Again, the type of data used did not have a statistically significant effect on student achievement outcomes.

The studies illustrate how researchers can use technology to gain insights into how CBM data might affect teachers' instructional decision making. Without the content analysis of Moodle discussions, it would appear that the type of CBM data has no impact, because student achievement did not vary as a result of different progress-monitoring approaches. However, the finding that teachers think about different types of data in different ways has potential implications for how they design their instructional programs, which may ultimately affect student achievement outcomes. This study sets the stage for future research, which could make use of similar technologies to examine whether teachers' actual instructional practices are impacted by the types of progress monitoring data they collect.

CBM in the Digital Age

In a recent article outlining future directions for CBM research, Lynn Fuchs (2004) noted the following:

> In this "age of the computer," it seems useful to explore the potential
> for technology to expand CBM's reach, by making data collection
> and management more efficient, by supplementing CBM graphed
> analyses with instructionally informative diagnostic profiles, and by
> designing teacher and student feedback systems that enhance CBM's

instructional utility. Some research involving CBM applications to increase efficiency and expand instructional helpfulness has already been accomplished . . . but additional strategies for using technology innovatively and inventively should be pursued. (p. 191)

"Expanding CBM's reach" is key: Whereas CBM has been demonstrated to produce reliable, valid, and instructionally useful data, it will have its greatest impact if teachers, schools, and districts are able to access and use it in efficient, effective ways. Indeed, teachers' use of the data still appears to be the most challenging aspect of CBM. Because student achievement effects are not likely unless teachers use the data for instructional planning, capitalizing on technological applications may be one way to aid teachers in examining data and in facilitating discussion about the implementation of appropriate instructional interventions.

One note of caution, though, may be in order. As data-based progress monitoring systems become increasingly sophisticated, such as computerized adaptive testing models where student responses dictate the difficulty of subsequent items or measures so that alternate forms are not equivalent, teachers may need more assistance with interpretation of data and appropriate application to instructional decision making. This possibility begs the question of whether unintended consequences may emerge from the use of some technological advancements (i.e., it may become more, rather than less, complex to use and interpret). Regardless of the sophistication of technological applications, developers of new CBM systems may be guided best by Deno's (1985, 2003) arguments for a data-driven system that is technically sound and easy for teachers, parents, and administrators to use and interpret. In this way, CBM will retain its original purpose, while at the same time meeting the needs of teachers and students in a constantly changing, technological world.

A Final Note

We believe it is noteworthy that Deno was one of the RIPM lead investigators and was instrumental in the Moodle research described previously. His continual influence in ongoing research is a testament to the significant impact he has had and continues to wield, not only on the field of special education, but also on the broader educational system. It is indeed remarkable that Deno, whose aim thirty years ago was to provide special educators with a simple tool that would help them make effective instructional decisions, continues to work at the forefront of cutting-edge CBM research and practical applications in the field.

Note

The three authors contributed equally and are thus listed in alphabetical order.

References

Deno, S. L. (1985). Curriculum-Based Measurement: The emerging alternative. *Exceptional Children, 52,* 219–232.

Deno, S. L. (2003). Developments in Curriculum-Based Measurement. *Journal of Special Education, 37,* 184–192.

Deno, S. L., & Mirkin, P. K. (1977). *Data-Based Program Modification: A manual.* Reston, VA: Council for Exceptional Children.

Espin, C., Deno, S., McMaster, K., Pierce, R., & Yeo, S. (2009). *Teacher use study: Reading aloud vs. maze selection* (Technical Report No. 31). Minneapolis: Research Institute on Progress Monitoring, University of Minnesota.

Espin, C., Deno, S., McMaster, K., Pierce, R., Yeo, S., Mahlke, A., & Zukowski, B. (2009). *Teacher use study: Progress monitoring with and without diagnostic feedback* (Technical Report No. 32). Minneapolis: Research Institute on Progress Monitoring, University of Minnesota.

Fuchs, L. S. (2004). The past, present, and future of Curriculum-Based Measurement research. *School Psychology Review, 33,* 188–192.

Fuchs, L. S., Deno, S. L., & Mirkin, P. K. (1984). The effects of frequent Curriculum-Based Measurement and evaluation on pedagogy, student achievement, and student awareness of learning. *American Educational Research Journal, 21,* 449–460.

Fuchs, L. S., & Fuchs, D. (2007). A model for implementing responsiveness to intervention. *Teaching Exceptional Children, 39*(5), 14–20.

Fuchs, L. S., Fuchs, D., Hamlett, C. L., & Allinder, R. M. (1991). The contribution of skills analysis to Curriculum-Based Measurement in spelling. *Exceptional Children, 57,* 443–452.

Fuchs, L. S., Fuchs, D., Hamlett, C. L., & Ferguson, C. L. (1992). Effects of expert system consultation within Curriculum-Based Measurement using a reading maze task. *Exceptional Children, 58,* 436–450.

Fuchs, L. S., Fuchs, D., Hamlett, C. L., & Stecker, P. M. (1990). The role of skills analysis in Curriculum-Based Measurement in math. *School Psychology Review, 19,* 6–22.

Fuchs, L. S., Fuchs, D., Hamlett, C. L, & Stecker, P. M. (1991). Effects of Curriculum-Based Measurement and consultation on teacher planning and student achievement in mathematics operations. *American Educational Research Journal, 28,* 617–641.

Fuchs, L. S., Fuchs, D., Hamlett, C. L., Stecker, P. M., & Ferguson, C. L. (1988). Conducting Curriculum-Based Measurement with computerized data collection: Effects of efficiency and teacher satisfaction. *Journal of Special Education Technology, 9*, 73–86.

Good, R. H., III, & Kaminski, R. A. (2002). *Dynamic Indicators of Basic Early Literacy Skills* (6th ed.) [Administration and Scoring Guide]. Eugene, OR: Institute for the Development of Educational Achievement. Available at http://dibels.uoregon.edu

Lee, Y.-S., Pappas, S., Ginsburg, H., & Lembke, E. (2008, March). Development and analysis of an integrated screening, progress monitoring, and cognitive assessment system for K–3 mathematics. Paper presented at the annual meeting of the American Educational Research Association, New York, NY.

Pierce, R. L. (2009, August). *Online peer collaboration: Teachers supporting each other's instructional use of CBM data* (Unpublished doctoral dissertation). University of Minnesota, Minneapolis.

Scullen, S., Werde, S., & Christ, T. J. (2006). Subskill analysis of reading fluency (SARF) 3.4: A review of miscue analysis and informal reading inventories (Tech. Rep. No. 1). Minneapolis: University of Minnesota.

Shinn, M. R. (Ed.). (1989). *Curriculum-Based Measurement: Assessing special children.* New York, NY: Guilford Press.

Stecker, P. M. (2007). Tertiary intervention: Using progress monitoring with intensive services. *Teaching Exceptional Children, 39*(5), 50–57.

Stecker, P. M., Fuchs, L. S., & Fuchs, D. (2005). Using Curriculum-Based Measurement to improve student achievement. *Psychology in the Schools, 42*, 795–819.

Wesson, C., King, R. P., & Deno, S. L. (1984). Direct and frequent measurement: If it's so good for us, why don't we use it? *Learning Disability Quarterly, 7*(1), 45–48.

IV

Applications in Secondary Education

11

Big Ideas and Core Values

*The Influence of Stanley Deno's Work on
Secondary Mathematics Progress Monitoring*

Anne Foegen

On a dusty shelf in my office sits a coffee-stained copy of *Data-Based Program Modification: A Manual*, authored by Stanley Deno and Phyllis Mirkin in 1977. This spiral-bound volume, with pale green graph paper and upward-sloping lines of data on its cover, is emblematic of past, present, and future advancements in Curriculum-Based Measurement. In this chapter, I draw from it and from my graduate school experiences to reflect on how Stanley Deno's career achievements in progress monitoring research have influenced and contributed to work in secondary mathematics progress monitoring.

Words of Wisdom: Big Ideas and Core Values

I am continually reminded of my good fortune in having Stanley Deno as my major professor. Regularly, whether through interactions with colleagues, experiences analyzing and interpreting data, or advising my own graduate students, I am reminded of catch phrases and ideas that I associate with him. One of those is the importance of focusing on big ideas. As a teacher and mentor, Deno encouraged his students to summarize major concepts from class readings, to teach in ways that focused on big ideas rather than minute details, and to interpret data with an eye for general patterns rather than isolated findings. More than thirty years ago, that same focus on big ideas was evident in the *Data-Based Program Modification Manual*. As I paged through the introductory material in the manual, I was struck by how well the five assumptions in the first chapter capture important aspects of work in secondary mathematics progress monitoring. In the sections that follow, I use these assumptions as organizational tools for outlining some of the big ideas in secondary math progress monitoring and their connections to Deno's early writings. I conclude the chapter with some reflections on the core values that Deno instilled in all his students and how these ideas continue to influence our work in the profession.

Big Ideas about Progress Monitoring

Big Idea 1: No intervention is guaranteed to be effective.

At the present time we are unable to prescribe specific and effective changes in instruction for individual pupils with certainty. Therefore, changes in instructional programs which are arranged for an individual child can be treated only as hypotheses which must be empirically tested before a decision can be made on whether they are effective for that child. (Deno and Mirkin, 1977, p. 11)

The need for an objective tool with which to determine instructional effectiveness is at the heart of Deno's work with Curriculum-Based Measurement. Progress monitoring measures were initially developed through the Institute for Research on Learning Disabilities at the University of Minnesota in the late 1970s and early 1980s (Tindal, Germann, Marston, and Deno, 1983). Since that time, they have been used to evaluate Individual Education Plan (IEP) goals (Wesson, Deno, and Mirkin, 1982), measure outcomes in research studies to develop intervention programs (Fuchs, Fuchs, Phillips, Hamlett, and Karns, 1995), and provide teachers with formative assessment data to systematically alter students' instructional programs and maximize achievement outcomes (Fuchs, Fuchs, Hamlett, and Stecker, 1991).

In recent years, progress monitoring has become an essential component of early prevention and intervention models around the country. Progress monitoring measures, such as those developed by Deno and colleagues, serve as technically adequate indicators of a student's response to an intervention. In many systems, progress monitoring measures are also used as efficient screening tools, providing teachers with data to indicate which students may need additional assessment or supplemental instruction.

As the use of progress monitoring has become more widespread, demand has been growing for an expanded range of tools. In particular, educators seek measures for subject areas and student populations that move beyond elementary basic skills. The development of secondary mathematics progress monitoring tools has reflected Deno's assertion that the first step in evaluating instructional effectiveness is the development of a measurement tool that will provide efficient and technically sound data. The majority of the research in secondary mathematics progress monitoring has been conducted within the past ten to fifteen years and has focused primarily on the technical adequacy of the measures (Foegen, 2000, 2001, 2008a, 2008b; Foegen, Jiban, and Deno, 2007; Helwig, Anderson, and Tindal, 2001; Helwig and Tindal, 2002). In the future, researchers in this area must shift their energies toward the application of secondary mathematics progress monitoring measures in classroom settings as a means of evaluating instructional effectiveness and refining instruction to improve student outcomes.

Big Idea 2: Time series designs are useful tools.

Time series research designs are uniquely appropriate for testing instructional reforms (hypotheses) which are intended to improve individual performance. (Deno and Mirkin, 1977, p. 11)

The vast majority of research to date on secondary mathematics progress monitoring has been conducted in general education mathematics classes in which students with disabilities are receiving instruction. Federal requirements that mandate special educators track students' progress toward IEP goals have made the application of time series designs commonplace among professionals serving students with disabilities. Special education teachers, school psychologists, and related service providers frequently receive training on progress monitoring as part of their professional preparation programs. In my own work in schools, I have found that while special educators are familiar with time series designs, their general education colleagues often have not been introduced to assessment approaches that involve repeated measurement over time on comparable tasks. I find that mathematics teachers participating in research projects often experience an aha moment after repeated opportunities to review their students' graphs and engage in interpreting data from a progress monitoring assessment paradigm that differs markedly from their usual mastery measurement approach in which assessments (chapter tests) are given on a limited set of content following the completion of instruction on that topic or chapter.

Deno's astute selection of a time series approach to assessment provides educators with data that can be compared over time to evaluate student growth on broad learning outcomes in a content area. Moreover, the use of quantitative metrics for scoring progress monitoring measures provides a means of quantifying students' rates of growth by determining slope values for trend lines drawn through the data, or more recently, by using more sophisticated statistical analysis techniques, such as hierarchical linear modeling and growth curve analyses (e.g., Espin, Shin, and Busch, 2005).

Big Idea 3: Many educational questions can be answered empirically.

Special education is an intervention system, created to produce reforms in the educational programs of selected individuals, which can (and, now, with due process requirements, must) be empirically tested. (Deno and Mirkin, 1977, p. 13)

I would speculate that nearly all of Deno's students could recall an experience in which a discussion resulted in Deno commenting, "I believe that's an empirical question." He consistently advocated the use of scientific methods to answer questions posed by his students, who found themselves encouraged to "run a little study" to gather data in response to a question they had. This reliance on empirical methods is evident in a paper published by Deno and Fuchs in 1987. The authors identified three critical questions that should guide the development of progress measures: (1) what to measure (with a focus on student behaviors that represent important outcomes, can be repeatedly measured, and are sensitive to instruction), (2) how to measure (with a focus on measurement procedures), and (3) how to use the data (with a focus on methods to summarize, display, and interpret the data in ways that support teachers' instructional decision making).

Deno and Fuchs's (1987) paper has been instrumental in shaping my work in secondary mathematics progress monitoring. It provided a framework for creating new measures that I have applied to my work on the Research Institute on Progress Monitoring (RIPM), which focused on the development of new middle-school measures that were conceptually connected to elementary and early numeracy measures, and in Project AAIMS (Algebra Assessment and Instruction: Meeting Standards), which focused on the development of measures for beginning algebra. Technical reports from these recent projects reflect the use of an incremental development process in which empirical methods are employed to evaluate which measures are most effective (what to measure) and which measurement procedures (e.g., duration and scoring) produce the strongest technical data (how to measure; Foegen and Lind, 2009; Foegen, Olson, and Perkmen, 2005).

Big Idea 4: Vital signs must be identified and monitored.

To apply time series designs to (special) educational reforms we need to specify the data representing the "vital signs" of educational development which can be routinely (frequently) obtained in and out of school. (Deno and Mirkin, 1977, p. 14)

The analogy of "vital signs" has been a consistent theme in Deno's work, notably in his seminal 1985 paper, "Curriculum-Based Measurement: The Emerging Alternative." The concept of "vital signs" or "indicators," however, has also proven to be one of the most difficult for educators to grasp. Deno (1985) clearly describes progress monitoring measures as indicators of competence in an academic domain, functioning in a manner similar to that of blood pressure or temperature measures as indicators of general health. Unfortunately, many educators struggle to grasp this aspect of progress monitoring and instead view the academic behaviors sampled in the measures as the test to which they should teach. As I teach progress monitoring to undergraduate teacher education students, they frequently respond to instruction about oral reading fluency by inferring that their task as teachers is to teach students to read fast.

The concept of "vital signs" is also relevant for the development of secondary mathematics progress-monitoring measures. At the middle-school level, the application of an approach Fuchs (2004) termed "curriculum-sampling" proved difficult to apply. Given wide variability in the instructional content for grades six, seven, and eight across regions of the country and commercial curriculum materials, the successful development of measures that were systematic samples of important instructional content at each grade level seemed unlikely. Instead, much of the work at the middle-school level has focused on measures that serve as "robust indicators" (to use Fuchs's 2004 language) of competence. These measures, which involve estimation (Foegen, 2000; Foegen and Deno, 2001) or numeracy concepts (Foegen, 2008b), do not represent the full instructional curriculum but have demonstrated acceptable levels of technical adequacy, suggesting they can serve as valuable indicators of students' proficiency in mathematics more generally. In algebra, the instructional content is more consistent across state curricula and commercial instructional materials. As a result, both the robust indicator and the curriculum-sampling approach to developing measures have proven fruitful (Foegen, 2008a; Foegen, Olson, and Impecoven-Lind, 2008).

Big Idea 5: Ongoing professional development is important for educators.

Testing program modifications (reforms) requires well-trained professionals capable of using time series data analysis to draw valid conclusions about program effects. (Deno and Mirkin, 1977, p. 15)

From the beginning, Deno recognized the importance of effective professional development to the successful implementation of progress monitoring. The Deno and Mirkin manual was designed to convey important concepts and skills to teachers. Deno's career includes numerous examples of working with preservice and inservice educators to build their knowledge of progress monitoring. A longstanding partnership with the Minneapolis Public Schools and with the Pine County Educational Cooperative (now the St. Croix River Education District) provided a means to work directly with teachers and establish collaborative partnerships within which research could be conducted to provide empirical data to address the pressing problems facing educators. School-based research activities, along with opportunities to assist with professional development workshops, were staples of the graduate program for Deno's students.

In addition to providing teachers with training in the use of progress monitoring tools, Deno was also committed to developing assessment tools and strategies that teachers could feasibly implement. This belief is evident in the design characteristics for Curriculum-Based Measures outlined in Deno's 1985 article. While the first characteristic (reliable and valid) emphasized the technical adequacy of the measures, the remaining three design characteristics (simple and efficient, easily understood, inexpensive) communicated a respect for the many demands and constraints teachers face and the importance of creating systems that are not only technically sound but also logistically practical, if they are to be of value to teachers.

The role of teachers in research on progress monitoring, as well as the importance of professional development to support teachers' implementation of progress monitoring, has been at the center of our work in secondary mathematics progress monitoring. The development of progress monitoring measures for algebra relied heavily on input from teachers in refining and revising the content of the measures and procedures for administration and scoring (Foegen et al., 2008). As teachers begin using these measures in their classrooms and as districts incorporate the data into their decision-making procedures, great opportunities exist for collaboration between researchers and practitioners (Foegen and Morrison, 2010). A recently funded project (Foegen and Stecker, 2008) will develop online training in algebra progress monitoring, as well as online scoring and data management tools, to support teachers' efforts to implement progress monitoring in algebra with their students.

While the five big ideas described earlier cannot begin to capture the magnitude of Stanley Deno's contributions to the field of education through his work on progress monitoring, they do provide a context from which one can draw insights about the nature of his work. In the next section, I briefly discuss some of the core values that he instilled during my graduate studies and that I strive to emulate in my work as a researcher, graduate advisor, and teacher educator.

Core Values

The lessons I've taken from studying under and later collaborating with Stanley Deno go far beyond academic knowledge and skills. Though my growth as a scholar has been important, even more critical were the life lessons I've derived from working with Deno. In closing this chapter, I believe it is important to address Deno's contributions not only to the knowledge base surrounding progress monitoring but also to the scholarly community evident among researchers in progress monitoring, many of whom were his students and their graduate students. In part, Deno's legacy lies not only in the academic papers and volumes he's published but also in the people whose careers were incubated while they studied with him.

The values I attribute to Deno were acquired not through formal presentations or direct instruction but by observing the manner in which he interacted with others and managed his own professional life. The first value is that of *integrity*. This was modeled through a consistent message that as graduate students, it was important to do our best work and to get it right. Statistical results that were surprising needed to be rechecked, along with the data files. Completion of a task was not sufficient; we understood that high quality work that reflected our best effort was always expected. The second value is that of *curiosity*. I can recall numerous conversations (often while reviewing output files from Statistical Package for the Social Sciences [SPSS]) in which Deno would ask, "Why do you think that is?" We were encouraged to ask questions, to explore new and related areas of study, and to not just obtain results from a research project but think carefully about them. The third value is a deep respect for *hard work and fun*. Graduate study was often a grueling experience involving late nights and weekend hours. At the same time, research meetings were enjoyable interactions and frequently included discussions of the outcome of the weekend's Gopher game or a review of Deno's most recent golf outing. The message communicated from these meetings was that hard work and fun were not mutually exclusive and that it was possible to be a careful scholar while still maintaining one's personal life. The final value is *compassion*. While a project deadline was important, the life circumstances affecting coworkers and students were also considered. As a graduate student, I was held to high expectations, but I also felt valued and cared about as a person who filled other roles in addition to that of graduate student.

Given the opportunity to reflect on Stanley Deno's contributions to the field and their influence on my work in secondary mathematics progress monitoring, I've found that they are many and broad. Deno is not only a notable scholar but also a mentor of future scholars who will continue to build and expand his efforts to develop efficient and inexpensive tools that teachers can use to track their students' progress. The greatest honor we can bestow on him is to continue this critically important work.

References

Deno, S. L. (1985). Curriculum-Based Measurement: The emerging alternative. *Exceptional Children, 52*, 219–232.

Deno, S. L., & Fuchs, L. S. (1987). Developing Curriculum-Based Measurement systems for data-based special education problem solving. *Focus on Exceptional Children, 19*(6), 1–17.

Deno, S. L., & Mirkin, P. K. (1977). *Data-Based Program Modification: A manual.* Minneapolis: Leadership Training Institute/Special Education, University of Minnesota.

Espin, C. A., Shin, J., & Busch, T. W. (2005). Curriculum-Based Measurement in the content areas: Vocabulary matching as an indicator of progress in social studies learning. *Journal of Learning Disabilities, 38*, 353–363.

Foegen, A. (2000). Technical adequacy of General Outcome Measures for middle school mathematics. *Diagnostique, 25*(3), 175–203.

Foegen, A. (2006). Evaluating instructional effectiveness: Tools and strategies for monitoring student progress. In M. Montague & A. Jitendra (Eds.), *Teaching mathematics to middle school students with learning difficulties* (pp. 108–132). New York, NY: Guilford Press.

Foegen, A. (2008a). Algebra progress monitoring and interventions for students with learning disabilities. *Learning Disability Quarterly, 31*, 65–78.

Foegen, A. (2008b). Progress monitoring in middle school mathematics: Options and issues. *Remedial and Special Education, 29,* 195–207.

Foegen, A., & Deno, S. L. (2001). Identifying growth indicators for low-achieving students in middle school mathematics. *Journal of Special Education, 35,* 4–16.

Foegen, A., Jiban, C., & Deno, S. (2007). Progress monitoring measures in mathematics: A review of the literature. *Journal of Special Education, 41,* 121–139.

Foegen, A., & Lind, L. (2009). *A replication of static use of six brief middle school mathematics measures* (Technical Report No. 21). Minneapolis: University of Minnesota, College of Education and Human Development, Research Institute on Progress Monitoring.

Foegen, A., & Morrison, C. (2010). Putting algebra progress monitoring into practice: Insights from the field. *Intervention in School and Clinic, 46,* 95–103.

Foegen, A., Olson, J. R., & Impecoven-Lind, L. (2008). Developing progress monitoring measures for secondary mathematics: An illustration in algebra. *Assessment for Effective Intervention, 33,* 240–249.

Foegen, A., Olson, J., & Perkmen, S. (2005). *Reliability and criterion validity of five algebra measures in districts B and C* (Technical Report No. 7). Ames, Iowa State University, Department of Curriculum and Instruction, Project AAIMS.

Foegen, A., & Stecker, P. M. (2008). *Professional development for algebra progress monitoring.* Grant proposal submitted to the Institute of Education Sciences, U.S. Department of Education.

Fuchs, L. S. (2004). The past, present, and future of Curriculum-Based Measurement research. *School Psychology Review, 33*(2), 188–192.

Fuchs, L. S., Fuchs, D., Hamlett, C. L., & Stecker, P. (1991). Effects of Curriculum-Based Measurement and consultation on teacher planning and student achievement in mathematics operations. *American Educational Research Journal, 28,* 617–641.

Fuchs, L. S., Fuchs, D., Phillips, N. B., Hamlett, C. L., & Karns, K. (1995). Acquisition and transfer effects of classwide peer-assisted learning strategies in mathematics for students with varying learning histories. *School Psychology Review, 24,* 604–620.

Helwig, R., Anderson, L., & Tindal, G. (2002). Using a concept-grounded, curriculum-based measure in mathematics to predict statewide test scores for middle school students with LD. *Journal of Special Education, 36,* 102–112.

Helwig, R., & Tindal, G. (2002). Using General Outcome Measures in mathematics to measure adequate yearly progress as mandated by Title I. *Assessment for Effective Intervention, 28*(1), 9–18.

Tindal, G., Germann, G., Marston, D., & Deno, S. (1983). *The effectiveness of special education: A direct measurement approach.* (Research Report No. 123). Minneapolis: University of Minnesota, Institute for Research on Learning Disabilities.

Wesson, C., Deno, S., & Mirkin, P. (1982). *Research on developing and monitoring progress on IEP goals: Current findings and implications for practice.* (Research Monograph No. 18). Minneapolis: University of Minnesota, Institute for Research on Learning Disabilities.

12

They're Getting Older . . . but Are They Getting Better?

The Influence of Curriculum-Based Measurement on Programming for Secondary-School Students with Learning Disabilities

Christine A. Espin and Heather M. Campbell

Prologue

Heather Campbell and I are pleased to be included in this volume and to have the opportunity to reflect on the question of how Curriculum-Based Measurement (CBM) research has influenced policy and practice at the secondary-school level. I (Espin) was a student of Stanley Deno's, and Heather was a "grand-student" of his—that is, she was a student of mine. Both of us are interested in the development of CBM progress monitoring for secondary-school students and are happy to see a growing interest in the topic in the schools. Twenty years ago such interest did not exist, and people such as Heather and I were often at a loss whether or not to pursue research in the area. Luckily, some wise words and advice from Stanley Deno helped us to find our way.

My (Espin) first meeting with Deno was at a national Council for Exceptional Children (CEC) convention. I was studying for my master's degree under the direction of Paul Sindelar, who had been Deno's first doctoral student. Sindelar had talked so often, and with such great admiration, about Deno that we were eager to meet him. Deno attended our CEC presentation and, afterward, offered Sindelar advice about the research design and results. This conversation must have surprised us, because at some point Deno looked at us and laughed and said, "Don't you know? Once an advisor, always an advisor!"

Although Deno referred to himself as Sindelar's advisor, Sindelar referred to Deno as his *mentor*. I came to understand why Sindelar used that term when I later moved to Minnesota to do my doctoral work with Deno. A *mentor*, according to Webster's dictionary, is a "trusted counselor or guide." Deno was just that to his students—a trusted counselor and guide, not only in terms of how to become an academic, but also in terms of how to live an academic life. Over the years, Deno offered his students many pearls of wisdom such as, "We all have one piece of baloney. We slice it up in different ways at different times, but it's still the same piece of baloney." Other pearls of wisdom were of a more serious nature, and it is one of these that forms the basis for this chapter.

In the late 1980s and early 1990s, there was little interest in the development of CBM measures for secondary-school students with learning disabilities (LD). The lack of interest was probably related to the general lack of interest in reading and writing instruction for secondary students with LD. Conventional wisdom at the time was, "If they haven't learned it by now, they never will." Instructional emphasis was placed on helping students to successfully graduate from high school. Although there *were* those who argued that continued reading and writing instruction might benefit secondary students with LD (e.g., Zigmond, 1990), it was difficult to test the validity of such arguments because there were no measures available to track individual growth and progress. This was a dilemma. To develop measures of progress, it was necessary to recruit research sites—and to recruit research sites, it was necessary for schools to be interested in the development of progress measures. It seemed to be a hopeless spiral.

I remember discussing this dilemma with Deno at some point, wondering if it made sense to pursue research on the topic of progress monitoring at the secondary-school level. Deno's response was, "Chris, you can do the research you think is important or the research others think is important. If you are lucky (and skilled), you can do both, but at some point, you may need to choose one or the other" (probably implying that he thought I would be neither lucky nor skilled). Fortunately for those of us interested in the development of CBM measures for secondary-school students, policy and practice began to change, and interest in progress monitoring at the secondary-school level began to grow.

The Influence of Policy and Practice on CBM Research

In the 1990s, policy and practice for secondary-school students began to change, and with that change came an increased interest in progress monitoring. One of the factors that heralded this change was the movement toward statewide testing in reading and writing. To illustrate, in the mid-1990s, a minimum competency reading test was introduced for eighth-graders in the state of Minnesota. Students were required to pass the test before they could graduate from high school. In the first two years that the test was implemented, 37 percent and 41 percent of eighth-graders failed. The newspaper headlines read, "Schools get more bad news ... more Minnesota eighth-graders failed the basic-skills tests they need to pass to graduate." The article went on to say, "Delivering another dose of disappointing news for public schools, state officials said Wednesday that 41 percent of Minnesota eighth-graders flunked a basic-skills test in reading" (Hotakainen, Smith, and Staff Writers, 1997). Suddenly, the public—and the schools—were very interested in reading instruction for secondary-school students. Suddenly, progress monitoring in reading seemed potentially important to schools and recruiting research sites and participants became easier.

The Influence of CBM Research on Policy and Practice

As illustrated in the previous example, policy and practice had an influence on CBM research at the secondary-school level. However, our charge for this chapter is to reflect on whether CBM research has had an influence on policy and practice at the secondary-school level. After much reflection and discussion, we decided that it has not—at least not yet. In our opinion, CBM research has not yet had a noticeable impact on policy and practice at the secondary-school level, perhaps because research in the area is still relatively young. Thus, in this chapter we reflect on the *potential* impact that CBM research may have on secondary-school policy and practice. We begin with a brief review of the CBM research at the secondary-school level in reading, writing, and content-area learning. (For a more complete review of research in these areas, see Espin and Tindal, 1998; McMaster and Espin, 2007; Wayman, Wallace, Wiley, Tichá, and Espin, 2007; for a discussion of research on mathematics, see Foegen, this volume, and Foegen, Jiban, and Deno, 2007.) We then return to the question of potential impact.

CBM Research at the Secondary-School Level

Two questions have guided the research at the secondary-school level (see Espin and Tindal, 1998). The first is, "What is the 'core curriculum' for secondary-school students with LD?" That is, what do we expect these students to learn? The second is, "What levels of proficiency do we expect secondary-school students with LD to reach in core curriculum areas?"

The early research was based on a set of assumptions: (1) "curriculum" for secondary-school students with LD includes content-area learning, reading, writing, and mathematics; (2) secondary-school students with LD *can* improve in these areas (including reading and writing) if provided with intensive, high-quality instruction; and (3) the amount of improvement attained will be meaningful. Such assumptions could later be tested with CBM progress measures—if technically adequate measures were to be found. The original CBM research at the secondary-school level focused on the development of measures in the content areas.

Content-Area Learning

The original work on the development of content-area progress measures was conducted by Tindal, Nolet, and colleagues (e.g., Nolet and Tindal, 1993; Nolet and Tindal, 1994; Tindal and Nolet, 1995; Tindal and Nolet, 1996). Subsequent research focused on three potential indicators of content-area performance: reading aloud from text, maze selection, and vocabulary matching (Espin and Deno, 1993a, 1993b; Espin and Deno, 1994–95; Espin and Foegen, 1996). For reading aloud, students read aloud from a passage for one minute, and the number of words read correctly was scored. For maze selection, every seventh word was deleted from a passage and replaced with a multiple-choice item consisting of the deleted word and two distracters. Students read silently for two to three minutes, circling a word at each multiple-choice item, and the number of correct choices was scored. For vocabulary matching, students were given five minutes to match selected content words with definitions. Each vocabulary probe consisted of twenty words selected randomly from a pool of words to be covered during the instructional period.

The measure that emerged from this research as the most promising indicator of performance and progress in content-area learning was *vocabulary matching*. For example, in social studies, correlations between vocabulary matching and scores on content knowledge and standardized achievement tests ranged from r = .59 to .84 (Espin, Busch, Shin, and Kruschowitz, 2001). In addition, the measure reflected interindividual differences in growth, and the amount of growth was related to student grades, to scores on the social studies subtest of a standardized achievement test, and to change in performance on a knowledge test (Espin, Shin, and Busch, 2005).

Reading

In the area of reading, the technical adequacy of *reading aloud* and *maze selection* as indicators of performance and progress were examined. In addition, the effects of different time frames and scoring procedures were examined. Dependent measures were performance on a state standards test and on standardized achievement tests in reading (see Espin, Wallace, Lembke, Campbell, and Long, 2010; Tichá, Espin, and Wayman, 2009).

Both reading aloud and maze selection measures emerged as reliable and valid indicators of *performance* (Espin et al., 2010; Tichá et al., 2009). Alternate-form reliability coefficients ranged from $r = .93$ to $.97$ for reading aloud and from $r = .79$ to $.96$ for maze selection. Correlations between the CBM and various criterion measures ranged from $r = .76$ to $.89$ for reading aloud and from $r = .75$ to $.88$ for maze selection. Few differences were found related to scoring procedures or time frame, with the exception that reliability of maze selection tended to increase somewhat with time frame.

With regard to *progress*, the results varied for the two measures (Espin et al., 2010; Tichá et al., 2009) and suggested that maze selection reflected change over time but reading aloud did not. Growth on the maze task was shown to relate to performance on a state reading test and improvements on a standardized achievement test.

Writing

As in the area of content learning, the original work in CBM writing was conducted by Tindal, Parker, and colleagues (Parker, Tindal, and Hasbrouck, 1991a, 1991b; Tindal and Parker, 1989a, 1989b; Tindal and Parker, 1991). In writing, students were given a prompt, provided a short time to think about what to write (e.g., thirty seconds), and then given a set amount of time to write (e.g., three to seven minutes). The writing samples were scored in various ways, including number of words written, words spelled correctly, correct word sequences, and correct minus incorrect word sequences. (A correct word sequence [CWS] was defined by Videen, Deno, and Marston [1982] as any two adjacent correctly spelled words used correctly within the context of the sentence.)

The initial research by Tindal, Parker, and colleagues revealed that the simple scoring measures that had been used at the elementary-school level—number of words written and number of words spelled correctly—were not the most appropriate measures for secondary school students. Support was found for a more complicated scoring approach that involved scoring the percent of correct words (%CW) or percent of correct word sequences (%CWS) written. Although percentage measures consistently correlated with criterion variables across studies, percentage measures were seen to be limited for growth monitoring because of their nonequal interval scale and potential ceiling effects.

In subsequent research (Espin, De La Paz, Scierka, and Roelofs, 2005; Espin, Shin, Deno, Skare, Robinson, and Benner, 2000; Jewell and Malecki, 2005; McMaster and Campbell, 2008; Weissenburger and Espin, 2005), the effects of various time frames (three, five, seven, and ten minutes of writing), scoring procedures (e.g., words written, correct words, correct word sequences, correct minus incorrect word sequences), and prompt type (expository, narrative, or picture prompts) on the technical adequacy of CBM writing measures were examined. Criterion variables across research studies included student performance on a standardized writing test (e.g., Test of Written Language), state or district writing tests (e.g., Minnesota Basic Standards Test of Writing [MBST]), teacher evaluation of student writing (teacher rankings), and other indirect measures of general writing ability (e.g., grades in a language arts class, scores on a language arts subtest of a standardized achievement test).

In general, the results of this later work replicated those of Tindal, Parker, and colleagues: Simple measures of words written and words written correctly were not valid indicators of writing performance for secondary-school students. Further, the results revealed that alternate-form reliability of writing samples increased with writing time (Espin et al., 2000; Espin et al., 2008; Weissenburger and Espin, 2005) and that scoring CWS or correct minus incorrect word sequences (CIWS) produced higher validity coefficients than other scoring procedures (Espin et al., 2000; Espin et al., 2008). For example, Espin et al. (2008) found that reliability coefficients increased from $r = .66$ to .85 for three to ten minutes of writing, and correlations between CBM writing and performance on a state graduation writing test were $r = .57$ to .60 for CIWS compared to $r = .23$ to .48 for other scoring approaches.

Two studies compared technical adequacy of the measures related to prompt type (Espin et al., 2000; McMaster and Campbell, 2008). Neither study found differences in reliability or validity of the measures between narrative and expository writing. Only two studies examined the sensitivity of the measures to change over time (Espin et al., 2005, McMaster and Campbell, 2008).

Espin et al. (2005) found that when intensive writing interventions were delivered to students with writing difficulties, significant pretest–posttest changes were seen on CIWS for students with learning disabilities and for low-, average-, and high-performing students. McMaster and Campbell (2008) found that five-minute samples written in response to expository prompts were sensitive to fall-to-spring growth for seventh graders. Samples written in response to narrative prompts were not sensitive to growth.

Summary of CBM Secondary-Level Research

In summary, CBM research at the secondary-school level has addressed content-area learning, reading, and writing (and math, see Foegen, this volume). In the content areas, the research to date has supported the technical adequacy of a five-minute vocabulary-matching probe (read silently by the students) as an indicator of performance and progress in content-area learning. In reading, the research has supported the technical adequacy of either a one-minute reading aloud or a two- to three-minute maze selection (three minutes for higher reliability) measure as an indicator of *performance* in reading, but only a two- to three-minute maze selection measure as an indicator of *progress*. In writing, the research has supported the technical adequacy of a five- to seven-minute writing sample written in response to a narrative or expository prompt and scored for CWS or CIWS as an indicator of performance. Note that the correlations in writing are somewhat lower than in reading or content-area learning. Little research in writing has addressed progress.

The Influence (or Potential Influence) of CBM Research on Policy and Practice

We now return to the original charge given to us in writing this chapter: What is the potential influence of CBM research on policy and practice for secondary-school students in reading, writing, and the content areas? We begin with reading and writing and then turn our attention to content-area learning.

Reading and Writing

In the areas of reading and writing, CBM progress measures might be used to answer questions such as the following: (1) Do students with LD plateau in skills—that is, is it true that "if they haven't learned it by now, they never will?" (2) If skills do improve, is it worth expending the instructional time and effort it takes to effect such improvements? (3) Do such improvements in performance lead to greater postsecondary school success? (4) If improvements do lead to greater success, can levels of performance be established that predict success?

In reading, a great deal of attention has been devoted to early intervention, with the hope that early intervention will prevent later difficulties. However, the reading difficulties of students with LD have proven to be both severe and persistent (see Espin et al., 2010; Roberts, Torgesen, Boardman, and Scammacca, 2008). An alternative view of reading intervention for students with LD is to begin early and then continue intensive instruction throughout students' educational careers, striving to lessen the long-term impact of reading difficulties. The influence of continued and intensive reading instruction for students with LD could be evaluated via progress-monitoring measures. Progress within, as well as across, academic years could be measured (for a discussion, see Wallace, Espin, McMaster, Deno, and Foegen, 2007; see also Espin, Wallace, Wayman, Tichá, Wiley, and Du, 2009). These same measures could be used to ascertain the reading proficiency levels needed for success in various postsecondary and employment settings and to monitor student progress toward those levels of proficiency.

With regard to writing, an important question to be addressed is what types of writing skills are necessary for students with LD to be successful in postsecondary settings? In the *Writing Next* report, Graham and Perin (2007) describe the writing demands faced by adolescents: "Most contexts of life (school, the workplace, and the community) call for some level of writing skill, and each context makes overlapping, but not identical, demands" (p. 9). It may be important to pinpoint exactly which skills are necessary to be successful in which contexts and then determine the best way to monitor progress in those skills.

To illustrate, the CWS and CIWS scores used in CBM progress monitoring most directly reflect the basic writing skills of capitalization, punctuation, sentence structure, word choice, spelling, grammar, and fluent writing. The research to date has revealed that these skills explain only a portion of the variance in judgments of overall writing quality. For example, in Espin et al. (2008), the number of CIWS written in seven minutes accounted for 34 percent of the variance in scores on a state writing test for high-school students. In Espin et al. (2000), the number of CIWS written in five minutes accounted for 53 percent of the variance on a district writing test for middle-school students. However, the question of importance for secondary-school students with LD might not be how well the measures relate to general ratings of writing quality but how well they relate to the type of writing needed in various postsecondary settings. CBM writing measures, with their emphasis on basic writing skills, might be used to examine the importance of basic writing skills in various secondary and postsecondary settings and might be used to examine the effectiveness of instruction in basic skills on various types of writing tasks (see Walker, Shippen, Alberto, Houchins, and Cihak, 2005, for an example).

Content-Area Learning

Thus far, we have discussed the potential influence of CBM progress monitoring in the areas of reading and written expression. The questions that might be answered in content-area learning are of a somewhat different nature than in the basic skill areas. These questions include the following: (1) How much do students with LD learn in content-area classes such as science and social studies? (2) How much do we expect them to learn? (3) Is earning a passing grade enough for students with LD, regardless of the amount learned?

Since passage of P.L. 94-142, The Education for All Handicapped Children Act, there has been an emphasis on educating students with disabilities in the Least Restrictive Environment, or to the maximum extent possible with students without disabilities. With passage of the Individual with Disabilities Education Act (IDEA) Amendments of 1997, the emphasis shifted to a focus on access for and meaningful inclusion of students in the general education curriculum and in statewide accountability assessments. At the secondary-school level, this shift meant a greater effort to include students in general education content-area classes, such as science and social studies. Although research has demonstrated that many students with disabilities can learn effectively in general education science classrooms if given appropriate instruction (e.g., Cawley, Hayden, Cade, and Baker-Kroczynski, 2002; De La Paz and MacArthur, 2003; Scruggs, Mastropieri, and Boon, 1998), the research also has revealed that such instruction may not occur, even when content-area classes are cotaught by content and special education teachers (Moin, Magiera, and Zigmond, 2008). Progress-monitoring measures might be used in the content areas to address questions related to how much students have learned under various instructional settings and approaches and might help to determine exactly how much knowledge is necessary for students to be successful on statewide accountability tests and in various post-secondary school settings.

Limitations and Questions yet to Be Answered

When evaluating the potential impact of CBM on practice at the secondary-school level, it is important to consider the limitations of the research conducted thus far. A major limitation is the absence of research focused on implementation. The majority of research to date has focused on measure development, not on the effects of implementation on teacher instruction and student performance.

A second limitation is that the majority of secondary-school research has been conducted at the middle-school level; it is unclear whether results from middle-school students generalize to high-school students. For example, in writing, correlation coefficients typically have been larger for middle-school than for high-school students (see, for example, Weissenburger and Espin, 2005).

A third limitation is that little research has focused on progress as opposed to performance, especially in the area of written expression. The progress studies that have been done in reading and content-area learning have taken place over relatively short periods of times (e.g., ten to twelve weeks). There is a need to examine the validity of the measures for tracking growth over an entire school year.

A fourth limitation is that in both content-area learning and reading, only a few studies have been conducted, and the sample sizes for those studies have been fairly small. It is important to replicate the existing studies with larger, more representative groups of students.

Finally, specific to content-area learning, the vocabulary-matching task is a selection task rather than a production task, which introduces limitations to the measure. Specifically, students can get answers correct by guessing. In addition, because there are a limited number of items on the measure (e.g., twenty vocabulary terms), it is possible for the scores to hit a ceiling. It would be useful to explore development of a vocabulary production measure, for example, the perception probes developed by Tindal and colleagues (Tindal, Nolet, and Blake, 1992).

Conclusion

To return to the beginning of this chapter, it is not yet clear what impact CBM progress monitoring will have on programming for students at the secondary-school level, but the research has progressed to a point where questions of impact should be addressed. That is to say, we should now be able to address whether or not students are not "just getting older, but also getting better." Keeping with Messick's (1989a, 1989b) conceptualization of validity, these are not merely questions of implementation but questions of validity. What are the outcomes or consequences associated with implementation of CBM progress measures? What effect does implementation have on the lives of secondary-school student with disabilities?

Deno's notion of validity (see Deno, 1985) fits nicely with that of Messick's. From the beginning, Deno focused not only on the technical but also on the practical adequacy of CBM measures and on the outcomes associated with implementation of the measures. We believe that it is this unique approach to measure development that explains the impact that CBM has had on policy and practice at the elementary-school level. In our research, we will continue to be guided by Deno's visionary work for, as you know—"once an advisor, always an advisor."

References

Cawley, J., Hayden, S., Cade, E., & Baker-Kroczynski, S. (2002). Including students with disabilities into the general education science classroom. *Exceptional Children, 68*, 423–435.

De La Paz, S., & MacArthur, C. (2003). Knowing the how and why of history: Expectations for secondary students with and without learning disabilities. *Learning Disability Quarterly, 26*, 142–154.

Deno, S. L. (1985). Curriculum-Based Measurement: The emerging alternative. *Exceptional Children, 52*, 219–232.

Espin, C. A., Busch, T., Shin, J., & Kruschwitz, R. (2001). Curriculum-based measures in the content areas: Validity of vocabulary-matching measures as indicators of performance in social studies. *Learning Disabilities Research and Practice, 16*, 142–151.

Espin, C. A., De La Paz, S., Scierka, B. J., & Roelofs, L. (2005). Relation between curriculum-based measures in written expression and quality and completeness of expository writing for middle-school students. *Journal of Special Education, 38*, 208–217.

Espin, C. A., & Deno, S. L. (1993a). Content-specific and general reading disabilities of secondary-level students: Identification and educational relevance. *Journal of Special Education, 27*, 321–337.

Espin, C. A., & Deno, S. L. (1993b). Performance in reading from content-area text as an indicator of achievement. *Remedial and Special Education, 14*(6), 47–59.

Espin, C. A., & Deno, S. L. (1994–1995). Curriculum-based measures for secondary students: Utility and task specificity of text-based reading and vocabulary measures for predicting performance on content-area tasks. *Diagnostique, 20*, 121–142.

Espin, C. A., & Foegen, A. (1996). Validity of three General Outcome Measures for predicting secondary students' performance on content-area tasks. *Exceptional Children, 62*, 497–514.

Espin, C. A., Shin, J., & Busch, T. W. (2005). Curriculum-Based Measurement in the content areas: Vocabulary-matching as an indicator of social studies learning. *Journal of Learning Disabilities, 38*, 353–363.

Espin, C. A., Shin, J., Deno, S. L., Skare, S., Robinson, S., & Brenner, B. (2000). Identifying indicators of written expression proficiency for middle school students. *Journal of Special Education, 34*, 140–153.

Espin, C. A., & Tindal, G. (1998). Curriculum-Based Measurement for secondary students. In M. R. Shinn (Ed.), *Advanced applications of Curriculum-Based Measurement* (pp. 214–253). New York, NY: Guilford Press.

Espin, C. A., Wallace, T., Campbell, H., Lembke, E., Long, J., & Tichá, R. (2008). Curriculum-Based Measurement in writing: Predicting the success of high-school students on state standards tests. *Exceptional Children, 74*, 174–193.

Espin, C. A., Wallace, T., Lembke, E., Campbell, H., & Long, J. D. (2010). Creating a progress-monitoring system in reading for middle-school students: Tracking progress toward meeting high-stakes standards. *Learning Disabilities Research and Practice, 25*, 60–75.

Espin, C. A., Wallace, T., Wayman, M. M., Tichá, R., Wiley, H. I., & Du, X. (2009). *Seamless and flexible progress monitoring: Age and skill level extensions in reading* (Technical Report No. 1). Minneapolis, MN: University of Minnesota, College of Education and Human Development, Research Institute on Progress Monitoring.

Foegen, A., Jiban, C., & Deno, S. (2007). Progress monitoring measures in mathematics: A review of the literature. *Journal of Special Education, 41*, 121–139.

Graham, S., & Perin, D. (2007). *Writing next: Effective strategies to improve writing of adolescents in middle and high schools—A report to Carnegie Corporation of New York*. Washington, DC: Alliance for Excellent Education.

Hotakainen, R., Smith, M., & Staff Writers. (1997, March 20). How students fared// Schools get more bad news// Reading test scores were better than last year's but the passing requirements were stricter. That means more Minnesota eighth-graders failed the basic-skills tests they need to pass to graduate [METRO Edition]. *Star Tribune*, p. 01.A. Retrieved January 23, 2010, from ProQuest Newsstand. (Document ID: 13866601)

Jewell, J., & Malecki, C. K. (2005). The utility of CBM written language indices: An investigation of production-dependent, production-independent, and accurate-production scores. *School Psychology Review, 34*, 27–44.

McMaster, K. L., & Campbell, H. (2008). Technical features of new and existing measures of written expression: An examination within and across grade levels. *School Psychology Review, 37*, 550–566.

McMaster, K., & Espin, C. A. (2007). Literature synthesis on Curriculum-Based Measurement in writing. *Journal of Special Education, 41*, 68–84.

Messick, S. (1989a). Meaning and values in test validation: The science and ethics of assessment. *Educational Researcher, 18*, 5–11.

Messick, S. (1989b). Validity. In R. L. Linn (Ed.), *Educational measurement* (3rd ed., pp. 13–103). New York, NY: Macmillan.

Moin, L. J., Magiera, K., & Zigmond, N. (2009). Instructional activities and group work in the US inclusive high school co-taught science class. *International Journal of Science and Mathematics Education, 7*, 677–697.

Nolet, V., & Tindal, G. (1993). Special education in content area classes: Development of a model and practical procedures. *Remedial and Special Education, 14*(1), 36–38.

Nolet, V., & Tindal, G. (1994). Instruction and learning in middle school science classes: Implications for students with disabilities. *Journal of Special Education, 28*, 166–187.

Parker, R., Tindal, G., & Hasbrouck, J. (1991a). Countable indices of writing quality: Their suitability for screening-eligibility decisions. *Exceptionality, 2*, 1–17.

Parker, R., Tindal, G., & Hasbrouck, J. (1991b). Progress monitoring with objective measures of writing performance for students with mild disabilities. *Exceptional Children, 58*, 61–73.

Roberts, G., Torgesen, J. K., Boardman, A., & Scammacca, N. (2008). Evidence-based strategies for reading instruction of older students with learning disabilities. *Learning Disabilities Research and Practice, 23*, 63–69.

Scruggs, T. E., Mastropieri, M. A., & Boon, R. (1998). Science education for students with disabilities: A review of recent research. *Studies in Science Education, 32*, 21–44.

Tichá, R., Espin, C. A., & Wayman, M. M. (2009). Reading progress monitoring for secondary-school students: Reliability, validity, and sensitivity to growth of reading aloud and maze selection measures. *Learning Disabilities Research and Practice, 24*, 132–142.

Tindal, G., & Nolet, V. (1995). Curriculum-Based Measurement in middle and high schools: Critical thinking skills in content areas. *Focus on Exceptional Children, 27*(7), 1–22.

Tindal, G., & Nolet, V. (1996). Serving students in middle school content classes: A heuristic study of critical variables linking instruction and assessment. *Journal of Special Education, 29,* 414–432.

Tindal, G., Nolet, V., & Blake, G. (1992). *Focus on teaching and learning in content classes* (Training Module No. 3). Eugene: University of Oregon, Research, Consultation, and Teaching Program.

Tindal, G., & Parker, R. (1989a). Assessment of written expression for students in compensatory and special education program. *Journal of Special Education, 23,* 169–183.

Tindal, G., & Parker, R. (1989b). Development of written retell as a curriculum-based measure in secondary programs. *School Psychology Review, 13,* 328–343.

Tindal, G., & Parker, R. (1991). Identifying measures for evaluating written expression. *Learning Disabilities Research and Practice, 6,* 211–218.

Videen, J., Deno, S. L., & Marston, D. (1982). *Correct word sequences: A valid indicator of proficiency in written expression* (Vol. IRLD-RR-84). University of Minnesota, Institute for Research on Learning Disabilities.

Walker, B., Shippen, M. E., Alberto, P. A., Houchins, D. E., & Cihak, D. F. (2005). Using the expressive writing program to improve the writing skills of high school students with learning disabilities. *Learning Disabilities Research and Practice, 20,* 175–183.

Wallace, T., Espin, C. A., McMaster, K., Deno, S. L., & Foegen, A. (2007). CBM progress monitoring within a standards-based system: Introduction to the special series. *Journal of Special Education, 41,* 66–67.

Wayman, M. M., Wallace, T., Wiley, H. I., Tichá, R., & Espin, C. A. (2007). Literature synthesis on Curriculum-Based Measurement in reading. *Journal of Special Education, 41,* 85–120.

Weissenburger, J. W., & Espin, C. A. (2005). Curriculum-based measures of writing across grade levels. *Journal of School Psychology, 43,* 153–169.

Zigmond, N. (1990). Rethinking secondary school programs for students with learning disabilities. *Focus on Exceptional Children, 23*(1), 1–22.

V

Applications in General Education Settings

13

Curriculum-Based Measurement at Larue Elementary

They Said It Couldn't Be Done!

*Amanda Kloo, Charles D. Machesky,
and Naomi Zigmond*

Proficient reading skills are integral to both school and life success. Decades of research have shown that early elementary-aged children with reading skill deficits experience persistent academic failure and difficulty as they progress through school (Chard and Kame'enui, 2000; Felton and Wood, 1992; Juel, 1988). Research has also evidenced, however, that reading failure can be prevented if identified early and treated vigorously (National Institute of Child Health and Human Development, 2000; National Research Council, 1998). Reading achievement of low-performing students can be significantly improved if systematic, explicit instruction and timely intensive intervention are delivered early in students' school careers (Chard and Kame'enui, 2000; Coyne, Kame'enui, and Simmons, 2001; Good, Simmons, and Kame'enui, 2001; Torgeson, 2000; Torgeson et al., 2001).

Building on this body of research, current educational reform initiatives have focused on preventing reading failure. Accountability legislation such as No Child Left Behind (2000) and the most recent reauthorization of the Individuals with Disabilities Education Act (2004) challenge schools to break the cycle of reading failure in the early elementary grades by preventing students from falling behind in the first place. A primary tool in the prevention arsenal is Curriculum-Based Measurement (CBM; Deno, 1985), a valid, efficient, and effective weapon in the battle against reading failure.

In August 2006, a team of Western and Central Pennsylvania researchers received Office of Special Education Programs (OSEP) funding to document and evaluate the implementation of a school-wide progress-monitoring model aimed at improving reading achievement in grades

K–4 and reducing unnecessary referrals to special education. The model was simple enough (see Kloo and Zigmond, 2009): we called it Monitoring Progress of Pennsylvania Pupils (MP³). The model consisted of the following components: (1) teach reading well the first time around; (2) monitor progress of all students at least three times each year to catch students falling behind; (3) provide daily more intensive interventions to students not making adequate progress within the core reading program; monitor progress of those (Tier 2) students monthly; (4) provide even more intensive, daily, small group interventions to students making minimal progress; monitor progress weekly for those (Tier 3) students; and (5) teach teachers to administer progress-monitoring assessments, interpret data, and make instructional changes based on group and individual trends.

Many school districts in Pennsylvania had already incorporated some parts of this model within a Response to Intervention (RTI)/progress monitoring initiative promoted by the Bureau of Special Education. The Central Pennsylvania team selected one of these school districts and documented the expansion and institutionalization of the RTI/CBM model. For the Western Pennsylvania team, the three-year model demonstration funding provided a unique opportunity to find a school district that had not yet adopted a progress-monitoring framework and to study real world adoption and application of CBM from scratch.

"Local Teachers Fare Poorly on State Tests"[1]

Larue Elementary School (grades one through five) was in desperate need to break a dangerous cycle of academic and behavioral failure. School and classroom visits confirmed the dismal state of academics, discipline, and motivation tied to years of student academic failure, teacher turnover, and a loss of interest and support by community and district partners. Table 13.1 summarizes the demographic and achievement characteristics of Larue in the spring of 2006. To establish baseline performance levels in reading, the DIBELS (Dynamic Indicators of Dynamic Literacy Skills; Good and Kaminski, 2002) and the *Reading Maze* (Shinn and Shinn, 2002) were administered to all students in grades one through four and two through four, respectively. Results showed fewer than 20 percent of students achieved at benchmark levels on the DIBELS Oral Reading Fluency (ORF) measure in first grade, and only 2 percent achieved at benchmark levels in the fourth grade. On the Iowa Tests of Basic Skills (Hoover, 2002), 12 percent of second graders scored above the 40th percentile. On the Maze measure, 10 percent of third graders scored at average or above average (see Table 13.2). These data were consistent with the school's performance on the annual statewide accountability measure, the Pennsylvania System of School Assessment (PSSA). In spring 2006, the target for Adequate Yearly Progress (AYP) for the state of Pennsylvania was set at 59 percent of students achieving proficient or advanced status. In Larue, only 29 percent of third graders and 21 percent of fourth graders scored at the proficient or advanced levels.

Larue was placed into Level One School Improvement status as a result of significantly depressed achievement and attendance school-wide. The school was a mess. According to the superintendent,

TABLE 13.1.

Larue Elementary School 2006 demographics and achievement

LARUE ELEMENTARY SCHOOL (GRADES 1–5)

Enrollment	252
Minority (%)	58
Free/reduced lunch (%)	92
Percent proficient/advanced fourth-grade state test	21
Percent proficient/advanced third-grade state test	29

TABLE 13.2.

Baseline reading performance by grade

	GRADE			
	1	2	3	4
Percent above 40th percentile on IOWA reading subtest	27	12	33	38
Percent "low risk" on DIBELS ORF	18	10	12	2
Percent "average/above" on maze	__	21	10	13

Prior to implementing the RTI model at Larue, the school atmosphere was negative and morale was low. The teachers at Larue were
fixed in the belief that it was a failing school with very little or no
hope of recovery. Members of the community had long ago given up
on Larue. (Superintendent, July 2006)

And this same sentiment was expressed publicly in the more than 150 articles
or editorials appearing in the local newspaper over the three-year period before model implementation. With headlines that proclaimed, "Uniontown
Educators Probe Possible Cheating on State Test" (Ostrosky, 2004); "State
Lists Schools that Failed to Reach Federal Guidelines" (Schiffbauer, 2005);
"*Larue* Students May Attend Another School" (Oravec, 2006), the local community was offered scathing reports of Larue's constant failure to achieve
and of parent frustrations and teacher failings.

Criticisms Justified: Reading Instruction before the Reading Program

Larue's reading curriculum was described as "balanced literacy" involving
small group, teacher-led instruction and independent work at learning centers. Instruction was centered on implementing Guided Reading (Fountas
and Pinnel, 1991) to small groups or pairs of students using instructional-
level material. The teachers supplemented their Guided Reading program
each Monday by teaching focus skills selected from the Harcourt Trophies
reading series (Beck, Farr, and Strickland, 2003). Reading instructional times
varied from forty to ninety minutes per day across classrooms, depending on
the proficiency level of the students, the number of small groups the teacher
organized, and the classroom management skills of the teacher.

In truth, Larue teachers reported that often reading groups would not receive any teacher-led reading instruction for days at a time because of the ro-
tation schedule, or because of schedule adjustments dictated by vacation days,
snow days, special school events, or another group's level of need. Monday
focus skills instruction occurred haphazardly or not at all. Instead, students
were exposed to a variety of texts, encouraged to explore literature independently and discover concepts about print; code-based reading instruction and
explicit strategy instruction occurred only incidentally. Teachers frequently
collected running record data on students and conducted miscue analyses
according to Guided Reading guidelines but rarely used the data to systematically influence instruction other than to move children between reading

groups and book levels. In fact, some teachers reported that the data collection was so time consuming that they feasibly could assess only a handful of students each week. Furthermore, though the teachers felt comfortable with coding student miscues, they were extremely uncomfortable interpreting these data to plan "what to do next" and "when and how to do it." Most student data records were simply filed away on a shelf somewhere, as the class went on with its daily instructional life. This instructional framework was clearly not meeting the needs of students at Larue.

The Classroom/Reading Teachers

The teaching staff at Larue were generally inexperienced and, admittedly, had limited knowledge of reading instruction and methodology. Average tenure at Larue was less than five years with the vast majority of teachers requesting transfers after one or two years at the school. Energetic teachers left Larue as quickly as they could; teachers who stayed took no responsibility for the dismal academic and behavioral climate of the school. No teachers (general or special educators) expressed any familiarity with the National Reading Panel's "5 Big Ideas" (2000) of reading instruction. Most had graduated from a local teacher preparation program that was fiercely committed to a whole language-based approach to reading instruction. Most believed they were simply not allowed to teach phonics rules or explicit reading strategies to their students because these practices conflicted with the whole language ideologies of the district. And most believed that their students' deficient reading skills were due to child-centered factors over which they had no control (e.g., socioeconomic status, race, limited parental involvement, lack of motivation, behavior problems, poor attitude, cognitive deficits, etc.) rather than instructionally centered factors that they could manipulate.

Enter CBM/MP[3]

Fortunately, the district was led by a committed and passionate superintendent who embodied many of the leadership qualities that research has shown to be closely related to sustained use of research-based reading practices (Klinger, Vaughn, Hughes, and Arguelles, 1999). He had trusted his curriculum leadership staff to select and implement an appropriate reading curriculum, but he came to realize that the instructional framework was not meeting the needs of students at Larue. He was ready to implement system-wide changes in reading instruction and to introduce CBM and data-based decision making to turn Larue and the rest of the district around. He was relentless in urging district administrators, principals, and teachers to accept MP³ staff suggestions for new ways to teach reading, to monitor student progress, and to provide tiered interventions to improve overall achievement in the elementary grades. Immediately, the district adopted and purchased a research-based core reading program that comprehensively addressed the "5 Big Ideas." They provided in-service training to the primary teachers on how to use the new reading program effectively. They established school-wide reading incentives and events to promote literacy and engage students and parents with reading data and achievement. Daily schedules were revised to include 120-minute reading blocks at each grade level. These blocks allowed for daily whole-group core instruction delivered to all students by general education classroom teachers plus multitiered skill-based small group reading interventions (again for all students) delivered by Title I staff, special educators, and general educators. Common planning time was scheduled to accommodate grade-level meetings, CBM data reviews, and collaboration. Monthly school-wide data review meetings were put on the calendar. Title I remedial reading staff were assigned to Larue to help collect progress-monitoring data and deliver small group interventions to students in response to those data. A literacy coach was appointed to support improved reading instruction and data-based decision making. Multiple opportunities for on-site ongoing professional development in effective reading instruction and intervention, progress monitoring/CBM, and RTI methodology were built into the school calendars. By pooling district funds, special education resources, and grant support, teachers were provided with the necessary materials, as well as training and daily on-site support to implement the model. Most importantly, Larue teachers began to take ownership of their students' reading achievement by learning to use screening and progress-monitoring data to set achievement goals, identify skill deficits, evaluate and plan for instruction, form instructional groups, and monitor reading progress for students with and without disabilities (Hosp and Hosp, 2003).

After One Year

Student achievement at Larue did not improve dramatically as soon as CBM was introduced. But there were remarkable changes in the school, even in that first year. According to the superintendent,

Perceptions began to change as early as the first year of implementation. Everyone recognized the value of frequently assessing students and using these data to plan for and provide reading instruction in which they could meaningfully participate and learn. When students were finally given the opportunity to actually learn to read we saw the data improve, the graphs go up, and the atmosphere at Larue change. Resistant teachers left or were transformed in their beliefs by what they had experienced. New staff who enthusiastically embraced the model flocked to Larue. Teachers now proudly claimed Larue as their school and the Larue students as their students. (Superintendent, December 2007)

Larue's principal agreed.

As a former special educator, the concept and practice of progress monitoring students' reading skills were familiar to me. Implementing these to improve reading instruction overall and benefit all students in a system that supports the use of data and evidence across all elementary classrooms just "made sense." My teachers are now committed to the idea that all of their kids "can learn"—we have the graphs to prove it. And they now know what to teach and how to teach so that they all "do learn." We are a school transformed. (Principal, September 2007)

And at the end of year one, even the newspaper coverage was slightly more optimist. The headlines exclaimed, "*Larue* Emphasizing Change" (Oravec, 2006); "Experts Help to Solve School's Problems" (Oravec, 2007); "*Superintendent* Promises a Better School" (Ferris, 2007). Change was in the air. The end of the school year brought the expected transfers of teaching staff—nearly half the teachers in grades one through four petitioned to leave Larue for a position in another district school, but those who stayed and those newly hired enthusiastically embraced the MP³ model of CBM, data-based decision making, and good instruction and intervention.

By the End of Year Three

Over the next two years, teachers at Larue found that they could make routine what had once been considered an extraordinary burden of data collection and instructional planning. As one classroom teacher put it,

How will I do it? When will I do it? What will I do it with? And why do we have to? These were all questions swimming around in my mind three years ago when the group from Pitt first started working at Larue. Now I'm training other teachers to progress monitor, analyze data, and deliver interventions! Imagine that! A teacher from Larue is actually a model for colleagues at "higher" performing schools. We [the teachers at Larue] no longer talk about when we will try to bid into another position somewhere; instead, we ask ourselves why we would ever want to leave Larue. There's nothing more rewarding than seeing my students' faces light up when they plot that higher data point on their progress-monitoring graph or when they grab the timer to see how much more fluent they are reading. The improvements of the Learning Support [Individualized Education Program] kids' skills have been impressive too. I'm ashamed to admit that I had really low expectations before, but now realize that the more they learn the more they can learn. I'm a better teacher now. I wish I could have progress monitored myself—my graph would be off the charts! (General education teacher, May 2009)

Table 13.3 summarizes Larue achievement across three years of implementing CBM practices within the MP³ model. At most grade levels, there was not only an increase in the percent of students meeting grade-level benchmarks but, more important, there was a decrease in the percent of students performing far below grade level. This change was most dramatic for fourth graders who had experienced the benefits of CBM/MP³ throughout their primary reading experience. Before implementing the model, and establishing data-based decision making linked to progress monitoring data, fourth graders were reading an average of sixty-seven words correct per minute (wpm)—a rate commensurate with most second graders midway through the second grade year. After implementing the model for three years, the mean fluency rate for fourth graders at Larue was 102 wpm—a rate closer to healthy readers in January of fourth grade. Furthermore, compared to typical fourth grade growth rates from fall to spring of 0.9 words per week, Larue's fourth graders grew on average 1.1 words correct per week. These students were now better positioned than their predecessors to avoid the long-term pitfalls and consequences of reading failure. And even parents noticed the changes.

TABLE 13.3.

Larue Elementary School 2006–9 achievement

	SPRING 2006 (BASELINE)	SPRING 2007 (YEAR 1)	SPRING 2008 (YEAR 2)	SPRING 2009 (YEAR 3)
Grade 1				
First-grade average oral reading fluency rates (wpm)	22	37	50	42
First-grade average growth rate (wpm)	___	1.1	1.4	1.2
First-grade % low risk on DIBELS ORF	18	35	46	46
First-grade % at risk on DIBELS ORF	65	45	32	29
Grade 2				
Second-grade average oral reading fluency rates	42	49	71	81
Second-grade average growth rate (wpm)	___	1	1.2	1
Second-grade % low risk on DIBELS ORF	10	13	26	40
Second-grade % at risk on DIBELS ORF	83	73	41	49
Grade 3				
Third-grade average oral reading fluency rates	83	82	80	90
Third-grade average growth rate (wpm)	___	1.3	1	1
Third-grade % low risk on DIBELS ORF	12	21	19	28
Third-grade % at risk on DIBELS ORF	36	44	45	20
Proficient/advanced third-grade state test (%)	29	37	32	44
Below basic on third-grade state test (%)	48	41	54	40
Grade 4				
Fourth-grade average oral reading fluency rates	67	77	89	102
Fourth-grade average growth rate (wpm)	___	.6	.9	1.1
Fourth-grade % low risk on DIBELS ORF	2	6	18	42
Fourth-grade % at risk on DIBELS ORF	85	65	60	45
Proficient/advanced fourth-grade state test (%)	21	38	38	33
Below basic on fourth-grade state test (%)	54	43	40	35

I appreciate that Mrs. M keeps me to date with how J.'s doin' with his readin'. I'm proud that he does better. We're not the kind to hang up work or nothin' but there's acoupla times that I showed his reports [progress-monitoring graphs] to his big sister or grandma. At first I was afraid they was office reports for bad behavior. Ya see, school ain't easy for J. Used to be a battle every day—cryin' and carryin' on. I was the same in school. Now, it ain't a piece a cake or nothin' but he's doin' better. He's even read a bedtime story to his baby cousin who's staying here. That would ain't never happened before. (Parent of Larue second grader, April 2009)

As student achievement improved, so did community perceptions and morale. By year three, local reporters were celebrating Larue Elementary as "innovative," "pleased with *PSSA* progress," and having "made significant gains" (Oravec, 2008). The superintendent acknowledged the positive impact CBM at Larue had had on the community as a whole.

Positive interactions with the home became frequent as student progress data was shared with parents. Parents were pleased not only at how their children were progressing academically but also at how significantly their disruptive behaviors diminished as learning improved. By implementing progress monitoring and MP³, we have succeeded in changing the academic expectations and achievement of this school as well as the school and community cultures, and we will continue to do so this year and in future years. (Superintendent, June 2009)

Most inspiring was a three-page color spread titled "Celebrating Achievement: New Approach Changes School" in the local newspaper (Oravec, 2009) announcing in the spring of year three that Larue Elementary had made "Adequate Yearly Progress (AYP)" in reading and math for the first time since state accountability testing began. The piece credited district leaders, the school principal, and teachers for their commitment to change and their passion for improving the emotional and educational lives of student at Larue. Moreover, the reporter highlighted the implementation of a progress-monitoring model that included data-based decision making and intensive interventions as playing a crucial role in transforming the school. The principal of Larue could not have been more proud.

Of course there is still so much room for us to grow to catch up and decrease the gap but the strides we have made in the past three years are nothing short of remarkable given where we began. The original mission to improve students' reading scores by monitoring progress and providing interventions in the RTI program grew into something that changed practice, changed instruction, changed perception, changed procedures, and changed students' lives. All of the pieces of the puzzle have come together for the first time. I'm reminded of that every time a child who never before crossed the library's threshold rushes in to show me the new book he's taking home to read to Grandma. Larue is a place for learning. (Principal, May 2009)

Clearly, the positive reach of progress monitoring was wide. School achievement data may not tell as inspiring or sentimental a story as testimonials, but they certainly tell a powerful tale. True, Larue is not yet a high-achieving school, nor even an average-achieving school, but Larue's progress has been nothing short of remarkable. Larue teachers, with limited teaching experience and only a superficial understanding of reading, are now engaging in daily conversations and debates about phonology, fluency, vocabulary, and comprehension. Instructional decisions that were once well intentioned, but certainly not data-based, are now thoughtful and intentional. Students who once believed that learning to read was beyond their reach and above their "station" are now burying themselves in books. School leaders who for years assumed that Larue would always be a failing school are now celebrating students' successes. Local newspaper reporters historically highlighting Larue's failings are now reporting that the school is transformed. The fight to combat reading failure has not been and will never be easy at Larue or at any of the hundreds of other low-performing schools across the nation. But CBM and MP^3 have brought success one step closer.

Note

1. Headline from Schiffbauer (2003).

References

Beck, I. L., Farr, R. C., & Strickland, D. S. (2003). *Trophies: A Harcourt reading/ language arts program*. Orlando, FL: Harcourt.

Chard, D. J., & Kame'enui, E. J. (2000). Struggling first-grade readers: The frequency and progress of their reading. *Journal of Special Education, 34,* 28–38.

Coyne, M. D., Kame'enui, E. J., & Simmons, D. C. (2001). Prevention and intervention in beginning reading: Two complex systems. *Learning Disabilities Research and Practice, 16,* 62–73.

Deno, S. L. (1985). Curriculum-Based Measurement: The emerging alternative. *Exceptional Children, 52,* 219–232.

Felton, R. H., & Wood, F. B. (1992). A reading level match study of nonword reading skills in poor readers with varying IQ. *Journal of Learning Disabilities, 25,* 318–326.

Ferris, S. (2007, July 12). [*Superintendent*] promises a better school. *Herald Standard.*

Fountas, I. C., & Pinnell, G. S. (1991). *Guided reading: Good first teaching for all children.* Portsmouth, NH: Heinemann.

Good, R. H., III, & Kaminski, R. A. (Eds.). (2002). *Dynamic indicators of basic early literacy skills* (6th ed.). Eugene, OR: Institute for the Development of Education Achievement. Available at http://dibels.uoregon.edu

Good, R. H., III., Simmons, D. C., & Kame'enui, E. J. (2001). The importance and decision-making utility of a continuum of fluency-based indicators of foundational reading skills for third-grade high-stakes outcomes. *Scientific Studies of Reading, 5,* 259–290.

Hoover, H. D. (2001). *Iowa tests of basic skills.* Chicago, IL: Riverside.

Hosp, M. K., & Hosp, J. L. (2003). Curriculum-Based Measurement for reading, spelling, and math: How to do it and why. *Preventing School Failure, 48,* 10–17.

Individuals with Disabilities Education Improvement Act (2004), Pub. L. No. 108–446, 20 Stat.145.

Juel, C. (1988). Learning to read and write: A longitudinal study of 54 children from first through fourth grades. *Journal of Educational Psychology, 80,* 437–447.

Klingner, J. K., Vaughn, S., Hughes, M. T., & Arguelles, M. E. (1999). Sustaining research-based practices in reading: A 3-year follow-up. *Remedial and Special Education, 20,* 263–274, 287.

Kloo, A., & Zigmond, N. (2009). Response to intervention: A reality check. In T. E. Scruggs & M. A. Mastropieri (Eds.), *Policy and practice: Advances in learning and behavioral disabilities* (Vol. 22, pp. 67–107). Bingley, UK: Emerald.

National Institute of Child Health and Human Development. (2000). *Teaching children to read: An evidence-based assessment of the scientific research literature on reading and its implications for reading instruction* (NIH Publication No. 00-4769). Report of the national reading panel. Washington. DC: U.S. Government Printing Office.

National Research Council. (1998). *Preventing reading difficulties in young children.* Washington, DC: National Academies Press.

No Child Left Behind Act (2001), PL 107–110, 15 Stat.1425.

Oravec, A. (2006, August 27). [*Larue*] students may attend another school. *Herald Standard*, A1, A4.

Oravec, A. (2006, November 1). [*Larue*] emphasizing change. *Herald Standard*, A1–A2.

Oravec, A. (2007, July 11). Experts help to solve school's problems. *Herald Standard*, A1–A2.

Oravec, A. (2008, September 21). Learning curve: Local school districts pleased with PSSA progress. *Herald Standard*, A1, A4.

Oravec, A. (2009, October 5). Celebrating achievement: New approach changes school. *Herald Standard*, A1–A2.

Ostrosky, S. (2004, March 26). Uniontown educators probe possible cheating on state test. *Herald Standard*, B1, B4.

Schiffbauer, K. (2003, January 12). Local teachers fare poorly on state tests, results show. *Herald Standard*, B1–B2.

Schiffbauer, K. (2005, December 31). State lists schools that failed to reach federal guidelines. *Herald Standard*, B1, B5.

Shinn, M. R., & Shinn, M. M. (2002). *Reading Maze-CBM*. Eden Prairie, MN: Edformation. Available at http://www.aimsweb.com

Torgeson, J. K. (2000). Individual differences in response to early interventions in reading: The lingering problem. *Learning Disabilities Research and Practice, 15,* 303–323.

Torgeson, J. K., Alexander, A. W., Wagner, R. K., Raschotte, C. A., Voeller, K., & Conway, T. (2001). Intensive remedial instruction for children with severe reading disabilities: Immediate and long-term outcomes from two instructional approaches. *Journal of Learning Disabilities, 34,* 33–58, 78.

14

Curriculum-Based Measurement Progress Monitoring and the Health of General Education

Deborah L. Speece

Before I describe how I view Curriculum-Based Measurement (CBM) contributing to the health of general education, I take a brief side trip to explain how Professor Deno's work and that of his students influenced my own development as a teacher and researcher. Although my memory is a bit hazy, I believe my first encounter was the Deno (1985) paper in *Exceptional Children* that explained the CBM research framework and provided the empirical support for the emerging CBM model. Shortly thereafter or possibly concurrently, I met Deno, along with Lynn and Doug Fuchs, as we were frequently on the same American Educational Research Association conference panels to present our work in the mid- to late 1980s. I remember being a bit amazed and flattered that Deno took the time to introduce himself and favorably comment on the work that we were doing. I didn't truly understand what CBM was all about, however, until I cotaught an assessment class with my University of Maryland colleague, Victor Nolet, who had been a student of Gerry Tindal's at the University of Oregon. Gerry, like Lynn and Doug, is a Minnesota alumnus. So there are two to three degrees of separation between me and Mt. Deno, but I have gained tremendously from his students and, by extension, from him. The knowledge gleaned from the Drs. Fuchs and Dr. Nolet set the stage for my own teaching and research. In every class I teach, regardless of the content, I find a way to work in information on CBM because of the solid empirical base that supports its use.

It was through Dr. Nolet that I learned the thermometer analogy for CBM: CBM is the vehicle through which you can "take the temperature" of a child's academic progress reliably, in a matter of minutes, and over time, just like taking your child's temperature multiple times when she becomes ill. CBM won't tell you everything you need to know, just as a thermometer will not: it is not a functional MRI, but you will learn if more time-consuming diagnostic instruments are required.

A Healthy Alternative

The thermometer analogy and Deno's (1985) use of growth charts to display data in the same manner as the height and weight charts pediatricians use prompted my thinking about CBM as a healthy alternative to usual practice in elementary education classrooms. When we began our first project that incorporated CBM measures (e.g., Case, Speece, and Molloy, 2003; Speece and Case, 2001), the one-minute measures were viewed with a bit of suspicion by our first- and second-grade general education colleagues. The Dynamic Indicators of Basic Early Literacy Skills (DIBELS) contagion lie ahead and the teachers were wedded to running records. Our purpose was not to convert the teachers (not overtly) but to use CBM techniques to test ideas about treatment validity (Fuchs, 1995; Fuchs and Fuchs, 1998), now known as Response to Intervention (RTI).

We learned a lot about the technique in our three-year project and became even more convinced that collecting, graphing, and interpreting CBM data could be instrumental in closing the assessment-instruction gap. The graphs were a key ingredient in our consultations with teachers. These meetings were focused on designing interventions to be implemented by the teachers in classrooms to improve the learning trajectory of children at risk for reading failure. There's something about a flat line that gets people's attention. This is certainly a healthy development in an environment that often relies on unvalidiated methods for measuring children's achievement.

Perhaps the most important quantitative findings from our work were (a) that children identified as reading disabled by CBM growth and level (i.e., dual discrepancy) were younger, more representative of the population demographics, and possibly more impaired than children identified as reading disabled by an aptitude-achievement discrepancy formula and (b) that at-risk children who were frequently identified as dual-discrepant over three years had poorer academic outcomes, received lower teacher ratings of academic competence and social skills, higher ratings of problem behaviors, and were more likely to receive attention at the school level than at-risk children not frequently identified (or not ever identified) as dual-discrepant. Taken together, the findings suggested that the RTI framework, based in part on work by Fuchs and Fuchs and powered by Deno's CBM, possessed criterion and social validity: another healthy development.

In addition to child measures, we collected measures of context, such as classroom reading slope, instructional quality, and teacher experience. The question asked was whether quantitative contextual differences differed for children more or less responsive to the general education setting. The answer was no; there were no significant differences between our at-risk groups on the contextual variables. Thus, as hypothesized by Fuchs and Fuchs (1998), persistent nonresponsiveness indexes a group of children who may need more than general education can provide.

The story behind the numbers is equally interesting. We also collected qualitative data based on our consultation meetings with the teachers and classroom observations of teachers, children, and instruction. These data provided a background from which to judge what was going on with our at-risk readers and their response, or lack thereof, to the general education environment. This approach—analyzing individual differences within the context they develop—was certainly not a new idea, but as we came to understand the interplay between child and context, we were even more appreciative of the role CBM could play in improving the reading achievement of children. We learned that four of our frequently nonresponsive students who had been selected for qualitative analysis had less access to learning than their peers. That is, the interaction between child characteristics and instructional environment produced a less robust context for learning. Sometimes the reason for this situation was more heavily influenced by the child, sometimes by the learning environment, but both were always involved. Access is a difficult variable to measure, but we speculated that CBM dual discrepancy as defined by level and slope might be the most direct measure of this construct. A dual discrepancy reflects child abilities and teacher skills and, thus, goes beyond a simple individual difference/context dichotomy. That CBM growth and level could provide insight to such a complex issue was an exciting possibility. However, not all were as enamored by our findings or similar findings from our colleagues.

Can CBM Be Unhealthy?

As scholars we must take seriously evidence that suggests CBM may not be a sound assessment procedure. Although the evidence summarized by the contributors to this volume would suggest otherwise, there are strong objections to the claim that CBM is a valid assessment technique. Sometimes these arguments are directed specifically at the DIBELS suite of assessments (International Reading Association, Standards for Assessment in Reading and Writing [revised]; Afflerbach, 2007) and sometimes at CBM oral reading fluency (Paris, Carpenter, Paris, and Hamilton, 2005). A quick review of these documents indicates that there are misperceptions about the purpose of CBM and its descendants and certainly philosophical differences. The arguments challenging the validity of CBM, however, are not strong. The Paris et al. (2005) chapter rests primarily on an unpublished study so the claims are impossible to evaluate. Their argument rests on the presumption that oral reading fluency distributions are skewed and that accuracy, not rate, is the driver behind any correlation between fluency and comprehension. There are data that refute these assertions (e.g., Deno, Fuchs, Marston, and Shin, 2001; Jenkins, Fuchs, van den Broek, Espin, and Deno, 2003), but it will be important to evaluate the Paris evidence when it becomes available.

Philosophical differences are more difficult to resolve. Afflerbach (2007) compares Marie Clay's Observation Survey of Early Literacy Achievement (OSELA) to Good and Kaminski's DIBELS in his reading assessment text. In a side-by-side comparison, Afflerbach lays out the strengths and weaknesses of each approach in terms of time required, consequences and usefulness, reliability, and validity. Afflerbach writes that selection of OSELA "reflects the fact that a school or school district values formative literacy assessment that is grounded in classroom instruction and learning" (p. 116). For DIBELS, he writes that it assesses "areas associated with successful reading" (p. 120) but that "it provides little information about how students coordinate skill and strategy to achieve the goal of reading: the construction of meaning" (p. 121). It is true that the DIBELS measures do not provide this information, but they do not claim to. The unstated inference is that OSELA does. There is no information supporting this inference other than Afflerbach's belief that the skills that are purportedly measured by OSELA support his construct of reading. Construct validity is always a judgment but one that should be supported by evidence that supports the claim.

However, and as detailed by Afflerbach (2007), DIBELS (and by association, CBM oral reading fluency) can be unhealthy when assessment is confused with instruction. If teachers believe that reading instruction should consist primarily of fluency lessons because the screening or progress monitoring system uses a fluency indicator, then the ideas behind CBM as described by Deno (1985) have gone astray. No doubt this has happened in classrooms, but it would be unfair to place this criticism at the doorstep of the assessment technique. It is equally likely that the results of the OSELA collection of assessments are completed as mandated and put away, without interpretation for instructional change, until the next benchmark is due. This situation may be a consequence of the assessment, but like CBM, the assessment itself is not the problem.

It seems obvious that the crux of the matter is educators' understanding of the interplay between assessment and instruction. In teaching preservice teacher candidates in an introductory assessment class, it is a hard sell to convince them that progress monitoring built on one-minute measures can provide the foundation for instructional change and child achievement. Part of the problem is the students' lack of familiarity with assessment in general and their background knowledge that is deeply embedded in their own assessment experiences. Oral reading fluency is a strange concept despite the impressive graphs of real performance by real children. Two years later in their student teaching experience, these teacher candidates design an instructional project to improve an academic or behavioral skill. Without fail, at least one student delights me with the selection of a CBM procedure to monitor growth and at the same time deflates me with an instructional plan that only includes a fluency component. There is more work to be done to assist preservice teachers in grasping the finer points of connecting assessment to instruction without making them identical. From the perspective of practicing professionals, the teachers we worked with in our research projects came to understand and value the CBM graphs "as long as we don't have to do it." We can solve the data-collection problem and at the same time take some solace in a positive view of data.

Prognosis

Even the most cursory review of the impact of CBM on the educational landscape suggests that Professor Deno's legacy will continue to influence scholars and practitioners. The work has progressed from single measures to multiple domains to conceptual frameworks of disability identification to screening applications across multiple years. The field of CBM has gone virile from its beginnings at the University of Minnesota to the present day that includes international studies. An electronic search of a single database using the term "Curriculum-Based Measurement" and stipulating peer-reviewed journals yielded 390 hits; deleting the peer-reviewed criterion yielded 958 hits. These are staggering numbers, but I suspect Deno is more interested in the unknowable number of children and teachers his academic agenda assisted. That they exist is not debatable, and this fact bodes well for the future health of the CBM enterprise. Thank you, Stanley Deno. Let's hope the next twenty-five years produce equally satisfying results.

References

Afflerbach, P. (2007). *Understanding and using reading assessment K–12*. Newark, DE: International Reading Association.

Case, L. P., Speece, D. L., & Molloy, D. E. (2003). The validity of a response-to-instruction paradigm to identify reading disabilities: A longitudinal analysis of individual differences and contextual factors. *School Psychology Review, 32,* 557–582.

Deno, S. L. (1985). Curriculum-Based Measurement: The emerging alternative. *Exceptional Children, 52,* 219–232.

Deno, S. L., Fuchs, L. S., Marston, D., & Shin, J. (2001). Using Curriculum-Based Measurement to establish growth standards for students with learning disabilities. *School Psychology Review, 30,* 507–524.

Fuchs, L. S. (1995, May). *Incorporating Curriculum-Based Measurement into the eligibility decision-making process: A focus on treatment validity and student growth.* Paper presented at the Workshop on IQ Testing and Educational Decision Making, National Research Council, National Academy of Science, Washington, DC.

Fuchs, L. S., & Fuchs, D. (1998). Treatment validity: A unifying concept for reconceptualizing the identification of learning disabilities. *Learning Disabilities Research and Practice, 13,* 204–219.

International Reading Association, Standards for Assessment in Reading and Writing (revised). Retrieved January 3, 2010, from http://www.reading.org/General/CurrentResearch/Standards/AssessmentStandards.aspx

Jenkins, J., Fuchs, L., van den Broek, P., Espin, C., & Deno, S. (2003). Sources of individual differences in reading comprehension and reading fluency. *Journal of Educational Psychology, 95,* 719–729.

Paris, S., Carpenter, R., Paris, A., & Hamilton, E. (2005). Spurious and genuine correlates of children's reading comprehension. *Children's reading comprehension and assessment* (pp. 131–160). Mahwah, NJ: Lawrence Erlbaum Associates.

Speece, D. L., & Case, L. P. (2001). Classification in context: An alternative approach to identifying early reading disability. *Journal of Educational Psychology, 93,* 735–749.

VI

Applications for Special School Populations

15

Curriculum-Based Measurement and English Language Learners

District-Wide Academic Norms for
Special Education Eligibility

Steven L. Robinson, Margaret J. Robinson,
and Lionel A. Blatchley

Curriculum-Based Measurement (CBM) was formally developed under the guidance of Stanley L. Deno, codirector of the Institute for Research on Learning Disabilities at the University of Minnesota in the late 1970s. The focus was primarily on children with learning disabilities who typically perform poorly in reading, mathematics, and writing. CBM provided an alternative approach to address the inadequacy of standardized achievement tests and the need to frequently monitor progress in core academics. However, early in the development of CBM, it became clear that the measures were useful and valid tools for establishing normative levels of performance and progress for nondisabled populations, such as English Language Learners (ELLs). During a doctoral internship in Saint Paul School District's Special Education Department, one of Dr. Deno's graduate students was assigned to the special education unit working with ELLs. The graduate student introduced department staff to CBM and its potential applications. Saint Paul special education staff and Dr. Deno met regularly to discuss the use of CBM to avoid discrimination in ELL assessment and to make eligibility decisions for supplementary educational services. This early work on the use of CBM led to the extensive application of CBM for ELLs in Saint Paul Schools and made an important contribution to meeting the needs of these students.

It is important that ELLs receive special education services due to a disability and not limited English proficiency. Traditional norm-referenced published tests of academic achievement are not useful for making special education decisions for ELLs due to lack of representation of ELLs in the normative sample or test content and format issues. The substitution of achievement tests in native languages (e.g., Spanish) may not improve validity due to the lack of relationship to the curriculum taught (Duran, 2008). Additionally, native language tests are not available for many language groups.

This chapter will focus on the use of CBM for making special education eligibility decisions for ELLs in Saint Paul Public Schools (SPPS), a large urban district in the Midwest. The process, procedures, data, and results of using CBM reading, writing, and mathematics to develop district-wide local norms for ELLs will be described. The norms presented can be used to repre-· sent typical progress for students who are learning basic skills while they are learning English. The progress of students referred for special education services can be compared to the progress of their peers. Comparisons can then be used for special education decision making (e.g., eligibility for placement in special education) and monitoring progress in academics.

Background

The development and use of local CBM norms has been a part of the special education decision-making process for over thirty years in SPPS, a district with large numbers of culturally and linguistically diverse students. SPPS experienced a large influx of Hmong Southeast Asian refugees starting in 1975. As these students entered the school system and moved through the grades, it was clear that traditional testing overidentified ELLs as having learning problems when, in fact, the larger issue was limited English language and acculturation. As noted earlier, SPPS Special Education Assessment Resource staff began using CBM with ELLs to determine current level of performance, to determine instructional level, and to monitor progress. Eventually, CBM was used to determine the typical progress ELLs made as they learned English. At first, CBM scores for students referred for special education services were compared to the CBM scores for six to ten grade-level ELL peers from the same culture. This model worked well as one method for determining ELL eligibility, but it required repeated identification and testing of peers. In the late 1990s, the SPPS Special Education Department began to develop district-wide ELL CBM norms. These norms were first collected in 1990–91 and have been updated every three to six years since then.

CBM for ELLs

CBM is a well-researched alternative assessment approach. CBM provides a systematic, research-based set of technically adequate procedures that can be used to make valid decisions about ELLs' achievement in reading, writing, and mathematics. CBMs are sensitive to growth and can therefore serve as indices of progress for ELLs. While research on the use of CBM for ELLs is sparse, existing investigations are supportive of the practice. Espin, Wallace, Campbell, Lembke, Long, and Tichá (2008) found that the technical adequacy of CBMs for written expression were adequate and similar between ELL and non-ELL tenth graders. Graves, Plasencia-Peinado, Deno, and Johnson (2005) reported that the progress of ELL first graders was similar to the progress of other first graders for CBM oral reading fluency (ORF) and nonsense word reading fluency measures. In an urban elementary school, Wiley and Deno (2005) found moderate to moderately strong correlations between the state standards test and both ORF and the maze task for ELLs. Moreover, the ORF measure functioned similarly for the bilingual and English-only groups. Baker and Good (1995) found that ORF was as sensitive to reading growth for bilingual students as it was for English-only students. They concluded that the reliability and validity for ORF were the same for bilingual and English-only students.

SPPS's use of CBM for ELL assessment has proven to be reliable, valid, low cost, feasible, and utilitarian at scale and over time. The remainder of this chapter will describe the process of norm development, explain the use of CBM in SPPS for ELL special education eligibility, and then present the normative data results for the 2007–8 school year.

Saint Paul Public Schools

SPPS serves 39,550 students in grades K–12. Enrollment is diverse: 29.3 percent Asian American, 30.2 percent African American, 25.3 percent Caucasian, 13.3 percent Latino, and 1.8 percent American Indian. Forty-four percent of students speak a home language other than English, and 70 percent are eligible for free and reduced lunch. Seventeen percent receive special education services. The district operates 101 sites including 65 schools and 36 programs.

Special education assessment staff in SPPS have collected district-wide elementary ELL academic norms in the fall, winter, and spring for the 1990–91, 1993–94, 1996–97, 2001–2, and 2007–8 school years. Data have been collected in grades one through six with a sample size of 150–200 ELLs per grade.

District-Wide Special Education Normative Assessment Process for English Language Learners

SPPS Special Education Assessment Resource staff collected district-wide elementary ELL academic normative data in the fall (October), winter (February), and spring (May) of the 2007–8 school year. The purpose was to update data last collected in 2001–2. For the 2007–8 assessments, twenty K–6 schools (out of forty-four in the district) were selected for participation based on ELL enrollment and the availability of special education staff in the schools who were trained to conduct the assessments.

Description of CBM Training and Administrative Process

A four-hour training session was conducted in early October by Special Education Assessment Resource staff for special education teachers in the schools selected for testing. Training included an introduction to the use of CBM; an overview of the district testing process for ELLs; the procedure for identification of students to be included in testing; and description of measures, administration, and scoring procedures. Packets of CBM probes for each grade level and written directions for administration and scoring were prepared and distributed during training. Packets included CBM probes of basic skills in reading, written expression, and mathematics using procedures outlined in Shinn (1989).

Letters from the SPPS director of special education and director of ELL programs were sent to the principals of the schools selected for testing. The letters described the purpose of the testing. In addition, the letter requested the reservation of testing dates and the release of special education staff for training and data collection.

ELL Normative Sample

Letters sent in the fall to the ELL teachers in the twenty schools explained the rationale and process for testing. The letters asked the teachers to provide class lists of the ELLs in their classrooms, identifying students who were receiving special education services and students who had not yet completed three years of school in English. To avoid singling out students, all students were tested, but the data of students receiving special education services or who had not completed three years of school in English were excluded from the norms. Only the scores of students who had either begun school in English in kindergarten or had completed at least three years of school in English were included in the norms.

For winter and spring administrations, the same students were included in addition to any new or transferred students. Total participants across the twenty schools were as follows: first grade (spring only; n = 185), second grade (n = 206), third grade (n = 205), fourth grade (n = 183), fifth grade (n = 189), sixth grade (n = 184).

Data regarding the specific demographics of students selected were not collected. However, except for ELL special education students, SPPS special education staff said students selected for the CBM assessments reflected the demographics of the district with respect to home language.

SPPS ELLs speak more than one hundred languages and non-American English dialects other than American English. The ten non-English languages most frequently spoken are Hmong, Spanish, Somali, Vietnamese, Cambodian, Amharic, Tigrinya, Oromiffa, Karen, and Chinese. Language groups enter the schools in waves or clusters. Hmong speakers began arriving in 1975. The number of Karen speakers has increased since 2006. The length of time in the United States for ELLs ranges from U.S. born to new arrivals from other countries.

CBM Measures

For math computation, students were given a math fact probe common to all grades and grade-level probes consisting of grade-level calculation problems. Both were scored for total number of correct digits.

Story starters were used to assess written expression. Students were given thirty seconds to think and five minutes to write. Stories were scored for total words written, correct word sequences, incorrect word sequences, and correct minus incorrect word sequences.

ORF was assessed through the use of a common probe written at the third-grade level. Special education teachers marked the words read correctly and errors during a one-minute timed reading sample. Errors in pronunciation were counted as incorrect due to the influence of the first language. Students in grades 3–6 were also given three two-minute maze passages written at the third-grade level. Maze passages were scored for number of correct and incorrect word choices. The median score was recorded for both correct and incorrect choices.

Administration and Scoring Process

The special education teachers arranged times with the classroom and English as a second language (ESL) teachers to conduct the testing. Testing was conducted with entire classrooms to avoid removing and singling out students in any way. Testing required approximately two days for each school (about thirty minutes per classroom). All testing for each time frame (fall, winter, and spring) was completed within a two-week period.

After administration, the special education teachers in each school scored all the probes in each packet and recorded the information on a summary cover sheet, which also included the administration date, student's name, school, grade, year of entry into the United States, and any other pertinent data.

After completion of testing in all schools, the packets were collected, reviewed, and spot-checked for scoring accuracy by Special Education Assessment Resource team members. The data were recorded and aggregated for reporting.

The entire process was repeated in the winter and spring of the 2007–8 school year. First graders were added to the spring testing following the same identification process as used in fall and winter.

CBM Normative Sample Results

The results of the testing showed that progress on the measures was evident across grade level (each successive grade was incrementally better than the previous one) and over time (each grade showed incremental progress over the school year). For example, during the fall data collection of ORF, sixth-grade ELLs read fifteen correct words per minute (CWPM) more than fifth graders, fifth graders read seventeen CWPM more than fourth graders, fourth graders read thirty-four CWPM more than third graders, and third-grade students read twenty-nine CWPM more than second graders. The spacing between grades was generally maintained across winter and spring assessments as well.

Progress within grade levels across the twenty-nine weeks from the fall to spring assessment was also evident with respect to CWPM gained. Second graders gained twenty-six CWPM (0.89 words per week) in twenty-nine weeks, third graders gained forty CWPM (1.4 words per week), fourth graders gained twenty-three CWPM (0.79 words per week), fifth graders gained twenty CWPM (0.69 words per week), and sixth graders gained twenty-three CWPM (0.79 words per week).

The gains within grade level over fall, winter, and spring administrations for ELLs also compared favorably with published national ORF norms. Hasbrouck and Tindal (2006) reported fall, winter, and spring ORF data for grades one through six with approximately sixteen thousand students in each grade level. Across the fall, winter, and spring administrations for second to sixth grade, there were gains (respectively) of 1.24, 1.24, 1.0, 1.0, and 0.79 words per week, which was similar to the SPPS ELL data.

SPPS ELL ORF level of performance scores by grade level were also comparable with national norms. For example, fifth-grade fall, winter, and spring ELL scores were 120, 129, and 140 CWPM, respectively. These were similar to the fiftieth percentile fall, winter, and spring data from the national sample (110, 127, and 139 CWPM, respectively). The similarity in performance and progress between SPPS ELLs and the norms reported by Hasbrouck and Tindal (2006) lend support to the validity of the SPPS data and the use of the data as normative standards for the typical academic level and progress of ELLs under consideration for special education services. The performance of ELLs referred for special education services can then be compared to this standard of typical progress.

Example Case of the Use of CBM Data for Determining Special Education Eligibility

The following case study is an example of how CBM is used as part of the ELL special education assessment process.

Kong was a fifth grader. Hmong was his first language. His family entered the United States when he was three. He began learning English in kindergarten. In fifth grade, his English proficiency was still poor. In addition, his progress in reading was slow. He did not retain previously learned skills, and his general performance was inconsistent. He had received ESL pullout instruction, tutoring by a volunteer, and shortened assignments as interventions.

These issues and a lack of response to interventions led to a winter referral for special education evaluation. CBM was conducted as part of the academic assessment. CBM written expression, reading, and math were administered.

In written expression, Kong wrote forty-five correct word sequences in five minutes, similar to the performance of fall scores for a fourth grader. Fifth-grade ELLs typically write sixty-six correct word sequences (see Table 15.1 and Figure 15.1).

TABLE 15.1.

Saint Paul Public Schools ELL academic norms, 2007–8 (student example: Kong)

		MATH						WRITTEN EXPRESSION									READING												
GRADE	# STUDENTS	Math facts			Grade level probe			Total words written			Correct word sequences			Correct minus incorrect word			Maze			Maze incorrect sequences			Common passage oral reading (CWPM)			Common passage errors		
		F	W	S	F	W	S	F	W	S	F	W	S	F	W	S	F	W	S	F	W	S	F	W	S	F	W	S
1		x	x	5	x	x	11	x	x	22	x	x	9	x	x	-1	x	x	x	x	x	x	x	x	37	x	x	9
2	206	5	7	9	11	14	18	29	40	47	12	22	26	-5	3	5	x	x	x	x	x	x	40	52	66	8	7	6
3	205	7	12	14	17	20	23	48	56	60	27	38	41	5	16	17	6	8	9	2	2	2	69	94	109	6	4	4
4	183	13	22	25	38	55	59	56	70	71	42	52	53	20	30	31	8	11	12	1	1	1	103	115	126	4	3	3
5	189	23	29	32	36	39	43	73	86	88	53	66	67	31	40	41	9	12	14	1	1	1	120	129	140	3	3	2
6	184	25	32	37	37	46	50	85	95	97	68	75	81	48	52	55	12	15	17	1	1	1	135	148	158	3	1	2

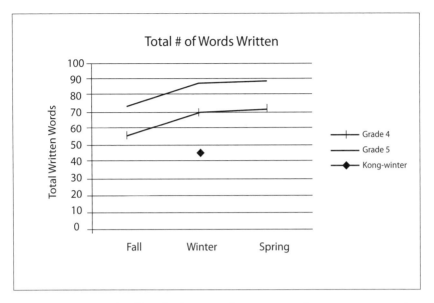

Figure 15.1. Saint Paul Public Schools ELL academic norm results: story starter—total words written, grades four and five

For reading, maze and common reading passages (ORF) were administered. On the maze task, Kong made three correct choices, similar to the fall scores of third graders. Fifth-grade ELLs typically make twelve correct choices. For common reading passages, Kong read forty-five CWPM, similar to fall scores for ELL second graders. Fifth-grade ELL winter scores averaged 129 CWPM (see Table 15.1 and Figures 15.2 and 15.3).

Mixed facts and grade-level facts probes were administered. Kong scored eighteen correct digits on mixed facts, which was similar to the performance of winter scores for fourth-grade ELLs. Fifth-grade ELL winter scores averaged twenty-nine correct digits. He scored twenty-five correct digits on grade-level facts, similar to third-grade winter scores. Fifth-grade ELLs averaged thirty-nine correct digits in the winter (see Table 15.1 and Figures 15.4 and 15.5).

The academic qualification standard used for special education services is that the student must be two times discrepant from his or her grade-level peers and two years behind the current grade placement. Kong's written expression scores were lower than his peers, but the difference was not considered significant. Based on the results of the CBM assessments, this example case indicates that Kong's reading scores met the standard for SPPS special education services. Criterion-referenced testing was also used to verify the CBM results.

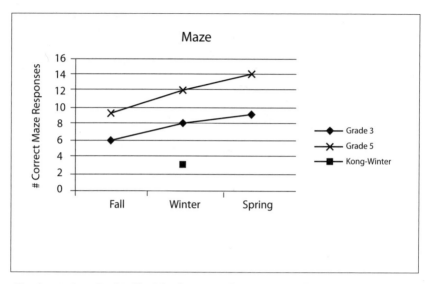

Figure 15.2. Saint Paul Public Schools ELL academic norm results: maze passages, grades three and five

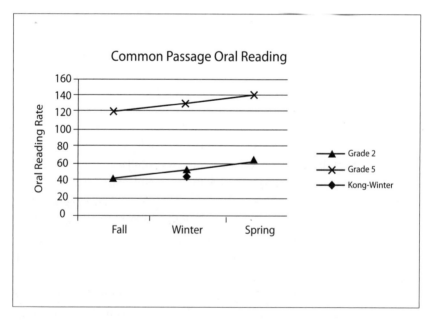

Figure 15.3. Saint Paul Public Schools ELL academic norm results: common passage oral reading, grades two and five

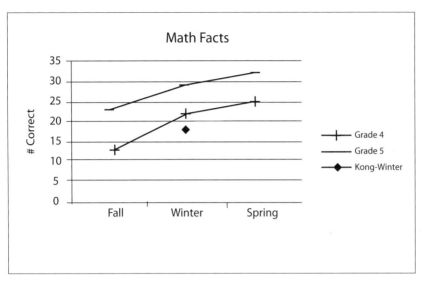

Figure 15.4. Saint Paul Public Schools ELL academic norm results: math fact probes, grades four and five

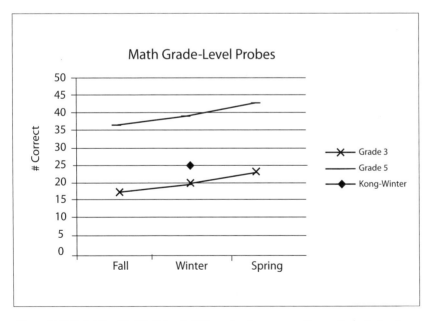

Figure 15.5. Saint Paul Public Schools ELL academic norm results: math grade-level probes, grades three and five

Referral and Evaluation of English Language Learners

Using CBM for academic assessment of Ells in SPPS is one element of a larger decision-making process. It is important to keep this larger process in mind to understand the use of CBM as part of the academic portion of an evaluation.

School psychologists, speech clinicians, special education interpreters, and teachers who participate in all elements and phases of ELL assessment are trained annually in the process. Training focuses on information and knowledge of acculturation, second language acquisition, academic language proficiency, working with interpreters, due process, state regulations, CBM, and principles of measurement. Training also covers basic knowledge of the most common cultures in SPPS.

Before referral to special education, the general education teacher must implement two consecutive eight-week interventions in each area of concern. An online referral form is then completed and processed. Hearing and vision are also checked. The form is sent to a child study team in the school. The team includes at least the principal, a special education teacher, speech clinician, school psychologist, and classroom teacher. The team reviews information, reviews the child's cumulative records, and sends the referral to the Special Education Assessment Resource Team. A highly trained professional special education interpreter conducts a parent interview. The assessment team reviews all information, and a recommendation is made.

An evaluation of communication skills is always conducted. Communication assessments help rule in or out a potential language disorder in the native language. All evaluations of ELLs include gathering language history, evaluating communication skills in the home language, and determining a current level of proficiency in English. Analysis is conducted to derive a picture of the individual's ability to convey meaning appropriate to their age and sociocultural background.

The primary, but not singular, focus of the academic evaluation is CBMs. These measures are used to determine ELLs' present level of performance, instructional level, and performance in comparison to local ELL norms and peers and to monitor progress over time.

The Brigance Comprehensive Inventory of Basic Skills, a criterion-referenced test, is used as an alternative to norm-referenced achievement tests. The tasks provide information about the skills a student can demonstrate and approximately the level of the skills.

The nonverbal subtests of the Wechsler Intelligence Scale for Children—Fourth Edition (WISC IV), Test of Nonverbal Intelligence (TONI), and Universal Nonverbal Intelligence Test are used for intellectual evaluation. The purpose of the intellectual evaluation is to determine the level of functioning, not to establish a norm-referenced IQ score.

Finally, if indicated, an adaptive evaluation of daily living skills is conducted using interview responses with parents based on a questionnaire developed by SPPS special education ELL staff. For Hmong families, this interview is conducted by a Hmong school social worker.

Summary and Discussion

This chapter described the use of CBM by a large urban school district as an important element in making decisions regarding eligibility of ELLs for special education services. For all children, placement in special education should be due to significant learning problems and not other factors. To avoid over- or underidentification of ELLs for special education services, accurate assessments of academic performance are required. Traditional norm-referenced achievement tests are not appropriate due to the biasing effect of limited English.

Research has indicated that CBM provides reliable, valid, and useful information about current levels of performance and progress in math, reading, and writing for ELLs. Poor performance in these areas is the most common reason for referral. CBM can be used to establish current levels of performance for ELLs and to monitor growth over time. More important for eligibility decisions, however, CBM provides appropriate assessment procedures to allow comparisons between ELLs referred for special education services and their limited English peers. Comparing performance to peers allows educators to determine the degree of discrepancy and, therefore, the severity of problem for the child under consideration while ruling out limited English proficiency.

SPPS Special Education Assessment Resource staff has employed CBM for ELL assessment for over twenty-five years. A key part of the process has been to implement a reiterative process to collect ELL CBM district norms. The use of SPPS district norms ensures that the performance comparisons between referred ELLs and their peers are appropriate and valid.

The SPPS special education ELL referral and evaluation process has been identified by the Minnesota State Department of Education as promising practice (Watkins, 2009). According to Minnesota Department of Education data, the representation of ELLs in special education in the district is close to the targeted proportionality of 1.0 (i.e., the proportion of ELLs in special education is the same as the proportion of ELLs in the district). For Asian students the ratio is approximately 0.85 for Specific Learning Disabilities (SLD) and 0.55 (underrepresentation) for all special education categories. For Latino students the ratio is 1.2 for SLD and approximately 0.85 for all special education.

The overall SPPS special education ELL referral, assessment, and evaluation process, including CBM, has proven to be a useful, scalable, effective model for districts with diverse ELL populations. In SPPS, Special Education Assessment Resource staff conducts all training, implementation and administration, scoring, and reporting. The process, including collection of district norms, has become fully institutionalized and maintained internally. Adoption and longevity of such a process in a large urban district is unusual. The success of this model in SPPS demonstrates the utility and importance of CBM for making important educational decisions.

References

Baker, S., & Good, R. (1995). Curriculum-Based Measurement of English reading with bilingual Hispanic students: A validation study with second-grade students. *School Psychology Review*, 24, 561–578.

Duran, R. (2008). Assessing English-language learners' achievement. *Review of Research in Education*, 32(1), 292–327.

Espin, C., Wallace, T., Campbell, H., Lembke, E., Long, J., & Tichá, R. (2008). Curriculum-Based Measurement in writing: Predicting the success of high-school students on state standards tests. *Exceptional Children*, 74(2), 174–193.

Graves, A., Plasencia-Peinado, J., Deno, S., & Johnson, J. (2005). Formatively evaluating the reading progress of first-grade English learners in multiple-language classrooms. *Remedial and Special Education*, 26(4), 215–225. Retrieved September 29, 2009, from Academic Search Premier database.

Hasbrouck, J., & Tindal, G. (2006). Oral reading fluency norms: A valuable assessment tool for reading teachers. *Reading Teacher*, 59(7), 636–644.

Shinn, M. (Ed.). (1989). *Curriculum-Based Measurement: Assessing special children*. New York, NY: Guilford Press.

Watkins, E. (2009, August 31). Personal communication.

Wiley, H., & Deno, S. (2005). Oral reading and maze measures as predictors of success for English learners on a state standards assessment. *Remedial and Special Education*, 26(4), 207–214.

16

A Tribute to Stanley Deno

Curriculum-Based Measurement for English Learners in First Grade

Anne W. Graves

Thank you, Stanley Deno, for bringing your sabbatical leave work to San Diego in 2001–2 and for the development of our investigation of the reading patterns of first-grade English learners at the end of the year using oral reading fluency and nonsense word fluency as Curriculum-Based Measures (CBM). Children and their families here in San Diego have been positively impacted by your work and our research team here at San Diego State University benefited immensely from the collaboration.

As other chapters in this book have recounted, Stanley Deno's work has spanned almost fifty years. His dedication to one line of research has yielded tremendous knowledge development in the area of progress monitoring and provides a seamless transition from research to practice. The field owes a great debt of gratitude to Stanley Deno and colleagues who have demonstrated the use and effectiveness of simple, timed measures. The body of work underscores the relative effectiveness of automaticity as a barometer in oral reading, math computation, and writing.

The purpose of this chapter is to summarize a study inspired by Deno (Graves, Plasencia-Pienado, Deno, and Johnson, 2005) that was conducted to examine norms and thresholds in nine multiple-language first-grade classrooms. The classrooms were termed "multiple-language" because often there were five or six native languages represented, including Spanish, indigenous dialects from Central America, Tagalog, Vietnamese, Hmong, Cambodian, Laotian, Cantonese, Somalian, Sudanese (Dinka language), and French. Bilingual instruction was not possible because of the multiple languages spoken; therefore, the first-grade teachers taught only in English.

Our intent was to extend the work that Russell Gersten, Scott Baker, Claude Goldenberg, myself, and others were doing here in San Diego from 1999 to 2002 in which we investigated literacy development instruction in the fourteen multiple-language classrooms. In our work with Deno, we obtained permission from nine of the teachers to conduct weekly progress monitoring using Oral Reading Fluency (ORF), which was measured using Curriculum-Based Measurement of Reading (CBM-R) for first graders in the final six weeks of school in June and July after the posttesting for the other study had reached completion. The primary purpose was to use Nonsense Word Fluency (NWF) and ORF measures taken from the set of already existing first-grade CBM-R measures, across six weeks, to examine thresholds and patterns of performance compared to non-English learners (Graves et al., 2005). We also wished to determine if either literacy development ratings or language levels could be mediating variables in patterns of performance among the English learners (ELs).

Background Information

ELs in the United States speak nearly five hundred different languages according a survey by Kindler (2002). Though Spanish speakers still total 77 percent of ELs, Vietnamese, Hmong, Korean, Creole (Haitian), Cantonese, Arabic, Russian, Navajo, Tagalog, Khmer (Cambodian), and unspecified Chinese languages represent another 15 percent of ELs. The remaining 8 percent of ELs include fairly large groups of students speaking Middle Eastern, Southeast Asian, South Asian, African, and European languages (Echevarria and Graves, 2010; Kindler, 2002).

Understanding English reading as a process and then deciphering how to teach reading to those who are learning the English language is a daunting task (August and Shannahan, 2006; Linan-Thompson and Ortiz, 2009; Ortiz and Graves, 2001). ELs often encounter the complex burden of attempting to learn to read a language while comprehending rudimentary aspects of that language (Chard and Linan-Thompson, 2008), placing untold cognitive demands on the learner (Fitzgerald and Noblit, 2000). As is the case for all students entering school, reading skills for ELs are the critical foundation for success in academic endeavors (August and Shannahan, 2006). It has been consistently reported that reading difficulties can often lead to special education referrals, and the imprecision and difficulties associated with diagnosing reading difficulties are compounded for ELs (Graves, Gersten, and Haager,

2004; Snow, Burns and Griffin, 1998). However, a number of studies have indicated that explicit reading instruction with a focus on reading subskills is effective for both native speakers and ELs (Gersten, Baker, Haager, and Graves, 2005; Graves, Gersten, and Haagar, 2004; Gunn, Biglan, Smolkowski, and Black, 2002; McIntosh, Graves, and Gersten, 2007). Several second-language studies conducted in Holland (Droop and Vanderhoeven, 2003) and Canada (Chiappe, Siegel, and Wade-Woolsey, 2002; Geva and Wang, 2001; Wade-Woolley and Siegel, 1997) are consistent with the U.S. research indicating that second language learners may learn to read at approximately the same rate as native speakers in the early grades. Our study was designed to extend previous work by examining the reading rates of ELs in multiple-language classrooms using CBM reading and NWF measures.

Method of Stanley Deno–Inspired Study

Setting and Participants

First-grade participants in our study from three elementary schools were largely ELs (98 percent), and 100 percent of them received free or reduced lunch. The classrooms were termed "multiple-language" because often there were five or six languages spoken with reportedly more than twenty-seven languages spoken in the three schools. Teachers taught only in English because it was the common language among the learners.

Using ORF scores from a total pool of 134 students, the three lowest scoring and the three highest scoring readers from each classroom formed the group of low readers (n = 27) and the group of high readers (n = 27) in the study. From the pool of remaining students who read between twenty and fifty words per minute in each classroom, three students were randomly selected to compose the middle group (originally twenty-seven were randomly selected, however, due to attrition, n = 23). The original intent was to select nine students from each of the nine classrooms, however, only students who participated in all six weeks of probes were included in the study (n= 77).

Measures

Reading Measures

To formatively evaluate both ORF and NWF, we used CBM-R to monitor ORF student progress using equivalent standardized grade-level passages and Dynamic Indicators Basic for Early Literacy (DIBELS; Kaminski and Good, 1996) for NWF. As had been done in previous work on ORF (Deno, 1997; Fuchs, Fuchs, Hamlett, Walz, and Germann, 1993; Silberglitt and Hintze, 2007), students read aloud for one minute, and the number of words correctly read were counted. For NWF, students read nonsense words aloud for one minute. The correctly read words were counted, according to consonant-vowel-consonant pronunciation rules.

Observation Measure

The English Language Learner Classroom Observation Instrument (ELL-COI), literacy development ratings for classrooms derived in previous investigations (Gersten, Baker, Haager, and Graves, 2005; Graves, Gersten, and Haager, 2004; McIntosh, Graves, and Gersten, 2007), was used to assess teachers' literacy practices. The literacy practices of the teachers in our study were rated from 1.0 to 4.0 on a Likert scale (for a full description of the ELL-COI, see Gersten et al., 2005).

Language Measure

No district language measures were available that reported English language levels at the end of first grade. We compared the IDEA Proficiency Test (IPT; Ballard, Dalton, and Tighe, 1995) scores given in kindergarten to gains on ORF and NWF. The test assisted the district in the designation of students as Non-English Speaker, Limited English Speaker, or Fluent English Speaker. The IPT tests four basic areas: vocabulary, comprehension, syntax, and verbal expression.

Procedures

Once a week, trained assessors administered the ORF and NWF measures to all seventy-seven students individually. Students in nine classrooms were taken out of the room for three or four minutes a week to be assessed for six weeks.

Results

A complete report of the results can be found in the published paper (Graves et al., 2005). A brief summary of the results is included here.

1. What ORF and NWF levels may be expected at the end of first grade for ELs in multiple-language settings?

The correlation between ORF and NWF at the end of the six-week period during the last month of first grade was strong ($r = .86$). However, the correlation between the gain on ORF and the gain on NWF across the six weeks was moderately weak ($r = .302$).

ORF Performances

An achievement status (low, middle, and high)-by-time repeated-measures analysis of variance ANOVA designed to investigate the number of words read revealed a significant interaction, $F (10, 74) = 4.22$, $p < .01$, and significant main effects both for groups, $F (2, 74) = 51.67$, $p < .01$, and for weekly ORF scores, $F (5, 74) = 36.6$, $p < .01$. The significant interaction indicates that ORF gains occurred in different patterns within achievement status on different passages across the six weeks. The average weekly ORF gain for the low group was 2.8 words per minute (wpm), 3.6 wpm for the middle group, and 1.8 wpm for the high group. The average weekly gain for all groups was 2.75 wpm. However, eight students in the low group gained four or fewer wpm across six weeks.

NWF Performances

An achievement status (low, middle, and high)-by-time repeated-measures ANOVA designed to investigate the number of nonsense words read revealed a significant interaction, $F (10, 74) = 3.57$, $p < .01$, and significant main effects both for groups, $F (2, 74) = 28.48$, $p < .01$, and for weekly NWF scores, $F (5, 74) = 37.6$, $p < .01$. Similar to the ORF findings, the significant interaction indicates that NWF gains occurred in a different pattern within achievement groups and on different nonsense word measures across the six weeks. Unlike the oral reading slopes, however, the NWF slopes increased consistent with group membership. The mean slope for students in the high group was the highest of the three slopes, and low group slope was the lowest. It is interesting to note that the ORF and NWF slopes for the low group were quite similar.

2. What is the nature of the relationship between teacher effectiveness and reading gain in the last six weeks of first grade?

We found a weak correlation between the ELLCOI ratings of literacy practices and gain scores on ORF ($r = -.06$). Similarly, we found a weak correlation between the ELLCOI classroom ratings and gain scores on NWF ($r = .15$). Thus our findings did not indicate that the strength of the classroom practices was related to the amount gained by students on ORF and Nonsense Word Fluency during the six-week period at the end of the school year. Examinations of fluency data by classroom indicate that gains were evenly distributed across students and groups; that is, teacher ratings did not appear to contribute to the amount students gained in fluency.

3. What is the nature of the relationship between language measures taken in kindergarten and reading gain in the last six weeks of first grade?

We found a weak correlation between the IPT scores from the beginning of kindergarten and ORF gains during the final six weeks of first grade ($r = .166$); similarly, we found a weak correlation between those same IPT scores and NWF gains in the final six weeks of school ($r = -.034$). Also, correlations were weak between the IPT score from beginning of kindergarten and the end-of-first-grade ORF score ($r = .062$) and end-of-first-grade NWF score ($r = .69$).

Discussion

The results of this study seem to indicate that reading fluency in ELs in multiple-language classrooms is similar to that of non-ELs (Fuchs et al., 1993; Silberglitt and Hintze, 2007) and that English language level of the students and skill of the teacher do *not* appear to be mediating variables. Further, in this case, ORF and NWF appear to be useful tools in identifying first grade students who might benefit from intensive instruction at the beginning of second grade.

Educational Implications and Future Research

Our study suggests that CBM can be a useful tool in assessing gains in reading for ELs, and the gains are similar to those for non-English learners. There is some evidence here that progress monitoring in and of itself may produce some positive effects given the inference that teacher ratings and language levels did not appear to be mediating variables. Perhaps due to the opportunity for practice reading aloud weekly, students progressed. An important point that should not be underestimated, and is a question for future research, is this: what is the potential power of individual reading out loud, particularly for ELs? Repeated trials of ORF and NWF provided a format and routine for speaking English out loud with individualized corrections. The modeling and practice of English reading regularly may have benefits to ELs perhaps even beyond those for non-ELs.

Stanley Deno's contributions to this study and to the field are irrefutable because his work on the measurement of fluency in different contexts continues to inform practice. However, as we begin to understand more about the interplay of literacy skills and language in the reading development of ELs, questions remain. Recently, Kung (2009) explored the relationship between ORF and passing a state-level achievement test and found that ELs who achieved the same ORF rate as their monolingual peers did not score as well on the state achievement test. This finding led Kung to posit that ORF may need to be coupled with reading comprehension and vocabulary development to improve scores on high-stakes tests, which is a logical conclusion. The need for continued instruction in academic language and test taking is critical, and these skills are *not* necessary on the typical CBM measures, so it makes sense that ELs need other skills for high-stakes testing and advanced academic achievement.

That said, our study indicates that ORF thresholds for non-English learners hold as a standard for ELs as well. With established fluency thresholds at forty wpm or more for first grade (Fuchs et al., 1993), our study suggests that the same threshold with a range of roughly twenty to sixty wpm is accurate for ELs in multiple-language settings. When an EL cannot read fluently, often it is because of limited decoding knowledge, limited vocabulary, limited syntax knowledge, and limited experience with reading in English. Fluency is something one can't guess about and one can't fake the results of. If someone reads fluently up to threshold standards, there is still a chance that reading comprehension performance on a test will not meet grade-level thresholds and standards. However, if someone meets reading comprehension thresholds and standards it is highly unlikely that the person would miss the ORF threshold for the grade.

It may be that while ORF is necessary for ensuring that students develop adequate foundational skills, there is also a need for the continued development of CBMs that measure the development of more complex reading skills such as comprehension and language component skills. Future research in these areas is critical but should not diminish the value and relative importance of the correlations of ORF to comprehension and the use of ORF as a measure of reading skill. In addition to the multiple generations of teachers and researchers who have been inspired by Stanley Deno, perhaps his greatest legacy is his tenacity and myopic pursuit of evidence to support the utility of ORF as a critical indicator of reading. Our work lends evidence to this simple truth, and Stanley Deno will not soon be forgotten.

References

August, D., & Shannahan, T. (2006). *Improving schooling for language-minority children.* Washington, DC: National Academies Press.

Ballard, W. S., Dalton, E. F., & Tighe, P. L. (1995). *IDEA oral language proficiency test in English* (5th ed.). Los Angeles, CA: Ballard and Tighe.

Chard, D., & Linan-Thompson, S. (2008). Introduction to the special series on systematic, multitier models: Emerging research on factors that support prevention of reading difficulties. *Journal of Learning Disabilities, 41,* 99–100.

Chiappe, P., Siegel, L. S., & Wade-Woolsey, L. (2002). Linguistic diversity and the development of reading skills: A longitudinal study. *Scientific Studies of Reading, 6,* 369–400.

Deno, S. L. (1997). "Whether" thou goest: Perspectives on progress monitoring. In J. W. Lloyd, E. J. Kameenuii, & D. Chard (Eds.), *Issues in educating students with disabilities* (pp. 77–100). New York, NY: Lawrence Erlbaum Associates.

Droop, M., & Verhoeven, L. T. (2003). Language proficiency and reading ability in first- and second-language learners. *Reading Research Quarterly, 38*(1), 78–103.

Echevarria, J., & Graves, A. (2010). *Sheltered content instruction: Teaching English-language learners with diverse abilities* (4th ed.). Needham Heights, MA: Allyn & Bacon.

Fitzgerald, J., & Noblit, G. W. (2000). Balance in the making: Learning to read in an ethnically diverse first-grade classroom. *Journal of Educational Psychology, 92,* 1–20.

Fuchs, L. S., Fuchs, D., Hamlett, C. L., Walz, L., & Germann, G. (1993). Formative evaluation of academic progress: How much growth can we expect? *School Psychology Review, 22,* 27–48.

Gersten, R., Baker, S., Haager, D., & Graves, A. W. (2005). Exploring the role of teacher quality in predicting reading outcomes for first grade English learners: An observational study. *Remedial and Special Education, 38,* 212–222.

Geva, E., & Wang, M. (2001). The role of orthography in the literacy acquisition of young L2 learners. *Annual Review of Applied Linguistics, 21,* 182–204.

Graves, A. W., Gersten, R., & Haager, D. (2004). Literacy instruction in multiple-language first-grade classrooms: Linking student outcomes to observed instructional practice. *Learning Disabilities Research and Practice, 19,* 262–272.

Graves, A. W., Plasencia-Peinado, J., Deno, S., & Johnson, J. (2005). Formatively evaluating the reading progress of first-grade English learners in multiple language classrooms. *Remedial and Special Education, 38,* 245–255.

Gunn, B., Smolkowski, K., Biglan, A., & Black, C. (2002). Supplemental instruction in decoding skills for Hispanic and non-Hispanic students in early elementary school: A follow-up. *Journal of Special Education, 36,* 69–79.

Kaminski, R., & Good, R. H., III. (1996). Toward a technology for assessing basic early literacy skills. *School Psychology Review, 25,* 215–227.

Kindler, A. (2002). *Survey of the states' limited English proficient students and available educational programs and services: 2000–2001 summary report.* Washington, DC: National Clearinghouse for English Language Acquisition.

Kung, S. H. (2009). *Predicting the success on a state standards test for culturally and linguistically diverse students using curriculum-based oral reading measures.* Unpublished doctoral dissertation, University of Minnesota, Minneapolis.

Linan-Thompson, S., & Ortiz, A. A. (2009). Response to intervention and English language learners: Instructional and assessment considerations. *Seminars in Speech and Language, 30,* 105–120.

McIntosh, A., Graves, A., & Gersten, R. (2007). The effects of response to intervention on literacy development in multiple language settings. *Learning Disability Quarterly, 30,* 197–212.

Ortiz, A., & Graves, A. W. (2001). English language learners with literacy-related learning disabilities. *International Dyslexia Association Commemorative Booklet, 58,* 31–36.

Silberglitt, B., & Hintze, J. M. (2007). A conditional analysis of R-CBM growth rates by level of performance. *Exceptional Children, 74*(1), 71–84.

Snow, C. S., Burns, S. M., & Griffin, P. (1998). *Preventing reading difficulties in young children.* Washington, DC: National Academies Press.

Wade-Woolley, L., & Siegel, L. S. (1997). The spelling performance of ESL and native speakers of English as a function of reading skill. *Reading and Writing: An Interdisciplinary Journal, 9,* 387–406.

17

Extending Curriculum-Based Measurement to Assess Performance of Students with Significant Cognitive Disabilities

Teri Wallace and Renáta Tichá

Background

Dr. Stanley Deno changed education when he and colleagues developed Curriculum-Based Measurement (CBM; Deno, 1985) in the 1980s. Since those initial years, CBM has been expanded in a variety of ways, all working toward providing educators with data to make informed instructional decisions about the performance and progress of students. One such expansion has been the recent development of General Outcome Measures (GOMs; of which CBM is a form) for students with significant cognitive disabilities—a term used to describe a group of students who both have an identified disability and who participate in state standards assessments through the alternate assessment based on alternate achievement standards. This chapter describes the challenges to teaching and assessing students with significant cognitive disabilities, as well as including them in state standards accountability. It goes on to describe the reading development and literacy framework used in two pilot studies examining newly developed GOMs, some initial results, and the need for future research.

Challenges to Teaching Students with Significant Cognitive Disabilities

There are a variety of challenges to teaching and assessing the performance and progress of students with significant cognitive disabilities. Recently, the field has focused on supporting students with significant cognitive disabilities in accessing the core curriculum. As this happened, teachers, administrators, and researchers realized that students were exceeding existing expectations. Specifically, students were showing reading, writing, speaking, and listening skills beyond what was anticipated (e.g., Kliewer, 1998; Ryndak, Morrison, and Sommerstein, 1999). In fact, as we move into the twenty-first century, students with significant cognitive disabilities are learning and doing more than many thought possible. Capturing this learning through assessment is important but challenging, and CBM might offer a solution.

Reading instruction for students with significant cognitive disabilities has most typically focused on sight words for functional reading. Browder (2001) defined the characteristics of functional reading as (1) the acquisition of specific sight words that have immediate functional use, (2) an alternative way to learn reading skills when literacy is not being achieved, and (3) a way to gain quick success in reading that could promote future reading. While research has found that students with significant cognitive disabilities can learn sight words (Browder and Xin, 1998) and are able to use them when cooking (Collins, Branson, and Hall, 1995), reading labels (Collins and Griffen, 1996), and self-instructing on the job (Browder and Minarovic, 2000), sight word instruction alone has several limitations. Browder, Courtade-Little, Wakerman, and Rickelman (2006) summarized some of these limitations with supporting research: (a) Browder and Xin (1998) found that most studies using sight words have not measured comprehension or functional use; (b) Conners (1992) and Katims (2000) suggest that reading instruction in general education requires gathering meaning from print rather than simply identifying a word; (c) Joseph and Seery (2004) found that sight-word instruction focuses on the whole-word recognition in absence of phonetic understanding; (d) Groff, Lapp, and Flood (1998) suggest explicit phonetic instruction for those struggling to read; and (e) Joseph and Seery (2004) found, in a review of the literature, that students with mental retardation can learn phonics skills but little research has been done in this area. In their chapter, Browder et al. (2006) conclude that it is not necessary to choose between a functional and a literacy-based approach to reading. They suggest that both can benefit students with significant cognitive disabilities in addition to information about literacy concepts, such as concept of print, words, and letters. In summary, they write that students need a balanced approach to literacy instruction, including alphabetic and phonological awareness, as well as shared reading and writing, guided reading and writing, and independent reading and writing (Ehri, 2000; Katims, 2001).

Literacy is important for all children, and while there has been debate over the components of reading and how it is best taught, its value has not been challenged (National Research Council, 1998; National Reading Panel, 2000). However, as noted earlier, the use of a separate functional curriculum for students with severe disabilities has been prominent since the 1980s (Browder and Spooner, 2006). It was not until the requirements of the No Child Left Behind Act (NCLB; 2002) were established that educators and researchers understood an increased focus on academics would be needed, even for students who take the alternate assessment.

Challenges to Inclusion in State Accountability Systems

The reauthorization of the Individuals with Disabilities Education Act (IDEA; 2004) and guidelines for using alternate assessments with alternate achievement standards for NCLB (Federal Register, December 9, 2003) both require determining adequate yearly progress for students with significant cognitive disabilities. Alternate assessments, in general, are intended for use with students with disabilities who are unable to participate meaningfully in general state and district assessment systems, even with accommodations and modifications (Roach and Elliott, 2006). Alternate assessments based on alternate achievement standards are intended for students with significant cognitive disabilities who cannot meet typical grade-level achievement standards. Noted by Roach and Elliott (2006), many states have struggled to develop alternate assessments that meet federal mandates for two primary reasons. First, the skills and concepts in the state academic standards were considered inappropriate or irrelevant for students with significant cognitive disabilities, which resulted in alternate assessments that focused on functional domains, and second, the development of alternate assessments was considered a special education function and deemed to be only somewhat connected to states' overall assessment systems.

While portfolios and mastery monitoring strategies have been used as alternate assessments, each has its limitations. CBM or GOM may be useful solutions as there is substantial evidence for their use with students with learning disabilities, to show both performance level and growth as well as to predict future performance (see Marston, 1989; Stecker, Fuchs, and Fuchs, 2005; Wayman, Wallace, Wiley, Tichá, and Espin, 2007). In addition, newly developed GOMs may be used in an individual student growth model for accountability as a value-added component to the existing alternate assessment. Capturing the performance and progress of students with significant cognitive disabilities in a meaningful way is important and GOMs may provide an avenue.

Support for Use of General Outcome Measures within Chall's Framework

In general, assessing the academic performance and progress of students with significant cognitive disabilities has long been a challenge to the field of education (Browder and Spooner, 2006). The information gained from using traditional standardized tests with students with significant cognitive disabilities may not provide useful information for teachers to use in educational decision making (Allinder and Siegel, 1999; Duncan, Sbardellati, Maheady, and Sainato, 1981; Sigafoos, Cole, and McQuarter, 1987). Additional assessment strategies may supplement traditional standardized tests, including criterion-referenced tests, adaptive behavior scales, observations, fluency measures, interviews, and others. These may provide useful data for educational decision making. Another useful assessment strategy is the recent work on CBM and GOM.

Initially we considered using CBM as the approach to measuring performance and progress. However, we later determined CBM had certain limitations that could affect its appropriateness for students who were not verbal, who usually had instruction focused on functional sight words rather than academic reading, and for whom consensus regarding progress within the general curriculum had not yet been determined. Therefore, we decided to use measures that provided an indicator of the general outcome area of reading. The intent was to create valid and reliable measures to assess students' progress in reading that link with state standards, as well as their Individualized Education Program (IEP) goals to provide teachers with information they could use to judge students' yearly progress and make meaningful instructional decisions throughout the year. However, students with significant cognitive disabilities do not typically follow a "grade-level" curriculum, and little is known about their reading potential. Therefore, we needed a framework to guide our thinking about measure development and found Chall's model useful in this regard.

Chall's model of reading development (1996) provides a framework for recognizing the possible usefulness of measures found to be applicable for typically developing emergent and early readers as well as for students with significant disabilities in a similar stage. For example, a letter identification measure—associated with Chall's Stage 0 (Pre-Reading) and often used in kindergarten—might assess performance of a fourth-grade student with significant cognitive disabilities who is at that developmental reading stage. However, determining whether this framework holds true for students with significant cognitive disabilities must be examined and the associated factors identified.

Extending CBM to Students with Significant Cognitive Disabilities: Measure Development and Some Results

As noted earlier, the instruction for students with significant cognitive disabilities has a history of focusing on functional skills, assessed primarily using mastery monitoring and task analysis. With the increasing emphasis on accountability and tying instruction for students with significant cognitive disabilities to general education standards, there is a need to develop assessments that are reliable and valid but also sufficiently sensitive to the improvement of these students in reading. Because of the recent shift in emphasis in teaching students with significant cognitive disabilities, research in this area is sparse. Al Otaiba and Hosp (2004), Tindal et al. (2003), and Wallace and Tichá (2007b) have recently begun work on developing progress measures in reading.

Al Otaiba and Hosp (2004) used CBM as one of their assessment measures to monitor progress while implementing a tutoring model with students with Down syndrome. Al Otaiba and Hosp used two CBMs typically recommended for beginning readers—letter sounds and passage reading—and added a third, more specific to the target skills for the participants, which was a measure including sight words. Additionally, Tindal et al. (2005) examined the possibility of developing a set of standardized tasks (CBM measures) for students with disabilities, which would assess the same construct as that of large-scale assessments. While successful, they did not include students with significant cognitive disabilities but provided support for the idea.

Wallace and Tichá (2007b) and Wallace, Tichá, and Gustafson (2008) have conducted initial pilot studies on the development and validation of GOMs in reading for use with students with significant cognitive disabilities. Because of the specific learning characteristics of the target population, Wallace, Tichá, and the research team at the University of Minnesota spent approximately three-quarters of a year simply researching and planning the format and administration procedures for the newly developed GOMs. Students with significant cognitive disabilities range broadly in their ability levels, both physically and intellectually. Consequently, the stimulus material requires students to be able to access the GOMs by any form of pointing. Following Chall's model of reading development, the GOM stimulus material content and structure was diversified by difficulty (i.e., from pictures to words and from matching to identification) to avoid ceiling or floor effects. In order to maximize student success in responding to the GOM stimulus material, a four-level prompting system—from an unaided response to physical guidance of the student's hand to point—was implemented. The question of timed measures used with students with significant cognitive disabilities also had to be examined. Taking into account opposing views of the appropriateness of timed versus untimed measures for students with significant cognitive disabilities, the time limit of measure administration was extended in the initial pilot study from the traditional one- to three-minute CBM reading measures to ten minutes. Finally, reflecting the shift in instructional focus for this population from largely functional to more academic as described earlier, the researchers faced a challenge when searching for appropriate criterion measures to be able to establish validity of the GOMs.

The purpose of the initial pilot study with thirteen students was to assess the feasibility of the format and content of the proposed GOMs for students with significant cognitive disabilities. The age range of the students was K–12. The primary disability label of the students was developmental cognitive disability (DCD) as identified in the students' IEPs. The results of the study showed that the format of the GOMs (i.e., 8.5-×-11-inch laminated cards) was suitable. The students were able to follow the administration directions and respond to the testing items of the GOMs by pointing. In most cases, prompts at levels 1, 2, and 3 were not required for the test items. A prompt was provided only on 3 percent of the total GOM cards administered. A three-minute administration was more appropriate for a thirty-card measure administration than longer time frames of seven and ten minutes as some students were able to finish before the time limit and students tended to lose their attention with time.

Based on the results of the first pilot study—Wallace and Tichá (2007b)—Wallace, Tichá, and Gustafson (2008) conducted a second pilot study with twenty-nine students across two years. Students ranged from K through grade 11 with DCD as the primary disability label. The purpose of the second study was to examine the technical adequacy of eight GOMs in reading (i.e., Functional Pictures and Signs, Mixed Letter Identification, Fry Sight Words Identification, K–4 Science Word Matching, K–4 Science Word Identification, Onsets, Rimes, and Simple Sentence Maze) administered with the same principles as the GOMs in the first pilot study. The GOMs in this two-year study, however, consisted of sixty rather than thirty cards and were administered for three minutes with a score recorded at one minute as well. Even though the results need to be interpreted cautiously because of the small and diverse sample, results of the study indicate promising reliability, criterion validity, and growth characteristics of the GOMs for students with significant cognitive disabilities. The average interobserver and interscorer reliability was 99.6 percent and 98.1 percent, respectively. Test-retest reliability coefficients ranged from $r = .75$ (Rimes) to $r = .95$ (K–4 Science Word Identification).

Establishing criterion validity of the newly developed GOMs was a more challenging task as measures that may be considered "gold standard," such as norm-referenced standardized measures of reading specifically for students with significant cognitive disabilities, are not available. Consequently, two commercially developed criterion measures, the Woodcock-Johnson Letter-Word Identification subtest (WJ-LW; Woodcock, 1987, 1998) and the Peabody Picture Vocabulary Test-III (PPVT-III) were chosen for the study on basis of (1) having students with significant cognitive disabilities or mental retardation in the norming sample and (2) containing reading or prereading tasks at the ability levels of the students in the study. Based on the suggestions of our advisory panel, dissatisfaction with the commercially developed criterion possibilities, and the more individualized nature of the teacher-student relationship with the students in the study, the researchers created the Early Literacy Knowledge and Reading Readiness Checklist (the Checklist; Wallace and Tichá, 2007a), which was completed by special education teachers with the aim to provide teachers with input regarding items associated with student literacy knowledge. In addition, the Minnesota state alternate test, the Test of Academic Skills in reading (Minnesota Department of Education, 2008), developed specifically for students with significant cognitive disabilities was used as a criterion measure. Based on the overall validity results with the different criterion measures, four GOMs appear to have the best potential for use as efficient indicators of student performance in the classroom. The validity coefficients for the four measures ranged as follows: Rimes ($r = .29–.79$), K–4 Science Word Identification ($r = .27–.89$), Simple Sentence Maze ($r = .22–.87$), and Fry Word Identification ($r = .28–.83$).

Student growth on all but two GOMs (Rimes and Onsets) was significant between the beginning and end of the study in year 1, with the greatest growth found on Functional Pictures and Signs, Mixed Letter Identification, and Fry Word Identification. The rate of growth for those three GOMs was between 1.2 and 1.4 pictures, letters, or words a month in year 1. Surprisingly, growth in year 2 was not significant on any of the GOMs. In addition, on four of the GOMs (except Simple Sentence Maze and Rimes; K–4 Science Word Matching was not administered in year 2) there was a decrease in student performance over the summer months ranging from 0.15 correct responses on Functional Pictures and Signs to 3.77 correct responses on Onsets. The results—while limited in their generalizability due to a small and diverse sample—suggest that GOMs may be a promising tool for special educators and general educators to use to assess, predict, and possibly monitor reading progress of students with significant cognitive disabilities. There is, however, a strong need for more research in this area.

Future Research Can Increase Promise

Students with significant cognitive disabilities—that is, those who take the alternate assessment based on alternate achievement standards—struggle with various needs, such as being nonverbal, experiencing physical and cognitive challenges, and more. Therefore, it is important to develop measures that have universal access (Gramm, 2007; National Center on Educational Outcomes). In other words, consideration must be given to the stimulus and response requirements of this student population (Buekelman and Miranda, 1998; Browder and Spooner, 2006; Koppenhaver, 2000; Kovach and Kenyon, 2003; McEwen, 1997). In addition, students with significant cognitive disabilities do not typically follow a "grade-level" curriculum. In fact, Al Otaiba and Fuchs (2002) suggest there is little information about predictors of future reading success for this population of students, yet we know there are significant individual differences in how students respond to instruction. Reading instruction for students with significant cognitive disabilities has most typically focused on sight words for functional reading, though Browder, Courtade-Little et al. (2006) conclude that it is not necessary to choose between a functional and a literacy-based approach to reading. They suggest both can benefit students with significant cognitive disabilities in addition to information about literacy concepts, such as concept of print, words, and letters. Both types of instruction should occur and technically adequate assessments should exist to measure performance (level) and progress (growth). Therefore, research is needed to develop valid and reliable and accessible measures for students with significant cognitive disabilities in reading (Browder et al., 2006).

There is presently no consensus regarding the progress students with significant cognitive disabilities should make within the general education curriculum, including performance and progress on state standards and assessments. Therefore, measures that can be linked to grade-level standards should be developed and examined for their technical adequacy and for use in assessing performance (level) and progress (growth). GOMs designed for young, typically developing readers may be appropriate for use with older students with significant cognitive disabilities who are at a similar developmental reading level. Understanding the complexity of factors that influence students' reading and writing development is challenging. Therefore, examination of the use of measures within subgroups should occur, and existing variance must be studied.

Initial work suggests promise regarding the reliability and validity of the newly developed GOMs; however, research will be needed to determine their practicality—will teachers use them for progress monitoring and adapting their instruction? Administration directions, prompting guidelines, and response requirements have an impact on the daily demands facing teachers; therefore, additional examination is needed though this approach to assessment and its practical utility appears promising.

Including students with significant cognitive disabilities in state standards assessments for accountability is required and necessary, and finding a way to do so that makes sense for students is critical. Even more important is determining a way to measure students' performance and progress in key academic areas—providing teachers and others with valid and reliable information to enhance their instruction, and ultimately to enhance student success. Teachers involved in this research continually expressed their surprise, optimism, and deep gratitude for development of measures for use with their students, which gave us a lot of encouragement to further our work. Dr. Deno's work has set the stage for many to follow and for some to expand. We are grateful.

References

Al Otaiba, S., & Fuchs, D. (2002). Characteristics of children who are unresponsive to early literacy intervention. *Remedial and Special Education, 23*(5), 300–316.

Al Otaiba, S., & Hosp, M. (2004). Providing effective literacy instruction to students with Down syndrome. *Teaching Exceptional Children, 36*(4), 28–35.

Allinder, R. M., & Siegel, E. (1999). "Who is Brad?" Preservice teacher's perception of summarizing assessment information about a student with moderate disabilities.

Education and Training in Mental Retardation and Developmental Disabilities, 34(2), 157–169.

Browder, D. (2001). Functional reading. In B. Wilson and D. Browder (Eds.), *Curriculum and assessment for students with moderate and severe disabilities* (pp. 179–214). New York, NY: Guilford Press.

Browder, D., & Xin, P. Y. (1998). A meta-analysis and review of sight word research and its implications for teaching functional reading to individuals with moderate and severe disabilities. *Journal of Special Education, 32,* 130–153.

Browder, D. M., Courtade-Little, G., Wakerman, S., & Rickelman, R. J. (2006). From sight words to emerging literacy. In D. M. Browder & F. Spooner (Eds.), *Teaching language arts, math, and science to students with significant cognitive disabilities* (pp. 63–91). Baltimore, MD: Paul H. Brookes.

Browder, D. M., & Minarovic, T. (2000). Utilizing sight words in self-instruction training for employees with moderate mental retardation in competitive jobs. *Education and Training in Mental Retardation and Developmental Disabilities, 35,* 78–89.

Browder, D. M., & Spooner, F. (2006). *Teaching language arts, math, and science to students with significant cognitive disabilities.* Baltimore, MD: Paul H. Brookes.

Browder, D. M., Wakeman, S. Y., Spooner, F., Ahlgrim-Delzell, L., & Algozzine, B. (2006). Research on reading instruction for individuals with significant cognitive disabilities. *Exceptional Children, 72,* 392–408.

Buekelman, D., & Mirenda, P. (1998). *Augmentative and alternative communication: Management of severe communication disorders in children and adults.* Baltimore, MD: Paul H. Brookes.

Chall, J. S. (1996). *Stages of Reading Development* (2nd ed.). Fort Worth, TX: Harcourt Brace.

Collins, B. C., Branson, T. A., & Hall, M. (1995). Teaching generalized reading of cooking product labels to adolescents with mental disabilities through the use of key words taught by peer tutors. *Education and Training in Mental Retardation and Developmental Disabilities, 30,* 65–75.

Collins, B. C., & Griffen, A. K. (1996). Teaching students with moderate disabilities to make safe responses to product warning labels. *Education and Treatment of Children, 19,* 30–45.

Conners, F. A. (1992). Reading instruction for students with moderate mental retardation: Review and analysis of research. *American Journal on Mental Retardation, 96*(6), 577–597.

Deno, S. L. (1985). Curriculum-Based Measurement: The emerging alternative. *Exceptional Children, 52,* 219–232.

Duncan, D., Sbardellati, E., Maheady, L., & Sainato, D. (1981). Nondiscriminatory assessment of severely physically handicapped individuals. *Journal of the Association of the Severely Handicapped, 6,* 17–22.

Ehri, L. C. (2000). Learning to read and learning to spell: Two sides of a coin. *Topics of Language Disorders, 20*(3), 19–36.

Gramm, S. (2007). *Cracking the code: IDEA and NCLB alternate assessment rules made simple.* Horsham, PA: LRP Publications.

Groff, P., Lapp, D., & Flood, J. (1998). Where is the phonics? Making a case for its direct and systematic instruction. *Reading Teacher, 52,* 138–141.

Individuals with Disabilities Education Act (1997), P.L. No. 105–117.

Individuals with Disabilities Education Improvement Act (2004), P.L. No. 108–446, 20 U.S.C. section 611–614.

Joseph, L., & Seery, M. E. (2004). Where is the phonics? *Remedial and Special Education, 25*(2), 88–94.

Katims, D. S. (2000). *The quest for literacy: Curriculum and instructional procedures for teaching reading and writing to students with mental retardation and developmental disabilities.* MRDD Prism Series (Vol. 2). Reston, VA: The Council for Exceptional Children.

Kliewer, C. (1998). Citizenship in the literate community: An ethnography of children with Down syndrome and the written word. *Exceptional Children, 64,* 167–180.

Koppenhaver, D. A. (2000). Literacy in AAC: What should be written on the envelope we push? *Augmentative and Alternative Communication, 16,* 270–279.

Kovach, T. M., & Kenyon, P. B. (2003). Visual issues and access to AAC. In J. C. Light, D. R. Beukelman, & J. Reichle (Eds.), *Communicative competence for individuals who use AAC: From research to effective practice* (pp. 277–319). Baltimore, MD: Paul H. Brookes.

Marston, D. (1989). A Curriculum-Based Measurement approach to assessing academic performance: What it is and why do it. In M. Shinn (Ed.), *Curriculum-Based Measurement: Assessing special children* (pp. 18–78). New York, NY: Guilford Press.

McEwen, I. R. (1997). Seating, other positioning and motor control. In L. Lloyd, D. Fuller, & H. Arvidson (Eds.), *Augmentative and alternative communication: A handbook of principles and practices* (pp. 280–298). Needham Heights, MA: Allyn & Bacon.

Minnesota Department of Education. (2008). *Minnesota Test of Academic Skills (MTAS): An alternate assessment for students with the most significant cognitive disabilities.* Division for Research and Assessment: Roseville, MN.

National Reading Panel. (2000). *Teaching children to read: An evidence-based assessment of the scientific research literature on reading and its implications for reading instruction.* Washington, DC: National Institute of Child Health and Human Development.

National Research Council. (1998). *Preventing reading difficulties in young children*. Washington, DC: National Academies Press.

No Child Left Behind Act (2001), Pub. L. No. 107– 110, 115 Stat. 1425.

Roach, A. T., & Elliott, S. N. (2006). The influence of access to general education curriculum on alternate assessment performance of students with significant cognitive disabilities. *Educational Evaluation and Policy Analysis, 28*(2), 181–194.

Ryndak, D. L., Morrison, A. P., & Sommerstein, L. (1999). Literacy before and after inclusion in general education settings: A case study. *Journal of the Association for Persons with Severe Handicaps, 24*, 5–22.

Sigafoos, J., Cole, D. A., & McQuarter, R. (1987). Current practices in the assessment of students with severe handicaps. *Journal of the Association for Persons with Severe Handicaps, 12*(4), 264–273.

Stecker, P. M., Fuchs, L. S., & Fuchs, D. (2005). Using Curriculum-Based Measurement to improve student achievement: Review of research. *Psychology in the Schools, 42*, 795–819.

Tindal, G., McDonald, M., Tedesco, M., Glasgow, A., Almond, P., & Crawford, L. (2003). Alternate assessments in reading and math: Development and validation for students with significant disabilities. *Exceptional Children, 69, 481–494.*

Wallace, T., & Tichá, R. (2007a). *Early literacy knowledge and reading readiness checklist—Version II*. Unpublished assessment.

Wallace, T., & Tichá, R. (2007b). *General Outcome Measures for students with significant cognitive disabilities: Pilot study*. Unpublished manuscript, University of Minnesota, Minneapolis.

Wallace, T., Tichá, R., & Gustafson, K. (2008). *Technical characteristics of General Outcome Measures (GOMs) for students with significant cognitive disabilities*. Manuscript submitted for publication.

Wayman, M. M., Wallace, T., Wiley, H. I., Tichá, R., & Espin, C. A. (2007).c Literature synthesis on Curriculum-Based Measurement in reading. *Journal of Special Education, 41*(2), 85–120.

Woodcock, R. W. (1987). *Woodcock reading mastery test—Revised*. Circle Pines, MN: American Guidance Service.

Woodcock, R. W. (1998). *Woodcock reading mastery tests—Revised*. Circle Pines, MN: American Guidance Service.

VII

Applications in State Assessments of Schools

18

How Curriculum-Based Measurement Progress Monitoring Contributes to the Alignment of Instruction and State-Adopted Standards and Assessments

Greg Roberts, Jeanne Wanzek, and Sharon Vaughn

The advent of Curriculum-Based Measurement (CBM) and the seminal work of Stanley Deno (1985) represent significant advances in educational research and practice, particularly in terms of the instruction for students at risk for and with disabilities. CBM has contributed greatly to the use of student assessment data in making instructional decisions. This chapter specifically examines the utility (Messick, 1989) of CBM for aligning classroom instruction with statewide standards and state-adopted tests of students' achievement. In the opening section, we briefly describe a utilitarian perspective on test validity and outline the challenges and potential value of using CBM to link instruction to state- or district-level standards. In the latter half of this brief chapter, we summarize research that estimates and compares aim lines using two criteria, the Stanford Achievement Test (SAT) and the Texas Assessment of Knowledge (TAKS). The criterion measures differ in the level of performance necessary to qualify as *proficient* (Wanzek et al., in press). We also consider form effects of the reading passages used to measure oral reading fluency (ORF) by evaluating differences in curriculum-based prompts and their effect on the student performance trajectories necessary to predict success on the SAT and the TAKS. Finally, we discuss the instructional implications of these prediction models using CBM.

Utility and Test Validity

A measure has high *utility* if it is appropriate for a specific purpose, in a given context, and with a particular population of test takers (Messick, 1989). Test validity, in this view, is not only a property of the measure itself but also of its use(s) and usefulness in addressing a particular purpose (Sireci, 2007).

Establishing utility requires multiple sources of evidence that are sufficiently persuasive to support the appropriateness of the measure's intended use. It is also an ongoing endeavor to the extent that circumstances change and purposes evolve (Sireci, 2007). The era of federally mandated high-stakes testing has introduced a relatively new purpose for CBM; increasingly, it is being used to screen for students at risk academically and to monitor progress in relation to future success on statewide tests. Tracking performance on CBM across the first three to four years of school provides a basis for calculating the likelihood that a student or a group of students will be successful on the high-stakes test. Remaining *on track* for passing the high-stakes test requires performance equal to or better than a predetermined trajectory. Students not on track are candidates for instructional intervention. The *utility* of this practice assumes that the CBM in question aligns with the high-stakes test and that a proposed or given level of student performance results in later success on the state-mandated measure. Both of these assumptions may be speculative, at best, in the absence of supporting evidence. We focus primarily on the latter of the two assumptions.

In general terms, this is a question of predictive validity, and in the context of CBM, it often is addressed using methods typically associated with screening measure validation, where sensitivity, specificity, and predictive value are the test's key attributes. Screening measure validation, as well as other predictive validity models, require a criterion, typically a more established or comprehensive measure of the same or similar attribute (in medical settings, presence or absence of disease is more common). These methods yield cut scores (e.g., ORF of forty words correct per minute by the end of first grade) that represent a minimal level of CBM performance necessary at given points in time for likely success on the criterion. Plotting cut scores across time defines the minimum performance *trajectory* (known also as *aim lines*) necessary for students to remain *on track* for meeting the criterion, as suggested earlier. These trajectories, in theory, vary for different criteria, suggesting that the requirements for being *on track* may also vary. In other words, the utility of a curriculum-based application is dependent on the criterion in use.

High-stakes testing is a relatively recent candidate as a criterion measure. The handful of reports on the relationship of different CBM applications and performance on state tests tend to fall into one of two groups in terms of the approach used to estimate cut scores and establish minimal trajectories. The first is what might be described as a segmenting or link-ing approach, where the criterion is students' performance on a subsequent administration of the same or an alternate form of the CBM (the predictive value of average performance in fall of first grade on performance in winter of first grade, the predictive value of winter of first grade on spring of first grade, etc.). Aim lines result when the individual cut scores are connected by line segments. This represents a very proximal criterion, with the idea that success on one screening occasion predicts success on the next occa-sion, which predicts success on the next, and so on. This may be reason-able in the context of high-stakes testing to the extent that scores from the measurement occasion that is most proximal to the mandated test are very highly predictive of performance on the high-stakes measure. A second approach establishes each point-in-time score in terms of the more distal criterion, rather than the subsequent CBM administration. Using the ear-lier example, the prediction of interest is between the average winter of first grade CBM performance and the average end of third grade scores on the high-stakes measure. Cut scores are estimated in terms of these relation-ships and minimal performance trajectories are again created by connect-ing these point estimates.

In this chapter, we present an alternative to these that uses latent vari-able growth modeling to represent performance over time on CBM. This approach makes sense given the distal nature of the criterion (high-stakes testing in general) and our interest in reliably comparing the effect of dif-ferent criteria, the SAT and the TAKS, on the performance requirements necessary for student success on the respective high-stakes measures (i.e., what is required to be *on track*). Growth models in a latent variable frame-work offer advantages over more traditional approaches. First, indices of model fit can be calculated as a means of testing the validity of the pro-posed model *and* for evaluating the relative fit of alternative models. Also, in a latent modeling approach, parameters representing growth (e.g., in-tercept, slope) are estimated using a factor analytic methodology (i.e., they are latent variable), which controls for measurement error, providing more precise estimates than more descriptive approaches. These highly reliable values are continuous-level data and can be subsequently manipulated ar-ithmetically. Finally, latent variable growth models use a full information maximum likelihood estimator that makes use of all available data. This contrasts with less efficient approaches to handling missing data such as list-wise deletion and imputation of missing values.

We also examined effects of different CBM prompts, specifically the reliability of performance estimates when the relative difficulty of the items (or passages in this case) varies in largely unknown ways. Measurement models that explicitly identify the difficulty of each item (e.g., item response models) rely on a range of difficulty levels that is aligned with the content being measured. Difficulty varies, but the nature of that variation is known. However, when information about item difficulty is less available, variation represents a potential confound in the estimation of performance trends. We examine this issue using Dynamic Indicators of Basic Early Literacy Skills (DIBELS) ORF passages with students from first through third grades, comparing use of the recommended DIBELS passages (passages that vary in difficulty by grade level, though difficulty is generally unknown) and use of a passage of the same difficulty across grade levels (Spache readability level of about 1.5) in terms of their validity in predicting performance on the both the SAT and the TAKS.

CBM's Utility for Improving Performance on High-Stakes Tests

Participants in this study were students from a high poverty, high minority, Title I school district (six elementary schools) in a near urban area in the Southwest. Students were included in the study if they had at least one ORF score on the DIBELS, one ORF score on the Growth Modeling Oral Reading Fluency Passages (latent variable growth modeling uses a full information maximum likelihood estimator instead of list-wise deletion or data imputation methods), and one valid score on both the TAKS and the SAT Comprehension in third grade during the 2005–6 school year.

Measures

Oral Reading Fluency

The DIBELS ORF measure (Good and Kaminski, 2002) was administered individually to students in the winter and spring of first grade, and the fall, winter, and spring of second and third grade. During administration, students were asked to read three passages aloud for one minute. Words omitted, substituted, and hesitations of more than three seconds were scored as errors. Words self-corrected within three seconds were scored as accurate.

The median score of the three passages was reported. Concurrent reliabilities ranged from $r = .89–.96$. Grade-level measures were administered.

Growth Modeling Oral Reading Fluency Passages

Growth Modeling Oral Reading Fluency Passages (GMORF) passages were also administered individually in the spring of first, second, and third grades. The difficulty of the GMORF passages was held constant at a first-grade level for each administration. Students read two GMORF passages aloud for one minute each and the mean score was reported. Scoring of the GMORF passages was conducted in the same manner as the DIBELS.

Stanford Achievement Test, Tenth Edition

The Stanford Achievement Test, Tenth Edition (SAT-10; Harcourt, 2003) is a group-administered, norm-referenced test of reading competence. The reading comprehension subtest (Form A) was administered in the spring of third grade. It requires students to read passages and respond to multiple-choice questions. The internal consistency reliability coefficient for Form A, Grade 3 is reported as $r = .93$ for the reading comprehension subtest.

Texas Assessment of Knowledge and Skills

The Texas Assessment of Knowledge and Skills (TAKS; Texas Education Agency, 2004) is a group-administered test measuring performance on Texas state reading standards in grades 3–9. The score in this study was from the test administered in April of the students' third-grade year. The TAKS measure of reading comprehension consists of thirty-six multiple choice questions related to narrative, expository, and mixed (both narrative and expository) passages read independently by the student. Passages range from five hundred to seven hundred words in length.

Analytic Strategy

ORF outcomes are generally treated as *observed* scores, meaning that a given value includes a generally unknown amount of measurement error. This error is often ignored when establishing aim lines and cut scores or when interpreting a given student's or group of students' ORF performance. Approaches that rely on correlations of the criterion with ORF scores at discrete points in time or on regressions with discrete time points as predictors of the criterion are poorly equipped to handle the error component of a given score or model. Similarly, screening test validity analysis (McCardle, Scarborough, and Catts, 2001) and receiver-operator curve analysis, while useful for demarcating a distribution of ORF scores into discrete categories and relating those categories to performance on the criterion, do not directly deal with measurement error. For example, it is possible that the same student will be classified differently on two occasions due merely to error in the measure.

In the analyses conducted for this study, measurement error was addressed by treating growth as a latent variable and directly estimating the error associated with measurement. Confounds related to missing data were addressed by treating data as missing at random and using full information maximum likelihood for estimation, which allows the inclusion of all cases with a criterion score and at least one ORF data point and one GMORF data point within each school year. Proficiency status on the SAT-10 and TAKS was regressed (logistic regression) on these growth parameters yielding estimates of the increased likelihood associated with changes in slope and/or intercept(s), expressed as odds ratios. Student growth and its effect on high-stakes performance (i.e., the logistic relationship of growth factors to outcome) were specified within a single model. The sample-adjusted Bayesian Information Criterion (cBIC) was used to evaluate the relative goodness of fit of the nonnested models, where *fit* is a function of a model's likely success in predicting the same criterion in a future sample from the same population using maximum likelihood estimation.

Results

A total of 154 cases met the selection criteria. On the TAKS, proficiency was indicated by a scaled score of 2100, the state-identified standard for *passing*, which represents mastery of the state-defined reading knowledge and skills necessary for advancing to the next grade level. *Proficiency* on the SAT-10 comprehension subtest was based on publisher-provided guidelines (Harcourt, 2003), where *proficiency* represents mastery of the grade-level skills necessary for success at the next grade level. Eighty-seven percent passed the TAKS on the first administration. Only 35 percent scored at a proficient level or higher on the SAT-10; 65 percent failed to meet the standard. Results on DIBELS and GMORF at each measurement point are summarized in Table 18.1.

TABLE 18.1.

Logistic regression results for TAKS and SAT given different prompts

	THRESHOLD		β INTERCEPT		β SLOPE	
	TAKS	SAT-10	TAKS	SAT-10	TAKS	SAT-10
DIBELS	1.45	5.49**	.147	.076	.113**	.150**
	(1.04)	(1.18)	(.096)	(.042)	(.040)	(.036)
GMORF	1.25	5.82**	.161	.081	.081*	.129**
	(1.11)	(1.34)	(.105)	(.046)	(.033)	(.034)

Note: *Significant at .05; **Significant at .01

For DIBELS data, the intercept of the growth model was 3.52 words read correctly ($p < .01$) with variance of 22.8. The average slope was 29.52 words read correctly (an increase of 29.52 words per minute per year), and its variance was 85.7. The average intercept for GMORF data was 3.17 words read correctly ($p < .01$) and variance was 18.5, while the slope was 37.01 words read correctly ($p < .01$) with variance of 87.8. The greater slope for the GMORF passages may reflect their relative ease for older students when compared to DIBELS passages, which increase in difficulty from one grade to the next; in other words, second graders and third graders are likely to read a first-grade passage with greater fluency (as in the GMORF model) than the second-grade and third-grade passages in the DIBELS model.

The growth models for DIBELS and for GMORF along with the TAKS and SAT-10 proficiency data were used in logistic regression to estimate four models: (1) DIBELS/TAKS; (2) DIBELS/SAT; (3) GMORF/TAKS; and (4) GMORF/SAT. Each term represents contributions to the estimated log-odds, such that for each unit change in X_j, there is a predicted change of b_j units in the log-odds in favor of Y = 1 (*proficiency* on the TAKS or SAT-10 in this case). Odds ratio is the exponentiation of log odds estimates and represents the relative frequency with which different outcomes occur (number of cases with the event in a group to the number of cases without the event). The probability of an event occurring is derived from odds using the logistic function. Probabilities of achieving proficiency scores on the TAKS and SAT-10 given different estimates of slope and intercept were a primary focus of this study.

For the DIBELS/TAKS model, coefficient values were 0.147 ($z = 1.53$) and 0.113 ($z = 2.82$) for the intercept and slope, respectively. The threshold estimate was 1.45 ($z = 1.40$). The odds ratios for the intercept and slope were 1.16 and 1.12, respectively. For the GMORF/TAKS model, the intercept and slope estimates were 0.161 ($z = 1.53$) and 0.081 ($z = 2.42$), the threshold was 1.25 ($z = 1.12$), and the odds ratios were 1.174 (intercept) and 1.084 (slope). For the DIBELS/SAT model, the coefficients were 0.076 ($z = 1.53$) and 0.150 ($z = 2.82$) for the intercept and slope, respectively. The threshold estimate was 5.49 ($z = 4.65$). The odds ratio for the intercept was 1.079. For slope, it was 1.161. The coefficients for intercept and slope in the GMORF/SAT model were 0.081 ($z = 1.76$) and 0.129 ($z = 3.78$), and the threshold value was 5.82 ($z = 4.35$). The odds ratio for intercept was 1.085, and for slope, it was 1.138.

The cBIC value for the DIBELS/TAKS model was 5,329 versus 5,335 for the GMORF/TAKS model, suggesting that DIBELS used as recommended may provide a more reliable fit in terms of predicting future performance on TAKS-like high-stakes tests. On the SAT-10, the DIBELS cBIC was 6,286 compared to the GMORF model value of 6,299, again suggesting a preference for DIBELS over GMORF for predicting later test performance. Note, however, that a formal test of the difference between estimates of cBIC is not available. Further, there is little guidance for qualitatively evaluating these differences, beyond the necessity to *minimize* the function. Given the relatively small difference in the cBIC values and the lack of clear guidance on what constitutes meaningful differences for information criteria, we plotted aim lines for all four models using the following logistic equations:

$$\pi\text{DIBELS\_TAKS} = e\,1.45 + .147(\text{intercept}) + .113(\text{slope})/1+$$
$$e\,1.45 + .147(\text{intercept}) + .113(\text{slope}) \qquad (1)$$

$$\pi\text{GMORF\_TAKS} = e\,1.25 + .161(\text{intercept}) + .081(\text{slope})/1+$$
$$e\,1.25 + .161(\text{intercept}) + .081(\text{slope}) \qquad (2)$$

$$\pi\text{DIBELS\_SAT-10} = e\,5.49 + .076(\text{intercept}) + .150(\text{slope})/1+$$
$$e\,5.49 + .076(\text{intercept}) + .150(\text{slope}) \qquad (3)$$

$$\pi\text{GMORF\_SAT-10} = e\,5.82 + .081(\text{intercept}) + .129(\text{slope})/1+$$
$$e\,5.82 + .081(\text{intercept}) + .129(\text{slope}) \qquad (4)$$

Solving for slope while holding initial status constant as the sample mean for the kindergarten ORF scores (these data included measures of ORF in kindergarten), we were able to represent the minimum ORF performance necessary for students to remain "on track" to pass the end-of-third-grade TAKS or SAT-10 with 80 percent probability, when ORF is measured according to DIBELS recommendations and when ORF is measured using the first grade passage at all time points. These are represented in Figure 18.1. The trajectories differed in expected ways (Wanzek et al., in press), with the GMORF passages having steeper slopes than the DIBELS passages, due to the higher ORF scores in second and third grades.

Utility of CBM and State Testing

This study demonstrates the contribution of CBM in aligning instructional decisions with performance on state outcome assessments. CBM measures of ORF can serve as reliable predictors of performance on both a nationally

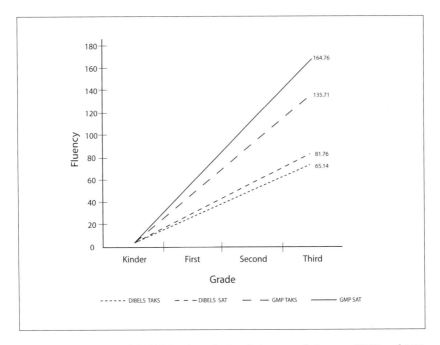

Figure 18.1. DIBELS and GMORF trajectories in relation to proficiency on TAKS and SAT

normed assessment and a state-normed assessment *across* grade levels. CBM can play an important role in improving students' performance on high-stakes tests to the extent that CBMs are reliably linked to the high-stakes standard in question. However, to be useful (and to avoid being harmful), performance on a CBM measure should be calibrated in terms of the high-stakes criterion in question. Failure to do so can compromise important instructional decisions, as suggested by the comparison or SAT and TAKS. While the SAT and TAKS may be similar in difficulty, the standard used by the two measures to determine proficiency differs, and the effect of this difference on suggested performance levels for ORF is dramatic with cut scores and aim lines for the same CBMs differing accordingly.

The difficulty of the DIBELS reading passages was established using the Spache readability formula, an approach that may not be as reliable as once thought. Unfortunately, the results of the prompt comparison are not definitive. While using a first-grade passage serves to standardize the difficulty of the prompt, it appears no more useful than the standard DIBELS approach for predicting performance on the TAKS and SAT and may be less so. DIBELS passages increase in difficulty, making the reasonable assumption that performance is a function not only of how a student responds but also item difficulty. Measurement models that were not available when CBMs were developed have made it possible to more precisely estimate passage difficulty. Their increasing use in selecting and organizing reading passages should further minimize concerns about form effects. In the interim, these results suggest that difficulty estimates for the DIBELS passages may be "close enough," at least compared to the GMORF alternative.

A Personal Acknowledgement

It is difficult when you have a famous mother in special education (Deno's cascade of special education services) to imagine that a son would find much motivation to also have a substantial influence—arguably one that is even more significant than his own mother. Stanley L. Deno has accomplished what most scholars can't even imagine. He has made a field-altering contribution to education. The notion of using the curriculum as a source of devising proximal measures to repeatedly assess students to determine whether the instruction provided is benefiting them and then furthermore determining how it should be altered provides an organizing framework for teaching and learning that radically shifts preservice instruction, professional development of teachers and school psychologists, and measurement development. S. L. Deno is one of the most influential educators of the last three decades and is likely to remain so for decades to come. For those who might wonder what evidence can be provided to warrant this claim, we offer two of many possible data sources: (1) Google Scholar (Deno, 2009) reports that just one of Stanley Deno's articles (1985) has had over six hundred citations, and (2) CBM has significantly contributed to the implementation of Response to Intervention, all assessment in special education, and many screening measures, and it is part of all research-based educational training programs for teachers and school psychologists across the United States and increasingly other countries as well.

References

Deno, S. L. (1985). Curriculum-Based Measurement: The emerging alternative. *Exceptional Children, 18*, 19–32.

Deno, S. L. (2009, August). *Curriculum-Based Measures: Development and perspectives*. Available at http://www.progressmonitoring.org/CBM_Article_Deno.pdf

Good, R. H., III, & Kaminski, R. A. (Eds.). (2002). *Dynamic indicators of basic early literacy skills* (6th ed.). Eugene: University of Oregon, Institute for the Development of Educational Achievement.

Harcourt Educational Measurement. (2003). *Stanford achievement test* (10th ed.). San Antonio, TX: Harcourt Assessment.

McCardle, P., Scarborough, H., & Catts, H. (2001). Predicting, explaining, and preventing children's reading difficulties. *Learning Disabilities Research and Practice, 16*, 230–239.

Messick, S. (1989). Validity. In R. Linn (Ed.), *Educational measurement* (pp. 13–103). New York, NY: Macmillan.

Sireci, S. G. (2007). On validity theory and test validation. *Educational Researcher, 36*, 477–481.

Texas Education Agency. (2004). *Texas assessment of knowledge and skills*. Austin, TX: Author.

Wanzek, J., Roberts, G., Linan-Thompson, S., Vaughn, S., Murray, C., & Woodruff, T. L. (in press). Differences in the relationship of oral reading fluency and high stakes measures of reading comprehension. *Assessment for Effective Intervention*.

19

Curriculum-Based Measures

Application with State Assessments

Gerald Tindal

In this contribution, I begin by highlighting the critical features of Curriculum-Based Measurement (CBM) that make it possible to use the measures in conjunction with current large-scale assessments. It is important to note the technical research on and essential features of CBM because of the importance of large-scale testing programs. When CBM measures are used in conjunction with large-scale tests, the measures come under increased scrutiny because of the potentially serious consequences that result from their use.

I next acknowledge that, under the leadership of Stanley Deno, those of us who have worked with CBM over the past four decades are ready to take the measurement system to a new level, as we interact with other measurement systems from state departments of education. This next level would involve the use of more precise scaling, presumably using some form of Item Response Theory (IRT).

Finally, I propose how CBM can provide critical information to help teachers make important decisions about student participation in large-scale testing programs. Presently, teachers make most of their decisions about participation in an informal manner, but with the emphasis on accountability, more systematic strategies are needed; CBM measures can provide this information, given their essential features.

Technical Research and Essential Features

In one of the early definitions of Curriculum-Based Measurement, Deno (1987) stated the following:

> The term curriculum-based assessment, generally refers to any
> approach that uses direct observation and recording of a student's

performance in the local school curriculum as a basis for gathering information to make instructional decisions . . . The term Curriculum-Based Measurement refers to a specific set of procedures created through a research and development program . . . and grew out of the *Data-Based Program Modification* system developed by Deno and Mirkin. (1977, p. 41)

Deno noted that CBM is distinct in two important respects: (a) the procedures incorporate technically adequate measures (the measures "possess reliability and validity to a degree that equals or exceeds that of most achievement tests" [p. 41]), and (b) "growth is described by an increasing score on a standard, or constant, task. The most common application of CBM requires that a student's performance in each curriculum area be measured on a single global task repeatedly across time" (p. 41).

CBMs, which originally sampled skills related to the curriculum material covered in a given year of instruction, provided teachers with a snapshot of their students' current level of performance and were a mechanism for tracking the progress students made toward desired academic skills. Historically, CBMs typically were very brief, individually administered measures (Deno, 2003; Good, Gruba, and Kaminski, 2002). Indeed, the history of research on CBM is rich and rather extensive, from the initial work in the late 1970s and early 1980s to more recent research in the 2000s. Wallace, Espin, McMaster, Deno, and Foegen (2007) summarized this research in a recent special series on CBM. In the initial twenty years, research on reading CBM focused on a number of technical characteristics, including the following:

1. Content-related evidence addressing domain size (Fuchs, Tindal, and Deno, 1984) and difficulty of material (Fuchs and Deno, 1992; Shinn, Gleason, and Tindal, 1989).
2. Criterion-related evidence regarding the relation of oral reading fluency to reading comprehension (Shinn, Good III, Knutson, and Tilly III, 1992) and secondary students' classroom performance (grades) in English and social studies (Fewster and MacMillan, 2002).
3. Construct validation with respect to rival hypotheses related to psychological variables, such as general cognitive ability, speed and efficiency of elemental cognitive processing, in addition to oral reading fluency in the prediction of reading comprehension

(Kranzler, Brownell, and Miller, 1998), as well as other theoretical and empirical concerns (Fuchs, Fuchs, and Hosp, 2001).
4. The effects of curriculum-based planning on grouping students (Wesson, Vierthaler, and Haubrich, 1989) and making instructional decisions (Allinder, 1996; Fuchs, Fuchs, and Stecker, 1989; Wesson et al., 1988).

Summary of CBM Features

In summary, research on CBM in reading has a long history that addresses many issues of technical adequacy (reliability, criterion-related validity, including both concurrent and predictive validity, and instructional decision making). The majority of studies have addressed reading (passage) fluency. More recently, this research has expanded to include early literacy as well. Although comprehension has been considered in some research, this focus has primarily been indirect (mostly achieved through the criterion-related evidence) and less so through the development of comprehension measures. And increasingly, mathematics measures are being developed and researched to address achievement in computation and application problems.

Although CBMs have appeared in various forms throughout this time, three essential features remain in which they reflect (a) repeated testing over time on material of comparable difficulty, (b) valid outcome indicators, and (c) qualitative as well as quantitative feedback (Fuchs and Deno, 1992). The first feature was a reflection of the common sense notion that to measure change, the repeated measures should not vary. The second feature addressed careful test design with attention to reliability and validity. The third feature considered the instructional program in relation to student change. In summary, the key issues appeared to be technically adequate measures of change over time with relevance for evaluating instruction.

The Next Generation of CBM

I argue, however, for a complete CBM system in which a comprehensive battery of assessments is available for teachers to use in making a number of decisions (not just evaluating instructional programs), with measures in reading of early literacy (decoding), fluency, and comprehension, and in mathematics of the main focal points (numbers and operations, algebra, geometry, and measurement—see National Council of Teachers of Mathematics; NCTM), this system for CBM needs to be appropriately scaled to ensure comparability and equivalence of forms. This requirement would then allow CBM to fit within the large-scale assessment system of states, virtually all of which are based on IRT. Finally, I argue that this unified and scaled CBM must meet traditional validity requirements as promulgated by the 1999 standards for educational measurement (AERA, APA, NCME, 1999) but, more important, must emphasize decision making and interpretations.

Most of the essential features of progress-monitoring measures have not changed since the 1970s. Such measures have been based on instructional material that sample from a year's worth of curriculum and have been designed to provide teachers with meaningful information about the progress students are making in mastering that material. In addition, to enhance their utility, ease of administration and scoring as well as interpretation continues to be necessary. However, whereas four decades ago researchers designed CBMs to not require any particular expertise for their development, the increasing stakes associated with assessment results as well as advances in psychometrics have significantly altered that perspective: We now recognize that the creation of reliable and valid progress measures requires specialized resources beyond what most public school teachers possess. This realization has spurred the creation of "next generation" CBMs, measures created using rigorous statistical modeling analytics that have previously been the exclusive feature of large-scale assessments.

An example of this next-generation system is easyCBM, which was developed using IRT during its construction. In reading, the skills range from early preskills, such as phonemic awareness and phonics; through midrange skills, such as developing automaticity in oral reading fluency; to the end skill of reading comprehension. In mathematics, skill sets previously used in CBM studies (computation and application problems) have been expanded to align with NCTM focal points. In both areas, IRT has been used to scale and calibrate CBMs for equivalence of alternate forms. With proper scaling, they can be used to help teachers not only monitor progress but also effectively make decisions about student participation in large-scale testing programs precisely because of their sensitivity in monitoring growth, their stability of alternate forms, and their sufficiency of information on a full range of student skills.

CBM to Support Teacher Decision Making on
Student Participation in State Testing Programs

The most significant area in which CBM is likely to make a contribution to large-scale testing programs is in helping teachers to make decisions about student participation in those testing programs. In particular, they can be used in helping teachers to decide whether or not accommodations are needed and, if so, what those accommodations might be. By using a high-quality assessment that is technically adequate, teachers can ensure not only appropriate access to the tests but also more positive outcomes. In the last ten years, this area of research has gained prominence and, in some ways, teachers now have more options than ever before but with little guidance on process.

The primary attributes to accommodations are that they reflect adaptations in tests (i.e., how they are given and taken) but *do not* change what the test means or how the results can be used. Schulte, Elliott, and Kratochwill (2001) define accommodations as "any change in an assessment that is intended to maintain or facilitate the measurement goals of the assessment so scores from the accommodated test measure the same attributes as scores from the unaccommodated test" (p. 2). Test accommodations are important to allow for valid interpretations and uses of assessment results because "inappropriate uses or withholding [them] . . . can invalidate scores, rob students of valuable information, and increase costs" (Helwig and Tindal, 2003, p. 213).

Accommodations for assessment may include changing the medium through which information is presented, allowing alternative response formats, altering the external environment, or adjusting the timing of the testing situation (Hopper, 2001) without altering the construct under investigation. Test accommodations are designed to enable students to demonstrate the depth and breadth of their content knowledge and understanding, and not just raise their performance levels. It is important to remember that the purpose of accommodations is not to "give disabled students a competitive edge, but eliminate competitive disadvantage" (Hartman and Redden, 1985, p. 2). In discussing accommodations for English Language Learners (ELLs), Wilner, Rivera, and Acosta (2008) comment that "effective accommodations for ELLs address the unique linguistic and socio-cultural needs of the student without altering the test construct. Accommodated scores should be sufficiently equivalent in scale that they can be pooled with unaccommodated scores" (p. vii).

Despite the need for care in creating accommodations, very few states have made the *process* for recommending and implementing accommodations explicit. For students with disabilities, the usual proscriptions warn against basing accommodations on the disability or introducing accommodations for the first time in testing (e.g., they should also be used in instruction). For ELLs, Wilner, Rivera, and Acosta (2008) report that, though all states now include ELL accommodation policies, more than half (64 of 104) of the accommodations allowed across all 51 state policies did not meet the criteria for ELL responsiveness (e.g., were appropriately specific to linguistic issues in testing rather than simply broad adjustments that ignored linguistic issues). Therefore, it has become critical to fully understand three important questions and dimensions of accommodations: (a) What are accommodations (definitional)? (b) How should accommodations be implemented (procedural)? (c) What are the effects of accommodations (interpretive)? Of these dimensions, the *definitional* aspects and *interpretive* outcomes have received the most attention; less research has been conducted on the *procedural* dimension.

One possible reason that the field of accommodations research is not reporting consistent and conclusive answers (see Sireci, Li, and Scarpati, 2003) is that too many variables mediate accommodation effects. Certainly, state-level policies and school-level practices are likely to be present; other variables include teachers' perceptions, students' perceptions, and students' access skills. Finally, teacher decision-making systems and Individualized Education Program (IEP) processes and systems are likely to be important for students with disabilities. However, for ELLs, because there is no IEP, little authority resides in the system. While the research on state policies has been documented for a decade by the National Center on Educational Outcomes, and while a nascent literature exists on IEP processes (e.g., DeStefano, Shriner, and Lloyd, 2001), the research on teacher and student perceptions is very limited. Yet these two variables may be among the most important for no other reason than that they are the closest to the process of actually implementing or receiving accommodations.

States need procedural practices that are consistent and replicable, otherwise it is difficult to train teachers in their use. These practices need to be based on the definitional aspects and will hopefully take into account the interpretive outcomes. However, the procedures need to be explicitly task analyzed so teachers can follow them, incorporating them into their classroom for teaching as well as testing for accountability. Training needs to be accessible to teachers and relevant for them; it needs to incorporate their perceptions and judgments. Likewise, it needs to fit students and address their perceptions as well as their learning needs. In summary, procedurally clear practices need to be centered on teachers and students when decisions about accommodations are being made.

Procedural clarity is particularly important because participation of students with disabilities in large-scale testing programs is standardized in terms of test administration; this feature allows their performance to be compared to others and to content as well as performance standards. However, without any information other than performance on the state test, it is not possible to determine whether or not they could access the test; in many instances, their access skills impede their performance. An obvious example is the influence of reading on mathematics tests: Many students perform poorly not because they lack skills in mathematical computation and application but because they cannot read the problems (see Tindal, Heath, Hollenbeck, Almond, and Harniss, 1998). However, more sophisticated follow-up analyses may be needed to more accurately document differential performance in both mathematics *and* reading skills (e.g., low readers with adequate math skills performed better on a standard version of a large-scale test over a video read aloud version [Helwig, Rozek-Tedesco, Tindal, Heath, and Almond, 1999]). As noted earlier, teacher judgment alone is unlikely to be accurate in helping determine this differential performance (Helwig and Tindal, 2003). Therefore, by using CBMs, teachers can better judge whether students with disabilities have adequate access skills to take a large-scale test in the standard manner or whether an accommodation is needed.

Such student information can include both performance on grade-level-benchmark CBMs as well as progress on instructional-level CBMs. Teachers' perceptions also can be used with performance and progress data. It is likely that when teachers are trained, they will show agreement between their perceptions of student performance and progress and actual student performance and progress. Recommendations for accommodations can be improved when perceptions are shaped to be more convergent and when decisions are validated using multiple measures. In Figure 19.1, CBM provides a critical role in helping generate a sufficient information system that allows teachers to make decisions about participation in large-scale testing programs. Critically, the use of CBM allows confirmation or disconfirmation of other information. As a consequence, the policy and practice environment of large-scale testing (noted on the left) can incorporate various types of teacher (and student) perceptions, which in turn are influenced by student data (both performance and progress) to eventually guide and direct appropriate participation.

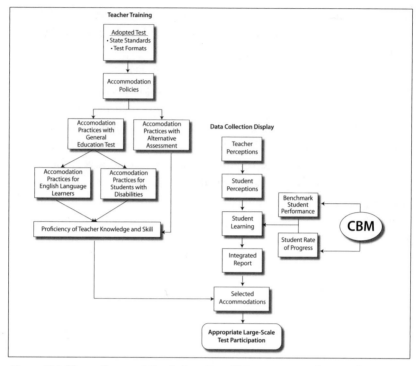

Figure 19.1. The confluence of Curriculum-Based Measurement and statewide testing programs

Conclusion

What began as a relatively simple question over forty years ago has become embedded in an extensive educational measurement environment today: Can students' performance and progress be measured in a straightforward manner that generates results quickly and is accessible to teachers, students, and parents? The answer has spawned research on various measures in both reading and mathematics along with their application in a number of decision-making frameworks (e.g., allocating resources with benchmark measures, monitoring instructional programs with progress measures, and ascertaining appropriate participation in large-scale testing programs). My purpose in addressing these issues has been to trace some of this development but, more important, to acknowledge the profound influence of Dr. Stanley Deno in bringing about a revolution of practice that has resulted in classroom measurement of student achievement (both performance and progress) becoming more scientific. And because of this, these data can be used with high-stakes decisions made from large-scale testing programs.

References

Allinder, R. M. (1996). When some is not better than none: Effects of differential implementation of Curriculum-Based Measurement. *Exceptional Children, 62,* 525–535.

American Educational Research Association (AERA), American Psychological Association (APA), & National Council on Measurement in Education (NCME). (1999). *Standards for educational and psychological testing.* Washington, DC: American Educational Research Association.

Deno, S. (1987). Curriculum-Based Measurement, program development, graphing performance and increasing efficiency. *Teaching Exceptional Children, 20*(1), 41–47.

Deno, S. L. (2003). Developments in Curriculum-Based Measurement. *Journal of Special Education, 37,* 184–192.

Deno, S. L., & Mirkin, P. M. (1977). *Data based program modification: A manual.* Minneapolis: University of Minnesota Leadership Training Institute/Special Education.

DeStefano, L., Shriner, J. G., & Lloyd, C. A. (2001). Teacher decision making in participation of students with disabilities in large-scale assessment. *Exceptional Children, 66,* 7–22.

Fewster, S., & MacMillan, P. D. (2002). School-based evidence for the validity of Curriculum-Based Measurement of reading and writing. *Remedial and Special Education, 23,* 149–156.

Fuchs, L. S., & Deno, S. L. (1992). Effects of curriculum within Curriculum-Based Measurement. *Exceptional Children, 58,* 232–243.

Fuchs, L. S., Fuchs, D., & Hosp, M. K. (2001). Oral reading fluency as an indicator of reading competence: A theoretical, empirical, and historical analysis. *Scientific Studies of Reading, 5,* 239–256.

Fuchs, L. S., Fuchs, D., & Stecker, P. M. (1989). Effects of Curriculum-Based Measurement on teachers' instructional planning. *Journal of Learning Disabilities, 22,* 51–59.

Fuchs, L. S., Tindal, G., & Deno, S. L. (1984). Methodological issues in curriculum-based reading assessment. *Diagnostique, 9,* 191–207.

Good, R. H., Gruba, J., & Kaminski, R. A. (2002). Best practices in using Dynamic Indicators of Basic Early Literacy Skills (DIBELS) in an outcomes-driven model. In A. Thomas & J. Grimes (Eds.), *Best practices in school psychology IV* (pp. 679–700). Washington, DC: National Association of School Psychologists.

Hartman, R. C., & Redden, M. R. (1985). *Measuring student progress in the classroom: A guide to testing and evaluation progress of students with disabilities.* Washington, DC: American Council on Education. (ERIC Document Reproduction Service No. ED295403)

Helwig, R., Rozek-Tedesco, M. A., Tindal, G., Heath, B., & Almond, P. (1999). Reading as an access to mathematics problem solving on multiple-choice tests for sixth-grade students. *Journal of Educational Research, 93,* 113–125.

Helwig, R., & Tindal, G. (2003). An experimental analysis of accommodation decisions on large-scale mathematics tests. *Exceptional Children, 69,* 211–225.

Hopper, M. F. (2001). *The implications of accommodations in testing students with disabilities.* Retrieved from ERIC database. (ERIC Document Reproduction Service No. ED463627)

Kranzler, J. H., Brownell, M. T., & Miller, M. D. (1998). The construct validity of Curriculum-Based Measurement of reading: An empirical test of a plausible rival hypothesis. *Journal of School Psychology, 36,* 399–415.

Schulte, A. A., Elliott, S. N., & Kratochwill, T. R. (2001). *Effects of testing accommodations on standardized mathematics test scores: An experimental analysis of the performance of students with and without disabilities.* Madison: Wisconsin Center for Education Research.

Shinn, M. R., Gleason, M. M., & Tindal, G. (1989). Varying the difficulty of testing materials: Implications for Curriculum-Based Measurement. *Journal of Special Education, 23,* 223–233.

Shinn, M. R., Good, R. H., III, Knutson, N., & Tilly, W. D., III. (1992). Curriculum-Based Measurement of oral reading fluency: A confirmatory analysis of its relation to reading. *School Psychology Review, 21,* 459–479.

Sireci, S. G., Li, S., & Scarpati, S. (2003). *The effects of test accommodation on test performance: A review of the literature* (Center for Educational Assessment Research Report No. 485). Amherst: University of Massachusetts Amherst, Center for Educational Assessment. Retrieved February 5, 2008, from http://www.education.umn.edu/NCEO/OnlinePubs/TestAccommLitReview.pdf

Tindal, G., Heath, B., Hollenbeck, K., Almond, P., & Harniss, M. (1998). Accommodating students with disabilities on large-scale tests: An empirical study of student response and test administration demands. *Exceptional Children, 64,* 439–450.

Wallace, T., Espin, C., McMaster, K., Deno, S., & Foegen, A. (2007). CBM progress monitoring within a standards-based system: Introduction to the special series. *Journal of Special Education, 41,* 66–67.

Wesson, C. L., Deno, S., Mirkin, P., Maruyama, G., Skiba, R., King, R., & Sevcik, B. (1988). A casual analysis of the relationships among ongoing Curriculum-Based Measurement and evaluation, the structure of instruction, and student achievement. *Journal of Special Education, 22,* 330–343.

Wesson, C., Vierthaler, J., & Haubrich, P. (1989). The discriminative validity of curriculum-based measures for establishing reading groups. *Reading Research and Instruction, 29*(1), 23–32.

Wilner, L. S., Rivera, C., & Acosta, B. D. (2008). *Descriptive study of state assessment policies for accommodating English language learners.* Washington, DC: The George Washington University Center for Equity and Excellence in Education.

20

Curriculum-Based Measurement, Progress Monitoring, and State Assessments

James G. Shriner and Martha L. Thurlow

State assessments of academic achievement are designed to provide a static indicator of the knowledge and skills of students in relation to state-defined academic content standards (Yell, Katsiyannis, and Shriner, 2006). Despite rhetoric about the instructional relevance of these large-scale assessments and attempts to increase their implications for classroom instruction, they have remained fairly far removed from the day-to-day decision making about instruction in the classroom (National Research Council, 2003). In contrast, Curriculum-Based Measurement (CBM) generally is defined by its relevance to instruction and instructional decision making (Deno, 1992, 2003; Gersten, Keating, and Irvin, 1995). This emphasis on instructional relevance is clearly attributable to the work of Stanley Deno. CBM is one of several approaches that involves "assessing student performance on a regular and frequent basis" (Quenemoen, Thurlow, Moen, Thompson, and Morse, 2004, p. 1). CBM is noted for its ease of use, sensitivity to change in student performance, technical characteristics (reliability, validity), and contribution to frequent measurement of student performance (Deno, 1992, 2003; Fuchs and Deno, 1991; Fuchs, Fuchs, Hamlett, Walz, and Germann, 1993; Hosp, Hosp, and Howell, 2007).

The importance of progress monitoring for evaluating the effectiveness of instruction has been emphasized with increased frequency during the past decade (e.g., Commission on No Child Left Behind, 2007; President's Commission on Excellence in Special Education, 2002; Popham, 1995; Stiggins, 2001). At the same time, the notion of static measurement of academic achievement for accountability purposes has evolved in response to demands for more instructionally relevant statewide assessments (Commission on Instructionally Supportive Assessment, 2001) and large-scale assessments that can be used more frequently (perhaps on a quarterly basis, such as formative or benchmark assessments) to better inform instruction (see McManus, 2008). Likewise, CBM has been pushed with increased frequency to provide information that will be relevant to state standards.

Statewide assessment activities and efforts surrounding CBM have become increasingly intertwined over time, especially during the past decade during which the use of assessments for accountability has dramatically increased. In this chapter, we address this intertwining by describing the value of the contributions of CBM to (a) assessments related to Individualized Education Programs (IEPs), (b) state regular grade-level and alternate assessments, (c) accommodations and modifications, and (d) new accountability provisions for growth models.

CBM, the IEP, and Assessment

Over time, Congress has placed increasing emphasis on the importance of meaningful programming that is articulated within annual, measurable goals and objectives. The procedural (compliance) requirements of the Individuals with Disabilities Education Improvement Act (IDEA, 2004) remain important pillars for educational programming, although the substantive (quality) elements of IDEA are becoming more important as the methods to evaluate students' progress toward their annual IEP goals receive increased attention by both legal and instructional experts (Etscheidt, 2006).

Substantive requirements refer to the characteristics of a student's special education program and compel schools to provide an education that confers meaningful educational benefit to a student. Thus substantive requirements address the implementation of the IEP and the extent of progress toward the student's individually determined goals. IDEA 2004 increased the emphasis on meaningful programming by requiring that IEPs include (a) special education services that are based on peer-reviewed research, (b) measurable annual goals, and (c) progress-monitoring systems. In fact, IDEA 2004 required that hearing officers ruling on cases involving IEPs base their decisions on "substantive grounds based on a determination of whether a child received a free appropriate public education" (IDEA, 20 U.S.C. § 1415(f)(3)(E)(I)).

Given this preference for substantive impact data, routine evaluations of students' classroom performance are part of best practice in communications with parents. For students who will be assessed using alternate assessments based on modified achievement standards (AA-MAS), federal rules go even farther, requiring that IEPs (a) include goals that are based on academic content standards for the grade enrolled and (b) be designed to monitor progress in achieving standards-based goals (Sec. 200.1(f)(2)(ii)(A)(B)).

Alternate Assessments for Students with Disabilities

IDEA 1997 (Section 612(a)(16)) required that all students with disabilities participate in state- and district-wide assessment programs and that alternate assessments be provided for students with disabilities who cannot participate in grade-level assessments, even with accommodations. Under the No Child Left Behind Act (NCLB; 2001), up to 1 percent of students in a school district may be assessed using an alternate assessment based on alternate academic achievement standards (AA-AAS). These assessments remain an evolving enterprise, with states using various assessment formats, including (a) portfolio-based/body-of-evidence approaches, (b) rating scales, (c) performance event formats, and (d) multiple-choice tests.

The importance of systematic measurement and monitoring of student progress is evident within AA-AAS approaches. As of the 2006–7 school year, thirteen states (25 percent) included student progress as a component of the AA-AAS (Cameto et al., 2009). Illinois was one state that required evidence of systematic measurement and graphical analysis of student progress on a defined task for its portfolio assessment. The use of systematic procedures for the presentation of evidence, summarizing and interpreting data as part of progress monitoring, allowed for portfolios to be scored, in part, on the degree of change in performance observed and displayed in graphs. The summative assessment (i.e., the Illinois Alternate Assessment) thus had built into its formal procedures aspects of the formative assessment model on which progress monitoring is based (Illinois State Board of Education, 2005).

Students with disabilities also may participate in an alternate assessment based on modified achievement standards (AA-MAS). Up to 2 percent of students may be counted as proficient via AA-MAS, and IDEA and NCLB specify with some precision how the education programming for these students is to be developed. Students assessed using an AA-MAS must have access to grade-level content so that they can work toward grade-level achievement. For example, their IEPs must include goals that are based on grade-level content standards and provide for monitoring of the students' progress in achieving those goals. The influences of progress monitoring or CBM are clearly evident in (a) decisions about which students might be eligible for the AA-MAS and (b) how standards-based educational opportunities are to be articulated and implemented within these students' IEPs.

Each year, a student's IEP team makes the decision about how the student will participate in state assessments. For students who might be assessed via the AA-MAS, the IEP team must make participation decisions for each content area (e.g., reading, math) and base its decision on evaluations of student progress in that content area (Sec. 200.1(e)(ii)). Progress must be based on multiple measures that indicate a student's progress over time. Clearly, CBM is a reasonable (though not required) option for IEP teams to use in determining student progress. The discussion document that accompanies the regulatory language for participation decisions includes examples of possible measures (e.g., portfolios, norm-referenced tests) and highlights CBM as an option because it offers "repeated measures from the student's curriculum that assess the specific skills being taught in the classroom and the effectiveness of instruction and instructional changes" (Title 1, 2007, 72 Fed. Reg., 177758). IEP teams are to restrict participation in AA-MAS to those students for whom progress rates based on valid assessments indicate that the student will not achieve grade-level proficiency within the year covered by the IEP. CBM can help IEP teams document the rate of progress a student is making because the data provided by routine progress monitoring (i.e., slope) establish a reliable data source for projecting the likelihood of the student achieving proficiency in content covered by the measures by year's end (i.e., time of state testing).

Fuchs, Seethaler, Fuchs, and Hamlett (2008) illustrated how CBM procedures might provide a way to "systematically assess whether the present instructional program is having its intended effect" (p. 157). CBM also indicates to the teacher whether additional well-researched instructional options should be added to the student's program.

The learning standards of a state are the basis for the AA-MAS group's goal. Periodic measurement of progress toward that goal and the culminating state assessment to determine students' status are group enterprises that are growing in importance. Quenemoen et al. (2004) discussed how progress monitoring options can be helpful in gauging within-year improvements at multiple levels of the educational system. By using formative assessment data obtained via progress monitoring, the connection between the individually referenced program goals of an IEP and the standards-referenced context of assessment and accountability systems can be examined.

Determination of the Likelihood of Success on State Assessments

State assessments required under NCLB have been the focus of much research and discussion since the law's passage in 2001. The group focus of Adequate Yearly Progress (AYP) determinations for all students, including students with disabilities, is different from the focus of most special educators, who emphasize the individual needs of the student. CBM as a progress-monitoring approach can inform both individual and group decisions. The relationship between the results of CBM and statewide tests of standards-based achievement has become the focus of research, especially in the content area of reading. A special issue of the *Journal of Special Education* was devoted to the research basis of CBM procedures in reading, mathematics, and writing (2007, Vol. 41, No. 2). In this issue, specific attention was given to CBM as a "means for predicting performance on and monitoring progress toward rigorous, state-defined academic standards for individual students" (p. 66). A special series on CBM for mathematics was also published in Assessment for Effective Intervention (2008, Vol. 33, No. 4). These journals provide thorough reviews of CBM research in each area.

Across studies, patterns of moderate to high correlations between CBM and state assessments for the areas of reading and mathematics and low to moderate correlations between CBM and state assessments in writing have emerged. Reviews in the area of reading by Shapiro, Keller, Lutz, Santoro, and Hintze (2006); Wayman, Wallace, Wiley, Tichá, and Espin (2007); and Yeo (2009) found that correlations for most CBM measures and state reading tests range from $r = .60$ to $r = .80$.

Studies in mathematics (e.g., Helwig, Anderson, and Tindal, 2002; Shapiro et al., 2006) found that correlations ranged from $r = .56$ for math computation tests to $r = .64$ for concepts and applications measures during winter months (when the strongest correlations were found) and that CBM predictions of success were obtained for over 85 percent of cases, with very similar predictive results for both general education and special education students.

Studies in writing show lower correlations between CBMs and state writing scores. McMaster and Espin (2007) reported that among the few studies to examine these relationships, correlations for CBM that allowed shorter writing times (i.e., less than five minutes) with district/state tests rarely exceeded $r = .60$ and that both the reliability and predictive power of CBM writing appeared to "strengthen with duration" of the CBM (p. 80).

These authors and others (Pemberton, Rademacher, Tyler-Wood, and Cereijo, 2006) suggested that a combination of measures (e.g., brief CBM sample and teacher assessments) might be needed to identify students' likely performance levels on measures relative to state or district standards. For example, if a student is working on a particular writing strategy, an abbreviated rubric focused on key standards or writing traits (e.g., organization, use of conventions) could be used in conjunction with CBM to provide a rich description of student performance relative to growth over time and status in relation to the standard or strategy. Use of a single student-generated writing sample for both scores (instead of obtaining a sample for each) may be a more efficient strategy for teachers to use for routine checks of students' writing skills. In a sense, this approach combines the progress-monitoring application of CBM with aspects of mastery measurement nested within the longer-range goals for the student (Zimmerman and Dibenedetto, 2008) and is similar to the skill-specific acquisition charts provided by some CBM products.

Monitoring Effects of Instructional Accommodations and Modifications

In addition to applications for alternate assessment options described previously, CBM models have influenced research and practice related to students' opportunities for access to and progress in the general curriculum, as well as their participation in traditional large-scale assessment programs. Following IDEA 1997, a series of research projects funded by the U.S. Department of Education, Office of Special Education Programs (see Rouse, Shriner, and Danielson, 2000, for a summary) focused national attention on issues of instructional and assessment adaptations (i.e., accommodations and modifications) for students with disabilities. Many of these efforts were conducted by researchers who had studied CBM and progress monitoring prior to IDEA 1997, and the basic theoretical framework for that work subsequently was applied to these "newer" issues of accommodations for instructional access and assessments. These influences remain relevant under NCLB and IDEA 2004.

Accommodations now are defined as changes in materials or procedures (for instruction or assessment) that do not change the intended content of what is taught or assessed (Lazarus, Thurlow, and Christensen, 2009; Thurlow, 2007). Modifications, in contrast, are defined as changes in materials or procedures that do change the intended content. Policymaking and research have been used to confirm whether a change should be considered an accommodation or a modification. In this discussion, we use the term *accommodation* generally to refer to any change that might eventually be determined to be either an accommodation or a modification.

A history of research on assessment accommodations (e.g., Johnstone, Altman, Thurlow, and Thompson, 2006; Thompson, Blount, and Thurlow, 2002; Tindal and Fuchs, 2000; Zenisky and Sireci, 2007) and instructional accommodations (e.g., Case, 2008; Salend, 2009) has shown that the studies produce mixed results. They vary depending on the nature of the students included in the research, the nature of the accommodation, and the nature of the content that is instructed or assessed. These results make it difficult for the practitioner to determine whether an individual student should receive a specific accommodation.

A consistent recommendation about improving the decision-making process for selecting classroom and assessment accommodations or modifications is to collect data on the effectiveness and feasibility of the accommodations (Elliott and Thurlow, 2006; Thurlow, Elliott, and Ysseldyke, 2003). Lynn Fuchs and colleagues investigated the effectiveness of CBM measures for assisting teachers in making decisions about accommodations (Fuchs, Fuchs, Eaton, Hamlett, Binkley, and Crouch, 2000a; Fuchs, Fuchs, Eaton, Hamlett, and Karns, 2000b). These studies, one focusing on mathematics and the other on reading, demonstrated the usefulness of CBM for decision making about accommodations. They showed that teachers tended to over-award accommodations and that data-based assessments predicted differential gains from accommodations better than teacher judgments. Although CBM approaches often are recommended for selecting appropriate accommodations for an individual student, particularly for instruction, research on the effects of accommodations rarely has used CBM. The exception is the work of Fuchs et al. (2000a, 2000b).

New Accountability Provisions for Measuring Growth

The reauthorization of the Elementary and Secondary Education Act in 2001 as NCLB required that all students participate in statewide assessments and that schools and districts be held accountable for student performance. Considerable angst emerged about the accountability requirements, in large part because they were static measures of student performance and failed to recognize students' growth (Choi, Goldschmidt, and Yamashiro, 2005;

Goldschmidt, Roschewski, Choi, Auty, Hebbler, Blank, and Williams, 2005; Linn, 2005; U.S. Department of Education, 2007).

Growth models were introduced through a pilot program announced by the U.S. Department of Education in April 2005. By October 2008, the growth model option was opened up to all states as long as they were approved after meeting numerous specific criteria (U.S. Department of Education, 2009). These criteria retained many of the rigorous requirements of NCLB, and perhaps as a result, their impact on accountability results was less than desired.

CBM researchers had already suggested that measuring growth was an important function of the measurement approach (Deno, 2003; Foegen and Deno, 2001), especially for documenting the need for interventions. But recently, several researchers have specifically looked at CBM as a mechanism for examining growth and growth patterns (Graney, Missall, Martinez, and Bergstrom, 2009; Jenkins, Graff, and Miglioretti, 2009). These researchers showed that (a) growth patterns may differ during different parts of the school year, depending on the measure (e.g., math CBM, reading CBM, or Maze); (b) growth slopes from CBM administered every three weeks and every nine weeks provided estimates of growth closest to an estimate of true growth; and (c) reducing the amount of measures (e.g., only one passage per time) limits the quality of the growth estimates. Looking at these types of findings reminds us of the wise words of Deno from a study he conducted with his colleagues (Deno, Fuchs, Marston, and Shin, 2001) in which they addressed the lower growth rates of students with learning disabilities. They indicated that the reasoning, under a normative approach to setting achievement expectations that assumes the growth rates are reasonable and predict future growth, reflects the "well-accepted fact that special education, as typically practiced in this country, fails to regularly incorporate demonstrably effective methods" (p. 515). In other words, given systematic educational interventions, typical growth rates might change, as well as their ability to predict future growth.

Conclusion

Deno and Mirkin (1977) introduced the foundations of CBM as "a set of procedures that the authors hope . . . will aid educators who are searching for effective instructional programs" (p. 5). As education has moved in and out of large-scale assessments and accountability systems, there is an intertwined interest in progress monitoring. Deno's work continues to emerge in conversations about how best to assess students with disabilities, how to ensure that they receive appropriate instructional interventions, and ways to determine whether they are progressing at sufficient rates. The strong and constructive influences of CBM on special and general education reforms (past, present, and future) that emphasize the importance and value of providing all students with opportunities to achieve to their highest levels possible is clear. Their hope, we believe, was not misplaced.

References

Cameto, R., Knokey, A. M., Nagle, K., Sanford, C., Blackorby, J., Sinclair, B., & Riley, D. (2009). *National profile on alternate assessments based on alternate achievement standards. A report from the national study on alternate assessments* (NCSER 2009-3014). Menlo Park, CA: SRI International.

Case, B. J. (2008). Accommodations to improve instruction and assessment of deaf students. In R. C. Johnson & R. E. Mitchell (Eds.), *Testing deaf students in an age of accountability* (pp. 51–62). Washington, DC: Gallaudet University.

Choi, K., Goldschmidt, P., & Yamashiro, K. (2005). Exploring models of school performance from theory to practice. In J. L. Herman & E. H. Haertel (Eds.), *Uses and misuses of data for educational accountability and improvement* (NSSE Yearbook, Vol. 104, Part 2, pp. 119–146). Chicago, IL: National Society for the Study of Education.

Commission on Instructionally Supportive Assessment. (2001). *Building tests to support instruction and accountability: A guide for policymakers*. Arlington, VA: American Association of School Administrators.

Commission on No Child Left Behind. (2007). *Beyond NCLB: Fulfilling the promise to our nation's children*. Washington, DC: Aspen Institute.

Deno, S. L. (1992). The nature and development of Curriculum-Based Measurement. *Preventing School Failure, 36*, 5–10.

Deno, S. L. (2003). Developments in Curriculum-Based Measurement. *Journal of Special Education, 37*, 184–192.

Deno, S., Fuchs, L., Marston, D., & Shin, J. (2001). Using Curriculum-Based Measurement to establish growth standards for students with disabilities. *School Psychology Review, 30*, 466–472.

Deno, S. L., & Mirkin, P. K. (1977). *Data-Based Program Modification: A manual*. Minneapolis: University of Minnesota, Leadership Training Institute/Special Education.

Elliott, J. L., & Thurlow, M. L. (2006). *Improving test performance of students with disabilities* (2nd ed.). Thousand Oaks, CA: Corwin Press.

Etscheidt, S. K. (2006). Progress monitoring: Legal issues and recommendations for IEP teams. *Teaching Exceptional Children, 38*(3), 56–63.

Foegen, A., & Deno, S. L. (2001). Identifying growth indicators for low-achieving students in middle school mathematics. *Journal of Special Education, 35*, 4–16.

Fuchs, L. S., & Deno, S. L. (1991). Paradigmatic distinctions between instructionally relevant measurement models. *Exceptional Children, 57*, 488–501.

Fuchs, L. S., Fuchs, D., Eaton, S. B., Hamlett, C. L., Binkley, E., & Crouch, R. (2000a). Using objective data sources to enhance teacher judgments about test accommodations. *Exceptional Children, 67*, 67–81.

Fuchs, L. S., Fuchs, D., Eaton, S. B., Hamlett, C. L., & Karns, K. M. (2000b). Supplementing teacher judgments of mathematics test accommodations with objective data sources. *School Psychology Review, 29*, 65–85.

Fuchs, L. S., Fuchs, D., Hamlett, C. L., Walz, L., & Germann, G. (1993). Formative evaluation of academic progress: How much growth can we expect? *School Psychology Review, 22*, 27–48.

Fuchs, L. S., Seethaler, P. M., Fuchs, D., & Hamlett, C. L. (2008). Using Curriculum-Based Measurement to identify the 2% population. *Journal of Disability Policy Studies, 19*, 153–161.

Gersten, R., Keating, R. J., & Irvin, L. K. (1995). The burden of proof: Validity as improvement of instructional practice. *Exceptional Children, 61*, 510–519.

Goldschmidt, P., Roschewski, P., Choi, K., Auty, W., Hebbler, S., Blank, R., & Williams, A. (2005). *Policymakers' guide to growth models for school accountability: How do accountability models differ?* Washington, DC: Council of Chief State School Officers.

Graney, S. B., Missall, K. N., Martinez, R. S., & Bergstrom, M. (2009). A preliminary investigation of within-year growth patterns in reading and mathematics curriculum-based measures. *Journal of School Psychology, 47*, 121–142.

Helwig, R., Anderson, L., & Tindal, G. (2002). Using a concept-grounded, curriculum-based measure in mathematics to predict statewide test scores for middle school students with LD. *Journal of Special Education, 36*, 102–112.

Hosp, M. K., Hosp, J. L., & Howell, K. W. (2007). *The ABCs of CBM: A practical guide to Curriculum-Based Measurement.* New York, NY: Guilford Press.

Illinois State Board of Education. (2005). *Illinois alternate assessment: Technical manual.* Retrieved May 22, 2009, from http://www.isbe.state.il.us/%5C/assessment/iaa.htm

Individuals with Disabilities Education Improvement Act (2004), Pub. L. No. 108-446, 1128 Stat. 2647.

Individuals with Disabilities Education Improvement Act Regulations (2004), 35 CFR §300 et seq.

Jenkins, J. R., Graff, J. J., & Miglioretti, D. L. (2009). Estimating reading growth using intermittent CBM progress monitoring. *Exceptional Children, 75*, 151–163.

Johnstone, C. J., Altman, J., Thurlow, M. L., & Thompson, S. J. (2006). *A summary of research on the effects of test accommodations: 2002 through 2004* (Technical Report No. 45). Minneapolis: University of Minnesota, National Center on Educational Outcomes.

Lazarus, S. S., Thurlow, M. L., Lail, K. E., & Christensen, L. (2009). A longitudinal analysis of state accommodations policies: Twelve years of change 1993–2005. *Journal of Special Education, 43,* 67–80.

Linn, R. L. (2005). *Test-based educational accountability in the era of No Child Left Behind* (CSE Report 651). Los Angeles: University of California, Center for Research on Evaluation, Standards, and Student Testing.

McManus, S. (2008). *Attributes of effective formative assessment.* Washington, DC: Council of Chief State School Officers.

McMaster, K., & Espin, C. (2007). Technical features of Curriculum-Based Measurement in writing: A literature review. *Journal of Special Education, 41,* 68–84.

National Research Council. (2003). *Assessment in support of instruction and learning: Bridging the gap between large-scale and classroom assessment* (Workshop report). Washington, DC: National Academies Press.

Pemberton, J. B., Rademacher, J. A., Tyler-Wood, T., & Cereijo, M. V. P. (2006). Aligning assessments with state curriculum standards and teaching strategies. *Intervention in School and Clinic, 41*(5), 283–289.

Popham, W. J. (1995). *Classroom assessment: What teachers need to know.* Boston, MA: Allyn & Bacon.

President's Commission of Excellence in Special Education. (2002). *A new era: Revitalizing special education for children and their families.* Washington, DC: U.S. Department of Education.

Quenemoen, R., Thurlow, M., Moen, R., Thompson, S., & Morse, A. B. (2004). *Progress monitoring in an inclusive standards-based assessment and accountability system* (Synthesis Report 53). Minneapolis: University of Minnesota, National Center on Educational Outcomes. Retrieved July 16, 2009, from http://education .umn.edu/NCEO/Online Pubs/Synthesis53.html

Rouse, M., Shriner, J., & Danielson, L. (2000). National assessment and special education in the United States and England and Wales. In M. McLaughlin & M. Rouse (Eds.), *Special education and school reform in the United States and Britain* (pp. 66–97). London, UK: Routledge.

Salend, S. J. (2009). Technology-based classroom assessments: Alternatives to testing. *Teaching Exceptional Children, 41,* 49–58.

Shapiro, E. S., Keller, M. A., Lutz, J. G., Santoro, L. E., & Hintze, J. M. (2006). Curriculum-based measures and performance on state assessment and standardized tests: Reading and math performance in Pennsylvania. *Journal of Psychoeducational Assessment, 24,* 19–35.

Stiggins, R. J. (2001). The unfulfilled promise of classroom assessment. *Educational Measurement: Issues and Practice, 20*(3), 5–15.

Thompson, S., Blount, A., & Thurlow, M. (2002). *A summary of research on the effects of test accommodations: 1999 through 2001* (Technical Report No. 34). Minneapolis: University of Minnesota, National Center on Educational Outcomes.

Thurlow, M. L. (2007). State policies and accommodations: Issues and implications. In C. C. Laitusis & L. L. Cook (Eds.), *Large-scale assessment and accommodations: What works?* Arlington, VA: Council for Exceptional Children.

Thurlow, M. L., Elliott, J. L., & Ysseldyke, J. E. (2003). *Testing students with disabilities: Practical strategies for complying with district and state requirements* (2nd ed.). Thousand Oaks, CA: Corwin Press.

Tindal, G., & Fuchs, L. (2000). *A summary of research on test changes: An empirical basis for defining accommodations.* Lexington, KY: Mid-South Regional Resource Center. (ERIC Document Reproduction Service No. ED442245)

Title I—Improving the Academic Achievement of the Disadvantaged; Individuals with Disabilities Education Act (IDEA)—Assistance to States for the Education of Children with Disabilities; Final Rule, 72 Fed Reg. 17748–17781 (April 9, 2007) (34 C.F.R. § 200 and 300).

U.S. Department of Education. (2007). *Growth models: Ensuring grade-level proficiency for all students by 2014.* Washington, DC: Author. Retrieved September 11, 2009, from http://www.ed.gov/admins/lead/account/growthmodel/proficiency.pdf

U.S. Department of Education. (2009). *Growth models: Non-regulatory guidance.* Washington, DC: Author. Retrieved September 11, 2009 from www.ed.gov/admins/lead/account/growthmodel/0109gmguidance.doc

Wallace, T., Espin, C. A., McMaster, K., Deno, S. L., & Foegen, A. (2007). CBM progress monitoring within a standards-based system: Introduction to the special series. *Journal of Special Education, 41,* 66–67.

Wayman, M. M., Wallace, T., Wiley, H. I., Tichá, R., & Espin, C. A. (2007). Literature synthesis on Curriculum-Based Measurement in reading. *Journal of Special Education, 41,* 85–120.

Yell, M. L., Katsiyannis, A., & Shriner, J. G., (2006). No Child Left Behind Act, Adequate Yearly Progress, and students with disabilities. *Teaching Exceptional Children, 38*(4), 32–39.

Yeo, S. (2009). Predicting performance on state achievement tests using Curriculum-Based Measurement in reading: A multilevel meta-analysis. *Remedial and Special Education, OnlineFirst.* Retrieved January 29, 2009. doi:10.1177/0741932508327463

Zenisky, A. L., & Sireci, S. G. (2007). *A summary of the research on the effects of test accommodations: 2005–2006* (Technical Report No. 47). Minneapolis: University of Minnesota, National Center on Educational Outcomes.

Zimmerman, B. J., & Dibenedetto, M. K. (2008). Mastery learning and assessment: Implications for students and teachers in an era of high-stakes testing. *Psychology in the Schools, 45,* 206–216.

VIII

Uses for Teacher Development

21

Stanley Deno's Contributions to Teacher Education Scholarship and Practice

Paul T. Sindelar, James L. McLeskey,
and Mary T. Brownell

This text is a paean to the significance and impact of Stanley Deno's scholarship on Curriculum-Based Measurement (CBM). Yet as significant as his scholarly accomplishments have proven to be, Deno also took seriously his role as a teacher educator. In his teaching, he endeavored to provide practitioners a practical means for solving the problems they encountered in their classrooms. In fact, we believe his *scholarly* interest in CBM grew out of his *practical* interest of helping teachers solve problems. At the very least, they were spawned together.

Deno may not have been a scholar of teacher education, but his scholarship has had a significant and positive impact on the work of teachers and the field of teacher education as well. This became apparent for one of us several years ago during a conference with his son's third-grade teacher. Robby had a reading problem, and to remedy it, his teacher had insisted on using Reading Mastery. We had told his teacher on several other occasions that a Direct Instruction approach had been tried with Robby and had failed, but she was determined to see for herself. After using CBM for several weeks and closely monitoring Robby's progress, she reached the same conclusion we had: Reading Mastery was not an effective approach for Robby.

This story is very nearly universal. Every parent who has a child with a reading problem can tell one just like it, as can teachers working with struggling readers and supervisors responsible for teachers who work with children who struggle in school. Such is the pervasiveness of Deno's influence on teaching practice. In teacher education programs across the country, students are taught to monitor their children's progress and to use this information to make critical decisions about what and how to teach. In fact, standards promulgated by the Council for Exceptional Children (2008) stipulate that "special educators regularly monitor the progress of individuals with exceptional learning needs in general and special curricula" (p. 49). In our judgment, effective special education practice requires it.

Initially, Deno's work influenced teachers in pragmatic, nuts-and-bolts ways as they monitored student progress and used performance data to make decisions about the effectiveness of methods they employed. More recently, his work has provided the foundation for more fundamental change in how we organize and differentiate instruction and how we ensure accountability for student outcomes. In his own words, "Special education is a problem-solving component of the general education program and . . . interventions designed to overcome those problems are, in effect, experiments that must be carefully evaluated to determine their effectiveness" (2007, p. 243). In this sense, special education may be used as "developmental capital" (as another Deno [1970] noted some years ago) to improve the education of all students. However, as significant as these ideas have been for school practice, their impact on teacher preparation was slow in coming.

Deno Has Influenced Teacher Education in Fundamental Ways

As a teaching assistant at the University of Minnesota, I (Sindelar) came to appreciate Deno's earnest interest in helping teachers solve nagging problems of classroom practice. He taught his students a process that involved the precise definition of a problem behavior and, to guarantee day-to-day comparability of the counts they were to maintain, had them express their counts as rates. Deno's students were to establish a baseline during which no intervention was attempted, then introduce an intervention and evaluate its effect on the behavior. This problem-solving process now is familiar to all special-education teachers and school psychologists, and it has a general education analogue in reflective teaching.

Early on, Deno focused on identifying standards with which the significance of a problem behavior could be judged. Standard setting required teachers to address the more difficult question of whether a problem was significant. However, equipped with the knowledge of the frequency of a problem behavior among other children, teachers could decide whether a problem was sufficiently severe as to warrant intervention. On academic tasks, which ultimately became Deno's focus, collecting normative performance data on standardized tasks was an initial step in extending the problem-solving process out of the classroom and into school and district-level decision making. As this process evolved, Deno and other proponents never lost sight of the features that made CBM appealing to practitioners—its efficiency, ease of implementation, and modest costs (Deno, 2007). Now, of course, CBM, or more generally progress monitoring, has become a cornerstone of Response to Intervention (RTI), which itself has prompted schools across the nation to reconsider how to conduct not only special education but general education as well.

We will leave to others the measurement of Deno's contribution to the development and refinement of CBM and how this body of work contributed to the thinking that brought about RTI. We would like to make one important point about the significance of these accomplishments as they pertain to teacher preparation. RTI provides teacher educators with both a new framework for understanding the work that special education teachers do and guidance about how teacher preparation may be reshaped to support contemporary school practice. These assertions apply equally well to the preparation of both general and special education teachers.

In special education's early years, teacher preparation was linked explicitly to school practice. Decades ago, those of us in teacher education prepared resource room teachers or teachers for self-contained classes. Then in the late 1980s and 1990s, as the inclusion movement created fundamental change in school practice, teacher preparation lost focus. Inclusion was practiced differently from school to school and from district to district, and no single model came to predominate. Furthermore, self-contained and resource room programs never went away completely. As a result, teacher educators were unable to prepare teachers for a universally agreed on role in a widely accepted model of service provision. Teacher educators recognized that collaboration with general education had become a central feature of teachers' work, but collaboration itself was not a simple construct that could be expected to unfold in a common manner from classroom to classroom or school to school. Simply put, the 1990s were a difficult era for teacher educators, because we could not predict with any degree of accuracy what role our graduates would assume in the schools.

RTI has changed all of that. In a paper two of us published recently (Brownell, Sindelar, Kiely, and Danielson, 2010), we argued that RTI provides a framework for understanding the work of both classroom teachers and special education teachers—a framework with which teacher education may be reshaped and revitalized. In this chapter, we also argue that in RTI, special-education teachers have an essential instructional role to which they bring distinctive expertise (in knowledge of and skill in implementing evidence-based practices). Recognition that special-education teachers contribute distinctive expertise to the process contrasts vividly with the monitoring role they often occupied in some inclusive coteaching models.

We have seen Deno's career-long commitment to helping teachers solve problems blossom and bear fruit. Now progress monitoring serves as the foundation for a new framework for service delivery that is likely to affect school practice and teacher education fundamentally. In their efforts to reach struggling students, RTI teachers will use the same process Deno taught decades ago. However, now generalists and specialists will work together to identify effective instructional approaches, and decisions about where students are instructed also will be informed by the knowledge of what has been tried and what has been found effective. These developments provide teacher educators with a concept of practice with which to rethink and reshape our work. We recognize that Deno has contributed instrumentally to this opportunity and thank him sincerely for it.

References

Brownell, M. T., Sindelar, P. T., Kiely, M. T., & Danielson, L. C. (2010). Special education teacher quality and preparation: Exposing foundations, constructing a new model. *Exceptional Children, 76*, 357–377.

Council for Exceptional Children. (2008). *What every special educator must know: Ethics, standards, and guidelines* (6th ed.). Arlington, VA: Author.

Deno, E. (1970). Special education as developmental capital. *Exceptional Children, 37*, 229–237.

Deno, S. (2007). The emerging alternative. In J. McLeskey (Ed.), *Reflections on inclusion: Classic articles that shaped our thinking* (pp. 239–249). Arlington, VA: Council for Exceptional Children.

22

The Impact of Curriculum-Based Measurement on Teacher Practice

Dana L. Wagner and Barbara J. Scierka

Curriculum-Based Measurement (CBM; Deno, 1985) is a central part of many special education teachers' vocabulary and practice. Monitoring students' basic academic performance using CBM procedures and assessments is widely considered best practice in special education, while its use is spreading within general education (Deno et al., 2009). We believe that several factors have contributed to the success of CBM within the teaching profession. First, CBM research began with teachers, taking a bottom-up approach. Second, it has been aligned with special education federal legislation, in turn helping teachers maintain due process compliance. Third, CBM has further professionalized the field of teaching by giving teachers the resources needed to do the professional work of problem solving. In this chapter, we describe how each of these three factors has contributed to the success of CBM within the teaching profession. We conclude with a case example that illustrates how one teacher used CBM to make decisions about reading instruction for an individual student.

Bottom-Up Approach

Dr. Deno's CBM research has a solid grounding in practice. While working with special education teachers in the 1970s, he noticed that they did not have a reliable and valid system for measuring and evaluating the effects of instruction on individual student performance (Wallace, Espin, and Deno, 2009). Out of this observation grew Data-Based Program Modification (DBPM). DBPM is a set of procedures that guides teachers to identify students' problems as discrepancies between actual performance and expectations, hypothesize solutions, and empirically test hypotheses (Deno and Mirkin, 1977). It was developed in close collaboration with teachers. In the DBPM manual, the first people Dr. Deno and Dr. Mirkin acknowledge are the special education teachers who worked with them throughout the project.

From the DBPM project, Deno identified the need for technically sound progress-monitoring assessments. To address this need, he conceptualized CBM. He wanted the assessments to fit within the functioning of a typical school. Therefore, CBM assessments are easy to collect, are inexpensive, and require little time, and any school personnel can gather the data with a little training (Deno, 1985). We believe that the solid foundation Deno's work has in teacher practice is one variable that has contributed to the significant impact of his work.

Alignment with Legislation

In addition to its grounding in practice, Deno's work has been explicitly connected to special education federal legislation. DBPM and CBM were developed in alignment with Public Law 94-142 (PL 94-142; 1975), in turn helping teachers implement policy. PL 94-142 called for special education students' goals to be connected to general education expectations and evaluated based on growth toward success in the general education setting. One of the first steps in the DBPM procedures is to identify the discrepancy between peer performance in the general education setting and an individual's performance. PL 94-142 also called for empirical evidence of the effects of special education programming on individuals' performance. The standardized scientific procedures of DBPM and the technical adequacy of CBM assessments gave teachers the power to generate empirical evidence of individual learning, a mandate that carried over from PL 94-142 to the Individuals with Disabilities Education Act (1997).

DBPM and CBM are two pieces from the same puzzle. Initially, DBPM was used to refer to the scientific process through which teachers used validated CBM assessments to evaluate instruction. Today, CBM refers to the scientific process, measurement procedures, indices, and graphical display of the data (Deno, 1985). In the remainder of this chapter, we use CBM to refer to the latter.

CBM helped teachers implement early special education policy. Recently, CBM ideas and research have been at the forefront of special education policy changes. The reauthorization of IDEA, Individuals with Disabilities Education Act (2004), gave local education agencies the option of using a Response to Intervention (RTI) approach to identify students who need special education services in the area of learning disabilities. An RTI approach begins with a technically adequate screening and progress-monitoring system. Although not the original intent of CBM, its robustness has led to its inclusion in screening for at-risk students and monitoring at-risk students' response to intervention. Special education teachers, who have used CBM for decades, are well prepared for the RTI movement.

Professional Work

By having a direct connection to federal legislation, Deno's early work was timely. What evolved, and continues to evolve, from CBM is timeless. The knowledge base of CBM has helped move teachers from the position of "teach and hope" to a more active role of teach, monitor, evaluate, and adjust. This paradigm shift has further professionalized the field of teaching. A defining feature of professional work is the use of problem-solving skills. Professionals use their specialized knowledge to make decisions that produce the best outcomes for clients. CBM gives teachers the tools they need to do the professional work of problem solving (Deno, 2005).

Increasingly, educators are using a problem-solving model that involves four or five steps; this model follows the scientific method. First, a problem is identified because of a discrepancy between actual and expected performance. Second, analysis is conducted to develop a hypothesis for why the problem may be occurring. Third, based on the hypothesis, an intervention plan is developed and implemented. Fourth, the intervention plan is evaluated for effectiveness based on continuous progress monitoring with valid and reliable measures.

When using CBM, teachers represent the problem-solving process on a graph. A student's initial datum point is plotted on a time series graph. Peer or expected benchmark performance is plotted to show a discrepancy. A long-term goal is set and illustrated with a straight line connecting the first datum point with the expected last datum point. A vertical line is inserted when an intervention is implemented. Regular progress-monitoring data are collected and plotted. The progress-monitoring data are evaluated to determine when an instructional change or goal adjustment is needed.

The CBM graph is a simple, elegant representation of the entire data-based decision-making or problem-solving model. A graph is a visual display of complex information. Its strength is in its ability to convey information in an easy-to-understand format. It is simple but not simplistic—simple as in straightforward and uncomplicated and elegant as in well-designed, neat, and pleasing to the eye.

Prior to CBM graphs showing students' growth toward long-term goals, many teachers assumed or hoped that initial instruction was effective. Using CBM has powerful effects on teachers' perspectives and instruction. The results of an early study showed that teachers who used CBM were more reliable reporters of the effects of instruction on student achievement than teachers who did not use CBM (Fuchs, Deno, and Mirkin, 1984). The results of additional studies have shown that teachers who use CBM modify instruction more frequently and have greater effects on student achievement than teachers who do not use CBM (Fuchs et al., 1984; Fuchs, Fuchs, and Hamlett, 1989; Fuchs, Fuchs, Hamlett, and Ferguson, 1992; Wesson, 1991). By changing teachers' perspectives and practice from teach and hope to teach, monitor, evaluate, and adjust, CBM has further professionalized the field of teaching.

While the CBM system gives teachers a reliable and valid way to determine *when* an instructional change is needed for an individual student, the system fails to consistently provide a reliable and valid way to determine *what* instructional change is needed. Teachers have reported that the problem-solving steps of analyzing individual students' instructional needs and planning instruction that is matched to the problem are difficult (Stecker, Fuchs, and Fuchs, 2005). Research results have shown that when teachers have access to CBM assessment results with an analysis of individuals' math skills, their instructional changes produce greater student achievement effects than those implemented by teachers who have access to CBM assessment results without skills analysis (Fuchs, Fuchs, Hamlett, and Stecker, 1990). Further, researchers have demonstrated preliminary evidence on the positive effects of teacher access to expert consultation when determining instructional changes for students in math (Fuchs, Fuchs, Hamlett, and Stecker, 1991). The results of studies that have examined the effects of CBM skills analysis and expert consultation on the effects of teachers' instructional changes in reading are less promising than those in math (Espin, Deno, McMaster, Pierce, Yeo, Mahlke et al., 2009; Fuchs et al., 1992; Wesson, 1991). Further research is needed in the area of CBM problem analysis and instructional planning.

Case Example

The CBM graph shown in Figure 22.1 illustrates the effectiveness of using CBM for one teacher and one student. The example comes from the second author's experience as a first-year special education teacher in the St. Croix River Education District. Although the graph is imperfect with gaps in data

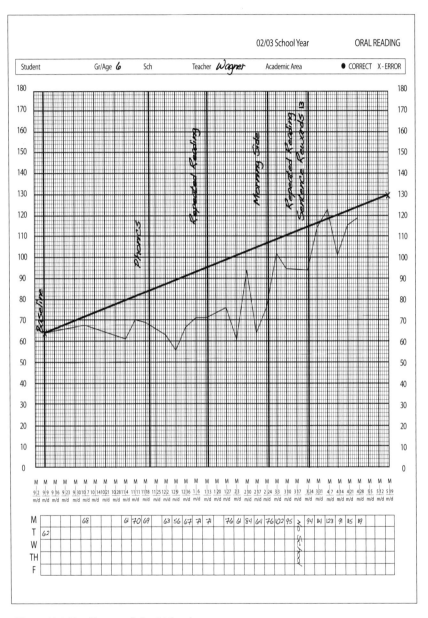

Figure 22.1. Reading graph for Richard

collection and decision rule violations, it illustrates the essence of CBM—persistent problem solving in response to formative data.

Several factors contributed to the success of using CBM for this teacher. First, the way CBM was developed to fit within the function of a typical school made the use of CBM doable for a novice special education teacher. Second, using the CBM system fostered compliance with special education due process laws. An Individualized Educational Plan goal, objectives, and progress reports were written using the CBM graph. Third, CBM empowered the teacher to be an empirically based problem solver. Her perception of the effects of her instruction was validated by the data. Imagine if the student's performance in the example was not graphed. The teacher would likely have stopped with the first instructional strategy, and the student would not have achieved at such a high level. In this case example, the implementation of the CBM system was a success for this student, and that is the real measure of success for CBM.

Curriculum-Based Measurement, as originally conceptualized by Dr. Deno and his colleagues at the University of Minnesota Institute for Research on Learning Disabilities, was developed to enable individual teachers to monitor the progress of individual students for the purpose of evaluating and adjusting their instruction, thereby maximizing student learning (Deno, 1985). While we have observed the systematic implementation of CBM at the group level, we have seen fewer individual examples of this than we would expect thirty years after the conception of CBM.

References

Deno, S. L. (1985). Curriculum-Based Measurement: The emerging alternative. *Exceptional Children, 52,* 219–232.

Deno, S. L. (2005). Problem-solving assessment. In R. Brown-Chidsey (Ed.), *Assessment for intervention: A problem-solving approach* (pp. 10–40). New York, NY: Guilford Press.

Deno, S. L., & Mirkin, P. (1977). *Data-based program modification: A manual.* Minneapolis, MN: Leadership Training Institute for Special Education, University of Minnesota.

Deno, S. L., Reschly, A. L., Lembke, E. S., Magnusson, D., Callender, S. A., Windram, H., & Stachel, N. (2009). Developing a school-wide progress-monitoring system. *Psychology in the Schools, 46,* 44–55.

Education for All Handicapped Children Act (1975), Pub. L. No. 94–142.

Espin, C., Deno, S., McMaster, K., Pierce, R., Yeo, S., Mahlke, A., & Zukowski, B. (2009). *Teacher use study: Progress monitoring with and without diagnostic feed-*

back (Technical Report No. 32). Minneapolis: University of Minnesota, College of Education and Human Development, Research Institute on Progress Monitoring.

Fuchs, L. S., Deno, S. L., & Mirkin, P. K. (1984). The effects of frequent Curriculum-Based Measurement and evaluation on pedagogy, student achievement, and student awareness of learning. *American Educational Research Journal, 21,* 449–460.

Fuchs, L. S., Fuchs, D., & Hamlett, C. L. (1989). Effects of instrumental use of Curriculum-Based Measurement to enhance instructional programs. *Remedial and Special Education, 10,* 43–52.

Fuchs, L. S., Fuchs, D., Hamlett, C. L., & Ferguson, C. (1992). Effects of expert system consultation within Curriculum Based Measurement using a reading maze task. *Exceptional Children, 58,* 436–450.

Fuchs, L. S., Fuchs, D., Hamlett, C. L., & Stecker, P. M. (1990). The role of skills analysis in Curriculum-Based Measurement in math. *School Psychology Review, 19,* 6–22.

Fuchs, L. S., Fuchs, D., Hamlett, C. L., & Stecker, P. M. (1991). Effects of Curriculum-Based Measurement and consultation on teacher planning and student achievement in mathematics operations. *American Educational Research Journal, 28,* 617–641.

Individuals with Disabilities Education Act (1997), 20 U.S.C. § 1400 et seq.

Individuals with Disabilities Education Act (2004), 20 U.S.C. § 1400 et seq.

Stecker, P. M., Fuchs, L. S., & Fuchs, D. (2005). Using Curriculum-Based Measurement to improve student achievement. *Psychology in the Schools, 42,* 795–819.

Wallace, T. (Interviewer), Espin, C. (Interviewer), & Deno, S. (Interviewee). (2009). *History of Curriculum-Based Measurement: An interview with Stan Deno* [Interview audio file]. Retrieved January 26, 2010, from http://www.progressmonitoring.org

Wesson, C. L., King, R. P., & Deno, S. L. (1984). Direct and frequent measurement: If it's so good for us, why don't we use it? *Learning Disability Quarterly, 7,* 45–48.

IX

Uses in Psychology and School Psychology

23

Data-Based Program Modification and the Launching of Careers

Edward S. Shapiro and Francis E. Lentz Jr.

It is amazing how one small book can have such a large impact on one's professional thinking and career. In 1982, we had both just recently become school psychology trainers at Lehigh University (Lentz was brand new) and prior to that had been involved in behaviorally oriented services, but not as school psychologists. We were not interested in the (at that time) traditional school psychology model and badly wanted to move the Lehigh model toward a behaviorally oriented, intervention-based program. As we were in the midst of this complicated process (more than we both had naively anticipated), we came across the 1977 volume titled *Data-Based Program Modification: A Manual* by Stanley Deno and Phyllis Mirkin. This discovery became a keystone event that was instrumental in allowing us to merge our emergent philosophy of practice, our behavioral training, and the use of effective interventions within an existing school-based behavioral consultation approach to service delivery (Bergan, 1977). For us, it was in many ways a practical catalyst for both the published articulation of a comprehensive model of behavioral school psychology service delivery and a more coherent behavioral curriculum for preservice training. Not only did this wonderful book inform both of us, but it was ready-made for inclusion in our classes and for student use.

Published by the Council for Exceptional Children, the spiral-bound text described a methodology for using a continuous data set to develop and implement intervention programs, set meaningful goals, and then repeatedly use these data to make ongoing decisions to improve student outcomes. Aimed primarily at special education teachers, Deno and Mirkin (1977) used their experiences in training resource teachers to develop this manual, and in almost every way it described what we felt school psychologists could help do as consultants in order to best serve children.

Most important for us, the volume basically said that to assess reading performance in order to improve outcomes, one should ask children to read. To assess math performance, ask children to do math. What a novel idea this was in the era of school psychologists as IQ test givers. We also interpreted this as the need to use the child's curriculum, rather than norm-based test results, as the reference point for both determining expectations and how children were doing to meet expectations.

Data-Based Program Modification (DBPM) started with five key assumptions. The first assumption raised the important point that instructional programs needed to be treated as empirically testable hypotheses to determine their effectiveness for academic outcomes. In particular, Deno and Mirkin (1977) recognized that at the level of the individual student, teachers needed an empirical methodology for determining if their instruction was working. The second assumption was that time series designs were uniquely appropriate for evaluating the impact of instructional interventions. In particular, DBPM was a methodology that derived its empirical base from the concepts embedded in single-case research design (e.g., Hersen and Barlow, 1976). As such, DBPM was equating teaching to a series of single-case experiments designed to increase the attribution of outcomes to the implementation of the instructional intervention.

Their third assumption was incredibly bold and indicated that special education is an intervention system that can be empirically tested. In particular, Deno and Mirkin (1977) identified the importance of accountability for special education intervention and viewed DBPM as a way to achieve this objective.

The fourth assumption of the DBPM model was probably one of the most important elements to impact the fields of both special education and school psychology for subsequent decades. Deno and Mirkin stated, "To apply time series designs to (special) educational reforms we need to specify the data representing the 'vital signs' of educational development, which can be routinely (frequently) obtained in and out of school" (1977, p. 14). Indeed, the concept of measuring a student's academic health through key indicators was the basis for Curriculum-Based Measurement (CBM), a concept of evaluation that has now sustained itself into one of the most crucial aspects of today's models of Response to Intervention (RTI; e.g., L. S. Fuchs and D. Fuchs, 2007). Within their description of this assumption, Deno and Mirkin introduced the practical idea of a discrepancy ratio, or "the relative difference between the individual's level of performance and the performance which is desired from individuals within the culture" (p. 14).

What was suggested here was a new way to look at the degree of discrepancy and thus provide a quantitative index that pointed to the importance of a problem. Not the discrepancy between ability and achievement, long associated with the administration of tests of intelligence and achievement, but a discrepancy between what is attained by a student and what is expected. All of these differences were related to the academic performance of the student and had nothing to do with cognitive potential. Clearly, this was a different way of looking at students who were struggling academically.

The final assumption of the DBPM was the recognition that implementation of DBPM required trained professionals who fully understood the concepts of data analysis, understood the time series design, and understood that instructional decisions needed to be data driven. Although Deno and Mirkin (1977) were talking about Special Education Resource Teachers, we saw, heard, and envisioned school psychologists.

The remaining details of the text described the methodology for implementing DBPM. This included the specific measures in reading, math, writing, or spelling that would be used; the steps for guiding (for Deno and Mirkin, 1977) the Special Education Resource Teacher's problem selection, program selection, program operationalization, program improvement, and program certification, all directly comparable to behavioral consultation (Bergan, 1977) in which we were very interested; how to graph the data (Deno and Mirkin still really liked equal-ratio as well as equal-interval graphs); and substantial detail on how to calculate discrepancy ratios and determine meaningful goals. The manual provided many case examples of how these decisions would be made and how the data drove the decisions. Altogether, the DBPM manual was an incredible recipe for how to provide empirical support for effective instruction.

The procedures in their book were presented in a very jargon-free manner and were not presented in an in-your-face behavioral way. However, the DBPM process was aligned (DBPM was a clinical methodology and not research, so the alignment was not perfect) in a very interesting way with many of the seven characteristics of applied behavior analysis as described in the seminal article by Baer, Wolf, and Risley (1968). DBPM was clearly *applied*, dealing with socially important problems in real settings—there were clear directions and descriptions involving the consultant, making clear why the problem was a meaningful one. It was certainly *behavioral*, always requiring clear definitions of behaviors so that reliable measurement was possible, although there was not a clear emphasis on data reliability (to ensure that student behavior, not the measurement behavior of staff, was what was changed). Certainly it described procedures in a *technological* manner, with heavy emphasis on written description of interventions and evaluation of intervention fidelity. The careful use of single-case design components in progress monitoring and evaluating change was *analytic*, although technically adequate designs for more pure attributions were not emphasized (it was a clinical service program after all). It was related to the *effective* characteristic of applied behavior analysis in very practical ways, requiring clear, data-related, consultant articulation of the social importance of goals and data-based decisions to reach effective outcomes with the resolution of the original discrepancy at the end of student programs. Most examples of interventions were *conceptually systematic* within the principles of behavior analysis. The *generality* of any interventions resulting from DBPM would need empirical support; however, the procedures of DBPM were intended to be, and were, a highly generalizable technology that could be used across practitioners, settings, and classroom problems.

Perhaps most important from our view, this manual sought to bring the behavior of change agents under the control of meaningful data and data-based decision rules. The behavioral school psychologist acts to collect valid data that in turn occasion decisions leading to important student outcomes. This is the explicit goal of behaviorally oriented school psychology—that the professional decisions of the behavioral school psychologist are controlled by data so that outcomes for clients are meaningful; the psychologist is in that sense appropriately self-managed, his or her behavior is also appropriately rule governed, and his or her important decisions are controlled by consequences related to student success.

Clearly, the foundations were sown in this one volume for what became CBM (and subsequent other General Outcome Measurement tools) and have influenced the current generation of thinking in school psychology as well as special education. Today the measures and decision-making processes so clearly articulated in DBPM for special educators are apparent for general education through RTI. It is amazing how much this approach has influenced not only our thinking but also several generations of graduates in school psychology that we have now trained (hopefully as self-managing, effective change agents). In looking at the references scattered throughout the DBPM text, the connections to our past training were quite evident. For example, the work of Don Campbell, the preeminent social scientist whose work shaped new ways of looking at quasi-experimental data and who actually ended his career while on the faculty at Lehigh. We were incredibly lucky to have been both been at Lehigh during his stay here. Tom Gilhool is mentioned in one of the references. Tom was the attorney for the parents in the Pennsylvania *Association for Retarded Children vs. Commonwealth of Pennsylvania* decision that led to the development of Public Law 94-142. In addition, Tom served briefly as the secretary of education in Pennsylvania, and to top it all, he was also a Lehigh graduate, class of 1960. References to the work of Jack Birch, one of the pioneers of mainstreaming, play a prominent role. Jack Birch was the major professor and dissertation advisor for one of us (Shapiro) in graduate school at the University of Pittsburgh. Jim Ysseldyke and John Salvia's 1974 article was cited, an article that was the beginning of a long and distinguished career that continues through today. Others are mentioned who are considered key figures in the development of their fields— Maynard Reynolds in special education and H. S. Pennypacker, who wrote one of the most influential text in behavior analysis. Clearly, Deno and Mirkin (1977) were connecting their work to others who likewise will be viewed for a long time as benchmarks in their field.

At the time we discovered the DBPM text, we were particularly searching for a way to better integrate concepts of behavioral assessment into the evaluation of academic skills and the subsequent connection between assessment activities and intervention planning that seemed missing in then-current school psychology practice. One of our personal concerns in the field of school psychology was the overreliance on standardized, norm-referenced tests in the evaluation of student performance. We were concerned about the equating of tests of intelligence as measuring student cognitive potential and were seriously concerned that the assessment process conducted by school psychologists had little impact on the educational outcomes of children. Our concern was ultimately greatly influenced not only by DBPM but subsequently by findings of the federally funded Institute for Research in Learning Disabilities (IRLD) at the University of Minnesota, with which both Deno and Mirkin were eventually associated. Our desire was to bring to the field of school psychology a methodology that would have better links between what we tested and what we did as a function of the testing.

The reports of the University of Minnesota IRLD were scathing in their examination of the testing practices used for the identification of students as having a specific learning disability. Jim Ysseldyke, Stanley Deno, and their colleagues pointed to the poor connection between the nature of problems presented at the point of referral and the subsequent selection of measures by school psychologists for conducting the assessment (Algozzine and Ys-seldyke, 1980; Ysseldyke and Algozzine, 1981). In particular, the work coming out of the IRLD chided school psychologists for their standard approach to assessment, selecting the same sets of measures regardless of the nature of the problem. Referred to as the "holy triad," psychologists would administer tests of intelligence, achievement, and personality, regardless of why the student was being referred.

Ed Shapiro came to Lehigh in 1980 after four years at the Western Psychiatric Institute and Clinic (WPIC), the University of Pittsburgh, Department of Psychiatry. Influenced by psychologists at WPIC and closely associated with the Association for the Advancement of Behavior Therapy and professionals such as Michel Hersen, Alan Bellack, Alan Kazdin, Rosemary Nelson, and C. Keith Conners, Shapiro began to recognize that the developing field of behavioral assessment as applied to clinical practice had a strong potential link to the field of school psychology. Other than the work of Jack Bergan and Tom Kratochwill in behavioral consultation, there was little influence of behavioral assessment being applied into school settings. However, translating these same concepts and principles to academic assessment and intervention had seemed elusive at the time we began our work at Lehigh. Given the high percentage of referrals for academic problems, finding a methodology that conceptually and practically could work was critical to a more effective role for school psychologists.

Ed Lentz joined Ed Shapiro at Lehigh in 1981, and we shared the same concern that the assessment of academic skills problems in schools needed a better connection between what we tested and what we subsequently taught. Having just spent several years with the Behavior Analysis Follow Through (BAFT) project of Don Bushell at the University of Kansas, Lentz brought a strong applied behavior analysis perspective to the problem. BAFT used standard curriculum-referenced progress data (not typically fluency based) across basic skill areas using both paper and pencil classroom group progress-monitoring graphs and a computer-based feedback system for all students across multiple sites, allowing continuous program decisions at the individual, classroom, and even project level (e.g., Bushell, 1978; Green, Eakins, Scott, and Weis, 1976). The BAFT experience, coupled with exposure to the ideas of Precision Teaching at Kansas and training experience with Richard Saudargas (at the University of Tennessee) with direct observation of behavior (e.g., Saudargas and Lentz, 1986), created high motivation for including data-based decision and behavioral techniques into school psychology training. One missing component, and what DBPM supplied, was a well-developed process for application to the range of school referrals. On reflection (and looking at citations in DBPM and the body of Deno's work), it is clear that behavior analysis and precision teaching also strongly influenced the procedures presented in DBPM.

The development and publication of our 1985 chapter and papers (Lentz and Shapiro, 1985; Shapiro and Lentz, 1985), followed closely by the 1986 paper (Shapiro and Lentz, 1986) detailing our view of the importance of the instructional ecology in assessing academic performance, was a direct function of the influence of the 1977 Deno and Mirkin text. Our perspective was not from that of a special education teacher but from that of the role of school psychologist. As such, our interests were particularly keen on the assessment and consultation process, two key aspects of the school psychologist's role. In particular, because we were very focused on shifting the role of the school psychologist from strictly assessment and diagnosis for special education eligibility to an interventionist and consultant within a problem-solving model, we needed to translate aspects of the DBPM into a language and a framework appropriate for school psychology.

Following the DBPM model, we established a set of seven assumptions regarding academic assessment. Specifically, the assessment must reflect what was happening in the natural environment, the assessment must be focused on the individual over time, what we test should be what we teach, there must be links between what we assess and what we target for intervention, the assessment methods must not only allow us to assess what is happening now but also must give useful information about ongoing performance, all measures we use must have empirical support for how we use them, and an assessment of academic skills must examine both skill and performance deficits (Shapiro and Lentz, 1985). From that basis, we then described a four-step process of assessment that incorporated much of what was contained in DBPM along with what we saw as a critical need to assess the instructional environment (Lentz and Shapiro, 1985, 1986). Added to that was the developing process of CBM as an evaluation tool, and a career path was set in motion for both of us as we pursued the effort to bring to the school psychology community the basics of DBPM.

The discovery of Deno and Mirkin (1977) was the catalyst that brought together our thinking and our early additions to the shaping of the future of academic problem assessment for school psychologists, a shaping that was taking place in multiple places in those years. We had the joint backgrounds and motivation to truly appreciate the potential of DBPM for our discipline, and (selfishly) for making our jobs so much more exciting. From a small, spiral-bound notebook a treasure was born. Unfortunately, Phyllis Mirkin passed away in 1982 and never got to see the full impact she had on the field. Thank you Deno, thank you Mirkin—you are treasures that started careers.

References

Algozzine, B., & Ysseldyke, J. E. (1980). Decision makers prediction of students' academic difficulties as a function of referral information. *Journal of Educational Research, 73*, 145–150.

Baer, D. M., Wolf, M. M., & Risley, T. R. (1968). Some current dimensions of applied behavior analysis. *Journal of Applied Behavior Analysis, 1*, 91–97.

Bergan, J. (1977). *Behavioral consultation.* Columbus, OH: Charles E. Merrill.

Bushell, D., Jr. (1978). An engineering approach to the elementary classroom: The behavior analysis follow-through project. In A. C. Catania & T. A. Brigham (Eds.), *Handbook of applied behavior analysis: Social and instructional processes* (pp. 525–561). New York, NY: Irvington.

Deno, S. L., & Mirkin, P. K. (1977). *Data-Based Program Modification: A manual.* Reston, VA: Council for Exceptional Children.

Fuchs, L. S., & Fuchs, D. (2007). The role of assessment in the three-tier approach to reading instruction. In D. Haager, J. Klinger, & S. Vaughn (Eds.), *Evidence-based reading practices for response to intervention* (pp. 29–42). Baltimore, MD: Paul H. Brookes.

Green, D. S., Eakins, D. J., Scott, J. W., & Weis, L. C. (1976, April). *The Behavior Analysis Follow Through evaluation strategy: A multifaceted approach.* Presented at the 60th Annual Meeting of the American Educational Research Association, San Francisco, CA. Retrieved October 1, 2009, from EBSCOHost ERIC database. (ERIC Document Reproduction Service No. ED126125)

Hersen, M., & Barlow, D. H. (1976). *Single case experimental designs: Strategies for studying behavior change.* New York, NY: Pergamon Press.

Lentz, F., & Shapiro, E. (1985). Behavioral school psychology: A conceptual model for the delivery of psychological services. In T. Kratochwill (Ed.), *Advances in school psychology* (Vol. 4, pp. 191–222). Hillsdale, NJ: Lawrence Erlbaum Associates.

Lentz, F., & Shapiro, E. (1986). Functional assessment of the academic environment. *School Psychology Review, 15*, 346–357.

Saudargas, R. A., & Lentz, F. E. (1986). Estimating percent of time and rate via direct observation: A suggested observational procedure and format. *School Psychology Review, 15*, 36–48.

Shapiro, E. S., & Lentz, F. E. (1985). Assessing academic behavior: A behavioral approach. *School Psychology Review, 14*, 327–336.

Shapiro, E. S., & Lentz, F. E. (1986). Behavioral assessment of academic behavior. In T. R. Kratochwill (Ed.), *Advances in school psychology* (Vol. 5, pp. 87–139). Hillsdale, NJ: Erlbaum.

Ysseldyke, J. E., & Algozzine, B. (1981). Diagnostic classifications as a function of referral information. *Journal of Special Education, 15*, 429–435.

Ysseldyke, J. E., & Salvia, J. (1974). Diagnostic-prescriptive teaching: Two models. *Exceptional Children, 41*, 181–185.

24

School Psychology as Problem Solving

Theodore J. Christ

Dr. Stanley Deno made substantial contributions to the field of school psychology. Perhaps the most noted and widely recognized of the contributions is the conceptualization, development, and dissemination of Curriculum-Based Measurement (CBM). As is true of many researchers in school psychology, the author of this chapter has spent a substantial amount of time and energy on the study of CBM procedures and instrumentation. As of 2009, more than three hundred studies that examined CBM were published in peer-refereed outlets. The scope of application and impact of CBM is substantial; perhaps one of CBM's most significant contributions is that it enables problem solving.

Although CBM has substantially influenced the field of school psychology, the conceptualization of problem solving as a guiding principle for practice stands as Dr. Deno's most considerable and enduring contribution to this field. The concept and practice of school psychology as a problem-solving enterprise (Tilly III, 2002) might seem obvious to those recently trained in the field of school psychology. Assuredly, that was not always the case. Contemporary practices in school psychology are drastically distinct from traditional and historical practices. Although the emphasis of this chapter is on what Deno wrote himself, there are innumerable contributions by his students and others he influenced. Indeed, the legacy of the chapter's author is traceable to those influenced by Deno. To make the lineage explicit, the author was trained in problem solving by Dr. Gary Stoner and Dr. Michelle Shinn (both influenced by Dr. Mark Shinn who was a student of Deno's) along with Dr. John Hintze (trained by Dr. Ed Shapiro who was influenced by Deno). What is true of this author is true for many other prominent practitioners, trainers, and researchers in the field of school psychology. The purpose of this chapter is to make explicit Deno's influence. I provide brief explanations and, more important, key excerpts that illustrate how a scholar in the field of special education so influenced the field of School Psychology.

Redefining the Role of the School Psychologist

As a researcher and trainer in the field of special education, Deno recognized the reciprocal relationship of the school psychologist and special educator. He recognized that the school psychologist could, and should, seek to provide useful information to guide intervention development and evaluation. He argued—as an outsider—that school psychologists must redefine their roles.

> Anyone outside the field of education or psychology rightfully might assume that a professional with such a noble purpose would be regarded highly by colleagues. Those who deliver school psychology services, however, are aware that efforts . . . are not always held in high esteem by consumers and related professionals. (1986, p. 358)

Further, "the current literature in school psychology reveals that clarity of purpose is lacking in the school psychologist's role" (Deno, 1995, p. 471). Deno argued that the diagnostic-prescriptive and task-analytic role of the school psychologist was faulty and provided insufficient information to guide service delivery within special education (Deno, 1986). He asserted that school psychologists were experts in assessment and evaluation, which is the use of data to guide decisions; however, he argued that the field was mired in the legal requirements for eligibility determination along with the faulty assumptions associated with the test-place diagnostic-prescriptive model of assessment and evaluation. At worst, the historical practices of school psychologists (i.e., high-inference assessment) identified neither what nor how to teach. At best, they identified what to teach (i.e., through task analysis and skills assessment) but not how to teach students within special education.

Deno was among the primary advocates for a systematic hypothesis-testing approach within school psychology and special education. More specifically, he advocated for an inductive hypothesis-testing model (as defined subsequently). Although the inductive nature of the proposed hypothesis-testing model is not stated explicitly as such, it is nevertheless apparent in his writing.

> While diagnosis and prescription cannot ensure effective treatment [because they are inductive], they are integral to the intervention process. The solution to our problem is neither to avoid diagnosis

and prescription, nor improve diagnosis and prescription—though improvements in this process would be welcome. Instead, school psychologists and special educators should be given tools and training to, in effect, conduct successive experimental tests of hypotheses . . . The goal of successive hypothesis testing is, of course, to determine empirically whether prescribed changes in education programs produce improvements in performance (brackets added). (Deno, 1986, p. 360)

Deno advocated for an experimental approach to service delivery, recognizing that hard-to-teach students respond to instruction in a manner that is unknowable a priori. That message is powerful and consistent with the conceptualizations of Response to Intervention models of service delivery (D. Fuchs, Fuchs, McMaster, and Al Otaiba, 2003; Gresham, 2001). Indeed, inductive hypothesis testing is at the very core of Response to Intervention. Deno and Mirkin (1977) presented five key assumptions that underlie the inductive hypothesis-testing approach that so influenced school psychology. As originally presented, they are as follows:

1. At the present time we are unable to prescribe specific and effective changes to instruction for individual pupils with certainty. Therefore, changes in instructional programs which are arranged for an individual child can be treated only as hypotheses which must be empirically tested before a decision can be made on whether they are effective for that child (p. 11).
2. Time series research designs are uniquely appropriate for testing instructional reforms (hypotheses) which are intended to improve individual performance (p. 11).
3. Special education is an intervention system, created to produce reforms in the educational programs of selected individuals, which can (and, now, with due process requirements, must) be empirically tested (p. 13).
4. To apply time series designs to (special) educational reforms we need to specify the data representing the "vital signs" of educational development which can be routinely (frequently) obtained in and out of school (p. 14).
5. Testing program modifications (reforms) requires well-trained professionals capable of using time series data analysis to draw valid conclusions about program effects (p. 15).

Some segments of the school psychology community adopted the proposed assumptions; moreover, those very assumptions influenced many leaders in school psychology (see Shapiro and Lentz, this volume; Marston, this volume). The assumptions underlie the very notion that education for special populations is a hypothesis-driven enterprise that requires ongoing use of data to evaluate effects.

The single criticism levied at Deno's conception is the undue pessimism associated with the potential for improvements in diagnosis and prescription techniques, especially those based on task and skills analysis to isolate intervention targets and hypothesize useful instructional routines. Christ (2008), for example, built on Deno's conception of hypothesis testing to propose that the efficiency and effect of instructional intervention can be improved with evidence-based, hypothesis-testing frameworks (i.e., diagnosis and prescription), and interventions that derive from those frameworks result in instructional recommendations/hypotheses likely to be especially effective and efficient. Emerging examples include various approaches to curriculum-based assessment and functional-based assessment. Problem solvers require such context and evidence-based guidelines to select and experiment with interventions.

The influence of Deno's conceptualization and promotion of the key assumptions that underlie inductive hypothesis testing is immeasurable. The tenets and national movement toward accountability and Response to Intervention are decedents of those very ideas.

School Psychologist as Problem Solver

Inductive hypothesis testing and the assumptions previously enumerated are foundations of problem solving. The earlier work of Deno laid out the rationale for inductive hypothesis testing, but it was his later work that provided a conceptualization for a systemic approach to problem solving (Deno, 1989). He proposed that effective systems of service delivery systemically engaged in problem solving, which includes (some version of) a multistep process: (1) identify the problem, (2) define the problem, (3) explore alternative solutions to the problem, (4) apply a solution, and (5) measure the effects (Deno, 1989, 1995, 2005). Deno's conceptualization of the school psychologist as a problem solver changed training programs around the country, especially those conceptualizations presented in 1989 and 1995. Those writings emerged as seminal sources in our field and spurred multiple derivations, including Tilly's (2002, 2008) influential conception of problem solving that is presented within critical chapters in each of the most recent versions of *Best Practices in School Psychology*.

Deno's work made key contributions to the conceptualization of problem solving that goes beyond the mere enumeration of the particular steps. In part, he made clear in his writing that the selection, definition, and measurement of problems are fundamental to the problem solving. His work provides the often-used definition of a problem, which is the discrepancy between what is expected and what is observed (Deno, 1989, 1995, 2005). His work also contributed to the conceptualization and technology of CBM as a General Outcome Measurement procedure for use to identify, define, and monitor the status of problems during intervention implementation (L. S. Fuchs and Deno, 1991). CBM is now widely used as a fundamental index of generalized basic skill achievement, especially for early reading development, but also for mathematics, written expression, and spelling. Those basic skills correspond with those valued by society and those that contribute fundamentally to academic health.

Deno's writing made clear that the context of the school paired with societal values (i.e., cultural imperatives) define the scope of relevant problems for school psychologists (Deno, 1989). School psychologists work within the school system to enhance child outcomes, and, Deno argued, their focus should be on the critical skills that enable people to function effectively within society. The emphasis and focus of the school psychologist is, therefore, on basic academic and social skills that enable individuals to function successfully in society. The narrowing and specification of purpose enhances school psychologists' potential to promote change.

> In developing a conception of school psychologists as problems solvers consider first the context in which they work. As participants in school environments . . . the problems to be solved by school psychologists are those generated out of the school's efforts to promote growth and development. (Deno, 1995, p. 471)

With regard to the selection of problem-solving targets—to promote growth and development—Deno indicates that there are priorities that guide the mission of both the school and school psychologist's problem-solving efforts. That is, not all problems are equally important, and the school psychologist must focus on the cultural imperatives before the cultural electives.

A useful framework for considering the distinction between important and unimportant handicaps is provided by the concept of the
"cultural imperative" . . . [which is] the implicit or explicit standards
of conduct or performance imposed on all who would be members of
a culture . . . the most commonly identified set of imperatives fall into
the category designated as "basic skills." (Deno, 1989, p. 8)

The focus of the school psychologist as problem solver is on well-defined
problems that are defined within context. That is, a problem is defined as
the discrepancy between what is expected and what is observed within a
particular context (Deno, 1989, 1995). The requirements of a clearly defined
problem and inductive hypothesis testing through time-series analysis make
a CBM-like assessment method necessary. Essentially, Deno's approach to
problem solving depends on the availability of a reliable and valid, simple
and efficient, easily understood, and inexpensive/accessible approach to
repeated assessment of basic skills (Deno, 1985). The challenge of attaining
these assessment features is more substantial than might be apparent. Deno
and many others have been spending their careers toward this end.

Research Institute on Problem Solving

The Research Institute on Problem Solving was recently established at the
University of Minnesota (http://www.cehd.umn.edu/EdPsych/RIPS) and
plans to continue the work of Deno. The institute's mission is as follows:

The mission of the Research Institute for Problem Solving (RIPS) is
to further the research, development, evaluation, and practices of
data-based problem solving in education. The Institute focuses on
the systematic use of data to guide the process of problem solving, a
recursive and iterative process that includes identifying a problem,
considering possible solutions, implementing proposed solutions and
using progress data to guide ongoing implementation, and evaluating
alternative solutions to guide future practice. The Institute functions to promote, conduct, and translate research to improve data-
based problem-solving by educators. This includes the procedures
and instrumentation associated with assessment and intervention.
Although the Institute functions to promote positive outcomes for all

children, there is a special emphasis on students with, or at risk for developing, academic, social-emotional, and behavioral disabilities.

The center will continue to develop, evaluate, and improve the methods and procedures that enable problem solving. Deno helped us define the philosophy, fundamental assumptions, and general processes to optimize service delivery. Deno contributed to the school psychology literature and published influential pieces in some of the most prominent outlets, which included *School Psychology Review* and the Best Practices in School Psychology series. His legacy is substantial, and it is left to those who come after to carry on the work and perfect the ideal of the school psychologist as a problem solver.

References

Christ, T. J. (2008). Best practices in problem analysis. In A. Thomas & J. Grimes (Eds.), *Best practices in school psychology* (pp. 159–176). Bethesda, MD: National Association of School Psychologists.

Deno, S. L. (1985). Curriculum-Based Measurement: The emerging alternative. *Exceptional Children, 52*, 219–232.

Deno, S. L. (1986). Formative evaluation of individual student programs: A new role for school psychologists. *School Psychology Review, 15*, 358–374.

Deno, S. L. (1989). Curriculum-Based Measurement and special education services: A fundamental and direct relationship. In M. R. Shinn (Ed.), *Curriculum-Based Measurement: Assessing special children* (pp. 1–17). New York, NY: Guilford Press.

Deno, S. L. (1995). The school psychologist as problem solver. In J. Grimes & A. Thomas (Eds.), *Best practices in school psychology III* (pp. 471–484). Bethesda, MD: National Association of School Psychologists.

Deno, S. L. (2005). Problem-solving assessment. In R. Brown-Chidsey (Ed.), *Assessment for intervention: A problem-solving approach* (pp. 10–42). New York, NY: Guilford Press.

Deno, S. L., & Mirkin, P. K. (1977). *Data-Based Program Modification: A manual.* Reston, VA: Council for Exceptional Children.

Fuchs, D., Fuchs, L. S., McMaster, K. N., & Al Otaiba, S. (2003). Identifying children at risk for reading failure: Curriculum-Based Measurement and the dual-discrepancy approach. In H. L. Swanson, K. R. Harris, & S. Graham (Eds.), *Handbook of learning disabilities* (pp. 431–449). New York, NY: Guilford Press.

Fuchs, L. S., & Deno, S. L. (1991). Paradigmatic distinctions between instructionally relevant measurement models. *Exceptional Children, 57*, 488–500.

Gresham, F. (2001). *Responsiveness to intervention: An alternative to the identification of learning disabilities.* Paper presented at the 2001 Learning Disabilities Summit: Building a Foundation for the Future, Washington, DC. Retrieved March 8, 2002, from http://www.air.org/ldsummit/download

Tilly, W. D., III. (2002). Best practices in school psychology as a problem-solving enterprise. In A. Thomas & J. Grimes (Eds.), *Best practices in school psychology* (Vol. 4, pp. 21–36). Bethesda, MD: National Association of School Psychologists.

Tilly, W. D., III. (2008). The evolution of school psychology to science-based practice: Problem solving and the three-tiered model. In A. Thomas & J. Grimes (Eds.), *Best practices in school psychology* (Vol. 4, pp. 17–36). Bethesda, MD: National Association of School Psychologists.

25

Cognitive Processes in Reading and the Measurement of Comprehension

Paul van den Broek and Mary Jane White

The ability to comprehend what we read is central to success and satisfaction in our lives. Indeed, individuals who experience difficulty with reading comprehension also experience difficulties in school, at the workplace, and in social life. The number of school-aged individuals with such difficulty is considerable (Paris, Carpenter, Paris, and Hamilton, 2005; Perie, Grigg, and Donahue, 2005; Verhoeven, Biemond, Gijsel, and Netten, 2007); moreover, the problems do not disappear with age, as difficulties understanding text at the word and discourse level often continue into adolescence and adulthood (Ehrlich, 1996; Greenberg, Ehri, and Perin, 1997; Perfetti, Yang, and Schmalhofer, 2008). Individuals with reading difficulties may not be able to partake fully in their social environments, to benefit from the same learning opportunities as individuals without reading difficulties, or to experience the enjoyment and informal knowledge that is attained from leisure reading. Besides the humanitarian cost to the individual, there also is an economic cost to both individual and society. Adult illiteracy costs the United States more than $10 billion a year and worldwide hundreds of billions of dollars each year in lost industrial productivity, unrealized tax revenues, poverty, and other, related social ills (Archer and Guttman, 2007; UNESCO, 2006). It is not surprising, then, that the identification and remediation of reading comprehension problems in children, and increasingly in adults, is a major focus of educational efforts.

To develop effective assessment and remediation methods, it is useful to know what is involved in understanding text—what the processes are and what can go wrong with them (Cain and Oakhill, 2007; Oakhill and Cain, 2007; Rapp, van den Broek, McMaster, Kendeou, and Espin, 2007). Recent cognitive-psychological investigations into reading and reading failures have provided insights in reading comprehension that are relevant to education.

In this chapter, we illustrate how understanding the cognitive processes involved in reading comprehension can inform our efforts to address the educational needs of struggling readers. In the first part we present an overview of what happens during reading comprehension as a reader proceeds through a text and where comprehension processes may fail. In the second part we discuss issues concerning the assessment of comprehension ability.

Success and Failure in Reading Comprehension

What does it mean to comprehend a text? A survey of the educational and psychological literature shows that there are many different answers to this question. For example, comprehension can refer to the ability to remember the text (Cain, Oakhill, and Lemmon, 2004), to extract the main idea (Baumann, 1983; van den Broek, Lynch, Naslund, Ievers-Landis, and Verduin, 2003), to apply the information in the text (Williams, Stafford, Lauer, Hall, and Pollini, 2009), or to build coherence within the text (O'Brien, 1995; Graesser, Singer, and Trabasso, 1994; van den Broek, Risden, and Husebye-Hartman, 1995). Such examples highlight the fact that reading comprehension is not a unitary concept but rather a cluster of distinct yet related activities and outcomes (Hoover and Gough, 1990; van den Broek, Rapp, and Kendeou, 2005; Whitehurst and Lonigan, 1998).

Diverse as these conceptualizations may seem, they all have as a common element an explicit or implicit notion that comprehension involves the construction of an integrated, coherent mental representation of the various parts of the text, as well as relevant background knowledge. The properties of such a representation and the processes by which it is constructed are described in detail by recent cognitive models of reading (Graesser et al., 1994; Kintsch, 1988; O'Brien and Myers, 1999; Trabasso, Secco, and van den Broek, 1984; van den Broek, Risden, Fletcher, and Thurlow, 1996).

Before summarizing these models, it is worth elaborating on the distinction between comprehension as a product and a process. The representation of text is a central part of the product of comprehension, the outcome that has been accomplished at the end of reading the text. The steps that were performed by the reader to arrive at that product form the *process* of comprehension. In theoretical models the product and process are labeled off-line and online, respectively. The focus in educational settings typically has been on the off-line aspects of comprehension (Pearson and Hamm, 2005; van den Broek, White et al., 2009). Children are asked to answer questions, to recall text information, or to perform other tasks once they are done reading the text. The results of these off-line tasks are used to gain insight into the strengths and weaknesses of the child and can be used to assess whether one intervention leads to better results than another.

Consideration of comprehension in terms of the outcome of reading is important—after all, this outcome frequently constitutes the primary purpose for reading the text. In recent years, however, attention for the processes involved during reading has increased (for an overview of the differences between these areas of research, see van den Broek and Gustafson, 1999). There are several reasons for this. One is the realization that it is the online processes that lead to the product and, therefore, largely determine whether readers succeed or fail. Thus, to be effective, interventions need to improve the process of reading. A second reason is that the theoretical understanding of the processes that take place during reading comprehension has greatly increased in recent years. Psychological models have described various components of reading comprehension with impressive precision (e.g., Graesser et al., 1994; Kintsch 1988; Myers and O'Brien, 1998; O'Brien and Myers, 1999; Rapp and van den Broek, 2005; van den Broek et al., 1996). Moreover, applications of these models to beginning and struggling readers have given insight into sources of difficulty as well as potential methods for remediation (Graesser, 2007; Rapp et al., 2007; van den Broek, Lorch, Linderholm, and Gustafson, 2001). We will now briefly describe the main properties of the products and processes of reading comprehension.

The Product of Comprehension

The product of successfully reading a text is a mental representation of the information in the text by the reader. In a successful representation, the elements (e.g., sentences, clauses) of the text are connected to each other by meaningful relations; moreover, relevant background knowledge is recruited and incorporated in the representation to create a *situation model*, an interpretation and coherent description of the information in the text (see Kintsch, 1998). Many types of meaningful relations can exist in a text and contribute to the coherence of the text. The relations identified during reading of a particular text depend on several factors, such as the reader's cognitive capacities, the reader's goals, the type of text, and so on (van den Broek, Fletcher, and Risden, 1993; van den Broek et al., 2001). However, two types of relations tend to be crucial for most reading situations, namely referential and causal relations (van den Broek, 1994). Referential relations provide connections between objects and persons across sentences, whereas causal relations indicate how the event described in one sentence causes the event in the other sentence. Consider, for example, the following pair of sentences:

The golf player hit the ball at a perfect angle.

It landed exactly where he wanted it to land.

The words "it" and "he" in the second sentence refer to the ball and the golf player, respectively, from the first sentence, thereby establishing referential coherence. The event described in the second sentence, the ball landing in the desired spot, is caused by the event in the first sentence, the player hitting the ball at a perfect angle. In this example, the relations are between adjacent sentences, but in real texts they may be separated by large segments (e.g., paragraphs or pages) of text. Further, relations may require considerable background knowledge or additional contextual knowledge supplied by the text. Imagine that the preceding sentence pair had read as following:

The golf player used a 7 iron.

The ball landed exactly where he wanted it to land.

In this case, the reader would need to know that "7 iron" refers to a particular type of golf club. Compared to the first sentence pair, here the reader must have rather detailed background knowledge about golf clubs—and perhaps more textual information about the specific setting for this golfing event—to determine whether use of the "7 iron" helped the ball to land so precisely.

Referential and causal relations are central to almost all reading situations, but other types of relations (e.g., spatial, temporal) may be recognized as well. These relations are likely to be identified when the text makes them particularly salient and easy to detect (e.g., chronological relations in the case of a history text, spatial relations in texts that give directions) or when the reader has a reading purpose that calls for particular relations (e.g., reading a description of a house read as a potential homebuyer versus as a potential burglar; see Pichert and Anderson, 1977).

Together, the text elements, the activated background information, and their semantic relations form a mental network representation that is the basis for further comprehension and for performing off-line tasks, such as retelling of the text, answering questions, applying the information, and so on (e.g., Graesser and Clark, 1985; Trabasso and van den Broek, 1985).

The Processes of Comprehension

How is coherence-building achieved as the reader proceeds through a text? What are the processes that take place *during* reading? Central to the comprehension process is the fact that direct relations between two elements are more likely to be established if the two elements are in the reader's working memory or attentional focus at the same time. Yet the capacity of working memory or attentional focus is strongly limited (Kintsch and Van Dijk, 1978; Miller, 1956). Thus, at each point during reading, only a small number of text and background-knowledge elements can be activated simultaneously. It is crucial, therefore, that the reader effectively allocate attention or working memory capacity to elements that are central to the comprehension of the text. If precious working memory capacity is spent on attending to unimportant textual information, then the ability to identify the relations that matter is compromised.

At each point during the reading of a text, information comes in the reader's focus of attention (i.e., activated in working memory) through various processes. The primary source is, of course, the sentence that is currently being read: By the nature of reading, the information in the current sentence will enter working memory. But additional information is activated from the preceding text and from the reader's background knowledge. This happens through a combination of automatic and strategic, reader-controlled processes. The central automatic process is spread of activation, by which concepts in memory of the preceding text or in the reader's prior knowledge that are associated to information in the current sentence receive activation as well (McKoon and Ratcliff, 1992; O'Brien, 1995).

Particularly interesting from an educational point of view is the allocation of attention that is under the reader's strategic control. For example, to comprehend the current sentence, the reader may reactivate information that has been processed during reading of prior sentences and attempt to meaningfully relate it to the current sentence (van den Broek et al., 1996). The reader can access this prior information by going back in the physical text and rereading or by retrieving the information from memory for the prior text. In similar fashion, a reader may search his or her background knowledge in order to provide explanations or retrieve other information that aids in the establishment of coherence. For both reactivation of prior text information and retrieval from prior knowledge, readers may use different search and retrieval strategies (e.g., Goldman and Saul, 1990; Rapp et al., 2007). Moreover, readers differ in their ability and strategies to execute the various cognitive processes that would allow them to establish coherence. For example, as a reader proceeds through a text, he or she employs *standards of coherence* that reflect the type and degree of coherence that the reader aims to maintain (van den Broek et al., 2001; van den Broek et al., 1995). The standards that a reader applies while reading a specific text specify both the types of relations (e.g., causal, referential, spatial, temporal) and the desired strengths of these relations (is it adequate that some relation is identified or does the reader strive for precise and complete relations?). Standards regarding both type and strength of relations vary not only as a function of reading goals, of course, but also as a function of fatigue, changes in involvement with the text, text difficulty, external distractions, and so on. Moreover, there are considerable differences between individual readers in their knowledge of what standards are important to maintain under particular circumstances (e.g., Rawson, Dunlosky, and McDonald, 2002). With experience, strategic processing may become automated, with their execution requiring less and less conscious directing by the reader (Laberge and Samuels, 1974).

Together, cognitive processes, such as spread of activation and retrieval of information from memory for preceding text and background knowledge, and metacognitive factors, such as one's standards of coherence and related strategies for directing strategic processes, provide the reader with a toolbox to establish coherence during reading (Rapp et al., 2007; Schraw and Bruning, 1999). They direct the dynamic allocation of attention to text and prior knowledge, thus fostering—if all goes well—the identification of meaningful relations and the construction of an integrated representation of the text. Success and failure in reading comprehension depends on the quality and coordination of these processes. Differences in the cognitive processes and the use of appropriate strategies constitute a major source of individual variation in reading skill.

Instruction and Assessment of Comprehension Skills

Besides basic language skills such a phonological awareness, letter knowledge, and decoding, beginning readers need to acquire language comprehension skills such as attention-focusing and inference-making strategies and knowledge about what it means to comprehend—including knowledge of types of standards of coherence and how to apply them (Kendeou, van den Broek, White, and Lynch, 2009; Oakhill and Cain, 2007; van den Broek, White, Kendeou, and Carlson, 2009). Educational reading programs play an important role in fostering the development of effective online comprehension processes in beginning readers.

To evaluate programs and to tune reading comprehension activities to the strengths and weaknesses in (meta) cognitive processes and strategies of students, both as a group and as individuals, assessment of the online processes of reading comprehension is central. Calls for the development of measuring tools that allow assessment of the reading process have increased in recent years (e.g., Pearson and Hamm, 2005; van den Broek, Kendeou et al., 2005) to complement the off-line, after-reading tests that are widely used (e.g., Keenan, Betjemann, and Olson, 2008; Nation and Snowling, 1997). The usefulness of the assessment of online processes is illustrated by a recent study by Rapp et al. (2007). In this study, struggling and proficient readers at three grade levels (fourth, seventh, and ninth) were identified using off-line standardized reading tests and teacher judgments. Investigation of the reading processes by these groups using eye-tracking and think-aloud methods revealed that within the group of struggling readers, two subgroups consistently emerged—at each age level and over several replications of the study. These subgroups were characterized by unique profiles of online reading processes, reflecting a weakness in building appropriate connections between text elements and a general lack of cross-sentence coherence building, respectively. Targeted interventions proved to be selectively effective for the intended subgroup. Buttressing the importance of the online assessment is the fact that the subgroups emerged *only* by consideration of the processes as they occurred during reading; they were indistinguishable in their performance on standard tests given after reading had been completed.

Unfortunately, the online assessment methods used in this study are not available or practical for teachers. Developing measurement methods that assess readers' standards of coherence and that are practically feasible would provide teachers and curriculum designers with a powerful tool in their toolbox of strategies for reading comprehension and, in turn, allow them to obtain crucial information. However, for many purposes a quick assessment of the general effectiveness of a reader's online processes is informative and useful. One method that is currently available is Curriculum-Based Measurement (CBM; Deno, 1985; Deno, 1989; Deno and Fuchs, 1987), which measures the speed and accuracy of word reading in a short period of time. One might contend that this task (word reading) is a far cry from the cognitively complex task of reading comprehension, but it is very useful as an *index* of processing efficiency as evidenced by correlations between CBM scores and other, more comprehension-oriented tasks. For example, in the previously mentioned study on struggling and proficient readers, differences in CBM measures were directly related to differences in processing profiles (Rapp et al., 2007). Furthermore, CBM has proven to be a valuable index of processing skills in other reading research contexts as well, such as in the study of second language reading (Lea, van den Broek, Cevasco, and Mitchell, 2007).

Concluding Remarks

A crucial component of successful reading comprehension is the construction of a coherent representation of the text. The mental representation is the outcome of an array of processes and skills, including the identification and application of proper standards of coherence and the availability and proper use of comprehension strategies. Educational practice is likely to benefit greatly from understanding the nature of these processes and the reasons why they may fail in an individual reader. Current reading comprehension assessment tools tend to measure the outcome of comprehension. The development and application of assessment tools that measure the process of comprehension provide a promising area of progress in educational efforts to improve the reading skills of students—children and adults.

References

Archer, D., & Guttman, C. (2007). Illiteracy costs more than literacy. *The UNESCO Courier, 10*. Retrieved from http://unesdoc.unesco.org/images/0019/001921/192180e.pdf#210819.

Baumann, J. (1983). Children's ability to comprehend main ideas in content textbooks. *Reading World, 22*, 322–331.

Cain, K., & Oakhill, J. (2007). Reading comprehension difficulties: Correlates, causes, and consequences. In K. Cain & J. Oakhill (Eds.), *Children's comprehension problems in oral and written language: A cognitive perspective* (pp. 41–75). New York, NY: Guilford Press.

Cain, K., Oakhill, J., & Lemmon, K. (2004). Individual differences in the inference of word meanings from context: The influence of reading comprehension, vocabulary knowledge, and memory capacity. *Journal of Educational Psychology, 96*(4), 671–681.

Deno, S. L. (1985). Curriculum-Based Measurement. *Exceptional Children, 52,* 219–232.

Deno, S. L. (1989). Curriculum-Based Measurement and alternative special education services: A fundamental and direct relationship. In M. R. Shinn (Ed.), *Curriculum-Based Measurement: Assessing special children* (pp. 1–17). New York, NY: Guilford Press.

Deno, S. L., & Fuchs, L. S. (1987). Developing Curriculum-Based Measurement systems for data-based special education problem solving. *Focus on Exceptional Children, 19,* 1–16.

Ehrlich, M. F. (1996). Metacognitive monitoring in the processing of anaphoric devices in skilled and less skilled comprehenders. In C. Cornoldi & J. V. Oakhill (Eds.), *Reading comprehension difficulties: Processes and remediation* (pp. 221–249). Mahwah, NJ: Lawrence Erlbaum Associates.

Goldman, S. R., & Saul, E. U. (1990). Flexibility in text processing: A strategy competition model. *Learning and Individual Differences, 2,* 181–219.

Graesser, A. C. (2007). An introduction to strategic reading comprehension. In D. McNamara (Ed.), *Reading comprehension strategies: Theories, interventions, and technologies* (pp. 3–26). New York, NY: Lawrence Erlbaum Associates.

Graesser, A. C., & Clark, L. F. (1985). *Structures and procedures of implicit knowledge.* Norwood, NJ: Ablex.

Graesser, A. C., Singer, M., & Trabasso, T. (1994). Constructing inferences during narrative text comprehension. *Psychological Review, 101*(3), 371–395.

Greenberg, D., Ehri, L. C., & Perin, D. (1997). Are word-reading processes the same or different in adult literacy students and third–fifth graders matched for reading level? *Journal of Educational Psychology, 89*(2), 262–275.

Hoover, W., & Gough, P. B. (1990). The simple view of reading. *Reading and Writing, 2,* 127–160.

Keenan, J. M., Betjemann, R. S., & Olson, R. K. (2008). Reading comprehension tests vary in the skills they assess: Differential dependence on decoding and oral comprehension. *Scientific Studies of Reading, 12*(3), 281–300.

Kendeou, P., van den Broek, P., White, M. J., & Lynch, J. (2009). Predicting reading comprehension in early elementary school: The independent contributions of oral language and code-related skills. *Journal of Educational Psychology, 4,* 765–778.

Kintsch, W. (1988). The role of knowledge in discourse comprehension: A construction-integration model. *Psychological Review, 95*(2), 163–182.

Kintsch, W. (1998). *Comprehension: A paradigm for cognition.* New York, NY: Cambridge University Press.

Kintsch, W., & van Dijk, T. A. (1978). Toward a model of text comprehension and production. *Psychological Review, 85*(5), 363–394.

Laberge, D., & Samuels, S. (1974). Toward a theory of automatic information processing in reading. *Cognitive Psychology, 6*, 293–323.

Lea, B., van den Broek, P., Cevasco, J., & Mitchell, A. (2007, November). *Bilingual resonance: Reactivating text elements between L1 and L2.* Presentation at the annual meeting of the Psychonomic Society, Long Beach, CA.

McKoon, G., & Ratcliff, R. (1992). Inferences during reading. *Psychological Review, 99*, 440–466.

Miller, G. A. (1956). The magical number seven, plus or minus two: Some limits on our capacity for processing information. *Psychological Review, 63*(2), 81–97.

Myers, J. L., & O'Brien, E. J. (1998). Accessing the discourse representation during reading. *Discourse Processes, 26*(2–3), 131–157.

Nation. K., & Snowling, M. (1997). Assessing reading difficulties: The validity and utility of current measures of reading skills. *British Journal of Educational Psychology, 67*, 359–370.

Oakhill, J., & Cain, K. (2007). Introduction to comprehension development. In K. Cain & J. Oakhill (Eds.), *Children's comprehension problems in oral and written language: A cognitive perspective* (pp. 41–75). New York, NY: Guilford Press.

O'Brien, E. (1995). Automatic components of discourse comprehension. In R. F. Lorch & E. J. O'Brien (Eds.), *Sources of coherence in reading* (pp. 159–176). Hillsdale, NJ: Lawrence Erlbaum Associates.

O'Brien, E. J., & Myers, J. L. (1999). Text comprehension: A view from the bottom up. In S. R. Goldman, A. C. Graesser, & P. van den Broek (Eds.), *Narrative comprehension, causality, and coherence* (pp. 35–53). Mahwah, NJ: Lawrence Erlbaum Associates.

Paris, S. G., Carpenter, R. D., Paris, A. H., & Hamilton, E. E. (2005). Spurious and genuine correlates of children's reading comprehension. In S. G. Paris & S. A. Stahl (Eds.), *Children's reading comprehension and assessment* (pp. 131–160). Mahwah, NJ: Lawrence Erlbaum Associates.

Pearson, P. D., & Hamm, D. N. (2005). The assessment of reading comprehension: A review of practices—past, present, and future. In S. G. Paris & S. A. Stahl (Eds.), *Children's reading comprehension and assessment* (pp. 13–69). Mahwah, NJ: Lawrence Erlbaum Associates.

Perfetti, C., Yang, C.-L., & Schmalhofer, F. (2008). Comprehension skill and word-to-text integration process. *Applied Cognitive Psychology, 22*(3), 303–318.

Perie, M., Grigg, W., & Donahue, P. (2005). *The nation's report card: Reading 2005*

(NCES 2006–451). U.S. Department of Education, National Center for Education Statistics. Washington, DC: U.S. Government Printing Office.

Pichert, J. W., & Anderson, R. C. (1977). Taking different perspectives on a story. *Journal of Educational Psychology, 69*, 309–315.

Rapp. D., & van den Broek, P. (2005). Dynamic text comprehension: An integrative view of reading. *Current Directions in Psychological Science, 14*, 276–279.

Rapp, D. N., van den Broek, P., McMaster, K. L., Kendeou, P., & Espin, C. A. (2007). Higher-order comprehension processes in struggling readers: A perspective for research and intervention. *Scientific Studies of Reading, 11*, 289–312.

Rawson, K., Dunlosky, J., & McDonald, S. (2002). Influences of metamemory on performance predictions for text. *Quarterly Journal of Experimental Psychology, 55A*, 505–524.

Schraw, G., & Bruning, R. (1999). How implicit models of reading affect motivation to read and reading engagement. *Scientific Studies of Reading, 3*(3), 281–302.

Trabasso, T., Secco, T., & van den Broek, P. W. (1984). Causal cohesion and story coherence. In H. Mandl, N. L. Stein, & T. Trabasso (Eds.), *Learning and comprehension of text* (pp. 83–111). Hillsdale, NJ: Lawrence Erlbaum Associates.

Trabasso, T., & van den Broek, P. W. (1985). Causal thinking and the representation of narrative events. *Journal of Memory and Language, 24*, 612–630.

UNESCO. (2006). *Education for all global monitoring report 2006: Literacy for life.* Paris, France: Author. Retrieved from http://unesdoc.unesco.org/images/0014/001416/141639e.pdf

van den Broek, P. (1994). Comprehension and memory of narrative texts: Inferences and coherence. In M. A. Gernsbacher (Ed.), *Handbook of Psycholinguistics* (pp. 539–588). New York, NY: Academic Press.

van den Broek, P., Fletcher, C. R., & Risden, K. (1993). Investigations of inferential processes in reading: A theoretical and methodological integration. *Discourse Processes, 16*, 169–180.

van den Broek, P., & Gustafson, M. (1999). Comprehension and memory for texts: Three generations of research. In S. R. Goldman, A. C. Graesser, & P. van den Broek (Eds.), *Narrative comprehension, causality, and coherence: Essays in honor of Tom Trabasso* (pp. 15–34). Mahwah, NJ: Lawrence Erlbaum Associates.

van den Broek, P., Kendeou, P., Kremer, K., Lynch, J. S., Butler, J., White, M. J., & Lorch, E. P. (2005). Assessment of comprehension abilities in young children. In S. Paris & S. Stahl (Eds.), *Children's reading comprehension and assessment* (pp. 107–130). Mahwah, NJ: Lawrence Erlbaum Associates.

van den Broek, P., Kendeou, P., & White, M. J. (2009). Cognitive processes during reading: Implications for the use of multimedia to foster reading comprehension. In A. G. Bus & S. B. Neuman (Eds.), *Multimedia and literacy development: Improving achievement for young learners* (pp. 57–73). New York, NY: Taylor and Francis.

van den Broek, P., Lorch, R. F., Jr., Linderholm, T., & Gustafson, M. (2001). The effects of readers' goals on inference generation and memory for texts. *Memory and Cognition, 29,* 1081–1087.

van den Broek, P., Lynch, J. S., Naslund, J., Ievers-Landis, C. E., & Verduin, K. (2003). The development of comprehension of main ideas in narratives: Evidence from the selection of titles. *Journal of Educational Psychology, 95*(4), 707–718.

van den Broek, P., Rapp, D. N., & Kendeou, P. (2005). Integrating memory-based and constructionist processes in accounts of reading comprehension. *Discourse Processes, 39,* 299–316.

van den Broek, P., Risden, K., Fletcher, C. R., & Thurlow, R. (1996). A "landscape" view of reading: Fluctuating patterns of activation and the construction of a stable memory representation. In B. K. Britton & A. C. Graesser (Eds.), *Models of understanding text* (pp. 165–187). Hillsdale, NJ: Lawrence Erlbaum Associates.

van den Broek, P., Risden, K., & Husebye-Hartman, E. (1995). The role of readers' standards for coherence in the generation of inferences during reading. In R. F. Lorch, Jr. & E. J. O'Brien (Eds.), *Sources of coherence in text comprehension* (pp. 353–373). Hillsdale, NJ: Lawrence Erlbaum Associates.

van den Broek, P., White, M. J., Kendeou, P., & Carlson, S. (2009). Reading between the lines: Developmental and individual differences in cognitive processes in reading comprehension. In R. Wagner, C. Schatschneider, & C. Phythian-Sence (Eds.), *Beyond decoding: The behavioral and biological foundations of reading comprehension* (pp. 107–123). New York, NY: Guilford Press.

Verhoeven, L., Biemond, H., Gijsel, M., & Netten, A. (2007). *Taalvaardigheid Nederlands: Stand van zaken in 2007* [*Reading proficiency in the Netherlands: The status in 2007*]. Nijmegen, The Netherlands: Expertisecentrum Nederlands.

Whitehurst, G. J., & Lonigan, C. J. (1998). Child development and emergent literacy. *Child Development, 69*(3), 848–872.

Williams, J. P., Stafford, K. B., Lauer, K. D., Hall, K. M., & Pollini, S. (2009). Embedding reading comprehension training in content-area instruction. *Journal of Educational Psychology, 101*(1), 1–20.

X

International Contributions

26

Current Status of Curriculum-Based Measurement in Korea

Dong-il Kim

A Reminiscence of the Riddle of "Curriculum-Based" Measurement

During my graduate-school years in the research room on the second floor of Burton Hall, I was always fascinated with "Deno-isms," words of wisdom delivered by Stanley Deno with humor and thoughtfulness. One of the lessons I learned at that time was that I was a part of a grand family tree, a branch that my good friend David Rogers called the "next generation of CBM." I have enjoyed the crew members of the "next generation of CBM," including many of my esteemed colleagues, such as Chris Espin (of course, she had already received her black belt in Tae Kwon Do, which earned my personal respect for her as my senior). However, during my first quarter at the University of Minnesota in 1988, the most puzzling jargon to me was that of Curriculum-Based Measurement (CBM; Deno, 1985). Because there is a national curriculum in each subject matter in Korea, my first impression of *curriculum-based* was that there should be a specific curriculum for CBM. After conducting a personal study on the term "curriculum-based," I realized that I should not be confused by the face value of curriculum-based. Several years later, when I was writing my dissertation, Deno suggested I use the term "generalized outcome measurement" instead of "Curriculum-Based Measurement."

When I returned to Korea, I began working on several research projects that were intended to develop the Korean version of CBM. At that time, I had to coin a new title for CBM because many professionals had a difficult time understanding the literal Korean translation of Curriculum-Based Measurement. In 2000, I finished the first edition of the Korean CBM, which was published under the title of Basic Academic Skills Assessment (BASA; Kim, 2000). Since that time, BASA has been applied actively in the field of Korean education. The Korean public education system has been dedicated to meet the educational needs of underachieving students, as well as those with learning disabilities, and the government has worked to improve the quality education for those students through the Basic Plan for National Human Resources Development (2001) and the Priority Area Support Project for Education Welfare Investment (2003). CBM has come to be viewed as an important tool to help students struggling with the acquisition of basic academic skills. The present chapter reports on a review of empirical research of CBM in Korea.

Current Status of Korean CBM: BASA

The review of CBM-related research was conducted in three steps. First, an electronic search of Korean research websites was conducted. These websites included the Academic Research Information Service (http://www .riss4u.net), the National Assembly Electronic Library (http://www.u-lib .nanet.go.kr), Noori Media (http://www.dbpia.co.kr), and Hakjisa Academic Research Service (http://www.newnonmun.com). Target words such as Curriculum-Based Measurement, CBM, Basic Academic Skill Assessment, BASA, reading fluency test, and basic school skills inventory were used to search for titles, key words, and abstracts. The words were searched in both English and Korean.

Second, irrelevant articles and papers were eliminated. Studies containing the content of simple reading fluency, pure curriculum, or cognitive behavior modification were identified as irrelevant. After the second step, a total of eighty-eight research articles were identified.

Third, a second exclusion round was implemented. Among the eighty-eight research articles, fifteen articles were excluded because they mentioned CBM but did not report empirical data. In addition, studies using teacher-made tools without standardized test forms were not included. These informal tools were considered to be curriculum-based assessments without norms and standardized procedures.

A total of seventy-three empirical research articles were obtained through the third step. *Field* and *topic* were used as the classification criteria to describe the research (for a detailed description of the analysis method on the research synthesis, see Kim, Koh, Jeong, Lee, Lee, Park, and Kim, 2009). The first CBM peer-reviewed article was my paper titled "Measuring Development and Change by Covariance Structure Analysis: With Special Regard to CBM Procedure for Children with Reading Difficulties," which was published in 1998 (Kim, 1998). Sixty-six (90.4 percent) of the seventy-three articles identified contained the application of BASA, which is the Korean version of CBM. A total of sixty-six articles were selected to be analyzed into two categories: field and topic. (The entire list of the articles can be obtained upon request.)

Field

CBM-related research broken down by field classification is displayed as follows:

As presented in Table 26.1 and Figure 26.1, a total of forty-four (60.2 percent) research projects were identified as CBM-related research in the field of special education. The special education research projects made up more than half of all the research reviewed and included research on children with learning disabilities or mild mental delays, research inspecting the effect of the Korean direct instruction reading program on the reading ability of students with poor reading skills (Kim and Jung, 2005), research examining the effect of reading instruction applied by a children's song on the reading ability of children with mental retardation (Kim, 2008), and research on students with math learning disabilities and the character of calculation errors in elementary school (Woo, Kim, and Shin, 2007).

TABLE 26.1.

CBM-related research trend by field

	NUMBER OF ARTICLES	PERCENT
Special education	44	60
Speech pathology	2	3
Early childhood	5	7
Clinical psychology	1	1
General education	21	29
Total	73	100

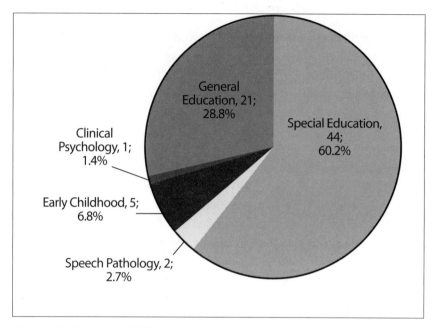

Figure 26.1. Diagram of CBM-related research trend by field

There were two research projects (2.7 percent) conducted in speech pathology. These included research on the reading aloud ability of mentally retarded children receiving language instruction through simultaneous reading (Jung, 2003) and research on the effect of question patterns of students and nonstudents with reading disabilities on problem-solving skills (Y. M. Kim, 2003). In early childhood, five research projects (6.8 percent) were found. These included research on children's reading error patterns and the level of family earnings (Koh, 2006), research on a reading intervention program for students in the lower grades with poor reading skills (Kim and Park, 2008), and research on the relationship between children's reading fluency and problematic family environment (S. H. Kim, 2003). In clinical psychology, there was one research project (1.4 percent) found that was an ADHD treatment case study using neuro-feedback (Kang et al., 2005). Lastly, there were twenty-one research projects (28.8 percent) found in general education for underachieving students or at-risk students, and these included research on the diagnosis and intervention of underachievers using a writing test system (Kim, Kim, and Bae, 2003) and research on the effect of a systematically repeated reading program on the reading fluency and reading comprehension of children with poor reading skills (Min and Lee, 2008).

Results revealed that more than half of the research projects targeted students with learning disabilities, mild mental delays, or developmental disabilities in special education in association with CBM. The remaining research articles targeted students with low achievement or at-risk students in general education. In addition, it was found that research studies in speech pathology, early childhood, and clinical psychology were only 5 percent of all research articles reviewed.

Topic

CBM-related research classified by topic in Korea is as follows:

Table 26.2 and Figure 26.2 display that CBM-related research studies by topic included a research article I published while developing BASA-Reading and five articles (6.8 percent) on test development and validation research. In intervention studies, there were sixty-seven articles (91.8 percent) located including research on repeated reading, SQ3R, reading comprehension strategy (Lee, 2007), readers theater program (Cho, 2008), and story-graphing strategy (Cho, 2006). These studies were related to testing the effect of intervention programs. In addition, there was one (1.3 percent) research article (Kim, Woo, Lee, and Ahn, 2008) that inspected the use of CBM in a variety of settings to evaluate intervention components of a Response to Intervention model in math.

TABLE 26.2.

CBM-related research trend by topic

CLASSIFICATION	NUMBER OF ARTICLES	PERCENT
Test development and validation	5	7
Intervention studies	67	92
Review	1	1
Total	73	100

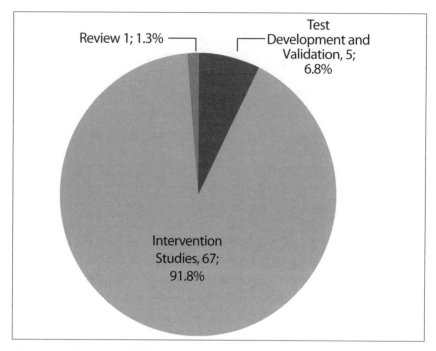

Figure 26.2. Diagram of CBM-related research trend by topic

Most of the CBM-related research studies in Korea were about intervention studies (91.8 percent); five test development and validation studies were conducted. After analyzing the intervention studies more specifically, it was concluded that there were nine (13.4 percent) research studies conducted using BASA as a diagnosis and screening tool and fifty-eight (86.6 percent) research studies using BASA as a test tool. This indicates that most of the research studies examined the use of CBM for verifying the effects of interventions or for examining developmental patterns.

Because BASA is the only pertinent CBM instrument developed in Korea thus far, research articles related to test development and validation were not conducted diversely. In the case of BASA, BASA-Writing was produced in 2008, and it has only been ten years since the first BASA (BASA-Reading) was developed. There is more to be done. However, on a positive note, intervention studies have been vigorously conducted.

Concluding Remarks

Currently, CBM in Korea has momentum to be applied and used in the public education system. Evidence-Based Practice (EBP) has become recognized as a means for narrowing the gap between educational needs and practice. An emphasis on EBP is well aligned with CBM. The research base on the use of CBM in Korea is growing. The next step is to investigate its application. The fact that BASA has already been developed in the areas of reading, math, writing, early numeracy, and phonemic awareness allows for its potential application and expansion in Korea. I predict that more and more research will be conducted in the near future using BASA.

As evidenced by the summary of the review of CBM research in Korea, CBM has had an influence on the Korean education system. Thanks to your influence, Deno, CBM is being used in Korea. In the future, CBM will move beyond special education and intervention to other diverse fields and topics.

References

Cho, G. H. (2006). *The effects of graphic organizers on reading fluency and comprehension of students with mental retardation.* Unpublished master's thesis, Chonnam National University, Gwangju, Korea.

Cho, K. H. (2008). *Readers theater: Its impact on reading fluency and reading comprehension of low achieving children in reading.* Unpublished master's thesis, Seoul National University, Seoul, Korea.

Deno, S. L. (1985). Curriculum-Based Measurement: The emerging alternative. *Exceptional Children, 52,* 219–232.

Jung, Y. B. (2003). *Effects of teaching speech through reading poems together on oral reading ability for the children with mental retardation.* Unpublished master's thesis, Dankook University, Seoul, Korea.

Kang, J. W., Park, J. G., Cheon, Y. W., Han, G., Park, H. C., Kim, L. H., Yoo, G., & Jeong, E. H. (2005). A case report of ADHD child treated with neurofeedback. *Journal of Oriental Neuropsychiatry, 16*(2), 243–249.

Kim, D. I. (1998). Measuring development and change by covariance structure analysis: With special regard to CBM procedure for children with reading difficulties. *Journal of Special Education, 5,* 85–99.

Kim, D. I. (2000). *Basic Academic Skills Assessment (BASA): Reading.* Seoul, Korea: Hakjisa.

Kim, D. I., & Jung, K. J. (2005). The effects of the Han-Geul reading program of direct instruction on the reading ability of elementary schools students with low achievement. *Journal of Emotional and Behavioral Disorders, 21*(3), 149–169.

Kim, D. I., Kim, M. S., & Bae, S. J. (2003). Development and validation of assessment of written expression for children with academic difficulties. *Asian Journal of Education, 4*(3), 43–67.

Kim, D. I., Koh, E. Y., Jeong, S. R., Lee, Y. R., Lee, K. J., Park, J. K., & Kim, I. N. (2009). The analysis of Korean learning disability research trend. *Asian Journal of Education, 10*(2), 283–347.

Kim, E. A. (2008). *The effects of a reading instruction using children's songs on the reading ability of children with mental retardation.* Unpublished master's thesis, Gwangju National University of Education, Gwangju, Korea.

Kim, M. S., & Park, C. H. (2008). The effectiveness of reading intervention on at-risk children in first through third grade. *Journal of Child Studies, 29*(5), 301–319.

Kim, S. H. (2003). *The relationship between children's reading fluency and home literacy environment.* Unpublished master's thesis, Yonsei University, Seoul, Korea.

Kim, Y. M. (2003). *Comparison of problem-solving abilities of children with reading disabilities and normal children on different types of questions in early elementary school.* Unpublished master's thesis, Dankook University, Seoul, Korea.

Kim, Y. W., Woo, J. H., Lee, S. H., & Ahn, J. A. (2008). A study on major components of response-to-intervention in mathematics. *Journal of Special Education: Theory and Practice, 9*(1), 279–302.

Koh, J. H. (2006). *Reading miscue analyses of children from low-income families.* Unpublished master's thesis, Yonsei University, Seoul, Korea.

Lee, T. S. (2007). Effects of repeated choral reading (RCR) and SQ3R strategy on reading fluency and reading comprehension of students with reading difficulties. *Korean Journal of Special Education, 41*(4), 133–147.

Min, H. S., & Lee, D. S. (2008). Effects of a systematic repetitive reading program on reading fluency and reading comprehension of underachieving elementary students. *Asian Journal of Education, 9*(4), 149–172.

Woo, J. H., Kim, Y. G., & Shin, J. H. (2007). A study on the characteristics of operation errors made by students with mathematics learning disabilities in elementary school. *Journal of Special Education: Theory and Practice, 8*(3), 575–596.

27

Footprints of Curriculum-Based Measurement in South Korea

Past, Present, and Future

Jongho Shin

The past directs the future and the future learns from the past. Curriculum-Based Measurement (CBM) has laid a foundation for making evidence-based, accountability-emphasized education systems for students with learning difficulties not only in the United States but also in South Korea. CBM, as a methodology, permits teachers to find out how students are progressing in basic academic areas such as math, reading, writing, and spelling using a systematic method. The research in this area by Professor Stanley Deno at the University of Minnesota has influenced much of the current research and practice for students with learning disabilities (LD); furthermore, future research and practice will derive their direction and agenda from what Stanley Deno has left us.

What Has Happened in the Past?

The concept of CBM was introduced to Korean researchers in the special education field during the late 1980s through journal articles and introductory textbooks on special education. In the 1980s, there were no experts with professional training on CBM; therefore, informational access to CBM was limited to documents (e.g., journal articles, special education textbooks, ERIC documents). As expected, the level of interest in CBM was only happening at the surface level at that time. Additionally, the usefulness and potential of CBM for monitoring basic skills of students with LD was only discussed within the narrow confines of the special education research community. Educational practitioners, including special education teachers, did not understand the methodology of CBM nor realize how to properly apply it to further educational practices for students with LD. This situation remained until the mid-1990s.

In the mid-1990s, Dong-il Kim returned to South Korea after receiving his doctoral degree under the academic supervision of Stanley Deno at the University of Minnesota. On his return, Dong-il gave many professional lectures on CBM to researchers and teachers in special education. As a result, Korean researchers and teachers gradually began to understand CBM and how CBM might be used in special education practice.

Dong-il developed a Korean-oriented version of CBM so that CBM could be disseminated at the classroom level. In 2000, he published the first Korean-version CBM in reading called the Basic Academic Skills Assessment (BASA)—Oral Reading (Kim, 2000). The BASA—Oral Reading has helped to bring CBM into widespread use in South Korea. After the development of the BASA—Oral Reading, Dong-il went on to publish the commercial BASA—Arithmetic and BASA—Writing tests in the mid-2000s.

The BASA instruments facilitated the use of CBM not only by practitioners but also by researchers who studied the psychometric characteristics of the BASAs. Most of this research was conducted by Dong-il and his graduate students at Seoul National University. Results of this research have revealed that the reliability and validity of the BASA instruments are similar to the reliability and validity of the CBM measures used in the United States. The BASA instruments also have been used as tools for evaluating educational programs for students with LD or low achievement. Most published articles on CBM in Korean journals can be categorized into this type of CBM use (e.g., Choi, 2008; Hur and Jeong, 2004; Jung and Kim, 2007; Min and Lee, 2008).

In South Korea, CBM has been used as an assessment tool not only for students with LD but also for low-achieving students. Although LD is stipulated as a category of special education services in South Korea, the type of formal special education services seen in many Western countries is not provided in South Korea. During the school day, students with LD are grouped with students without LD. Students with LD do not receive independent special education programs within the regular school hours. Instead, special basic-skills programs are provided for both students with LD and students who are low-achieving after the school day is over. Even though special education services have increased to a large extent over the past two decades, the services are still organized mainly for students with intellectual disabilities and students with sensory disorders.

What Is Happening Now?

The special education community is still relatively small in South Korea. To advocate for better educational services for students with learning difficulties (including LD), a professional organization was established in 2004 called the Korea Learning Disabilities Association (KLDA). The KLDA is composed of professionals in the areas of learning disabilities, educational psychology, educational counseling, and communication disorders. Since 2008, KLDA has conducted professional training workshops for teachers and professionals. These workshops include an assessment training workshop focused on the use of CBM in reading, arithmetic, and writing. As a result of these workshops, the use of CBM for monitoring and assessing students with learning difficulties has increased in recent years.

In the last five years, research on CBM in South Korea has been directed toward the development of a progress-monitoring system for students with learning difficulties. Thus far, the CBM measures (BASA) have been found to have good psychometric characteristics (Hong, Jung, and Kim, 2006; Kim, 1999; Kim, Kim, and Bae, 2003). With the increased use of advanced statistical techniques such as Hierarchical Linear Modeling, more systematic research can be directed toward the characteristics of the measures as growth-monitoring measures (see Shin, Espin, Deno, and McConnell, 2004, for details).

Researchers in Korea have noticed the strengths of CBM as a growth-monitoring system and have been involved in the development of norms for growth rates in reading and arithmetic. Plans are under way to use the norms to monitor the students' progress over a year and to evaluate the educational programs provided after school.

What Do We Expect for the Future?

One emerging topic in South Korea is the development of a reliable and valid system for identifying students with LD in order to provide independent services for these students. Influenced by the research outcomes conducted in the United States, Korean researchers have been questioning the practical validity of the discrepancy model and have moved toward a Response to Intervention (RTI) model. They have considered CBM to be an important component in developing the Korean RTI model. Considering the current situation, CBM will be influential in setting up an independent educational service system for students with LD in South Korea in the near future.

An additional topic of interest for CBM researchers in South Korea is the development of CBM measures in the content areas. In the United States, researchers such as Espin, Foegen, and Tindal (see Espin and Tindal, 1998, and Foegen, this volume) have extended the horizon of CBM research beyond the basic skill areas. A CBM vocabulary measure in social sciences is an example (see Espin, Shin, and Busch, 2005, for details). In South Korea, efforts are being made to expand the borders of CBM to the content areas (e.g., social sciences, sciences, and technology subjects).

Finally, the use of CBM is expected to expand into the areas of educational counseling and communication disorders. In South Korea, educational counseling is becoming more specialized, and the counselors are now conducting various academic consulting activities with students with severe learning difficulties and their parents. Many counselors attend the CBM workshops offered by the KLDA and show high interest in the use of CBM for addressing students' academic problems in the basic skill areas. Additionally, professionals in communication disorders are becoming interested in using the CBM oral reading to assess reading fluency of students with communication disorders. We can expect more professional exploration of the possibility of using CBM reading measures for students with communication disorders in educational and clinical settings.

A British historian, Arnold J. Toynbee, in his book titled *A Study of History*, suggested that the continuation and development of a civilization depends on how it deals with the challenges it faces. CBM is helping educators and educational researchers in South Korea to face the challenges associated with the education of children with disabilities. As I illustrated in this chapter, Deno's work is not just historical in nature but paving a path to the future. It is in this way that Deno's work will remain with us forever and continue to thrive and improve education in future generations.

References

Choi, J. K. (2008). A study on the meaning of goal setting and effects of intervention within Curriculum-Based Measurement. *Asian Journal of Education, 9*(2), 89–112.

Espin, C., Shin, J., & Busch, T. (2005). Curriculum-Based Measurement in the content areas: Vocabulary-matching as an indicator of social studies learning. *Journal of Learning Disabilities, 38*, 353–363.

Espin, C. A., & Tindal, G. (1998). Curriculum-Based Measurement for secondary students. In M. R. Shinn (Ed.), *Advanced applications of Curriculum-Based Measurement* (pp. 214–253). New York, NY: Guilford Press.

Hong, S. D., Jung, E. J., & Kim, D. I. (2006). Math Curriculum-Based Measurement for the students with learning disabilities. *The Korea Journal of Learning Disabilities, 3*(2), 1–27.

Hur, S. J., & Jeong, J. H. (2004). Effects of story retelling strategy on the reading comprehension and fluency of students with learning disabilities. *Journal of Special Education Theory and Practice, 5*, 369–387.

Jung, K. J., & Kim, D. I. (2007). The effects of the Korean reading program of applying direct instruction principles on special need students who are reading disability students in primary schools. *Asian Journal of Education, 8*, 169–196.

Kim, D. I. (1999). Developing reading inventories with the Curriculum-Based Measurement procedure. *Journal of Special Education, 6*, 103–116.

Kim, D. I. (2000). *Basic Academic Skills Assessment (BASA): Reading*. Seoul, Korea: Hakjisa.

Kim, D. I., Kim, M. S., & Bae, S. J. (2003). Development and validation of assessment of written expression for children with academic difficulties. *Asian Journal of Education, 4*, 43–67.

Min, H. S., & Lee, D. S. (2008). Effects of a systematic repetitive reading program on reading fluency and reading comprehension of underachieving elementary students. *Asian Journal of Education, 9*(4), 149–172.

Shin, J., Espin, C. A., Deno, S. L., & McConnell, S. (2004). Use of hierarchical linear modeling and Curriculum-Based Measurement for assessing academic growth and instructional factors for students with learning difficulties. *Asia Pacific Education Review, 5*, 136–148.

28

Expanding the Use of Curriculum-Based Measurement

A Look at Nicaragua

Sylvia Linan-Thompson

In 2005, a public service video showing young children from Peru reading a passage about a dog named Dogo and answering questions introduced parents, educators, and policymakers to the utility of Curriculum-Based Measurement (CBM) for determining who could read fluently and who could not (*Metas Claras Para Aprender Mejor*, 2005). It also introduced the notion that quick assessments are useful for setting the direction in education reform by providing "comprehensible and actionable information on student performance" (Abadazi, Crouch, Echegary, Pasco, and Sampe, 2005, p. 137). The report that followed confirmed what is often assumed but rarely documented—that students in the most disadvantaged areas of developing countries are functionally illiterate even after two or three years of schooling (Abadazi, 2006). The video, along with the report and a concerted effort by numerous agencies, is changing the manner in which developing countries are using assessments and approaching educational reform. This chapter will provide a brief introduction to assessment practices in developing countries, the United Nations Educational, Scientific and Cultural Organization (UNESCO) initiative that propelled a shift in the use of assessment, the development process of the Early Grade Reading Assessment (EGRA), and the implementation of EGRA in Nicaragua.

At the time the video and report were released, little was known about the utility of CBM in developing countries. Whereas students are assessed in many countries regularly, particularly in core areas such as reading and mathematics as a means of determining promotion into the next grade or level, few educational systems use formal assessments to screen students or to monitor their progress in basic skills. Thus educators and policymakers have little information about the rate at which students acquire basic literacy skills to inform educational policy or to make systemic changes. For example, results from the few low-income countries that participate in international assessments such as the Programme for International Student Assessment (Organisation for Economic Co-operation and Development, 1997) indicate that the median child in a low-income country performs at about the third percentile of children from a high-income country (Organisation for Economic Co-operation and Development, 2004). Scores in the third percentile are indicative of students who fail to score or who have very low scores, giving a clear indication of what students do not know. The very low scores that children below the third percentile achieve, however, are not useful in determining what students *do* know (Research Triangle Institute International, 2009).

Improving basic instruction is one of the goals of UNESCO's Education for All Initiative (Dakar Framework for Action, 2000). More specifically, one of the goals of this initiative states that educators should strive to "improve all aspects of the quality of education and ensure excellence of all so that recognized and measurable learning outcomes are achieved by all, especially in literacy, numeracy and essential life skills" (UNESCO, 2005, p. 29). The use of CBM is providing educators in developing countries a means to respond to UNESCO's initiative. General Outcome Measures (GOMs) of reading are gaining acceptance in developing countries as a means of not only tracking achievement but also informing instruction. However, this process has to be conceptualized and operationalized in countries that, to date, have focused on measuring student achievement on outcomes only in third and sixth grade, if that. The results of these measures, like those of the international assessments, are often disappointing and do not help educators identify the source of students' difficulties or the specific areas to address.

Curriculum-Based Measurement

CBM, as defined by Deno (1985), refers to the evaluation of instructional needs through ongoing measurement of student performance within the local school curriculum (Tucker, 1987). Deno's work and the research that followed led to the establishment of a measurement system that was (a) easy to construct, (b) easily administered and scored, (c) technically adequate, and (d) available in alternate forms to allow for the monitoring of student progress. Initially, CBM was used to track student progress in reading and spelling. Currently, CBM is also used for screening, normative decision making, and benchmarking. In recent years, CBM has become increasingly important in classrooms as a form of standardized measurement that is highly related to and relevant for understanding students' progress toward achievement of state standards.

In the United States, the use of CBM in the classroom to determine the effects of instruction and curricula is prevalent. The measures used (e.g., oral reading fluency, letter naming, letter sound fluency, and word reading) assess basic skills necessary for efficient reading. The tasks used to assess these skills are not necessarily specific to a particular curriculum but are considered GOMs of proficient reading (Fuchs and Deno, 1994).

CBM in Developing Countries

Recently under EdData II (see https://www.eddataglobal.org for a description), an initiative funded by the U.S. Agency for International Development with additional support from the World Bank, and with the collaboration of ministries of education and development professionals in the World Bank, the United States Agency for International Development (USAID), and other institutions (Abadzi, 2006; Center for Global Development, 2006; Chabbott, 2006; World Bank: Independent Evaluation Group, 2006), the use of GOMs has been introduced in several countries. This initiative has led to the creation of simple, effective, and low-cost measures of student learning outcomes in reading.

Research Triangle Institute (RTI) International (2009) developed a protocol for the individual oral assessment of students' foundational reading skills. The development of a set of measures that could be used across countries and languages began in fall of 2006. As a starting point, the evidence for reading acquisition in English that supports a comprehensive approach based on five essential components identified by the U.S. National Reading Panel (2000; phonics, phonemic awareness, vocabulary, fluency, and comprehension) was used to propose key components. A group of cognitive scientists, early grade reading instruction experts, research methodologists, and assessment experts were tasked with reviewing the proposed key components. In addition to reviewing the reading literature, cognitive science research, and assessment practices, the group considered issues related to designing a multicountry, multilingual, early grade reading assessment protocol. Finally, the assessment had to be method-independent because the approaches used to teach reading across countries varied in response to the structure of the language, resources, and level of teacher training.

EGRA includes between eight and ten subtests with tasks that assess letter recognition, phonological awareness, alphabetic principle, reading fluency, and comprehension. EGRA has been adapted into twenty-three languages and implemented in eighteen countries. Each subtest is developed following criteria that allows for flexibility to adjust for differences in the structure of each language. Because there are no data on beginning reading skills across grade levels and high rates of illiteracy in the countries using EGRA, the same measures are used with students in grades one through three. This set of common measures allows researchers to begin to get a sense of gain against a constant instrument, which is helpful in beginning to think about setting growth norms and targets.

Initially, the goal was to develop measures that provided stakeholders with a comprehensive approach to improve student reading outcomes by identifying areas for improvement at the system level. Across countries, ministries of education now have a baseline of student reading skills in the primary grades. They have data on what reading skills students have acquired and when they acquire them.

According to the EGRA Toolkit, the baseline data have been used in a number of ways across countries. General benchmarking and the creation of goals for future applications have been the most common uses. Ministry personnel and educators at all levels have used the results to critically examine current curricula, existing programs, and preservice and in-service teacher programs and to begin to identify areas to modify. The intent is that parallel forms of EGRA will be developed and used to screen and monitor the progress of students.

Use of EGRA in Nicaragua

The development of EGRA followed a slightly different trajectory in Nicaragua. The first version of the Spanish EGRA was implemented in Nicaragua. Additionally, it was the first site to have two forms of the measures (Form A and Form B). These parallel forms were validated in the initial collection of pilot data in November of 2007. As in other countries, a version using the most commonly used indigenous language, Miskito, was developed and piloted. The measures were piloted in forty-seven schools in four departments. The sample was composed of 2,206 children in grades one through three; of these, 1,927 were assessed in Spanish and 282 were assessed in Miskito (Laguna, 2009).

The baseline data were collected in April and May of 2008 from a sample of second to fourth grade students in 126 randomly selected public and private schools. The sample was composed of 6,649 students, with about equal numbers females (n = 3,322) and males (n = 3,327). Of these, 44 percent (n = 2,927) of students attended rural schools, and the remaining students attended urban schools. The sample included just over 2,000 students at each grade level (n = 2,164 for second grade; n = 2,218 for third grade; and n = 2,267 for fourth grade). Results indicated that although the students in Nicaragua were acquiring early reading skills at levels that were higher than other developing countries, they were still performing at rates that were considerably lower than developed countries. For example, the mean for letter naming at second grade was 39.4 correct letters per minute (CLPM). The beginning of first-grade benchmark for low-risk status on *Indicadores Dínamicos del Éxito en la Lectura* (Dynamic Indicators of Reading Success; Good, Bank, and Watson, 2003) *Fluidez en Nombrar Letras* (Letter Naming Fluency) is greater than 35 CLPM. The end-of-first-grade benchmark for low-risk status on nonword reading fluency is greater than 90 correct words per minute (CWPM). The mean correct words per minute read by students in Nicaragua across the three grades was 22.9 in second grade, 35.1 in third grade, and 41.9 in fourth grade. Finally, the oral reading fluency means on a 50-word passage written at a first-grade level were 46.5 CWPM at second grade, 82.7 CWPM at third grade, and 106.5 CWPM at fourth grade. Oral reading fluency benchmarks on *Indicadores Dínamicos del Éxito en la Lectura* are greater than 65 CWPM at the end of second grade and greater than 85 CWPM at the end of third grade. However, these benchmarks are on grade-level passages, and the Nicaraguan scores are on a first-grade passage.

Students did not perform well on measures of phonological awareness, letter sound fluency, or on the nonword reading measure relative to their performance on letter naming fluency, word reading fluency, and oral reading fluency. Educators confirmed that phonological awareness is not a part of the national curriculum and that letter sounds are not taught. Teaching letter names and not sounds is standard practice in Spanish literacy instruction in Central America.

Across the measures there was an increase in scores from second to fourth grade, indicating that on average students are learning, just not at a rate that allows the majority to be proficient readers by the time they finish third grade. One of the greatest challenges Nicaragua faces is the high level of school desertion and grade retention. There is a 25 percent drop in school enrollment between first and second grade, presumably due to retention and desertion by students who after at least two attempts at first grade have failed to learn to read.

One limitation in interpreting the scores is the lack of Nicaraguan benchmarks on basic reading skills. Benchmarks from other Spanish language measures provide a point of reference that indicates that the large contextual differences between Nicaragua and the United States. These baseline data provide a starting point, and as more data are collected and alternate forms developed, correlational studies will provide the additional data needed to develop Nicaraguan benchmarks.

Based on the results of the baseline data and the research on the use of CBM in improving instruction, the Ministry of Education of Nicaragua asked that teachers be trained to use CBM to monitor student progress and plan instruction. A four-day workshop was developed and provided in three regions to 142 teachers, district personnel, teacher educators, and Ministry of Education personnel in April of 2009 by RTI International staff and the author in collaboration with staff and consultants from *Centro de Invesitagcion y Accion Educacativa Social* (Center for Research and Educational Social Action), a Nicaraguan research organization. The attendees were to return to their homes to train the teachers in their area. Implementation of CBM to benchmark student learning began in the fall of 2009.

Challenges in Using CBM in Developing Countries

Though the promise of CBM for benchmarking, screening, and progress monitoring is recognized, there are challenges in large-scale implementation in developing countries. Measures like EGRA can be used to fulfill a diverse range of assessment needs, including screening and progress monitoring in developing countries, but funding and the capacity for developing parallel forms and validating them is not readily available in most countries. The work continues, nonetheless.

Although the goal in all developing countries and of UNESCO's Education for All initiative is to ensure that all children acquire literacy and numeracy, the realistic approach is to set attainable goals in the short term with an eye toward meeting the benchmarks set in more developed countries. The use of CBM is the process that is enabling educators in many parts of the world to make decisions and to make changes to their education system to improve outcomes for their children by providing data about student learning.

References

Abadazi, H. (2006). *Efficient learning for the poor: Insights from the frontier of cognitive science.* Washington, DC: World Bank.

Abadazi, H., Crouch, L., Echegary, M., Pasco, C., & Sampe, J. (2005). Monitoring basic skills acquisition through Rapid Learning Assessments: A case study from Peru. *UNESCO Prospects, 35*(2), 137–156.

Center for Global Development. (2006). *When will we ever learn? Improving lives through impact evaluation.* Retrieved January 12, 2007, from http://www.cgdev .org/files/7973_file_WillWeEverLearn.pdf

Chabbott, C. (2006). *Accelerating early grades reading in high priority EFA Countries: A desk review.* Retrieved June 20, 2009, from http://www.equip123.net/docs/E1-E GRinEFACountriesDeskStudy.pdf

Dakar Framework for Action. (2000). *Education for all: Meeting our collective commitments.* Retrieved June 20, 2009, from http://www.unesco.org/education/efa/ ed_for_all/dakfram_eng.shtml

Deno, S. L. (1985). Curriculum-Based Measurement: The emerging alternative. *Exceptional Children, 52*, 219–232.

Fuchs, L. S., & Deno, S. L. (1994). Must instructionally useful performance assessment be based in the curriculum? *Exceptional Children, 61*, 15–24.

Good, R. H., Bank, N., & Watson, J. M. (Eds.). (2003). *Indicadores dinámicos del éxito en la lectura* [Dynamic Indicators of Reading Success]. Eugene, OR: Institute for the Development of Educational Achievement.

Laguna, J. R. (2009). *Informe de Resultados EGRA 2008* [Report on the Results of the EGRA 2008 Pilot Assessment]. Unpublished report.

Metas claras para aprender mejor [Teaching with clear goals]. (2005). Retrieved June 20, 2009, from https://www.eddataglobal.org

National Reading Panel. (2000). *Teaching children to read: An evidence-based assessment of the scientific research literature on reading and its implications for reading instruction* (NIH Publication No. 00-4769). Washington, DC: National Institute of Child Health and Human Development.

Organisation for Economic Co-operation and Development. (1997). *Programme for International Student Assessment.* Paris, France: Author.

Organisation for Economic Co-operation and Development. (2004). *Learning for tomorrow's world: First results from PISA 2003.* Retrieved January 2008 from http:// www.oecd.org/document/55/0,3343,en_32252351_32236173_33917303_1_1_1_1,00 .html

Research Triangle Institute International. (2009). *Early grade reading assessment toolkit*. Retrieved May 25, 2009, from https://www.eddataglobal.org/documents/index.cfm?fuseaction=pubDetail&ID=149

Tucker, J. A. (1987). Curriculum-based assessment: An introduction. *Exceptional Children, 52*, 199–204.

United Nations Educational, Scientific and Cultural Organization. (2005). *EFA global monitoring report: Education for all literacy for life*. Paris, France: Author.

World Bank: Independent Evaluation Group. (2006). *From schooling access to learning outcomes—An unfinished agenda: An evaluation of World Bank support to primary education*. Washington, DC: World Bank: Independent Evaluation Group.

29

The Use of Curriculum-Based Measurement Maze in Greek

A Closer Look at What It Measures

Panayiota Kendeou and
Timothy C. Papadopoulos

Reading comprehension is a multidimensional construct. This conclusion is consistent with recent initiatives in the field that involved exploring the relative contribution of component skills to performance on well-known reading comprehension tests (Cutting and Scarborough, 2006; Keenan and Betjemann, 2006). The findings of these studies have revealed that a reader's performance on these tests depends on different component skills. This finding raises the possibility that commonly used tests of reading comprehension may tap different language and cognitive processes and highlights the need for a systematic investigation of the relative contribution of these component skills to performance on different reading comprehension tests. In the study described in this chapter, we investigated the relative contribution of cognitive, phonological, rapid automatized naming (RAN), orthographic, and word reading fluency measures to Curriculum-Based Measurement (CBM) Maze (see Espin, Deno, Maruyama, and Cohen, 1989; Deno, Maruyama, Espin, and Cohen, 1989; Fuchs and Fuchs, 1992). CBM Maze has considerable psychological validity and is commonly used in the fields of reading and learning disabilities as a general index of reading. Even though it is often considered a proxy of reading comprehension, we know very little about the exact processes it assesses.

To attain our objective, we examined the degree to which different cognitive and language component skills explain unique variance in performing a reading task such as CBM Maze. With respect to cognitive skills, we focused on the assessment of children's simultaneous and successive processes, which have been found to be strong correlates of word reading

(Das, Parrila, and Papadopoulos, 2000; Papadopoulos, 2001). With respect to language skills, we focused on phonological, reading fluency, RAN, and orthographic measures, all of which have been investigated in the context of reading comprehension (Cain, Oakhill, and Bryant, 2004; Kendeou, van den Broek, White, and Lynch, 2009). Furthermore, we investigated the contribution of these skills longitudinally. We consider it important to establish the longitudinal continuity of these component skills, particularly in early elementary school, because most of these skills tend to measure different processing skills at different points in time in the early years (Papadopoulos, Georgiou, and Kendeou, 2009).

Component Skills and Reading Comprehension

With respect to cognitive skills, we focused on the assessment of children's simultaneous and successive processes in the context of the Planning, Attention, Simultaneous, and Successive (PASS) processing theory (Das, Naglieri, and Kirby, 1994). Because thorough reviews of the PASS model and related research are presented elsewhere (e.g., Naglieri and Rojahn, 2004; Papadopoulos, Das, Parrila, and Kirby, 2003), only a brief summary of the two component skills that were used as predictors in the present study is provided here.

The PASS theory of cognitive processes is based largely on the psychological work of Luria (e.g., 1980). The maintenance of attention, the processing and storing of information, and the management and direction of mental activity comprise the activities of the operational units that work together to produce cognitive functioning (Das et al., 1994). *Simultaneous and successive coding* of information composes the second functional unit of the PASS theory. Simultaneous processing involves the arrangement of incoming information into a holistic pattern, or a gestalt, that can be surveyed in its entirety. For example, recognition of whole words by sight involves this kind of processing, as does comprehension of the meaning of a sentence or a paragraph (Papadopoulos, 2001). Simultaneous processing, therefore, contributes to what has become known as *outside-in* skills of emergent literacy (Whitehurst and Lonigan, 1998).

Successive processing refers to coding information in discrete, serial order where the detection of one portion of the information is dependent on its temporal position relative to other material. It is used in skills such as word decoding and spelling where the maintaining of the exact sequence or succession of letters in the word is crucial for completion (Naglieri, 2001; Papadopoulos, 2001). Successive processing, therefore, is relatively broader than the specific tests for phonemic awareness, syntax awareness, or even short-term memory (Papadopoulos, Georgiou, and Douklias, in press) and contributes to the deployment of what has become known as *inside-out* skills of emergent literacy (Whitehurst and Lonigan, 1998).

With respect to language skills, we focused on phonological, word reading fluency, RAN, and orthographic measures, all of which have been investigated in the context of reading comprehension (Cain et al., 2004; Kendeou et al., 2009). The terms *phonological awareness* and *phonological sensitivity* are used interchangeably to refer to a wide range of skills involved in manipulating the sounds of speech. There is irrefutable evidence for the significant role of phonological abilities in reading development across different languages (Anthony and Lonigan, 2004; Ziegler and Goswami, 2005). Phonological abilities are among the best predictors of how well children acquire reading during the first two years of formal reading instruction (Savage, Carless, and Ferraro, 2007). For many, training in phonological skills may have benefits for subsequent reading in later years (Bus and van Ijzendoorn, 1999).

Fluency is one of several critical factors necessary for reading comprehension and involves reading orally with speed and accuracy (Fuchs, Fuchs, Hosp, and Jenkins, 2001). A key component of reading fluency is automaticity. As automaticity in the context of word reading develops, readers can move away from the laborious and slow unit-by-unit decoding and can allocate their attentional resources to higher-order processes such as comprehension (Perfetti, 1985). Indeed, it has been shown that readers who lack reading fluency also have impaired comprehension (Schwanenflugel et al., 2006); therefore, it is no surprise that reading fluency reliably distinguishes skilled from less-skilled readers (Juel, 1988).

RAN is a multicomponent skill and is assumed to measure the ability to access and retrieve phonological representations from long-term memory and the ability to form orthographic representations (e.g., Torgesen, Wagner, Rashotte, Burgess, and Hecht, 1997). There is evidence that RAN skills are a significant predictor of reading (de Jong and van der Leij, 1999; Georgiou, Papadopoulos, and Parrila, 2008). Furthermore, there is also evidence for its relation to reading fluency (e.g., Compton, 2003).

Spelling is the productive ordering of the letters that compose a word (Vellutino, Tunmer, Jaccard, and Chen, 2007) and is often measured using orthographic processing measures. Spelling skills, in turn, depend heavily on children's phonological awareness and knowledge of the alphabetic system (Ehri, 2005). Furthermore, there is direct evidence that spelling skills predict word reading and vocabulary (Protopapas, Sideridis, Simos, and Mouzaki, 2007). Indeed, spelling instruction results in better reading. Several studies have demonstrated that orthographic processing impacts reading acquisition and accounts for a significant amount of variance in reading comprehension (e.g., Torgesen et al., 1997).

What Does CBM Maze Measure? Empirical Evidence in Greek

We conducted an empirical investigation of the extent to which different language and cognitive skills contribute to a child's performance on CBM Maze. Participants in the study were 280 Greek-Cypriot children (141 males and 139 females). The children were native Greek speakers with no reported history of speech, language, or hearing difficulties. The mean age of the group in the initial assessment (grade 1) was six years, six months, and in the second assessment seven years, seven months.

We used a battery of language measures to assess phonological awareness, RAN, word reading fluency, and spelling and a battery of measures to assess cognitive skills central to reading. Participants' phonological skills were assessed using the phoneme elision and phoneme blending tasks from a larger comprehensive phonological battery that has undergone extensive development and validation (Papadopoulos, Kendeou, and Spanoudis, 2009; Papadopoulos, Spanoudis, and Kendeou, 2009). RAN was assessed using tasks of naming letters and digits. Word reading fluency was assessed using real word and pseudoword reading tasks within sixty seconds (Papadopoulos, 2001). Spelling was assessed using tasks of orthographic choice and word chains (Papadopoulos, Georgiou, and Kendeou, 2009). Three measures (one simultaneous processing and two successive processing) taken from the Das-Naglieri Cognitive Assessment System (DN-CAS; Naglieri and Das, 1997) standardization in Greek by Papadopoulos, Georgiou, Kendeou, and Spanoudis (2007) were used to assess participants' cognitive processing skills. These measures included verbal-spatial relations, sentence repetition and sentence questions, and speech rate.

The CBM Maze (Espin, Deno, Maruyama, and Cohen, 1989; Deno, Maruyama, Espin, and Cohen, 1989; L. Fuchs and D. Fuchs, 1992) was adapted in Greek and required students to read passages that included incomplete sentences. Participants were asked to choose the correct word among three options (one correct and two incorrect) to appropriately complete the sentence as they read the text. Three written passages were presented, one at a time, in a booklet form. These passages were similar to text that participants were exposed to in their own reading or in school, with the exception that they had multiple-choice sentences embedded within them. Participants had one minute to read as much of each passage as possible and, while reading, circle the appropriate words to accurately complete the target sentences. This same pattern was repeated for all three passages. Students' scores consisted of the average number of correct words chosen minus the number of incorrect words chosen.

We used Structural Equation Modeling to explore which skills were measured by CBM Maze. In evaluating the goodness of fit of the model to the data, we report the model chi-square statistic associated with the p-value, the comparative fit index (CFI), and the root mean square error of approximation (RMSEA). A nonsignificant value of the chi-square statistic indicates a good fit; however, the test is sensitive to sample size and should be considered in relation to its degrees of freedom (i.e., dividing chi-square value by its degrees of freedom should result in a value below two, indicating a good model). A CFI index equal to or superior to 0.90 indicates a good fit (Hu and Bentler, 1999). Finally, the RMSEA is an absolute fit index that considers the complexity of the model; values less than 0.05 are considered a good fit (Cudeck and Browne, 1992).

The model included five latent variables at each time point. The five latent variables were cognitive processing skills, phonological awareness, RAN, word reading fluency, and spelling. Indicators for cognitive processing skills were DN-CAS verbal-spatial relations, sentence repetition and questions, and speech rate measures. Indicators for phonological awareness were phoneme elision and phoneme blending measures. Indicators for RAN were RAN digits and RAN letter measures. Indicators for word reading fluency were word identification and word attack measures. Finally, indicators for spelling skills were orthographic choice and word chains measures. We hypothesized that the latent variables were interrelated. We also hypothesized that the latent variables possessed longitudinal continuity—that is, skills at time point 1 (grade 1) predicted skills at time point 2 (grade 2), and thus, grade 1 scores were applied as autoregressors on grade 2 scores. Finally, we hypothesized that all five latent skills in grade 2 predicted CBM Maze in grade 2.

The conceptual model is presented in Figure 29.1. As indicated by the fit indexes [χ^2 (193, N = 289) = 405.83, p < .001; CFI = .92; RMSEA = .06 (90 percent confidence interval = .05 to .07)], the model yielded a good fit to the data. The relative magnitude of the standardized coefficients showed that reading performance on CBM Maze was significantly predicted by word reading fluency (7.3 percent) and RAN (9 percent). Cognitive, phonological, and spelling skills did not significantly predict performance on CBM Maze.

Conclusions and Implications for the Use of CBM Maze

Inferences about how well an individual reads and comprehends are based on the material and the task that is completed during or after reading (Fletcher, 2006). Indeed, comprehension is typically assessed by requiring students to

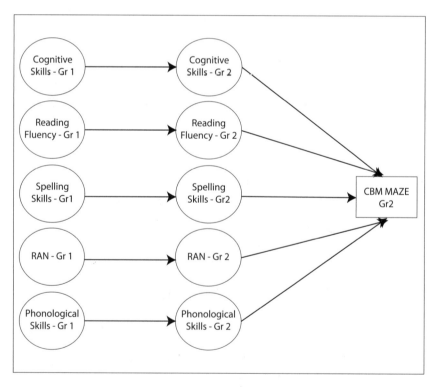

Figure 29.1. Conceptual model of component skills contributing to CBM Maze from grade 1 to grade 2

read short passages and then respond either by retelling, selecting among multiple-choice answers, or filling in the missing words (van den Broek et al., 2005). These traditional measures can yield useful information about reading comprehension if we better understand the cognitive and linguistic skills that are involved during reading (Kendeou, van den Broek, White, and Lynch, 2007; Kendeou, Bohn-Gettler, White, and van den Broek, 2008; Kendeou et al., 2009; Rapp et al., 2007). In the absence of such understanding, these measures provide only a basic indication of how well a child understands text and offers little information about why some students may struggle with comprehension when others succeed, in turn, making remedial instruction a burdensome task for teachers and psychologists alike.

On the basis of our approach and results, we reached a better understanding of the predictive validity of different cognitive and linguistic predictors of reading comprehension. Our findings show that despite the use of a number of predictors, such as phonological, RAN, word reading fluency, spelling, and cognitive measures, performance on CBM Maze depends primarily on two of these predictors: RAN and word reading fluency, both of which require speed and accuracy of processing. The conclusion, therefore, that the type of measure used to determine the child's reading competence does matter, is consistent with recent initiatives in the field that explored the relative contribution of component skills to performance on well-known measures of reading comprehension, such as the Gates-MacGinitie, Gray Oral Reading Test, and Wechsler Individual Achievement Test (Cutting and Scarborough, 2006; Keenan and Betjemann, 2006). The clear consensus across these studies and ours is that the measurement issues are complicated, reflecting the complex, multidimensional nature of reading comprehension.

Even though any single attempt to assess a complex construct such as reading comprehension will be by definition imperfect, using CBM Maze in a school context as a reading comprehension proxy measure has important implications for instructional decision making, including early diagnosis and intervention of reading problems. With respect to early diagnosis, the measure taps into language and cognitive skills that have been identified to be central to reading comprehension, but mostly on word reading fluency and RAN. Therefore, low performance on CBM Maze likely indicates difficulty with speed and accuracy of decoding. This information can be used to tailor interventions appropriately and address the child's specific weakness. A fruitful future direction would be to investigate the degree to which higher-order comprehension skills (e.g., inference making) also contribute to CBM Maze.

Knowing the degree to which performance on CBM Maze also depends on those skills will contribute significantly to its psychological validity.

Furthermore, using CBM Maze in a school context can be advantageous for several reasons beyond the knowledge of the exact component skills it taps into. First, the test is simple and easy to administer. Second, training of teachers is quick and reliable. Third, large numbers of students can be tested simultaneously, frequently, and in only a few minutes. Finally, frequent testing can allow the teacher to track student progress over the school year.

To the best of our knowledge, this is the first attempt at using CBM Maze in Greek. We believe that the potential of the CBM approach is reliable and cost-effective, and we hope that it will find supporters in our educational system.

References

Anthony, J. L., & Lonigan, C. J. (2004). The nature of phonological awareness: Converging evidence from four studies of preschool and early grade school children. *Journal of Educational Psychology, 96*, 43–55.

Bus, A. G., & van Ijzendoorn, M. H. (1999). Phonological awareness and early reading: A meta-analysis of experimental training studies. *Journal of Educational Psychology, 91*, 403–414.

Cain, K., Oakhill, J., & Bryant, P. (2004). Children's reading comprehension ability: Concurrent prediction by working memory, verbal ability, and component skills. *Journal of Educational Psychology, 96*, 31–42.

Compton, D. L. (2003). Modeling the relationship between growth in rapid naming speed and decoding skill in first-grade children. *Journal of Educational Psychology, 95*, 225–239.

Cudeck, R., & Browne, M. W. (1992). Constructing a covariance matrix that yields a specified minimizer and a specified minimum discrepancy function value. *Psychometrika, 57*, 357–369.

Cutting, L. E., & Scarborough, H. S. (2006). Prediction of reading comprehension: Relative contributions of word recognition, language proficiency, and other cognitive skills can depend on how comprehension is measured. *Scientific Studies of Reading, 10*, 277–299.

Das, J. P., Naglieri, J. A., & Kirby, J. R. (1994). *Assessment of cognitive processes: The PASS theory of intelligence*. Boston, MA: Allyn & Bacon.

Das, J. P., Parrila, R. K., & Papadopoulos, T. C. (2000). Cognitive education and reading disability. In A. Kozulin & Y. Rand (Eds.), *Experience of mediated learning: An impact of Feuerstein's theory in education and psychology* (pp. 274–291). Oxford, UK: Pergamon Press.

de Jong, P. F., & van der Leij, A. (1999). Specific contributions of phonological abilities to early reading acquisition: Results from a Dutch latent variable longitudinal study. *Journal of Educational Psychology, 91,* 450–476.

Deno, S. L., Maruyama, G., Espin, C. A., & Cohen, C. (1989). *The Basic Academic Skills Samples (BASS).* Minneapolis: University of Minnesota.

Ehri, L. C. (2005). Learning to read words: Theory, findings, and issues. *Scientific Studies of Reading, 9,* 167–188.

Espin, C. A., Deno, S. L., Maruyama, G., & Cohen, C. (1989, March). *The Basic Academic Skills Samples (BASS): An instrument for the screening and identification of children at risk for failure in regular education classrooms.* Paper presented at the National Convention of the American Educational Research Association, San Francisco, CA.

Fletcher, J. M. (2006). Measuring reading comprehension. *Scientific Studies of Reading, 10,* 323–330.

Fuchs, L. S., & Fuchs, D. (1992). Identifying a measure for monitoring student reading progress. *School Psychology Review, 21,* 45–58.

Fuchs, L. S., Fuchs, D., Hosp, M. K., & Jenkins, J. R. (2001). Oral reading fluency as an indicator of reading competence: A theoretical, empirical, and historical analysis. *Scientific Studies of Reading, 5,* 239–256.

Georgiou, G. K., Parrila, R., & Papadopoulos, T. C. (2008). Predictors of word decoding and reading fluency across languages varying in orthographic consistency. *Journal of Educational Psychology, 100,* 566–580.

Hu, L. T., & Bentler, P. M. (1999). Cutoff criteria for fit indexes in covariance structure analysis: Conventional criteria versus new alternatives. *Structural Equation Modeling: A Multidisciplinary Journal, 6,* 1–55.

Juel, C. (1988). Learning to read and write: A longitudinal study of 54 children from first through fourth grades. *Journal of Educational Psychology, 80,* 437–447.

Keenan, J. M., & Betjemann, R. S. (2006). Comprehending the Gray Oral Reading Test without reading it: Why comprehension tests should not include passage-independent items. *Scientific Studies of Reading, 10,* 363–380.

Kendeou, P., Bohn-Gettler, C., White, M., & van den Broek, P. (2008). Children's inference generation across different media. *Journal of Research in Reading, 31,* 259–272.

Kendeou, P., van den Broek, P., White, M., & Lynch, J. (2007). Preschool and early elementary comprehension: Skill development and strategy interventions. In D. S. McNamara (Ed.), *Reading comprehension strategies: Theories, interventions, and technologies* (pp. 27–45). Mahwah, NJ: Lawrence Erlbaum Associates.

Kendeou, P., van den Broek, P., White, M. J., & Lynch, J. (2009). Predicting reading comprehension in early elementary school: The independent contributions of oral language and decoding skills. *Journal of Educational Psychology, 101,* 765–778.

Luria, A. R. (1980). *Higher cortical functions in man* (2nd ed.). New York, NY: Basic Books.

Naglieri, J. A. (2001). Using the Cognitive Assessment System (CAS) with learning-disabled children. In A. S. Kaufman & N. L. Kaufman (Eds.), *Specific learning disabilities and difficulties in children and adolescents* (pp. 141–177). Cambridge, UK: Cambridge University Press.

Naglieri, J. A., & Das, J. P. (1997). *Das-Naglieri cognitive assessment system.* Itasca, IL: Riverside.

Naglieri, J. A., & Rojahn, J. (2004). Construct validity of the PASS theory and CAS: Correlations with achievement. *Journal of Educational Psychology, 96,* 174–181.

Papadopoulos, T. C. (2001). Phonological and cognitive correlates of word-reading acquisition under two different instructional approaches. *European Journal of Psychology of Education, 16,* 549–567.

Papadopoulos, T. C., Das, J. P., Parrila, R. K., & Kirby, J. R. (2003). Children at-risk for developing reading difficulties: A remediation study. *School Psychology International, 24,* 340–366.

Papadopoulos, T. C., Georgiou, G. K., & Douklias, S. (in press). Modeling of dyslexia: Is a unitary model of dyslexia possible? In H. D. Friedman and P. K. Revera (Eds.), *Abnormal psychology: New research.* Hauppauge, NY: Nova Science.

Papadopoulos, T. C., Georgiou, G. K., & Kendeou, P. (2009). Investigating the double-deficit hypothesis in Greek: Findings from a longitudinal study. *Journal of Learning Disabilities, 42,* 528–549.

Papadopoulos, T. C., Georgiou, G. K., Kendeou, P., & Spanoudis, G. (2007). *Standardization in Greek of the Das-Naglieri cognitive assessment system.* Department of Psychology, University of Cyprus, Nicosia, Cyprus. (Original work published 1997)

Papadopoulos, T. C., Kendeou, P., & Spanoudis, G. (2009). *Development and factor structure of phonological abilities in Greek.* Manuscript submitted for publication.

Papadopoulos T. C., Spanoudis, G., & Kendeou, P. (2009). The dimensionality of phonological abilities in Greek. *Reading Research Quarterly, 44,* 127–143.

Perfetti, C. A. (1985). *Reading ability.* New York, NY: Oxford University Press.

Protopapas, A., Sideridis, G. D., Simos, P. G., & Mouzaki, A. (2007). The development of lexical mediation in the relationship between text comprehension and word reading skills in Greek. *Scientific Studies of Reading, 11,* 165–197.

Rapp, D. N., van den Broek, P., McMaster, K. L., Kendeou, P., & Espin, C. A. (2007). Higher-order comprehension processes in struggling readers: A perspective for research and intervention. *Scientific Studies of Reading, 11,* 289–312.

Savage, R., Carless, S., & Ferraro, V. (2007). Predicting curriculum and test performance at age 11 years from pupil background, baseline skills and phonological awareness at age 5 years. *Journal of Child Psychology and Psychiatry, 48,* 732–739.

Schwanenflugel, P. J., Meisinger, E., Wisenbaker, J. M., Kuhn, M. R., Strauss, G. P.,

& Morris, R. D. (2006). Becoming a fluent and automatic reader in the early elementary school years. *Reading Research Quarterly, 41*, 496–522.

Torgesen, J. K., Wagner, R. K., Rashotte, C. A., Burgess, S. R., & Hecht, S. A. (1997). The contributions of phonological awareness and rapid automatic naming ability to the growth of word reading skills in second to fifth grade children. *Scientific Studies of Reading, 1*, 161–185.

van den Broek, P., Kendeou, P., Kremer, K., Lynch, J. S., Butler, J., White, M. J., & Lorch, E. P. (2005). Assessment of comprehension abilities in young children. In S. Stahl & S. Paris (Eds.), *Children's reading comprehension and assessment* (pp. 107–130). Mahwah, NJ: Lawrence Erlbaum Associates.

Vellutino, F. R., Tunmer, W. E., Jaccard, J. J., & Chen, R. (2007). Components of reading ability: Multivariate evidence for a convergent skill model of reading development. *Scientific Studies of Reading, 11*, 3–32.

Whitehurst, G. J., & Lonigan, C. J. (1998). Child development and emergent literacy. *Child Development, 69*, 848–872.

Ziegler, J. C., & Goswami, U. (2005). Reading acquisition, developmental dyslexia, and skilled reading across languages: A psycholinguistic grain size theory. *Psychological Bulletin, 131*, 3–29.

Reflections on the Influence of Curriculum-Based Measurement on Educational Practice and Policy . . . and Its Progenitor

Mark R. Shinn

It is a distinct honor, and significant challenge, to write the summary piece for *A Measure of Success*. In the introduction to this book, the question was posed, "How has CBM research influenced educational practice and policy?" Considering the depth and breadth of the chapters, and the varied backgrounds of the authors, one would have to conclude that the influence has been substantial. Chapters were contributed by noted authorities in the field of special education (e.g., Vaughn, L. Fuchs, D. Fuchs, Sindelar, Zigmond), educational psychology (e.g., van den Broek) and school psychology (e.g., Shapiro, Christ), from university professors (e.g., Graves, Shriner, Tindal, Yell), school-based leaders (e.g., Gibbons, Germann), and U.S. Department of Education personnel (e.g., Bradley).

After reading the powerful chapters included in this volume, I struggled with a way to say *more* than the chapters themselves said. I settled on an organizational structure that may be unconventional: to organize the big ideas I gleaned from the contributors' chapters around a set of *Ps*; that is, some themes that might capture characteristics of the impact of Curriculum-Based Measurement (CBM) research on the field of education, special education, and school psychology.

I first encountered the set of *Ps* organizational structure in a presentation years ago by one of the book's authors, Gary Germann. In that presentation, he stressed that schools currently are organized around a set of *Ps*, including politics, power, personalities, provincialism, parochialism, promises, and philosophies. Gary characterized this set of *Ps* as adult issues. In other words, schools, in his opinion, are based on the needs of adults, not students. What attracted me to this organizational structure was that Gary was determined to create conditions where schools were driven by a new set of *Ps*: (a) *performance* and (b) *progress*.

In reading this volume, it is clear that among the ties that bind all the authors' reflections on CBM is the collective effort to drive what schools do by this new set of *Ps*. I intend to include the *Ps* of performance and progress implicitly throughout this summary. However, I will also explicitly highlight other *Ps* including (a) progenitor, (b) parsimonious, (c) prescient, (d) powerful, (e) principled, (f) programmatic, (g) participatory, (h) passionate, and if I may stretch the structure a bit, (i) phish and phishing. In addressing this set of *Ps*, I do not intend to be exhaustive with respect to repeating all that is written by every single contributor, at greater length and detail, and also with better quality than I can in this summary. Instead, I hope that the selections I use here are representative of the concepts I am trying to communicate.

Progenitor

Let me begin with the most obvious of the *Ps* in this book, that of *progenitor*, or originator. It must be obvious to the reader that all the chapters in this book were contributions from persons with a relationship to Stanley L. Deno, from the University of Minnesota, whether as former graduate students (e.g., Espin, Foegen, Lembke, Marston) or as long-standing contemporaries and colleagues (e.g., Jenkins). Other chapters were written by persons with a less obvious relationship with Deno but, from my reading, were influenced strongly by his development of CBM (e.g., Dion, Linan-Thompson).

Certainly educators were aware of the importance of authentic assessment of student performance, especially oral reading before the development of CBM. However, from my knowledge of the field, no one had taken the concept of authentic assessment with measures like oral reading and validated them as psychometrically sound yet practically efficient instruments and built them into key components of today's data-based service delivery systems (e.g., Response to Intervention). That is Deno's legacy. Thus, to me, it is not possible to de-couple CBM from its progenitor, and thus, I will interpret the remaining *Ps* with respect to CBM as well as the person, Stanley Deno.

Another definition of progenitor includes ancestor. For more than thirty-five years, my professional work and, indeed, my worldview on schools and schooling has been influenced by Deno and the simple lens into student progress and performance that CBM provided me.

Parsimonious

In the first paragraph of the first chapter of this book, Jenkins and Fuchs adeptly capture the overarching theme of Deno's work on student progress monitoring, data-based decision making, and CBM. This theme is one of the most important *Ps, parsimony*: "Simple indicators of academic competence could be used to capture the overall academic strength of an individual student at a given point of time, and such data could be used to track the trajectory of development. His emphasis was solidly on the idea of simplicity" (p. 7).

In all likelihood because of Deno's own graduate training as a scientist, Ockham's Razor drove the research efforts for all the years of his work on CBM. If there was an oversight in the book, it was the chronology of the labels used to describe the major efforts of Deno's scholarly work. The Jenkins and Fuchs chapter describes how the measurement concepts that became CBM emerged out of the Applied Behavioral Analysis of social behavior, such as graphing an observable behavior over time, and from expanding the educational psychology research on reading assessment, including Precision Teaching (White, 1974; White and Haring, 1980). Other chapters note the influence of the school practice philosophy summarized in *Data-Based Program Modification: A Manual* (DBPM; Deno and Mirkin, 1977). But the importance of parsimony to Deno was reflected in the progress monitoring test development principles published in a seminal article by Jenkins, Deno, and Mirkin (1979). I was surprised that this important article was not referenced in the chapters. The importance of parsimony also was shown in the titles of the early research publications, *simple measures of progress*. See for example, the following citations for the early research directed by Deno at the Institute for Research on Learning Disabilities (IRLD). In the interest of explicitness, I have modified APA format.

Deno, S. L., Mirkin, P. K., Chiang, B., Tindal, G., Fuchs, L. S., Martson, D., & Kuehnle, K. (1980). **Simple** approaches to assessing learning disabled students' spelling performance, social status and written expression.

Deno, S. L., Mirkin, P. K., Lowry, L., & Kuehnle, K. (1980). Relationships among **simple** measures of spelling and performance on standardized achievement tests.

Fuchs, L. S., Tindal, G. A., & Deno, S. L. (1982). Use of aggregation to improve the reliability of **simple** direct measures of academic performance.

Marston, D., & Deno, S. L. (1981). The reliability of **simple**, direct measures of written expression.

Marston, D., Lowry, L., Deno, S. L., & Mirkin, P. K. (1981). An analysis of learning trends in **simple** measures of reading, spelling, and written expression: A longitudinal investigation.

At some point, *simple measures* evolved into Data-Based Assessment (DBA) briefly around 1982–85, as noted in the chapter by Marston, but the concept of parsimony was expressed in the title of one of the first published articles on CBM reading:

Deno, S. L., Marston, D., Shinn, M. R., & Tindal, G. (1983). Oral reading fluency: A **simple** datum for scaling reading disability. *Topics in Learning and Learning Disability, 2*, 53–59.

After a brief sojourn as Curriculum-Based Assessment (CBA), by 1985, simple measures were formalized as Curriculum-Based Measurement (Deno, 1985), but the defining attribute of Deno's work was not lost on the field nor on the contributors of the book.

Parsimony was the guiding principle for research and, importantly, *for practice.* From the beginning, the goal was to provide teachers with a simple tool for decision making. Indeed, the most frequently used metaphor was to provide educators with the equivalent of the thermometer or a weight scale. Jenkins and Fuchs's chapter included a quote by the noted medical scientist Atul Gawande (2007) that captured the key to Deno's contributions: "All patients deserve a simple measure that indicates how well or badly they have [responded to medical intervention] . . . and that pushes the rest of us to innovate" (Gawande, 2007, p. 199).

Numerous contributors echoed the theme of parsimony as it related to teacher decision-making practices, including but not limited to Hosp and Hosp (this volume): "Deno's work on CBM has focused on technical adequacy *and* utility—producing measures that are useful for educators, parents, and students to make consistent and valid decisions about a student's progress" (p. 52).

Principled

The second major theme that emerged from my reading of the book was that Deno's work on CBM was *principled.* I consider two interpretations of this *P*. The first interpretation is principled with respect to (a) research and (b) practice. Research and practice surrounding CBM have consistently been guided by a set of explicit underlying big ideas. These ideas were first laid out in DBPM, expanded in Jenkins, Deno, and Mirkin (1979), and further articulated in the Problem-Solving Model (Deno, 1989, 1995, 2002).

The second interpretation is principled with respect to meeting the needs of children and families. It was this meaning of the *P* that I derived by reading the chapters on school practice, especially special education practices in the chapters by D. Fuchs and Bradley on Special Education Resource Teachers (SERTs) and by Yell and Busch on Individualized Education Programs (IEPs).

Principled Research and Practice

It is evident to the contributors that Deno's research on CBM was guided by a consistent set of guidelines for a progress monitoring system, described in Deno and Mirkin (1977), in Jenkins, Deno, and Mirkin (1979), and revisited in various forms throughout the subsequent years, including two pieces that I believe should be required readings for all educators serious about assessment:

Deno, S. L. (1991). Individual differences and individual difference: The essential difference of special education. *Journal of Special Education, 24*(2), 160–173.
Fuchs, L. S., & Deno, S. L. (1991). Paradigmatic distinctions between instructionally relevant measurement models. *Exceptional Children, 57*(6), 488–500.

Among the key concepts of Deno's research efforts was attention to solid technical adequacy (i.e., reliability, validity), sensitivity, utility, efficiency, and efficacy. Jenkins and Fuchs attribute this consistent adherence to principles to Deno's graduate school training in classical measurement theory. It is not at all difficult to see these concepts in every article that Deno has published that has a Method section.

What is equally compelling, if not more so, is that Deno's impact on school practices also has been principled. A set of guiding assumptions (or principles) for practice as well as research was first laid out in the DBPM manual (Deno and Mirkin, 1977), a book that was referenced in thirteen of the twenty-nine chapters I read. Three of these DBPM assumptions were referenced consistently in the chapters (e.g., D. Fuchs and Bradley):

1. Educators cannot with any certainty prescribe specific and effective instruction for individuals. Prescribing a form of instruction for an individual should be treated only as a hypothesis that must be empirically tested to ascertain its effects.
2. Time-series analyses are uniquely appropriate for testing instructional hypotheses.
3. Progress monitoring should focus on those academic performances that represent "vital signs" of educational development.

That these principles for practice affected the field was expressed well in chapter 23 by Shapiro and Lentz:

> It is amazing how one small book can have such a large impact on one's professional thinking and career. In 1982, we had both just recently become school psychology trainers at Lehigh University . . . and badly wanted to move the Lehigh model toward a behaviorally oriented, intervention-based program. As we were in the midst of this complicated process . . . we came across the 1977 volume titled *Data-Based Program Modification: A Manual* by Stanley Deno and Phyllis Mirkin. This discovery became a keystone event that was instrumental in allowing us to merge our emergent philosophy of practice, our behavioral training, and the use of effective interventions within an existing school-based behavioral consultation approach to service delivery (Bergan, 1977). (p. 277)

Principled as Reflecting Strong Social Values

Embedded in many of Deno's writings is a compelling argument regarding the need to improve educational outcomes for all students, but especially for those students who receive special education services. In an era where CBM is used widely for general education student screening and progress monitoring, it was refreshing to see chapter 3 on the use of CBM in IEPs by Yell and Busch. These contributors point out the long-standing problems of IEPs and progress monitoring and remind the reader of the original intent of what became CBM—to provide a basis for writing IEP goals and monitoring their attainment. Quoting a famous court case, Yell and Busch (this volume) report that the judge wrote the following: "Without a clear identification of [the child's] present levels, the IEP cannot set measurable goals, evaluate the child's progress and determine which educational and related services are needed" (*Kirby v. Cabell County Board of Education*, 2006, p. 694).

Under Deno's guidance, and through leadership from Phyllis Mirkin, the IRLD research on CBM was an effort to fulfill the *vision and promise of the IEP* under circumstances where procedural compliance was high but substantive compliance in use of IEPs to improve outcomes was low. At the IRLD, IEP goal writing and progress-monitoring manuals were completed and delivered to school personnel in order to provide IEP teams with a research-validated assessment tool (i.e., CBM) that could be used to write goals and monitor student progress (Deno, 1985). Important early works related to IEP development include the following:

Deno, S. L., & Mirkin, P. (1980). Data-based IEP development: An approach to substantive compliance. *Teaching Exceptional Children, 12*, 92–97.

Deno, S. L., Mirkin, P. K., & Wesson, C. (1984). How to write effective data-based IEPs. *Teaching Exceptional Children, 16*, 99–104.

Fuchs, L., Deno, S. L., & Mirkin, P. K. (1981). *Teacher efficiency in continuous evaluation of IEP goals* (No. IRLD-RR-53). Minneapolis: University of Minnesota Institute for Research on Learning Disabilities.

Mirkin, P. K., Deno, S. L., Fuchs, L. S., Wesson, C., Tindal, G., Marston, D., & Kuehnle, K. (1981). *Procedures to develop and monitor progress on IEP goals*. Minneapolis: University of Minnesota Institute for Research on Learning Disabilities.

Powerful

It was clearly expressed in a number of chapters that although Deno's work was predicated on building a parsimonious, efficient, and effective system for progress monitoring (i.e., *simple* methods of gauging students' response to intervention), the impact of his work extended beyond just the development of CBM. A sizeable proportion of chapters (e.g., Germann; Marston; Robinson, Robinson, and Blatchley; Gibbons and Casey) detailed how this simple measurement system became a critical and *powerful* tool in creating and implementing a new service delivery *system*. In chapter 2, D. Fuchs and Bradley, among others, describe Deno's very early work with Minneapolis Special Education Research Teachers to transform school practices. Other chapters, notably chapter 6 by Germann, describe how CBM was a cornerstone in a new service delivery system in the Pine County Special Education

District. It was Pine County, a rural cooperative, that not only served as a field-testing site for the original CBM research but also helped to develop a different way of conceptualizing schooling. Two years after Germann's Pine County implementation, systems changes began to occur in urban schools in Minnesota, including Minneapolis (described by Marston) and St. Paul (described by Robinson, Robinson, and Blatchley). In less than three years, CBM and Deno's work had moved from small *n* research and field testing to the progress monitoring of hundreds, if not thousands, of special education students as standard practice.

Robinson, Robinson, and Blatchley describe it this way:

> During a doctoral internship in Saint Paul School District's Special Education Department, one of Dr. Deno's graduate students was as-signed to the special education unit working with ELLs. The graduate student introduced department staff to CBM and its potential applica-tions. Saint Paul special education staff and Dr. Deno met regularly to discuss the use of CBM to avoid discrimination in ELL assessment and to make eligibility decisions for supplementary educational ser-vices. This early work on the use of CBM led to extensive application for ELLs in Saint Paul Schools and made an important contribution to meeting the needs of these students. (p. 189)

Marston echoes these sentiments on the effects of Deno's work on Minne-apolis Public Schools: "His research and development at the University of Minnesota on CBM has inspired the implementation of data-based decision making in screening, eligibility, instructional planning, progress monitoring, program evaluation, school improvement planning, problem solving, and Response to Intervention. The work of Deno has indeed had a profound ef-fect on the Minneapolis Public Schools and improved our ability to make informed educational decisions for our students" (p. 77).

Today, these school improvement efforts, driven by data-based decision making and attention to student performance and student progress, have led to a multitier, coordinated early intervening services model or Response to Intervention (RTI). The evolution of CBM as a simple assessment tool to a key component of the nationwide RTI effort is described well by Kloo, Machesky, and Zigmond in chapter 13 as they describe the impact of CBM on a *single school* that was not succeeding: "Perceptions began to change as early as the first year of implementation. Everyone recognized the value of frequently assessing students and using these data to plan for and provide reading instruction in which they could meaningfully participate and learn. When students were finally given the opportunity to actually learn to read we saw the data improve, the graphs go up, and the atmosphere at Larue change" (p. 173). This quote reminded me of one of the Deno-isms from my own graduate years: "What works, wins." How the power of Deno's CBM work and his DBPM principles are winning by being a critical component of RTI is a common theme of a number of contributors.

Shapiro and Lentz put it this way: "Indeed, the concept of measuring a student's academic health through key indicators was the basis for Curriculum-Based Measurement (CBM), a concept of evaluation that has now sustained itself into one of the most crucial aspects of today's models of Response to Intervention" (p. 278). Speece says the following: "Taken together, the findings suggested that the RTI framework, based in part on work by Fuchs and Fuchs and powered by Deno's CBM, possessed criterion and social validity: another healthy development" (pp. 182–183).

Finally, given the quantitative nature of Deno's research efforts, I would be remiss if I didn't organize the *power* of his CBM work from the book's contributors in a single place in the volume.

In chapter 18, Roberts, Wanzek, and Vaughn say the following: "We offer two of many possible data sources: (1) Google Scholar (August, 2009) reports that just one of Stanley Deno's articles (1985) has had over six hundred citations, and (2) CBM has significantly contributed to the implementation of Response to Intervention, all assessment in special education, and many screening measures, and it is part of all research-based educational training programs for teachers and school psychologists across the United States and increasingly other countries as well" (p. 237). In chapter 14, Speece says the following: "An electronic search of a single database using the term 'Curriculum-Based Measurement' and stipulating peer-reviewed journals yielded 390 hits; deleting the peer-reviewed criterion yielded 958 hits" (pp. 185–186). And in chapter 1, Jenkins and Fuchs say the following: "In 2004, the Research Institute on Progress Monitoring (Espin and Wallace) identified 585 CBM research reports, 307 of which were published in journals (121 were unpublished documents, 131 were dissertations, 26 were unclassified). Among the 307 publications, 141 reported empirical studies addressing questions of technical adequacy, instructional utility, and the logistics of implementation in reading, writing, spelling, and math" (p. 16).

I wanted to conclude the section on *Powerful* on a less quantitative note but one that is perhaps the most important index of the effect of Deno's work. This part of the Sindelar's chapter 21 struck me the most. "Such is the pervasiveness of Deno's influence on teaching practice. In teacher education programs across the country, students are taught to monitor their children's progress and to use this information to make critical decisions about what and how to teach. In fact, standards promulgated by the Council for Exceptional Children (2008) stipulate that 'special educators regularly monitor the progress of individuals with exceptional learning needs in general and special curricula' (p. 49). In our judgment, effective special education practice requires it" (pp. 263–264).

Programmatic

The original simple measurement research began in 1979 not only with measures of language arts, especially reading, but also with spelling and written expression, and somewhat less successfully, behavior. From this beginning, whether by Deno or by his graduate students or colleagues, an ongoing *program* of research was initiated. In looking at this book's chapters, it is clear that the original work has expanded to other (a) measures (e.g., early literacy, early numeracy, algebra), (b) student populations (e.g., English Learners, persons with severe disabilities), (c) assessment decisions (e.g., high-stakes tests, special education assessment accommodations), and (d) other languages and countries (e.g., Korean, Greek). It is not surprising then that chapters describe the generalization of CBM to young children in prereading (i.e., Good et al., this volume) and to older students in middle and high school in language arts, including reading, reading comprehension, and writing (Espin and Campbell, this volume).

Mathematics CBM research has paled in comparison to reading, although it is not without its own modest size research base (Foegen, Jiban, and Deno, 2007). What struck me was an increasing and very important set of advances in mathematics, especially algebra. If the National Mathematics Advisory Panel (2008) recommendations come to fruition in practice, then more national attention will be directed to this area. However, given that so many students struggle to master the content, and given that instruction remains largely whole group, a new frontier for progress monitoring in content-area instruction is opening. Foegen's contribution is especially exciting in expanding the tools in the mathematics progress-monitoring toolbox.

That CBM expands into other populations and languages is not at all surprising, although I would speculate the robust nature of the measures' validity and utility must confound some persons with "culturally centric" perspectives—that is, the perspective that each culture learns to read differently and thus assessment must be different. In contrast, it seems that reading aloud works the same way (i.e., as a valid measure of general reading ability) regardless of language and culture. In the fields of psychology and education, implementation often begins with students more at the margins, and Deno's work with CBM is no exception. Still, as I read the chapters, I couldn't help but think how this volume could be used in an assessment class to communicate the concepts of "educational indicators" (i.e., the thermometer) across multiple dimensions, including, but not limited to (a) academic subject areas, (b) student language and cultures, (c) ages, and (d) assessment decisions.

Prescient

In reading the chapters, and in my own experience with CBM and Deno's work, the theme of *prescience* struck me. Among the definitions of the word are "knowing in advance" or "prophetic." One of the comments that occasioned my choice to use this term to describe Deno's impact was in chapter 10 by Lembke, McMaster, and Stecker: "When Curriculum-Based Measurement (CBM) research was beginning in the 1970s, members of the University of Minnesota's Institute for Research on Learning Disabilities (IRLD) would probably have scarcely believed that thirty years later, educators and psychologists would be collecting CBM data using handheld devices or laptop computers or that teachers would be sharing and discussing CBM data with their peers online" (p. 127).

My first reaction to this quote was that I'm not so sure. One of the remarkable features of Deno's work was his vision toward the future, not only building on attempts to remedy past concerns and attending to *past* research outcomes, but also seeing how prior simple solutions in other fields had led to widespread practice use. In particular, I recall a research meeting in 1979 in which Deno predicted that by the twenty-first century, all students in the country would have their reading progress monitored by a simple oral reading assessment. His prediction was close, although current nationwide use is not *all* students. I doubt it was hubris, especially given that at the time, obtaining participants for the early CBM research demanded miles of travel.

And certainly, the exact technological *how to's* described in terms of current CBM and progress-monitoring practices by Lembke, McMaster, and Stecker weren't there at the time. But the basic structures for widespread practice were (a) parsimony and (b) strong social utility. *What* was measured had the potential for considerable expansion. *How* it was measured (and reported) was a different question.

Lembke et al. note that Deno's early CBM research was well aware of assessment logistics. They note that in a publication by Wesson, King, and Deno (1984), many teachers reported that they were using CBM data but reported also that they perceived it as time consuming. The awareness of limited teacher time was always reflected in the IRLD where research addressed efficiency of measurement, including systematically evaluating the length of time it took to collect student progress-monitoring data (e.g., thirty seconds vs. one minute vs. five minutes of reading), finding the simplest ways to score specific measures (e.g., total words written vs. total word sequences vs. correct word sequences), and organizing and reporting the outcomes (e.g., equal interval vs. six-cycle graphs). It should also be noted that by 1982, Gary Germann had already developed *SHERI*, an Apple IIe program that graphed and reported CBM data.

Participatory, Phish, Phishing, and Maybe Potpourri

A few of the chapters speak about the effect that CBM had on the authors' own research or as a tool in their research toolbox. These chapters clearly outline the impact of Deno's work with CBM on the authors' own research programs. For example, in chapter 8, Dion et al. describe their efforts to address the floor effects of oral passage reading with kindergartners and beginning first graders. Likewise in chapter 18, Roberts et al. examine CBM and its linkage to high-stakes tests, demonstrating that CBM aligned with instructional decisions on state outcome assessments. Like these researchers, all chapter contributors learned content such as CBM, reliability, validity, sensitivity, graphing, and so on directly and indirectly through Deno's work. In pushing the alliteration, we learned about the *phish*.

What especially struck me, however, was that many of the chapters moved *beyond* a description of learning content to learning process; that is to say, a number of chapters, including this one, report learning not only about phish but also about *phishing*—the process of becoming an academician, from advising, to scholarship, and to inquiry. In large part, this came from the nature of how Deno conducted business; graduate students and colleagues were expected to *participate*. Jenkins and Fuchs note the etiology of this approach in chapter 1: "Deno worked with Jerry Gross, Minneapolis's director of special education, to develop a field-based training site at Seward School. There he introduced preservice special education teachers to Precision Teaching methods. Using a 'general rounds' model, he met with groups of practicum students to review and discuss their children's performance charts . . . his leadership qualities and capacity for working constructively with colleagues and research teams allowed him to take advantage of university and government resources" (p. 12, 21).

Deno's work was always done in teams, and with a few notable exceptions, nearly all the writing and reporting came in the form of multiauthored papers. An interesting part of the phishing process was the unrelenting feedback about work that Deno gave away. Many contributors, such as Graves, comment on how Deno would visit their institutions and projects and join *their* team.

Some particular comments about "phishing" stood out. In chapter 11, Foegen, one of Deno's doctoral advisees, says the following: "I would speculate that nearly all of Deno's students could recall an experience in which a discussion resulted in Deno commenting, "I believe that's an empirical question." He consistently advocated the use of scientific methods to answer questions posed by his students, who found themselves encouraged to "run a little study" to gather data in response to a question they had" (p. 144).

Similarly, chapter 12 by Espin and Campbell, former advisees and colleagues, puts it this way: "From the beginning, Deno focused not only on the technical but also the practical adequacy of CBM measures and on the outcomes associated with implementation of the measures. We believe that it is this unique approach to measure development that explains the impact that CBM has had on policy and practice at the elementary-school level. In our research, we will continue to be guided by Deno's visionary work for, as you know—'once an advisor, always an advisor'" (p. 161).

Passionate

I'll conclude this summary with a word typically *not* used by academicians, especially researchers. Of all the adjectives used to describe Deno or his work in these chapters, none of them included the word *passionate*. Science is designed to be *dispassionate*, objective, and neutral. In more than forty years of work, there is definitely that scientific theme in Deno's numerous publications in refereed journals. Yet the outcomes of Deno's work have formed the basis of a passion (a) for a new and better educational system and (b) for inquiry as a form of higher-education practice. The passion for practice is best expressed in chapter 6 by Germann, whose voice in this book and in his career has been for a better, more equitable educational service delivery system. As Germann translated DBPM into widespread practice, he did so with the passion embedded in Deno's conception: "Unfortunately, federal law based on a deviant status classification system resulted in the wrong labels, identified with the wrong instruments, given for the wrong purposes, by people trained in the wrong methodology and implementing the wrong interventions . . . It focused attention on process, not progress, to the detriment of all. It perpetuated a model that blames the child for instructional failure, with the unintended consequence of delaying instructional improvements in the general education programs" (p. 83).

I found passion in nearly all the chapters in one form or the other, including passion for "the work" in inquiry as a way of higher education life that was most evident in chapter 11 by Foegen and in chapter 23 by Shapiro and Lentz who state the following: "It is amazing how one small book [DBPM] can have such a large impact on one's professional thinking and career" (p. 277, brackets added). I believe Christ in chapter 24 also said it well: "Although CBM has substantially influenced the field of school psychology, the conceptualization of problem solving as a guiding principle for practice stands as Dr. Deno's most considerable and enduring contribution to this field" (p. 287).

Needless to say, I concur. Yes, CBM is highly quantitative and objective; until another better method comes along, it provides educators a fine way to judge whether an intervention is making a difference. Yet at the heart of Deno's work and the use of CBM is social values, a fact that is often overlooked by many—not by many of the chapters' authors and certainly not by me.

References beyond the Chapters in the Book

Deno, S. L. (1989). Curriculum-Based Measurement and alternative special education services: A fundamental and direct relationship. In M. R. Shinn (Ed.), *Curriculum-Based Measurement: Assessing special children* (pp. 1–17). New York, NY: Guilford Press.

Deno, S. L. (1991). Individual differences and individual difference: The essential difference of special education. *Journal of Special Education, 24,* 160–173.

Deno, S. L. (1995). School psychologist as problem solver. In A. Thomas & J. Grimes (Eds.), *Best practices in school psychology III* (pp. 471–484). Washington, DC: National Association of School Psychologists.

Deno, S. L. (2002). Problem-solving as best practice. In A. Thomas & J. Grimes (Eds.), *Best practices in school psychology IV* (pp. 37–55). Bethesda, MD: National Association of School Psychologists.

Deno, S. L., Marston, D., Shinn, M. R., & Tindal, G. (1983). Oral reading fluency: A simple datum for scaling reading disability. *Topics in Learning and Learning Disability, 2*, 53–59.

Deno, S. L., & Mirkin, P. K. (1977). *Data-Based Program Modification: A manual.* Reston, VA: Council for Exceptional Children.

Deno, S. L., & Mirkin, P. (1980). Data-based IEP development: An approach to substantive compliance. *Teaching Exceptional Children, 12*, 92–97.

Deno, S. L., Mirkin, P. K., Chiang, B., Tindal, G., Fuchs, L. S., Martson, D., & Kuehnle, K. (1980). *Simple approaches to assessing learning disabled students' spelling performance, social status and written expression.* Minneapolis: University of Minnesota Institute for Research on Learning Disabilities.

Deno, S. L., Mirkin, P. K., Lowry, L., & Kuehnle, K. (1980). *Relationships among simple measures of spelling and performance on standardized achievement tests* (No. IRLD-RR-21). Minneapolis: University of Minnesota Institute for Research on Learning Disabilities.

Deno, S. L., Mirkin, P. K., & Wesson, C. (1984). How to write effective data-based IEPs. *Teaching Exceptional Children, 16*, 99–104.

Foegen, A., Jiban, C., & Deno, S. L. (2007). Progress monitoring measures in mathematics: A review of the literature. *Journal of Special Education, 41*, 121–139.

Fuchs, L. S., & Deno, S. L. (1991). Paradigmatic distinctions between instructionally relevant measurement models. *Exceptional Children, 57*, 488–500.

Fuchs, L., Deno, S. L., & Mirkin, P. K. (1981). *Teacher efficiency in continuous evaluation of IEP goals* (No. IRLD-RR-53). Minneapolis: University of Minnesota Institute for Research on Learning Disabilities.

Fuchs, L. S., Tindal, G. A., & Deno, S. L. (1982). *Use of aggregation to improve the reliability of simple direct measures of academic performance* (No. IRLD-RR-94). Minneapolis: University of Minnesota Institute for Research on Learning Disabilities.

Jenkins, J. R., Deno, S. L., & Mirkin, P. K. (1979). Measuring pupil progress toward the least restrictive environment. *Learning Disability Quarterly, 2*, 81–92.

Marston, D., & Deno, S. L. (1981). *The reliability of simple, direct measures of written expression* (No. IRLD-RR-50). Minneapolis: University of Minnesota Institute for Research on Learning Disabilities.

Marston, D., Lowry, L., Deno, S. L., & Mirkin, P. K. (1981). *An analysis of learning trends in simple measures of reading, spelling, and written expression: A longitudinal investigation* (No. IRLD-RR-49). Minneapolis: University of Minnesota Institute for Research on Learning Disabilities.

National Mathematics Advisory Panel. (2008). *Foundations for success: National Mathematics Advisory Panel final report.* Washington, DC: U.S. Department of Education.

Mirkin, P. K., Deno, S. L., Fuchs, L. S., Wesson, C., Tindal, G., Marston, D., & Kuehnle, K. (1981). *Procedures to develop and monitor progress on IEP goals.* Minneapolis: University of Minnesota Institute for Research on Learning Disabilities.

White, O. R. (1974). *Evaluating educational process* (working paper). Seattle: University of Washington, Child Developmental and Mental Retardation Center, Experimental Education Unit.

White, O. R., & Haring, N. G. (1980). *Exceptional teaching* (2nd ed.). Columbus, OH: Merrill.

Contributors

Laurence Bergeron is a special education teacher who works with young, underprivileged students in Montréal, Québec, Canada. Her master's thesis focuses on the sustained effects of a preventive intervention. She is also interested in children's literature.

Lionel A. Blatchley received his PhD in school psychology in 1973 from the University of Rhode Island. He was employed by the Saint Paul Public Schools, Saint Paul, Minnesota, as a school psychologist from 1973 to 2006. The assessment and programming of ELL students with disabilities was one of his areas of concentration.

Renee Bradley is a former teacher, teacher trainer, and consultant in special education. She currently works at the U.S. Office of Special Education programs.

Dr. Mary T. Brownell is a professor in the special education program at the University of Florida. She also directs, along with her colleague Dr. Paul Sindelar, the Center for Policy and Practice in Special Education Professional Development. Her research interests include teacher quality issues as they relate to working with students with disabilities, professional development, teacher preparation, and literacy instruction for students with learning disabilities. Over the course of her career she has secured approximately $13 million in federal research and preparation monies to address her research interests. Additionally, she has published over fifty book chapters and papers in some of special education's most prestigious journals, including *Exceptional Children*, *Journal of Special Education*, and *Learning Disability Quarterly*. Recently, she has completed a book to be published by Guilford Press titled *Inclusive Instruction: Using Evidence Based Practices for Teaching Students with Disabilities*.

Dr. Todd W. Busch is currently an associate professor in the Special Education Department at the University of St. Thomas. Dr. Busch has trained nationally on the topics of RTI and progress monitoring. His publications include articles and book chapters on alternative assessment, General Outcome Measures, and Response to Intervention. Before entering higher education, Dr. Busch worked as both a general and special education teacher in secondary-level schools.

Heather M. Campbell, PhD, is an associate professor of education at St. Olaf College. In addition to teaching courses on special education and English learners, she has worked with colleagues to develop education opportunity programs for low-income and first-generation students. Her research interests include measuring the effectiveness of underprepared college students' metacognitive strategy use and helping teachers to design and implement research-based assessments of written expression for English learners.

Ann Casey is the executive director of special education for the Minneapolis Public Schools. Both prior to this experience and in her current position, she has been an advocate for systems and structures that provide students with the supports they need to be successful in schools. She has served as the director of the MN RTI Center and worked with the RTI Action Network to provide schools with the skills needed to implement this framework of student support. Ann received her PhD from the University of Minnesota where Dr. Stanley Deno provided significant mentorship to her and the foundational skills she relies on in her daily work of using data to make decisions.

Theodore J. Christ, PhD, is an associate professor with the school psychology program in the Educational Psychology Department at the University of Minnesota. Dr. Christ is engaged in research to develop, evaluate, and improve assessments that are used to enhance data-based decisions, problem solving, and Response to Intervention. Dr. Christ has numerous publications and national presentations on topics related to Curriculum-Based Measurement (CBM), data-based decision making, and Direct Behavior Rating. He is the principal and coprincipal investigator of multiple projects funded through the Institute of Education Sciences and Office of Special Education Programming. Dr. Christ received the 2008 Lightner Witmer Early Career Award for outstanding early career scholarship from Division 16 of the American Psychological Association.

Kelli D. Cummings, PhD, NCSP, is a research associate at the University of Oregon, Center on Teaching and Learning. Her areas of research interest include K–12 school improvement and the development of language and social behavior in elementary children. She has provided formal technical assistance and training on problem solving, Response to Intervention, and the use of Curriculum-Based Measurement for eight states in both the United States and Canada.

Éric Dion is a professor of special education at the Université du Québec à Montréal and director of the Research Group on Evidence-Based Teaching Strategies. He conducts research on the prevention of reading disabilities using class-wide regular education classroom strategies, including peer-mediated activities.

Isabelle Dubé is majoring in psychology at the Université du Québec à Montréal. Her research interests center on the development of word-recognition skills among underprivileged first graders.

Christine A. Espin, PhD, is a professor at Leiden University in the Department of Education and Child Studies, Special Education. Dr. Espin's research interests are the development of Curriculum-Based Measurement procedures in reading, writing, second-language learning, and content-area learning for secondary students with learning disabilities and on teachers' use of data for decision making. Dr. Espin began her career as a special education teacher for high school students with learning disabilities in grades 9–12.

Hank Fien is a research associate at the Center on Teaching and Learning at the University of Oregon. Currently, he serves as coprincipal investigator on several IES-sponsored research and development grants studying the feasibility and efficacy of early reading and early math curricula and interventions. His research interests include reading and mathematics development in young children, instructional design, and empirically validating interventions aimed at preventing or ameliorating student academic problems.

Anne Foegen, PhD, is an associate professor in the Department of Curriculum and Instruction at Iowa State University, where she teaches graduate and undergraduate classes in assessment, learning disabilities, and instructional methods in mathematics for struggling learners. Dr. Foegen's research interests include the development and implementation of progress monitoring measures in mathematics, with a particular emphasis on middle school and high school mathematics.

Douglas Fuchs, PhD, is Nicholas Hobbs Professor of Special Education and Human Development. His research focuses on the assessment and instructional components that are foundational to responsiveness-to-intervention instructional reform, learning disabilities classification issues, and the efficacy of and mechanisms by which instructional programs promote learning among students with or at risk for reading disabilities.

Lynn S. Fuchs, PhD, is Nicholas Hobbs Professor of Special Education and Human Development. Her research focuses on classroom assessment for improving teachers' instructional decisions and student learning, as well as the efficacy of and mechanisms by which instructional programs promote learning among students with or at risk for mathematics or reading disabilities.

Gary Germann is retired from education. He holds degrees in general and special education and taught at both the training and K–12 levels. He was the director of the Pine County Special Education Cooperative when it developed a nationally recognized data-based special education system. For ten years he was the director of the St. Croix River Education District. In this capacity he led member districts' efforts to develop a continuous database of all students' academic performance and its associated electronic data management system. He was the president and CEO of Edformation Inc. and developed AIMSweb, a web-based electronic data management and reporting system. He is the author of several book chapters and has published in professional journals, as well as presented at numerous local, state, and national conferences.

Kim Gibbons, PhD, currently is the executive director of the St. Croix River Education District (SCRED) located in Rush City, Minnesota. SCRED has received national recognition for its use of RTI systems and received a legislative appropriation to fund the Minnesota Response to Intervention Center for two years. Dr. Gibbons obtained her doctoral degree in school psychology from the University of Oregon where she received extensive training in the problem-solving model, Curriculum-Based Measurement, and research-based practices. Prior to her role as the executive director, Dr. Gibbons has worked as a director of special education, staff development coordinator, and school psychologist.

Dr. Roland H. Good III is an associate professor at the University of Oregon who teaches measurement, statistics, and research design courses at the graduate level and conducts research on assessment of early literacy skills.

He also works part time for Dynamic Measurement Group, Inc. He is coauthor of Dynamic Indicators of Basic Early Literacy Skills, Next Edition. Dr. Good received his undergraduate degree in elementary and special education and has two years teaching experience in elementary general education and special education classrooms. He earned his doctorate from Pennsylvania State University in school psychology.

Dr. Anne W. Graves, professor and chair, Department of Special Education, teaches and conducts research on instruction in reading and writing for learners with disabilities from diverse backgrounds. She has been a teacher and a professor in special education for thirty-five years with numerous presentations at professional conferences, journal articles, and chapters. Recently, she was project director on a study of Tier II instruction for literacy development in sixth grade English language learners with and without disabilities.

John L. Hosp is an associate professor in the Department of Teaching and Learning and codirector of the Center for Disability Research and Education at the University of Iowa. He received his PhD in education and human development from Vanderbilt University. His research focuses on aspects of implementing Response to Intervention, including disproportionate representation of minority students in special education and aligning assessment and instruction, particularly in the areas of Curriculum-Based Measurement and curriculum-based evaluation (CBE). Dr. Hosp has presented at several national and international conferences as well as conducted workshops nationally on reading, the Reading First Program, and RTI. He is also an author of over thirty journal articles, monographs, and book chapters and has produced a video on assessment in education. His books include *The ABCs of CBM: A Practical Guide to Curriculum-Based Measurement*, and *Designing and Conducting Research in Education*.

Dr. Michelle K. Hosp is a nationally known trainer and speaker on problem solving and the use of progress monitoring data. Her background is in school psychology and special education. She has published articles, conducted workshops both at the state and national level, and is coauthor of the book, *The ABCs of CBM*. She is a trainer with the National Center on Response to Intervention and is currently employed by the Iowa Department of Education as a consultant for data-based decision making and program monitoring.

Joseph R. Jenkins, PhD, is professor emeritus of special education at the University of Washington where he teaches classes in the master's and doctoral programs in special education and in the elementary teacher education program. Dr. Jenkins has conducted research and written extensively in special education (more than one hundred articles, chapters, and books) and has since 1982 directed OSEP leadership, personnel development, model demonstration, and research projects. In 2000, he was awarded the American Education Research Association's Distinguished Research Award for Special Education Research. In 2009, he was awarded the Council for Exceptional Children's Distinguished Research Award and the Division for Learning Disabilities Jeannette Fleischner Award. His work has focused on developing research-based practices for serving students with learning disabilities—reading assessment and intervention, inclusive education, and effective service delivery models for students with disabilities.

Ruth A. Kaminski is director of research and development at Dynamic Measurement Group, in Eugene, Oregon. She has been involved in research investigating assessments and interventions designed to promote early school success for the past twenty-five years and is currently one of a team of nationally recognized researchers collaborating on the national Center for Response to Intervention in Early Childhood (CRTIEC). Dr. Kaminski is also coauthor of Dynamic Indicators of Basic Early Literacy Skills (DIBELS).

Panayiota Kendeou, PhD, is an assistant professor of educational psychology at Neapolis University Pafos, Cyprus. Her current research focuses on the cognitive processes that support memory and learning across development in the context of reading comprehension. She can be contacted at Neapolis University Pafos, 2 Danaes Avenue, 8042 Pafos, Cyprus, or by e-mail at p.kendeou@nup.ac.cy.

Dong-il Kim is a professor in the Department of Education (Counseling and Special Education) at Seoul National University, Seoul, Korea. He is the co-author of *Basic Academic Skills Assessment: Reading, Math, Written Expression, Early Reading, Early Math, Introduction to Learning Disabilities*, and *Counseling for Special Children*.

Dr. Amanda Kloo is a research assistant professor of special education in the Department of Instruction and Learning at the University of Pittsburgh. Her research and professional interests focus on early literacy practices, effective reading intervention strategies, and data-based decision making for students with disabilities and those at risk for academic failure. She is also principal and coinvestigator of a variety of federal and state research projects investigating best practices in instruction and assessment with exceptional children. Dr. Kloo is a former classroom teacher who is certified in special, early childhood, elementary, and secondary education, as well as a reading specialist.

Danika Landry is an advanced doctoral student in educational psychology at the Université du Québec à Montréal. She is a school psychologist. Her research interests center on vocabulary learning and development of word-recognition skills among underprivileged kindergarteners and first graders.

Dr. Erica Lembke is an associate professor in the Department of Special Education at the University of Missouri, a trainer for the National Center on Response to Intervention, and vice president on the national board of the Division for Learning Disabilities. Dr. Lembke has numerous publications in peer-reviewed outlets on the topics of Curriculum-Based Measurement and Response to Intervention. She has presented over 150 national/international and state presentations on the topics of progress monitoring and Response to Intervention. Prior to receiving her PhD from the University of Minnesota, Erica was an elementary special education teacher for six years.

Francis E. Lentz Jr. is professor of school psychology at the University of Cincinnati, where he has taught since 1986. He received his PhD in psychology from the University of Tennessee, Knoxville, in 1982 and spent five years at Lehigh University before his current appointment. His current and career interests have been in the use of applied behavior analysis in educational settings.

Sylvia Linan-Thompson is an associate professor in the special education department at the University of Texas at Austin. Her research interests include the development of reading interventions for struggling readers who are monolingual English speakers, English language learners, and bilingual students acquiring Spanish literacy and the implementation of RTI. Additionally, she has worked in Latin America, Africa, Asia, and Eastern Europe on various projects related to literacy instruction and teacher professional development.

Dr. Charles D. Machesky is currently completing his tenth year as superintendent of the Uniontown Area School District in Uniontown, Pennsylvania. His prior education experiences include eighteen years as a special education teacher, six years as an elementary-middle school principal, and four years as a supervisor of special education. His wife, Mary, recently retired after thirty-four years as a classroom teacher and their two daughters, Elizabeth and Angela, are currently teachers of students with severe disabilities, including students with autism. Their third daughter, Suzanne, is employed as a business consultant with Bumble and Bumble of New York City. Dr. Machesky earned his bachelor's and master's degrees in special education from California University of Pennsylvania and supervisor of special education certification and doctorate in educational administration at the University of Pittsburgh.

Doug Marston is currently the administrator for research, evaluation, and assessment for the Special Education Department of the Minneapolis Public Schools where he is responsible for teacher training in assessment and data utilization, grant writing, program evaluation, and implementation of the Problem-Solving Model and Response to Intervention models. In addition, Dr. Marston is an adjunct faculty member in the special education program at the University of Minnesota, where he has taught classes in assessment and has been coprincipal investigator for several federal-funded grants with University of Minnesota faculty. He received his PhD in educational psychology from the Psychology in the Schools Training Program at the University of Minnesota in 1982. Since then he has published extensively in the areas of Curriculum-Based Measurement, student progress monitoring, reading interventions for students with mild disabilities, the Problem-Solving Model, and Response to Intervention. He has published over thirty-five journal articles and ten book chapters and coauthored *Classroom-Based Assessment: Evaluating Instructional Outcomes.* In 2006 he was the recipient of the Ysseldyke Distinguished Best Practices Award from the Minnesota School Psychology Association. In 2006 he was also named one of the "100 Distinguished Alumni" of the College of Education, University of Minnesota. He currently serves on the National Advisory Board for the National Research Center on Response to Intervention.

James L. McLeskey is a professor of special education at the University of Florida. He has extensive experience in teacher education and professional development activities related to providing high-quality, inclusive services for students with disabilities. His research interests include effective methods for achieving school reform/improvement, the role of the principal in developing effective, inclusive schools, and issues influencing teacher learning and the translation of research based methods into practice.

Kristen L. McMaster, PhD, is an associate professor of special education in the Department of Educational Psychology, University of Minnesota. She received her PhD in special education from Vanderbilt University. Her research interests include creating conditions for successful response to intervention of students at risk and students with disabilities. Specific research focuses on (1) promoting teachers' use of data-based decision making and evidence-based instruction and (2) developing individualized interventions for students for whom generally effective instruction is not sufficient.

Timothy C. Papadopoulos, PhD, is an associate professor of educational psychology at the University of Cyprus, Cyprus. His current research focuses on the cognitive and linguistic skills underpinning reading development, reading difficulties and different subtypes of reading disability, and the cognitive remediation for the enhancement of reading skills. He can be contacted at the Department of Psychology, University of Cyprus, P.O. Box 20537, 1678 Nicosia, Cyprus, or by e-mail at tpapadop@ucy.ac.cy. This research was supported by EU-UCY Grants for Applied Research Projects for Cyprus to the second author (Grant No. 8037-16013).

Kelly A. Powell-Smith, PhD, NCSP, is a senior research scientist with Dynamic Measurement Group, where she conducts research on assessment and intervention related to early childhood language and literacy development. She is also a nationally certified school psychologist. Dr. Powell-Smith obtained her doctorate in school psychology from the University of Oregon in 1993. She is a former associate professor of school psychology at the University of South Florida. She also was a faculty associate of the Florida Center for Reading Research (FCRR) and a consultant with the Eastern Regional Reading First Technical Assistance Center (ERFTAC). She has provided training in formative assessment and academic interventions in sixteen states and Canada. Over the past twenty years, Dr. Powell-Smith has conducted research related to children with various learning and behavioral difficulties and has conducted over 175 national, state, and regional workshops and presentations.

Greg Roberts, PhD, is the director of the Vaughn Gross Center for Reading and Language Arts and the associate director for the Meadows Center for

Preventing Educational Risk at the University of Texas at Austin. Dr. Roberts is the principal investigator of the Content Center on Instruction, Special Education Strand. He has directed evaluations of several federally funded programs related to literacy, disability, and school change and has extensive experience managing large extant data sets and successfully managed several large data-collection efforts.

Margaret J. Robinson, MEd, has worked as a diagnostic teacher in the area of special education evaluation of English language learners in St. Paul Public Schools, St. Paul, Minnesota, for twenty-five years. Approximately 40 percent of St. Paul's students live in homes where a language other than English is spoken.

Steven L. Robinson is an associate professor in the College of Education Special Education Department at Minnesota State University—Mankato. He teaches in and coordinates the master of science program in emotional disturbance and learning disabilities. Research interests include the use of technology to enhance instruction for children with disabilities.

Susan Rose is an associate professor at the University of Minnesota in the Department of Educational Psychology—Special Education Programs. She has conducted several studies related to monitoring progress of students who are deaf or hard of hearing and the application of CBM principles to monitoring progress in American Sign Language.

Catherine Roux is an advanced doctoral student in educational psychology at the Université du Québec à Montréal. She has worked eight years in classes for autistic students. Her research interests center on developing strategies to teach reading comprehension to atypical readers, especially high-functioning autistic students.

Barbara J. Scierka is a math collaborative planner for St. Croix River Education District in East Central Minnesota. Her interests include using data with grade-level and problem-solving teams to develop effective interventions for students in mathematics. Barbara was a special education teacher for twelve years, working with students with learning disabilities and cognitive disabilities. She earned a doctoral degree in educational psychology from the University of Minnesota.

Edward S. Shapiro, PhD, is director of the Center for Promoting Research to Practice and Professor, School Psychology Program, at Lehigh University, Bethlehem, Pennsylvania. Dr. Shapiro is author/coeditor of many books including the fourth edition of *Academic Skills Problems: Direct Assessment and Intervention*, the *Academic Skills Problems Workbook*, and *Models for Implementing Response to Intervention*, all by Guilford Press. Over the past five years, Dr. Shapiro has been working as a consultant with the Pennsylvania Department of Education and Pennsylvania Training and Technical Assistance Network to facilitate the implementation of Response to Intervention across the state. Best known for his work in Curriculum-Based Assessment, Dr. Shapiro's current research interests focus on the process of implementation and evaluation of Response to Intervention models in schools.

Jongho Shin is an associate professor in the Department of Education, Seoul National University. He is an author of *Research in Educational Psychology* and a coauthor of *Introduction to Children with Learning Disabilities*.

Mark R. Shinn, PhD, currently is a professor of school psychology at National Louis University in Chicago. He received his educational psychology doctoral degree at the University of Minnesota where he had the special opportunity to work with Jim Ysseldyke and Stanley Deno at the University of Minnesota Institute for Research on Learning Disabilities (IRLD). After working in Minneapolis and St. Paul Public Schools on special assignment, he joined the University of Oregon in 1984 where he led efforts to stabilize its school psychology program and obtain NASP and APA accreditation. He has published two edited books on CBM and more than seventy-five refereed journal articles and book chapters on screening, progress monitoring, and SLD identification. He also edited three books on evidence-based intervention. In 2003, he received the APA Division 16 Jack Bardon Distinguished Career service award.

James G. Shriner, PhD, is an associate professor of special education at the University of Illinois at Urbana-Champaign. Prior to coming to Illinois, he was an assistant professor of education at Clemson University and a senior researcher for the National Center of Educational Outcomes (NCEO) at the University of Minnesota. Dr. Shriner's work includes research on the effects of both ESEA and IDEIA on students with disabilities' educational services. Recently, he has been principal investigator of an Institute of Education Sciences (IES) research grant (R324J06002), IEP Quality Improvement: Research and

Development of Web-Based Decision Support, as well as state grants for IEP development from Illinois and South Dakota.

Dr. Paul T. Sindelar is professor of special education at the University of Florida. He got his PhD from the University of Minnesota and was Stanley Deno's first doctoral graduate. Dr. Sindelar also served on the special education faculties at Penn State and Florida State Universities and chaired departments at all three institutions over a fifteen-year span. He also served a term as associate dean for research in UF's College of Education.

Deborah L. Speece is professor of special education at the University of Maryland. Her research interests include the identification of children at risk for reading disabilities and the investigation of models of Response to Intervention to prevent reading problems and ameliorate risk.

Pamela M. Stecker presently is professor of special education at Clemson University in South Carolina. Her teaching focuses on assessment practices and academic interventions in reading and mathematics for students with learning disabilities or who are at risk. Pam's research interests include the use of progress-monitoring systems for improving teacher planning and student achievement in language arts and mathematics. Pam has served as a trainer for the federally funded National Center on Student Progress Monitoring and currently serves as a consultant on the National Center on Response to Intervention.

Martha L. Thurlow is director of the National Center of Educational Outcomes, where she addresses the implications of contemporary U.S. policy and practice for students with disabilities, including national and statewide assessment policies and practices, accommodations, alternate assessments, and graduation requirements. She has published extensively on these topics; presented at numerous state, regional, national, and international conferences; testified before Congress on the inclusion of students with disabilities in accountability systems; and is often called on by individuals at all levels of the educational system to provide input on challenging issues surrounding the inclusion of special needs students.

Renáta Tichá, PhD, has received her PhD from the University of Minnesota in educational psychology, special education programs. She works as a research associate in the Institute on Community Integration at the University of Minnesota. She has extensive experience in the development, implementation and conducting research on materials (i.e., assessments and interventions) for individuals with intellectual and developmental disabilities (IDD). Dr. Tichá currently coordinates two longitudinal randomized control trials with adults with intellectual and developmental disabilities in community residential settings as part of the Research and Training Center on Community Living (RTC) as well as a Leadership Training Grant focused on training doctoral students in Response to Intervention. She is also a data analyst on a National Core Indicators Survey dataset to assist with answering questions pertaining to the quality of life for adults with IDD.

Dr. Gerald Tindal is currently the Castle-McIntosh-Knight Professor in the College of Education—University of Oregon. He is the department head of Educational Methodology, Policy, and Leadership and directs Behavioral Research and Teaching (BRT). His research focuses on integrating students with disabilities in general education classrooms using Curriculum-Based Measurement for screening students at risk, monitoring student progress, and evaluation instructional programs. Dr. Tindal also conducts research on large-scale testing and alternate assessments, investigating teacher decision making on test participation, test accommodations, and extended assessments of basic skills. Finally, he teaches courses on assessment systems, data-driven decision making, research design, and program evaluation.

Dr. Paul van den Broek is professor of educational sciences at Leiden University, the Netherlands, and of Cognitive Sciences at the University of Minnesota. His research interests concern the cognitive and neurological processes involved in reading comprehension, in adults and children. In addition, he has a long-standing interest in the application of insights into these processes to educational practice.

Dr. Sharon Vaughn, H. E. Hartfelder/Southland Corp. Regents Chair in Human Development, is the executive director of the Meadows Center for Preventing Educational Risk an organized research unit at the University of Texas at Austin. She is the recipient of the AERA SIG distinguished researcher award, the University of Texas Distinguished faculty award, and the Jeannette E. Fleischner Award for Outstanding Contributions to the Field of LD from CEC. She is the author of more than fifteen books and 150 research articles. She is currently investigator on several Institute for Education Sciences, National Institute for Child Health and Human Development, and U.S. Department of Education research grants.

Dana L. Wagner is an assistant professor of Special Education at Augsburg College in Minneapolis, Minnesota. Her primary interests include teacher preparation and development in the areas of academic assessment and instruction and research involving older struggling readers.

Teri Wallace, PhD, is associate professor and chair of the Department of Special Education at Minnesota State University, Mankato. She was a researcher for more than twenty years at the University of Minnesota where she worked with Dr. Stanley Deno on the research contained in this chapter. Dr. Wallace's research interests include General Outcome Measurement development for students with significant cognitive disabilities, RTI, and the use of data for decision making at the individual, classroom, school, and district level. In addition, she is interested in the continuous improvement of teacher preparation.

Jeanne Wanzek, PhD, is an assistant professor in the school of teacher education at Florida State University. She is a former special educator and elementary teacher. Dr. Wanzek conducts research examining effective reading instruction and intervention focusing primarily on prevention and remediation for students with reading difficulties and disabilities.

Dr. Miya Miura Wayman is a consultant at the University of Minnesota. She received her PhD and MA in educational psychology/special education from the University of Minnesota and her BS in special education and mathematics education from Winona State University. Her current research interests include developing progress monitoring measures for beginning readers and English learners and improving teachers' use of data for instructional decision making.

Mary Jane White is a research associate at the University of Minnesota working as project coordinator for both the FAIP-R and MRC, IES-funded grants. She completed her PhD in educational psychology from the University of Minnesota with an emphasis in cognition and learning. Her research includes both theoretical and practical applications of cognitive science to memory, learning, and language in the context of reading and writing. Publications include developmental and adult studies of discourse comprehension, interventions for reading and writing, and motivation.

Mitchell L. Yell is the Fred and Francis Lester Chair of Teacher Education at the University of South Carolina. His research interests include special education law, IEP development, and progress monitoring. Dr. Yell was fortunate to be a doctoral student under Stanley Deno at the University of Minnesota from 1985 to 1988.

Naomi Zigmond has been an active special education researcher and teacher for more than forty years; her focus has been on the organization of special education services for students with disabilities in elementary and secondary schools and the impact of program organization on student achievement. Her work has focused on the various roles of the special education teacher (consultant, coteacher, resource teacher, self-contained class teacher, etc.) and how best to improve academic and social outcomes for students with disabilities in public schools. For the last decade, Dr. Zigmond has also led a team of researchers and practitioners in the development, production, distribution, scoring, reporting, and validation of the Pennsylvania Alternate System of Assessment, the statewide alternate assessment for students with significant cognitive disabilities. Throughout her career, Dr. Zigmond has published many articles, book chapters, and books.

Index

accommodations: for academic assessment, 241–42, 252–53, 350; research on, 241–42

accountability testing: in CBM, 58; high-stakes, 237; in Minneapolis Public Schools, 68–72, 71; in reading, 69; standards-referenced context of, 250. *See also* assessment; measurement; progress monitoring; testing

Acosta, B. D., 241, 242

Adequate Yearly Progress (AYP) determinations, 251

Afflerbach, P., 182

African American students, in special education programs, 67

aim lines, for performance, 226, 227

AIMSweb (educational data application), 128

algebra, progress monitoring in, 142, 144, 145, 350

alternative assessment-alternate academic achievement standards (AA-AAS), 249. *See also* assessment, academic: alternatives for

alternative assessment-modified achievement standards (AA-MAS), 249–50; group goals for, 250

analysis of covariance (ANCOVA) design, 65

Apgar, Virginia, 17–18, 19

Appleton, J. J., 69

Applied Behavioral Analysis, 343

assessment, academic: accommodations for, 241–42, 252–53, 350; alignment with instruction, 225–35; alternatives for, 49–55, 213, 218, 248, 249–50; of basic skills, 111–14; behavioral, 279–81; of cognitive disabilities, significant, 211–19; confusion concerning, 88; continuous, 81; in DBPM, 81; demystification of, 49, 50, 54; in developing countries, 5, 321–24, 326–27; discrepancies in, 81, 180, 181, 276–77; district-wide, 51–54, 53, 144, 225; federally required, 88, 226, 248–49, 265, 266–67, 354; as formative process, 81, 249; high-stakes measures of, 88, 90; in IEPs, 38–39 41, 42, 81; multiple-choice tests for, 249; in native languages, 188; of 1950s, 85; against normative groups, 87; parents in, 49, 52, 248; alternate formats of, 249; for performance outcomes, 4, 18, 112; portfolio-based, 249; procedural clarity in, 242–43; progress monitoring and, 88, 92–95; psychometric, 78; rating scales for, 249; of reading, 51–54, 69, 99–108, 111–14, 113, 293; relationship to instruction, 61, 113, 180, 183; replicable procedures for, 242; schools' role in, 53; screening in, 88, 89–92; by specialists, 49; standards-referenced context of, 250, 251; statewide, 4,

decision making: for accommodations: parsimony in, (*continued*) 344; in Saint Paul Public Schools, 188; software for, 125

decision making, data-based, 3, 49, 53, 58, 73, 111, 343; at Larue Elementary, 170; in school psychology, 278, 280–81

Demonstration of Response to Intervention (RTI) Project, 58

Deno, Stanley, 1; career achievements and influence of, 139, 145–46, 183, 234–25, 244, 264, 266, 285, 315, 342, 349, 353; citation of works, 349; collaboration with Minneapolis Public Schools, 57, 73, 144, 347–48; compassion of, 146; contributions to education, 1, 7, 20–21, 53, 77, 85, 261; contributions to school psychology, 4, 275–76, 285–91; contribution to English learner research, 4; core values of, 145–46; curiosity of, 145; DBPM model of, 4, 13, 27–35, 37, 122, 126, 265; development of assessment tools, 144; development of CBM, 10–15; early research of, 10–11; Edcheckup program of, 128; educational partnerships of, 144; on English Language Learners, 189; evaluation tools of, 73; focus on big ideas, 139; goal-oriented monitoring work, 111; graduate studies of, 10, 343; on hypothesis testing, 287, 288; IEP work, 13, 346–47; importance of parsimony for, 343–44; influence on teacher education, 1, 261–64, 350; integrity of, 145; investigation of teachers' data use, 126; leadership qualities, 353; learning disabilities work, 79–82, 255; as mentor, 149–50; participatory approach of,

353; partnership with Pine County Special Education Cooperative, 144, 347–48; passion for education, 353–54; Precision Teaching work, 13–15, 20, 343; prescience of, 351–52; principled work of, 344–45; problem-solving work of, 288–90; on professional development, 144; progress-monitoring work of, 3, 94, 270; quantitative work of, 349, 354; and RAFT skills, 9; SERT model of, 2, 27–35; study of writing skills, 153; teamwork under, 353; time series work, 141; training of, 10, 20; use of empirical methods, 142, 265; view of leadership, 5–6; vision of measurement, 7; work with English learners, 201–2, 207–8; work with Moodle, 133. Works: "Curriculum-Based Measurement: The Emerging Alternative," 125; Data-Based Program Modification: A Manual, 37, 57, 80, 139, 144, 238, 265–66, 275–76, 343, 346; Instructional Alternatives for Exceptional Children, 57

developing countries: CBM in, 5, 321–24, 326–27; GOMs in, 322, 323

developmental cognitive disability (DCD), 216. *See also* cognitive disabilities, significant

Dion, Éric, 3, 352

discrepancy ratios, 276–76

Down syndrome, tutoring model for, 215

Drasgow, E., 40

Dubé, Isabelle, 3

Dynamic Indicators of Basic Early Literacy Skills (DIBELS), 3, 111, 128, 180; benchmark assessments in, 112, 116, 120, 166; challenges to validity of, 182; Data System (DDS) of, 112,

mainstreaming: case against, 32–34; in general education, 28–30, 31

Marston, Doug, 2, 58, 60, 71, 348; Edcheckup program of, 128; study of writing skills, 153; on test administration, 67

mastery measurement, 7, 13; for cognitive disabilities, significant, 213, 215; CBM's role in, 8–10; technical difficulties with, 8. *See also* progress monitoring

mathematics: big ideas in, 139–40; CBM assessment in, 9–10, 239–40, 254, 268, 350; handheld data systems for, 131; influence of reading skills on, 243; interventions in Minneapolis Public Schools, 64; Korean students' difficulties with, 39; learning disabilities in, 152; progress monitoring tools for, 13, 42–43, 142, 146; secondary, 3; state assessments in, 251. *See also* algebra

maze. *See* reading maze tasks

McLeskey, James L., 1

McMaster, Kristen L., 3, 155, 238, 351

measurement, academic: accountability provisions for, 253–54; arbitration of instruction, 15; assessment of outcome using, 82; clinical concept of, 18; error reduction in, 20; establishment of utility for, 225–28; of global achievement, 42; link to teaching, 12; for long-term goals, 12; 1977 standards for, 240; one-minute sample, 180, 183, 216; of proximal instructed content, 15; repetition of, 142; separation from lessons, 15; in SERT model, 30; standard tasks for, 15; technically sound data from, 141. *See also* assessment, academic; Curriculum-Based Measurement;

General Outcome Measurement; progress monitoring; testing

Mehrens, William, 10

Merwin, Jack, 10

Metas Claras Para Aprender Mejor (video, 2003), 321

Minneapolis Public Schools (MPS): accountability testing in, 68–72, 71; administration of tests in, 67; African American students in, 67; agreement with Office of Civil Rights, 66–69, 71; Basic Skills Reading Center, 29; Classroom Intervention Worksheet, 71, 72; Cooperative Teaching Project in, 65–68; CBM in, 2, 57–75; data-utilization strategies of, 62–65; Demonstration of Progress-Monitoring Project, 71, 73; Deno's collaboration with, 57, 67, 144, 347–48; IEPs in, 62, 68; instructional planning in, 61–64; interventions in general education, 66–69; math interventions in, 64; NCLB in, 68–72; Problem-Solving Model of, 66–70, 71; proficiency benchmarks of, 69, 70, 71; program evaluation in, 64–67; progress monitoring in, 62–65; reading interventions in, 65; reading performance in, 58–62, 63, 64, 67, 151; RTI in, 57, 58, 65, 67, 68, 71; screening procedures of, 58–61; special education effectiveness in, 64–67, 347; special education eligibility in, 58, 59–63; Student Data Warehouse of, 71; Students Needing Alternative Programming in, 66; survey level assessment in, 59; tiered interventions in, 71, 73; web-based data system of, 71

Minnesota Basic Standards Test (MBST), 69

Minnesota Comprehensive Assessments (MCA), 69
Minnesota State Department of Education, 199–200
Mirkin, Phyllis, 1, 77; Data-Based Program Modification: A Manual, 37, 57, 80, 139, 144, 238, 265–66, 275–76, 343, 346; DBPM model of, 4, 13, 27–35, 37, 126; death of, 85; investigation of teachers' data use, 126; and RAFT skills, 9; service delivery for disability model of, 79–82; SERT model of, 2, 27–35; work with Precision Teaching, 13–14
Monitoring Basic Skills Progress (MBSP, computer application), 127
Monitoring Progress of Pennsylvania Pupils (MP3), 166; at Larue Elementary School, 169–75
Moodle (virtual learning application), 130, 131; Deno's work with, 133
Moores, Don, 29
Muyskens, P., 71

National Council of Teachers of Mathematics (NCTM), 240
National Longitudinal Transition Study database, 34–35
National Mathematics Advisory Council, 350
Nicaragua: CBM in, 5, 321–27; EGRA in, 321, 324–26; reading fluency in, 321; school desertion in, 326
No Child Left Behind Act (NCLB, 2001), 251; accountability under, 87, 89, 90; alternative standards for, 213, 249; in Minneapolis Public Schools, 68–72; program development specifications under, 249; reading under, 165; state assessments under, 251, 253
Nolet, Victor, 179

Nonsense Word Fluency (NWF), 53, 111, 114–19, 189; benchmark goals for, 121, 122; for English learners, 202, 203–6, 207; indication of skills, 112, 113; raw scores in, 113
Normalization Principle, 28

Observation Survey of Early Literacy Achievement (OSELA), 182–83
obstetrics, newborn health measurement in, 17–18
Office of Civil Rights (OCR), agreements with Minnesota Public Schools, 66–69, 71
Office of Special Education Programs (OSEP): Demonstration of Progress-Monitoring Project, 71, 73; Model Demonstration project, 65; Monitoring Progress of Pennsylvania Pupils funding, 165–66
online collaboration technologies, 125
oral reading fluency (ORF), 111–16, 115, 182, 189; assessment of, 51–54; average scores in, 116; benchmark goals for, 120–21, 122, 166; for English Language Learners, 191, 192, 193, 195, 196, 202, 203, 205–8; in first grade, 116, 120–21, 122; in high-stakes testing, 228, 229–30, 233; at Larue Elementary, 166; observed scores in, 229. See also Dynamic Indicators of Basic Early Literacy Skills; reading, oral
Organisation for Economic Co-operation and Development, 322
Otaiba, Al, 215, 218
outcomes: definitional aspects of, 242; effect of standardized norm-referenced assessments on, 279; interpretive aspects of, 242; measurement of, 82; progress monitoring for, 142; screening in, 89–92; skills in